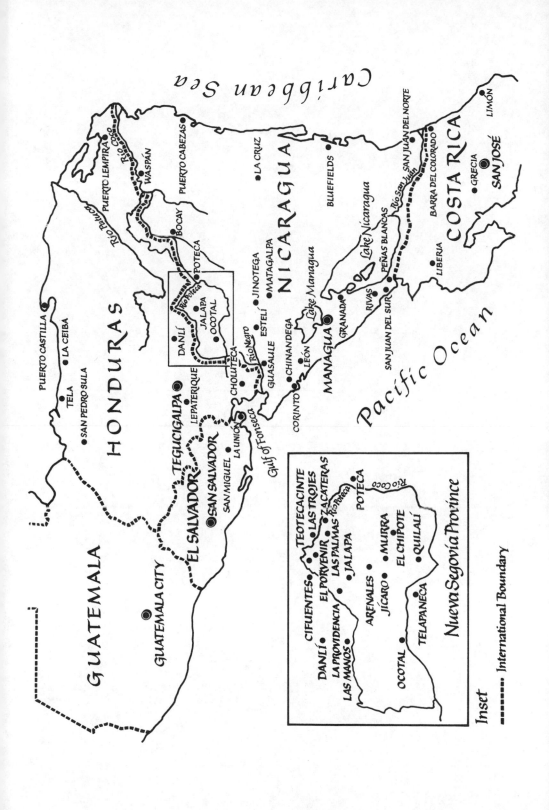

Caribbean Sea

GUATEMALA

GUATEMALA CITY

HONDURAS

PUERTO CASTILLA
TELA
LA CEIBA
SAN PEDRO SULA

Río Patuca

PUERTO LEMPIRA

Río Coco

WASPÁN

PUERTO CABEZAS

BOCAY

POTECA

Río Poteca

JALAPA
OCOTAL
DANLÍ

Río Negro

CHOLUTECA

GUASAULE

ESTELÍ

JINOTEGA

MATAGALPA

LA CRUZ

NICARAGUA

BLUEFIELDS

Lake Nicaragua

Río San Juan

SAN JUAN DEL NORTE

BARRA DEL COLORADO

COSTA RICA

LIMÓN
SAN JOSÉ
GRECIA

LIBERIA

PEÑAS BLANCAS

SAN JUAN DEL SUR

RIVAS

GRANADA

Lake Managua

MANAGUA

LEÓN

CHINANDEGA

CORINTO

Pacific Ocean

Gulf of Fonseca

LA UNIÓN

SAN MIGUEL

SAN SALVADOR

EL SALVADOR

LEPATERIQUE

TEGUCIGALPA

TELA

Inset

Río Poteca

POTECA

ZACATERAS

LAS TROJES

TEOTECACINTE

CIFUENTES

EL PORVENIR

LAS PALMAS

JALAPA

ARENALES

JÍCARO

MURRA

EL CHIPOTE

QUILALÍ

Río Coco

DANLÍ

LA PROVIDENCIA

LAS MANOS

OCOTAL

TELPANECA

Nueva Segovia Province

------ International Boundary

WITH THE
CONTRAS

*A Reporter in the Wilds
of Nicaragua*

Christopher Dickey

SIMON AND SCHUSTER   NEW YORK

Copyright © 1985 by Christopher Dickey
All rights reserved
including the right of reproduction
in whole or in part in any form
Published by Simon and Schuster
A Division of Simon & Schuster, Inc.
Simon & Schuster Building
Rockefeller Center
1230 Avenue of the Americas
New York, New York 10020
SIMON AND SCHUSTER and colophon are registered trademarks of Simon & Schuster, Inc.
Map by Ozzie Greif
Designed by Eve Kirch
Manufactured in the United States of America

10 9 8 7 6 5 4 3 2 1

Library of Congress Cataloging in Publication Data

Dickey, Christopher.
    With the Contras: a reporter in the wilds of Nicaragua.
    Includes index.
    1. United States—Military relations—Nicaragua.
2. Nicaragua—Military relations—United States.
3. Nicaragua—Politics and government—1979–   .
4. United States—Foreign relations—1981–   .
5. Dickey, Christopher. I. Title.
E183.8.N5D53   1985   327.7307285   85-22151
ISBN: 0–671–53298–7

Acknowledgments

The first people to be thanked for their help on a book such as this should be one's sources. It is unfortunate indeed that many of mine cannot, for their own protection, be named, and have to be identified in the notes at the end of this volume in generic terms or sometimes simply by the approximate time or the location of our conversations. But it is with deep respect that I think of many men and women from the Central Intelligence Agency, the Defense Department, the State Department, the Congress, the Nicaraguan Democratic Force and the Sandinista National Liberation Front who have shared their time, thoughts and information with me over the last six years. Those I could name, I did, and mostly with great thanks.

James LeMoyne, formerly with *Newsweek* and now with *The New York Times*, literally kept me alive during the most difficult personal moments in this narrative. My gratitude, affection and respect for him are beyond expression.

John Herman, my editor, is a man of great talent and unbelievable patience, who found the book in a pile of pages.

From *The Washington Post*, where I could easily thank everyone from the owners to the copy aides, I especially want to thank Howard Simons, now curator of the Nieman Foundation, for making me a journalist. Jim Hoagland taught me to be tough and thoughtful. Karen

DeYoung taught me about Central America. Patrick Tyler gave me the nudge that started the book. Peter Harris kept track of me for six years and kept me solvent. Peyman Pejman, meanwhile, did me no end of invaluable favors.

The Council on Foreign Relations, through its unique Edward R. Murrow Fellowship, gave me the time to think and the resources to investigate that helped me find a way to start the book. Many thanks to Winston Lord, John Temple Swing, Margaret Osmer-McQuade, Frances P. Himelfarb and Merle Dalziel for all their support during my year there.

WGBH Television, especially producers Austin Hoyt and Elizabeth Deane, gave me a tremendous chance to pursue my reporting on this project while working on theirs. The transcripts of interviews for the WGBH Frontline television series *Crisis in Central America* were indispensable in writing the initial chapters.

Theron Raines, my agent, spent years waiting for this book—for any book—from me. I hope he enjoys it.

Free-lance journalist Brian Barger, a long-standing authority on the contras, provided me with invaluable files.

Martin Andersen gave me eyes and ears in Argentina. I look forward to his own book about the Dirty War.

Independent researcher Eddie Becker, a master sleuth of the National Archives, took me into fascinating corners of the historical record.

My wife, Carol, did valuable research as well as typing and editing what must have seemed interminable transcripts in English and Spanish. She put up with me, my computer and my book for more than a year in a tiny apartment. She knows how much I owe her for that. But I also thank her, along with my son James, for putting up without me for so many months and years.

To Carol
For her bravery and love

Contents

"They are our brothers, these freedom fighters, and we owe them our help. . . . They are the moral equivalent of the Founding Fathers and the brave men and women of the French Resistance. We cannot turn away from them. For the struggle here is not right versus left, but right versus wrong."

—President Ronald Reagan,
March 1, 1985

"An armed guerrilla force always carries with it implicit terror because the population, without saying it out loud, fears the arms can be turned against them."

—"Psychological Operations
in Guerrilla Warfare,"
Central Intelligence Agency,
October 1983

Prologue

"In this war there are so many passions," said the Nicaraguan in the O. Henry Bar, "people are changed into beasts."

He said this sincerely, with a kind of weary amazement one afternoon in January 1984 in Tegucigalpa, Honduras. He was a man of conventional bourgeois sensibilities caught up in a crazy war that no longer had any reason to it; an casygoing Miami exile thrust to the fore of the Central Intelligence Agency's campaign as the kind of moderate whom Washington wanted to see leading the fight against communism in Nicaragua.

The overhead lights dimmed and blue stars from a little mirrored ball flickered across the empty dance floor as this Miami contra talked about the field commanders he had known, the ones who did the killing.

"They have, like, double personalities," he said, and again there was the note of incredulity. "Very tender, very cruel."

The one whose troops were then working part of Jinotega province across the border in Nicaragua, for instance, was called Tigrillo, little tiger, or wildcat. He had honey-colored eyes, sensitive in the sun, penetrating in the dark. "He is lively and quick," said the Miami contra. "I've seen him this side of the border and he plays the idiot. '*Mi comandante*' this and '*mi comandante*' that. But you cross the river with him and he *becomes* a tiger. He hangs people. He rapes. He shoots

15

people who don't obey him. Whatever is necessary in the jungle. I once saw one of his soldiers challenge him and he pulled out his pistol and shot him. He doesn't have any doubts about killing. But he is also tender with his troops, caring for them and watching over them.

"You know," continued the Miami contra in the O. Henry Bar, leaving his drink untouched as his mind dwelled on all of this, "there are people who learn to kill and who love it."

That, he was trying to explain, was what had happened to the commander called Suicida and his men. That—he was groping for some rationale behind the madness of the summer of 1983—that was how the bloodbath began.

And all the while President Ronald Reagan had talked of "freedom fighters."

"Here," the Miami contra mused, "fiction and reality, they're the same thing."

He was talking about the hidden history of men who fought a secret war, and in those first months of 1984 few other people knew, or would say, what had happened.

The witnesses to the worst madness were scattered all over Central America and the United States. Some of the survivors were in a field hospital outside the Honduran capital. One was a young man broken in the cells of the Sandinistas, where prisoners spend long days and nights naked in the darkness. Others were in a suburban home in Memphis, Tennessee, and in a Burger King in Miami. A night watchman at a condominium in southern Florida knew about the denouement. A family in one of the slums of the Honduran capital led me to more details on the slaughter. It all kept coming back, kept confirming what the Miami contra had said.

"If you know too much you owe too much," he had said, looking at the dim blue lights flickering across the dance floor. "There are times when it is better not to know too much."

The odyssey of the men who loved to kill began in the summer of 1979, in the last days of the fighting between the troops of Nicaragua's dictator and the forces of the Sandinista National Liberation Front, when their Central America became a world turned upside down.

For three generations the entire region had been balanced on the edge of revolution and this time, it seemed, there might be no pulling it back. In the 1930s there were uprisings that threatened to cover the isthmus in blood, but they were crushed by the presence and technology and training of U.S. troops or by the brutality of local ones. There was a democratic awakening in the 1940s, but it was aborted by the Central Intelligence Agency in the 1950s for fear the Soviets would take advantage. There was economic and technical progress through the 1960s, and the economies of the nations grew richer, but most of the people grew poorer. The greatest difference in their condition was that more of them survived to be poor, and their expectations were raised by new visions of a life they still were unable to have. The land that could be worked often was filled to overflowing and the cities became collections of hovels where frustration built to the point of explosion. Armies that were trained and armed and in some cases established by the United States saw it as their duty to keep the peace and to keep the power, and in the 1970s the generals ruled every nation of the Central American isthmus except Costa Rica.

Violent rule spawned violent opposition, and violent opposition was used to justify violent rule. In Guatemala, Marxists had begun a war against the generals in 1960, and through reigns of terror and brief respites of relative calm, it was still being waged in 1979. In El Salvador in 1979 the cities had degenerated to the edge of chaos and the streets were controlled by the poor of the slums and the idealists and Communists of the university marching in the face of repeated massacres. In Honduras a clique of officers known mainly for their drinking, drug running and bribe taking dominated the life of a nation still so poor that rising expectations were not yet a volatile problem. In Panama, a man with the rhetoric of a revolutionary and the wit to confront the United States about dominion over the Canal, ruled in the name of the people but with the rank of a general and the guns and clubs of his soldiers to crush those who questioned his policies.

The United States expressed concern from time to time about the political, economic and social conditions among its neighbors to the south and repeatedly called for reform, but it remained essentially complacent about the status quo in nations that had no voice, direct or indirect, in U.S. politics, countries where its domination could lapse easily into neglect and no one would be heard to question the process. The State Department, certainly, had little interest. Its envoys did not acquire ambassadorial rank until the 1940s; its ambassadors had little prestige and, in many cases, little talent. As late as the 1970s, when the Central Intelligence Agency had to cut back its budget, it found little reason to maintain a major presence in Central America. The agency's station in El Salvador was shut down altogether at mid-decade. Rela-

tions were mainly a matter for the Pentagon. The United States cultivated the region's officers and trained its best recruits at Leavenworth
and Benning and Bragg and in the long white bungalows among the
manicured lawns of the School of the Americas in Panama. Policymakers hoped that U.S.–trained armies could be moderated and molded to
become forces for positive social change while crushing any hints of
communism.

In most of Central America the faces of the generals changed periodically in elections that were decided by the top commanders and
ratified by ballots that the army counted—and marked and recounted
if necessary. The generals served their terms, took their money and
retired to make way for colleagues anxious to take their share of wealth
and power. If this system was abused, if the turnover at the top did not
come fast enough, then the generals were replaced by younger officers,
colonels and majors, in what were usually bloodless coups.

But in Nicaragua, while the dictators wore the uniforms of generals, and while their power was built on the training and arms of the
United States, and while they held electoral shows to mollify the people
and the world, their faces changed very little, and their names not at
all, from father to older son and then younger son, through almost half
the century: Somoza.

The Somozas portrayed themselves as the engineers of regional
stability, their country as the keystone of regional peace. When they
were challenged they fought and, for better or worse, they always won.
So it was a surprise to many, maybe even to those who fought against
them, when, in the summer of 1979, they fell. Journalists recorded the
events there as the culmination of nineteen months of strikes and fighting and negotiations and more fighting in Nicaragua. The dictator, re-
treating in anger before a swell of revolutionary excitement, blamed his
difficulties on two and a half years of Jimmy Carter in the White House.
His traditional ally, the United States, had questioned him, scolded him
and finally cut him off for running his country much as he had always
run it. The revolutionaries themselves saw their triumphs as the reward
for decades of organizing, plotting and suffering and building fragile
alliances. In order to win they had planned and trained and finally
agreed on strategies for everything—except how they would run the
country if they did win, and how they would treat their enemies, and
who exactly would be their friends.

ENDINGS—1979

I.

San Juan del Sur, Nicaragua, July 19, 1979

The war was over, but the soldiers were still in the field. On the seventeenth of July 1979, the dictator Anastasio Somoza Debayle had left. After forty-five years, finally, the family was gone. It took its money, which was much of the money the country had. And it left its army. And now, almost minute by minute, the army was falling apart. But not from the bottom, as you might expect. The disintegration had started from the top. The dictator left. The generals left. The colonels. They fled by helicopter and airplane, by car and on foot. They fled in clouds of promises and solemn vows. And by the nineteenth they were, almost all of them, gone. But the soldiers remained.

San Juan del Sur, on the Pacific coast of Nicaragua, had not known much of the war. Only a few kilometers to the south and east in this last offensive the toll had been enormous. But in San Juan del Sur, no. The war was not here.

Lieutenant Briceño and his little group of *guardias* had spent these months nervously but in peace, as the town had, and then, on the morning of the eighteenth, Briceño was gone. His men, too, had disappeared in the night. And the town, that morning, seemed strangely

19

empty without them. Many people were afraid to come into the streets. Along the beach the little fried-fish stands stood empty and in the Hotel La Estrella, which had been closed for three months, the breeze coming in off the half-moon bay moved over empty chairs, then out through the kitchen (still with its smell of old chicken flesh) and up the dirt street toward the church, past shuttered windows and closed doors.

The family downstairs in the old high school looked out warily across the counter where they used to sell Coca-Colas to tourists. Over the years the school above them had become a ruin. Its shutters had once been closed and the entire front of the building painted with the dictator's name during one of his many elections. But the shutters had dropped off or been carried away or burned and now his name appeared toothless and faded and gray on the rotting boards at the front of the building. SO___ZA S___OZ__74. The family sat far back in the shadow of its little stand, ready to fall back farther still, behind the door and into the humid darkness of the cellar and hit the floor and pray to God and Jesus and the Virgin if the war should fall suddenly upon them. Only the boy ventured into the streets. He and the other boys, who had seen nothing but had heard so much of what the boys were doing in Managua and Estelí, found the guns the *guardias* had left behind. They grabbed them up from the floor of the little barracks and the street outside. Galils and M-16s. The boy held his tentatively, as if it might turn on him. He slipped the strap over his shoulder. The action lay across his crotch, and the barrel nestled in his hand like some misformed electric guitar. Everyone laughed. But they listened, too. Faintly, from behind the shutters, you could hear the radios.

The Father came down the hill and people began opening their doors to get word of the world beyond the low ridge that was San Juan's horizon, that had been until now its protection from the war. In the last day, seven hundred of Somoza's *guardias* had gathered on the road above the town. They had come from Sapoá, Cárdenas and Naranjo, Peñas Blancas and La Virgen. They had fought until they were, most of them, out of ammunition and not one of them had surrendered. But now the *guardias* were trapped between the strongest units of the rebel army and the sea. And San Juan del Sur and these people of the port, as they call themselves, were trapped between the sea and the *guardias*.

So the war was over, and still it was threatening to arrive in all its horror where it had not arrived before.

*   *   *

PEÑAS BLANCAS, NICARAGUA

Pastora's body tensed and the rebel commander angled his watch to see it in the dawn light. 5:30. Son of a *bitch!* 5:30. He should have waked to the thunder of the howitzers and the ratcheting blast of the machine guns. Where were the mortars? He and his lieutenant Pichardo had decided (what was it? two hours ago?) that the attack would start at 4:30. And nothing was happening. Where the hell was Pichardo?

Edén Pastora, the Sandinistas' *Comandante Cero,* took a long breath of the wet air. It seemed he had been tired all his life, that only his anger and his balls kept him going. No guns. What was he going to fight with now? Maybe there was nothing left? Maybe now, with Somoza gone, with the junta arriving in León, with the war won, maybe the whole victory was going to fall apart because of the goddamn Costa Ricans and gringos and Humberto Ortega, Pastora's chief in the Sandinista Directorate. If the Guardia held out today and tomorrow . . . shit. Pastora grabbed up his AR-15. Where were the goddamn howitzers?

Exhaustion had spread like an epidemic among the boys on the line. They were used up. Physically, there was no reserve left.

Fifty-two days since the final offensive began, and the whole time Pastora had been bottled up on this narrow strip of land that separates Lake Nicaragua from the Pacific. The dictator had thrown his best people down here: Bravo, Montenegro, the Rattlesnakes, the Wild Geese, the Black and White. Of course, part of the strategy had been to put Pastora on the line as a decoy so advances could be made in the north. The hero of the National Palace could be counted on to draw the dictator's fire and the strategy had worked. But you don't want your men to die just to be decoys. You don't want your command to take all the casualties and see nothing of the victory. And with the war almost won, on the tenth Pastora had ordered an advance. They were going to push the son-of-a-bitch *guardias* off Hill 50, set up the guns there at Ostional and catch the bastards with an enveloping maneuver. They were going to break the bottle's neck at last.

And the Directorate didn't have the slightest fucking idea what was going on down here. They were getting ready for victory and they'd left him with the war. Every shouted word on the radio made that clear.

"Humberto, listen," Pastora had pleaded earlier in the week. "The Ticos"—the Costa Ricans—"are cutting off our logistics. They're tired of us, Humberto, and I think the gringos are tightening the screws on them. They've given in and they've cut off the mortars and the rounds and the guns that are coming in from Cuba. . . . We use up in a day what we get from Cuba. . . .

"Look, Humberto, the situation is critical," Pastora had said on the seventeenth. "We got 150,000 rounds yesterday. We got 250,000 rounds today. We have got to have 250,000 more."

And what Humberto had said was, "Why don't you control your people? Sounds like you're shooting off a lot of rounds."

"Listen, Humberto, we're not fighting a fucking guerrilla war here. This is a war of positions. Since six this morning along the whole length and breadth of the line we've been *fighting*. Do you hear! *Do you hear that?*" Pastora had held the microphone up to the staccato of the guns.

But now the guns were silent. He had to find Pichardo.

The hills were small and menacing in the black shadows of dawn. On the approach to Sapoá they stood separately like oddly rounded burial mounds on the flat surface of the land as it neared the lake. Nothing grew on them but the low, blowing grass and, sometimes at the very summit, a palm tree. And guns grew on Hill 50, which dominated the key routes up the isthmus. The Guardia had refused now for weeks to give it up, and every assault had been cut to pieces. There might be nothing left when the boys took it, but Pastora was going to give his boys a victory today. He was going to beat the *guardias* until they were beaten for good, if only they could get this damned assault started.

The road straightened out and Pastora's jeep picked up speed. In the distance were the enormous volcanoes in the lake. The halo of the sun flamed around them and the water stretched out before them like a prehistoric sea.

The car, racing as if it could outrun a sniper's bullet, nearly missed Pichardo. He was coming back from Sapoá, where he was supposed to have led the infantry attack covered by the mortars. His face, normally so civilized—sometimes you thought he should be running an export company if you just looked at his face—his face was furious. More than an hour now and no mortars, and Pichardo didn't know—and Pastora didn't know—what the hell had happened.

They went together to the silent artillery and found the commander. He was just a kid and he had gone to sleep at 3:30 when the plan had been finished and he thought he would be able to rest for just a few moments. But he had slept and stayed asleep and the artillery had slept with him.

Pichardo was breathless with anger. He grabbed up his binoculars and took off for the front line to direct fire on Hill 50. Pastora waited for him to call out the first coordinates as the mortar crews armed the shells. Boxes were strewn everywhere. The Chileans who had trained these boys never had succeeded in imposing much discipline. Most of the boxes were empty.

"Nothing," was the word from Pichardo. "Nothing. I don't see any signs. We fire and there's no answer."

"What?"

"They don't answer our fire. They're gone, *Comandante*. They've given up the position."

San Juan del Sur, Nicaragua

Julio César Herrera and Sergeant Pedro Pablo Ortiz Centeno and the rest of the Rattlesnakes had staked out a small territory for themselves among the hundreds of *guardias* there on the road above San Juan del Sur. Some lay in the shade beneath a *guanacaste* tree; others leaned against the tires of the trucks or the Bearcat armored car. Others cleaned their weapons, although many no longer cared about guns. In two months the world had fallen apart. Now there was nothing left to do but survive and escape and, at this moment, to wait as the priest took their demands back down to the people of the port. They knew that some of the boys there had picked up guns, and there might be some Communists. They wanted every last person in the port locked behind his doors. No one on the streets. Any shot, any explosion, any mistake that sounded like one and they would burn the town in five minutes. Those were the terms. If they boarded the boats and barges without being attacked, the town would be spared. That was the deal.

There was supposed to be a plan. When their commander, Bravo, left in the helicopter, it was with the idea that when things fell apart this would be the retreat. They would sail north to El Salvador. He would meet them there. Montenegro was overseeing the preparations. But who could be sure of that? Nothing was sure except that they were fucked if they didn't get out of here.

Julio César studied the Sergeant's face: broad and dark and flat, the eyes oriental and black, pure *indio* and impenetrable except when he smiled. He smiled when he won at dice or cards. He smiled when he saw La Negra. He smiled when the fighting started. He used the smile. At moments like this he would pick up the dice and look at Julio César, and Julio César would wait for some sign. The Sergeant taunted him with his inscrutability. He rolled and won and smiled.

Julio César's eyes were red with fatigue and fighting and the pills he had been taking for days to keep going. Maybe the town should be burned anyway. It didn't matter what was left behind now. Except for the men here of the Rattlesnakes who had become his brothers, he was abandoned and alone. His mother in Chinandega—who knew how she was or what had happened to her or when he would see her again? There might be dreams of coming back home someday, but the Communists were going to hunt *guardias* like dogs and there was nobody who was going to help them but themselves. Julio César knew that. All of them knew that. This was a world of betrayal. Only in the ranks could you find real trust.

Julio César had joined the Guardia in 1973 thinking it would be a chance to live better than anyone he knew. He was eighteen years old then and in the Guardia you were taught how to read. You carried a gun and you were respected, they said, and it was true.

All this time there had been the threat of the Communists. Always the officers had talked about this. Some had said that those who were in league with the subversives should be burned in the plazas of their towns to make examples. Julio César had heard all of this and thought, many times, that the officers must be right. But there was also the business of the money. There were a lot of ways to make extra *córdobas* here and there, and in the meantime his family was going to be better taken care of because he was of the Guardia. They got better doctors and schools and houses, and the government helped pay for their food and clothes. There were many good reasons to become a member of the Guardia Nacional, and many more people would have done it if they could have except that there were very few slots. When Julio César joined there were only eight thousand *guardias* in the whole country.

You got a chance, if you were good or if you knew the right people, to travel. Many of the recruits went to Panama to train at the School of the Americas. Some of them went to the United States, which had been, until this Communist Carter became president, the great friend of Nicaragua.

In the Guardia Nacional you learned quickly, though, that for all you were respected, you were not really like other people, even other members of your family. You were set apart by your privilege, by your discipline. That was one reason that the courts for the Guardia were special. If you had to be tried in regular courts the civilians would try to screw you.

That was what had saved the Sergeant. He killed a man in 1970. They put him in the stockade. But he was there only a few months, which was not so bad for killing a man. The military understood what could happen. The Sergeant had gotten in trouble for beating one of the recruits. But Julio César understood that. You had to understand authority. You could not be weak.

Sometimes the officers were weak. The higher up they got, the richer they got. And the richer, the softer. But the Sergeant was never weak and he knew whom to talk to among the officers. He had been the driver for a general and knew how to fix things for himself and for his people if there was trouble. That was part of what Julio César admired about him. He knew how to do good for his people. And that was partly why it was so good to be one of his people.

Julio César would never have used the word when he was sober, but the feeling he had for the Sergeant was something like love. It was the feeling you get when you take great risks with someone, but more than that.

Julio César Herrera often found it hard to say how he felt. He liked to express himself with his body or with his gun. As the buzzards soared on the air currents overhead he might easily have shot one of them for the hell of it. It felt good to pull the trigger. Really, it made him laugh sometimes. It was strange about him that when he was safe and his hair got long and his wisp of a beard grew, people often thought that he was a fool, or that he was stoned. His face lost its expression and he seemed not to care, much, what happened around him. He sat passively and waited for orders and if he had any resentment of them, any ideas about them, he kept them to himself. Only when he was near the fight did his mind seem to come alive. Only then did his brain seem to begin to work.

The Sergeant was not like that. The Sergeant was thinking all the time, looking for the chance to get ahead. It was a shame, some of the soldiers said, he was only a peasant, a *campesino* like them. He might have made a good officer. They thought he would make a much better officer than the lieutenants and captains, and a hell of a lot better than the colonels and generals. But it was also true that the Sergeant's strength was that he was not better born. He understood Julio César and Caramalo and the rest of the Rattlesnakes. He was born one of them. When you got to know him his smile of approval was like a gift.

The Sergeant had taken them into some fights that nobody should have gotten out of alive. Suicida, the officers began to call him. And he was going to get them out of this alive, no matter if the officers fucked up, no matter what the people of the town tried to do.

Word came down the line. The deal had been made. They would

go down to the barges tomorrow in the morning if they weren't attacked tonight.

LA VIRGEN, NICARAGUA

The last Guardia convoy had left a half-hour before Pastora arrived in La Virgen. Now every one of the positions was abandoned and the road was open to Managua, but the question remained of what to do about San Juan del Sur. Pastora would say, later, that his first instinct was to move against the Guardia regrouping there, but some of his lieutenants advised him not to, that it was crazy. They were supposed to be several hundred strong, maybe a couple of thousand. They were in bad shape, they were strung out, but they were crazy and if they decided to fight, anything could happen. The objective was Managua, and the situation there was incredibly confused. Communications had fallen apart and only the reporters coming up from Costa Rica seemed to have any idea what was happening. Somoza had cut a deal with the Americans to turn over the government to the rebel junta, but also to save the Guardia. Then the deal fell apart. Most of the raw recruits had stripped off their uniforms, running away in the civilian clothes they had worn beneath them for several days. But the men from the unit under Somoza's son, the newest Anastasio Somoza—the EEBI or Basic Infantry Training School—might still hold on. In that case Pastora's troops from the Southern Front should be there. And if the EEBI did not hold out, the junta was prepared to arrive in Managua tomorrow. If that happened the triumph would be celebrated without Pastora.

Twenty fucking years of fighting and of exile—this would be one hell of a way for it to end. The Directorate, Tomás Borge himself, and Humberto and the rest would get the credit. No. If the *guardias* are broken and fleeing from San Juan del Sur, then let them go. The main thing is the fighting in Managua, Pastora said. "I have artillery with me and if there's no communication, that must mean they're fighting hard and they need me. Let's go for Managua."

Pastora arrived on the twentieth, just in time for the party.

In San Juan del Sur that morning the tugboat pilot Antonio Calderón lay sweating in his narrow wooden bed. He had been sick for days, unable to sail. But, of course, there was no work anyway. The port had been as still as death even before the *guardias* began coming down the hill.

Some rode in trucks, others came in jeeps or on foot, dragging their rifles behind them. They had gathered at the pier, ready at last to escape, when they had been stopped by a simple fact. There was no one to sail the boats. There was no one who knew how to sail who would volunteer, certainly, and no one else even wanted to tell the *guardias* who the tugboat pilots were or where they could be found.

Calderón's house was a few hundred feet behind the docks, up a dirt track littered with garbage. Made of cast-off scraps of wood, it was dark and smelled of the mud beneath it and of the sewage that ran in rivulets down the hill beside the door. Pigs snuffled at the front step below the gaze of the Virgin on the opposite wall. Calderón's wife and his nearly grown children were nervous, walking back and forth from the front room down into the mud-floored kitchen. Over the loud-speaker of the church the priest had told everyone to stay inside; that any attempt to oppose the *guardias* would cause them to burn the entire port. They would do it, they had said, in five minutes if they had to. They had grenades and rockets and the the guns of the Bearcat and there was no reason at all not to believe them. They must have become very angry by now, so close to escape, so sure of getting away, so unsure of when they might be attacked. Would the town continue to try to protect the pilots of the tugs? It did not seem, really, that such a thing would be possible.

The sound of the jeep rolling up to the wall below his house told Antonio that finally someone had broken. He heard the voice of a boy he knew. "Antonio Calderón. They want you."

Lieutenant Colonel Franklin Montenegro, the young Guardia commander of Rivas up the road, was meeting with some of his officers and a committee made up of the Father and some townspeople. Two other tug pilots had also been found and they were there and, at first, it seemed as if the situation might not be as bad, quite, as had been feared. Perhaps they would be able to take the *guardias* south down the coast just a few miles to Costa Rica and leave them there. They could do that. They would do that. That, apparently, had been part of the understanding when the *guardias* came into the town.

"No," one of the officers said angrily. "You do not set the terms here. We are going to El Salvador. We want nothing to do with Nicaragua and not with Costa Rica either. It is full of the Communists. You have got to take us to El Salvador, to La Unión, and there is no choice and there is no discussion."

Antonio Calderón and the other captains argued that they did not know the coast to the north, certainly not as far north as the Gulf of Fonseca and El Salvador. It was days away in these boats. There was no fuel, no food or water to sail that far. But the *guardias* did not care and would not listen and the threats they had made before they entered the town now came back.

The pilots—everyone in the town—believed that if they left with the *guardias* for El Salvador they would be killed. But if they stayed, the *guardias* would burn the port. That much was clear. That was the choice.

Calderón looked around him. Some of these *guardias* were broken and desperate and only wanted to escape. They tried to be kind; they talked as if, suddenly, they could all be friends. Some had found their women and some their entire families in the retreat to San Juan del Sur and they were anxious not only for themselves but for these people. But there were some, too, whose faces showed only hate and contempt. There were even a couple of Honduran mercenaries who seemed, because they were foreign and had no stake in any of this but the killing, particularly cruel.

At fifty-three, Antonio Calderón was sick. He thought of himself as an old man. "We decided we would die. This is where our families were."

One by one he and the other pilots pulled their tugs and the open barges up to the end of the pier. Into each barge went two hundred men or more. Others clambered onto the boats. The officers were trying to keep some discipline, but men were stripping off their gear. Some hurled their M-16s far out into the bay. Some let them slip into the water among the oyster shells and the skeletons of fishes and the crabs below the dock.

Others kept their arms. Those from the unit called the Rattlesnakes threw nothing away, not even the heavy 75mm recoilless rifle.

At 5:30 the evening of July 20, 1979, the boats pulled out past the rock outcroppings that mark the limits of the bay at San Juan del Sur.

II.

MANAGUA, NICARAGUA, JULY 20, 1979

Long before dawn on the twentieth the victorious rebel troops began arriving in Managua from León, Masaya, Chinandega, Matagalpa. "A people united will never be defeated," some of them shouted. "A free fatherland or death," they chanted. Or just "A free fatherland. A free fatherland." There wasn't going to be any more death. Highways were filled with ragged soldiers singing about love and revolution, martyrdom and joy, fighting, and freedom after the decades of torpor under the dictators and these last months of escalating slaughter. Radio Sandino, still broadcasting from a hidden location, began calling people to the Plaza de la República. But they were there already.

For almost seven years Nicaragua's capital had been a hollow city, never rebuilt after the earthquake in 1972 that had destroyed its entire center. The answer of the dictatorship to reconstruction had been to bulldoze the buildings that were mostly collapsed and to leave standing without repair those few that were mostly intact. So now, in the rainy season, what had been the downtown was mostly weeds and rubble. On a hill overlooking the destruction the pyramid-shaped Intercontinental Hotel was still standing. And, surrounded by a few shells of other buildings, the Bank of America stood, a skyscraper above the emptiness.

During the fighting, Managua's center had seemed deserted except for the killers and the dead. But now it was suddenly filled with life. Guns were firing, but into the air and out of happiness. There were no more ambushes near the ditches through the highways. No one hid behind the barricades made of paving stones. People climbed through the rubble of the cathedral and waved the red-and-black banners of the Sandinistas from its crumbling windows. The women who sold cigarettes by the pack or singly on the sidewalks, the men who labored over the repair of tires that should have been thrown away years before, the children who wore no clothes until they were almost old enough to ask for them, all found their way to the plaza. The girls who had grown up knowing that at any moment a *guardia* could look at them and like them and have them, and the boys who had seen their friends stretched out on sidewalks, questioned, crying, and shot through the head and burned on the streets, they found their way to the plaza. They came from the dusty slums made of plywood and unfinished boards and cardboard and they came, too, from the cool white houses of Las Colinas. They came from the *mercados* around the bus stations and the slick Miami-style shopping centers, Plaza España and Ciudad Plástica. They packed themselves along the balustrades of the National Palace, where the dictator's congress had met. They burned tires and they danced.

Later, even a few months later, it would be hard for some people in Nicaragua to remember the ecstasy of that moment. It would haunt some of them like a mistaken love, the recollection of happiness only deepening the disillusionment, the embarrassment, the regret. Others would see it in perspective as the beginning of a long struggle and look to it for inspiration, but the joy would be lost to them, impossible to describe, a feeling that haunted like a taste or smell from childhood.

A world of exiles had arrived in the first hours. Some had fought alongside the troops, others only claimed to. Some had been in the background advising. Chileans and Argentines in exile had been with Nicaragua's rebels. They had fought the fight against Somoza that they had lost against Pinochet in the slaughter at the soccer stadium in Santiago de Chile; they were survivors of the reign of terror called the Dirty War that crushed them in Buenos Aires and in Cordova. There were three full columns of Argentine *montonero* guerrillas and support personnel, and members of the Argentine Ejercito Revolucionario del Pueblo (ERP) had helped the Sandinistas run their intelligence apparatus. There was Spadáfora and his Panamanians and Costa Ricans. There were Cubans. There were Palestinians. There were guerrillas from El Salvador looking, now, to pursue their own war at home, just across the Gulf of Fonseca. This was the first great battle for the revolution which had been won in the Western Hemisphere in twenty years. It had been two decades since Fidel marched into Havana. Twenty years since the capital of Cuba had felt this same joy. Now other capitals seemed certain to follow. The internationalists saw this as part of their own struggle. They had lost their battles, but they had survived and they would soon go home again. Nicaragua was the first new step toward their return. All they had to do was make it work.

In the plaza the people waited for the arrival of the new junta and for the Sandinistas' Directorate. The Ortega brothers—Daniel, who looked as if his mind were somewhere else, Humberto with his face thin and his arm withered with the pain of an old wound—were coming; Jaime Wheelock, whose boyish face was made to excite young girls and whose approach to the revolution was cool, urban, Chilean; and Tomás Borge, the last of the original founders of the Sandinista National Liberation Front, his voice powerful, his body small and oddly formed and showing the suffering of so many years in jail. These were the leaders of the Front's three factions. They had been together and split apart and plotted against each other as much as against Somoza until the war and Fidel had pulled them together in March. Now they had led the revolution to victory. So the people cheered them. But the people were waiting, too, for Pastora.

"Freedom in Managua and in the whole country of Nicaragua today has new meaning," shouted a Costa Rican television reporter in the crowd. "Freedom to gather together, freedom to shout, freedom to welcome their new government of National Reconstruction. The fight, the fight has been really long. There were seven weeks in the final offensive. Today it all ends. Today is joy. Today here is the Fiesta of Free Nicaragua. This is Managua that we observe at this moment."

In front of the old stadium, the statue of the first General Somoza, ridiculous astride a horse, was pulled down and dismembered. The bunker from which the last General Somoza had run his war was first occupied by the boys, many of them barefoot and in ragged, thrown-together uniforms of green and blue jeans. They posed for the television cameras brought by the journalists who lived next door at the Intercontinental. They pointed their rifles in a pose as old as daguerrotypes, but there was nothing at which to aim. Having suddenly found themselves in the most inner sanctum of the dictator with no one to oppose them they were befuddled. But soon the Argentine exiles in the Sandinista intelligence operation arrived and began sifting through the drawers. And in a few hours the new commanders of the new army had made the bunker their own. They renamed it El Chipote, after the stronghold of Sandino. But in the windowless conference room Somoza's hand-drafted map of the city was left spread out over the entire length of the long table. On one corner was scribbled the phone number of the dictator's favorite commander for easy reference: "Bravo 26781."

When Pastora arrived, the Directorate was meeting there with a handful of other commanders. Pastora entered like a bull, whirling to face first one commander and then another, oblivious to protocol and full of good spirits. This was, after all, a time for celebration, not for ceremony. The members of the Directorate looked up at him. He looked at Humberto Ortega, who sat stiffly, his dead arm resting limp on the map. There was a pause.

"Humberto, I've got the entire South at El Retiro," Pastora said. He had brought two thousand men from the Southern Front to Managua and had left them on the edge of the city because he had no idea where to put them, or how to feed them. "What do I do with these people? Who do I turn them over to? Where do I take them? Do I disarm them? What do I do?"

Pastora heard later that he had burst in on the Directorate as they were discussing how to surround his men and disarm them. He heard, he said, that the Cubans were in fact the ones who opposed that idea, warning that it would start fighting and butchery on both sides in the new army. The Cubans were always pushing for unity, always guarding it. But Pastora said later, without any apparent sense of irony, "I was always afraid of treason."

III.

NICARAGUA, 1937–1979

Edén Pastora came from the high forests and wide-open fields of Matagalpa province, where men—even men who were not rich men—owned the mountains on which they lived and, in some cases, for as far as they could see. Nicaragua had a lot of land and few people. When Pastora was born, one of a family of five children, there were scarcely more than a million Nicaraguans. It was a nation of pioneers and cowboys, of peasants and aristocrats, and some families seemed to include all categories. The Pastoras' mountain was almost five thousand acres near the village of Ciudad Darío. Edén Pastora was born there on the twenty-second of January 1937, the son of Pedro Panfilo Pastora and Elsie Gómez de Pastora. When he was seven years old, his father died. "On the road to the farm, they caught him with a shotgun blast between the shoulders." He had owned land that a Guardia general had wanted, and when he fought to keep it, the Guardia's thugs killed him.

Edén was the youngest of the five Pastora children who had lived, and he was, it seems, his mother's favorite.

"She was white, so white, she looked like a gringo, with chestnut-colored hair," Pastora remembered. She had gone to a convent school in Louisiana in the United States, Pastora said, and "she spoke an English like I've never heard. It was an English that was breathy. I remember the way she would say 'New Orleans' and 'Jesus Christ.' "

When Pastora was thirteen he was sent to the Jesuit boarding school in the old capital of Granada, the Colegio Centroamerica. El Indio, the others called him, perhaps because of his own dark skin, or perhaps because he was so rough and crazy and because he had so little money.

"From the time of his youth he was a little resentful," remembered a schoolmate. "It was like a complex, feeling that he was from the poor Pastora family, because there was also a rich Pastora family."

Edén built his life around sports, playing everything except bas-

ketball "because it was for queers. You bump somebody and
BRRRRRRR, it's a foul." And Pastora always called attention to himself. Other boys, even others from Matagalpa, fitted in more easily:
handsome young Jorge Salazar, for instance, whose family owned the
mansion-hotel where the gringos stayed at Santa Maria de Ostuma and
who grew up to be a leader of the country's businessmen. Jorge was a
cousin. Pastora called him Patelana and they got along well enough,
but Jorge was always smoother, better spoken, and in his last years of
high school he went away to the United States, to the Culver Military
Academy.

Pastora's mother had to sell two cows to buy Edén Pastora a
uniform for the Colegio's marching band, but he eventually became its
leader. It was called, in Spanish, the "band of war," and "El Indio"
Pastora loved to parade before it giving commands with his cornet.

Alfonso Robelo, who grew up to make millions making the vegetable oil that Nicaraguans used to cook their tortillas, and who then
became the private sector's representative on the revolutionary junta,
served with the band on the snare drum. José Francisco "El Chicano"
Cardenal played the bass drum. He was also Pastora's closest friend
on the soccer team. They broke their legs playing against bigger boys.
Cardenal went off to Catholic University in Washington and then
helped lead the businessmen who opposed the Somozas.

How the tangle of friendships formed at the Colegio would sort out
in the midst of civil war could never have been predicted. But the
Colegio was in Granada, the capital of the Conservative party and the
heart of aristocratic opposition to the Somozas. So when Edén Pastora
told his classmates that his father had been killed by Somoza's general,
and that he would take his vengeance someday, his friends may have
thought him melodramatic, but the idea was not exotic or rare. And
Pastora always talked.

It was in Guadalajara, Mexico, while biding time as a medical
student, that Pastora first began reading seriously about Augusto César
Sandino, the Nicaraguan "general of free men" who fought against the
American occupation and the Guardia Nacional the United States had
created in the 1920s and 1930s. He was Pastora's perfect hero, full of
fire and intensity, fighting against enormous odds and practically on his
own, defying the power of his nation's armies and those of the vast and
magically powerful United States with a mystical and indefatigable determination. It was not an ideological thing. It was purely visceral.

Pastora first raised a red-and-black flag and joined a movement named after Sandino to fight the Somozas in the late 1950s when there were almost as many movements as there were revolutionaries. There were student groups and there were bourgeois groups. There were Marxists and there were Conservatives, all disunited in their opposition to the dynasty. Former generals in Sandino's army had survived, in a few cases, to pull together a few men and to fight on.

In 1956 a young poet had assassinated the founder of the dictatorship. But the sons had held on to their fief. In 1958 their men had massacred students at León and the country had been filled with indignation. Then the Cuban revolution in 1959 had inspired new hopes and new ambitions. But only slowly did the groups coalesce around the young ideologues Tomás Borge and Carlos Fonseca in the Frente Sandinista de Liberación Nacional in the 1960s as it became clear that the young Somozas were never going to give up their power.

From the beginning there were antagonisms among the revolutionaries, and Pastora was party to many of them, especially with the diminutive, intense Borge.

Borge was an intellectual and a poet. Pastora was a peasant and a fighter. Borge was the plotter, Pastora the romantic. Borge was a Marxist strategist, Pastora a dreamer about democracies. But both were born to be demagogues or dictators.

"The quarrel between us is historical, brother," Pastora said. "If you want to make it simple, I started into the struggle in '58 and '59. Tomás was making revolution in the cafés of Tegucigalpa after he got out of jail, where he'd landed after the business with the execution of Somoza. He was knocking around there, a Nicaraguan exile in the Jardin de Italia there while *we* were in the mountains. So then he takes off for Cuba. He wants to cut a figure and get the prestige among the Communists."

The world, even the world of Nicaragua, took little notice for most of those years. The Alliance for Progress was bringing some limited improvement to Nicaraguan life. An election in 1967 brought some disillusionment. With that, the second General Somoza formally established his dynasty. But in the same year, at a village in Matagalpa province called Pancasán, the Guardia crushed the fledgling rebel organization of the Sandinista Front.

It did not resurrect itself until seven years later. Its leaders were in hiding or in prison. Some had lent themselves to Chile's attempt at democratic revolution. Others had trained with Palestinians in the Middle East. Still others, led by Tomás Borge, had plotted and trained in

Cuba. Not until 1974 did the Sandinistas re-emerge in a burst of gunfire, breaking in on a Christmas party and taking hostage much of the diplomatic corps in Managua.

Yet Pastora, for all his own restless movement through the revolution, managed to miss many of the watershed events in the development of the Sandinista Front. He missed Pancasán; he was not involved in the Christmas party raid. And he was not jailed. Partly for the latter failing he was never quite accepted by the rest. Their view of the world was shaped by the life they had led in the prisons of the Somozas.

Daniel Ortega would talk of five jailings, seven years in continuous confinement, as "a time of rich experiences."

Borge was beaten and tortured and his tiny body shrunken from repeated hunger strikes. He would remember the hood that cut off his breath, the handcuffs, the suffering that lasted week after week and then month after month. Borge would remember 59 days without food. And, even when that was over, he would remember the terror of the loneliness in an isolated cell. "I was always afraid," he said, "that I would be murdered while I was alone." Nine months of torture. Two years alone. "It is not pleasant to be alone."

While Ortega was in jail and Borge in Cuba in the 1960s, Edén Pastora was in Mexico and in Los Angeles and in Italy and in Switzerland (as an illegal alien and a kitchen helper in Geneva). He was in and out of the mountains; he accepted amnesties and grew tobacco in Nicaragua; he was detained, but only briefly, in Venezuela as a presumed Communist.

At one point Pastora tried, and failed, to go to Cuba. Tomás Borge, he thought, blocked his way by advising Fidel that he was an unreliable social democrat. The bitterness between them grew. But Borge's power was increasing in the Front. Pastora steadily was squeezed out. There were rumors he might be killed.

In 1973, Pastora retreated to the fishing village of Barra del Colorado on the northeast coast of Costa Rica along the border with Nicaragua, where the Rio San Juan merges with the sea. He was there when Borge plotted the Christmas hostage-taking. He was there when Somoza began his state of siege and the systematic elimination of anyone, especially anyone in the northern mountains, who might have supported the Sandinista guerrillas. Pastora was in Barra del Colorado when the organization of the Sandinista Front was shattered by internal divisions. And when the main intellectual force in the Front, Carlos

Fonseca, was killed by the Guardia in 1976 while trying to repair the schism, Pastora was still safe in Barra del Colorado by the sea.

"I lived on the beach in a fisherman's hut, with my woman and my children, on the sand of the beach! The roof was made of straw, the floor of sand. I was a fisherman and I lived from the fish.

"I didn't know how to catch them, didn't know how to gut them. Hell, the first shark I hooked, I gaffed it and I brought it into the boat alive. And it damn near ate me, the son of a bitch, in the bottom of the boat. I didn't know how to row, and I went out in a rowboat. Son of a bitch.

"So after two years I wasn't a fisherman, I was a businessman. I bought shark. I bought coconuts. One day one thing, the next the other. And I'd built my house in the town . . . and I was getting things together. I already had a speedboat. I had launches and boats, skiffs, I had several coolers and a freezer.

". . . One day," said Pastora, "I was surprised to see, coming into Barra, Sergio Ramírez and Carlos Coronel." Ramírez was an author and intellectual with long ties to the Front. He had once sold his Volvo to help them raise money. The other, from a distinguished old family, was a professional conspirator, plotter, gun smuggler and an old friend.

"The boys want to talk to you," said Sergio.

"What boys?"

"The Directorate."

"What directorate?" Pastora asked.

"The Directorate of the Sandinista Front."

By now Borge was in jail again. Others of Pastora's old enemies were incommunicado in the mountains. But Daniel and Humberto Ortega were in San José and they were pushing a new approach to the fight, one that Pastora just might like. It was being called Tercerismo, the third way.

Ideas about how to bring about the revolution, often theoretical, sometimes ludicrous, sometimes tragic, were always evolving. First there was the notion of building an invasion force, going out of the country, training and arming, then moving back in across the borders from Costa Rica in the south or Honduras in the north and, so, marching toward victory. In 1962, Borge and the others had moved in from Honduras and had achieved nothing but suffering. So the strategy began to change, under the influence of the Cubans and of Ché Guevara and the Frenchman Regis Debray. Now the strategy called for building *focos*. They would go to the mountains, congregate there, train there and try to create an uprising in the region, building an insurrection that eventually would be projected into the cities. For more than a decade they followed these plans, and there was no revolution. Then Wheelock had come back from Chile with his notion that the revolt would be built in the cities by slow and careful organization of the workers there, and that the mountains were not important. But still there was no revolution.

Now, when Pastora went to San José to talk to the Ortegas he was being presented with a plan to join forces with businessmen and landowners, Conservative party leaders—all the people the other revolutionaries scorned but whom he knew so well. The Ortegas were going to attempt to build, quickly, a mass following capable of rising up at once all over the country. Pastora's old contacts, even his old schoolmates, would be useful for this. There was a great role for Pastora to play as a leader of the *tercerista* faction, they said, and he could not resist.

"We left Barra as poor as when we'd arrived, leaving the home I'd made, the refrigerators, the freezers, boats, motors, the estate with five thousand acres that I'd bought, all left to my sons."

The first *tercerista* attempts at insurrection in 1977 failed. Of all the towns and villages targeted for uprisings, only three saw any action at all. But the military move was followed by a political ploy. Twelve respected and moderate men were pulled together in public opposition to the dictator: economists, businessmen, priests and the intellectual/author Sergio Ramírez. They flew back to Managua together and their return provoked more rioting, more opposition to Somoza.

In January 1978, the enormously popular publisher of *La Prensa*, Pedro Joaquín Chamorro, was blown away by shotgun blasts as he drove through the barren lots of Managua's center on his way to work. He had long been the most powerful voice of the Conservative party; and the middle-class opposition to Somoza, and nearly everyone else, assumed that Somoza or his men had killed him. The country seemed to break open. The momentum of the revolution seemed unstoppable.

But there were hardly any guns with which to fight.

Now the new "democratic" face of the revolution began to pay off. With Pastora and Carlos Coronel setting up many of the connections, old José "Pepe" Figueres, the father of Costa Rican democracy and a longtime hater of the Somozas, started channeling guns from his personal arsenals and stockpiles to the Sandinistas working out of Costa Rica: 300 old M-1 rifles, bazookas, five .50-caliber machine guns and 30,000 rounds for them, grenades, mortars. The liberal dictator of Panama and the social democratic president of Venezuela also began to send arms. Contacts were made with what Pastora called la cosa nostra to buy still more guns. Weapons came from Miami and from Portugal as the arsenals grew for the insurrection.

The members of Borge's faction still dreamed of a prolonged war in the mountains, certain that it was the only true way to a genuine revolutionary triumph, and they hated those who divided their forces and questioned their tactics. Borge himself, even from jail, managed to communicate his fury. The Ortegas and their *terceristas* were called "putschists" and adventurers, allies of the bourgeoisie and traitors.

By mid-1978 the *terceristas* had organized in Granada and Rivas in the south, and there had been several attacks staged in the north. "To take over a little Guardia headquarters was not news anymore." So the planning began for a spectacular—for the palace where the Somoza congress met. It was a project worthy of Errol Flynn. And Pastora had dreamed of it for years.

Borge heard of this in jail and tried to influence the decision about who would lead the attack, about the size of the force. But he had difficulty getting his messages out of the prison, and when he succeeded, they were ignored.

On the morning of August 22, 1978, two olive-green pickup trucks, their beds shaded with olive-drab tarps, pulled up to the doors of the National Palace as the Somoza congress met inside. Pastora and a dozen of his people entered from the east and another thirteen entered from the west. They wore the uniforms of the Guardia's EEBI.

A private posted at the door jumped to attention, startled. "What's happening?" Pastora looked at him as if to say, you dumb bastard, you don't know? "The boss is coming," he said. "You cannot be armed. Give me your weapon." The startled private handed over his rifle and Pastora ordered him to leave. The private stared for a second and started running. Pastora and his squad sprinted up stairs that were polished and worn by the feet of so many years of bureaucrats and politicians and the supplicant peasants who petitioned them here. Another guard. Again, the question, What's happening? "The boss is coming. Give me your weapon." Now Pastora's squad, stepping sharply and with authority, marched to the door of the Blue Room, where the congress met. Three more guards surrendered to the ruse of the officer's uniform.

On the west side of the building, Hugo Torres was playing out the same scene. The sound of shots was beginning to echo in the corridor. Torres found his way to the door of the interior minister's office, burst in on him and took him prisoner.

Pastora crashed through the doors of the Blue Room, and hundreds of faces turned to him. "Eight years," he thought, remembering a hungry night in León when he first imagined this moment. "Eight years." He brandished his assault rifle and waited, smiling slightly at the hush and fear before him as five of his commandos sprinted to positions along the back benches. He sprayed bullets toward the ceiling. "Guardia Nacional. Hit the floor."

The negotiations went on for three days. More than a thousand people were held hostage in the National Palace by this group of terrorists led by a man calling himself Commander Zero, and the story was reported all over the world. The dictator's officers wanted Somoza to attack the palace, to show how tough he was. But he refused. His family, in many respects his world, was hostage to Pastora and the other Sandinistas there. Finally the Archbishop of Managua succeeded in negotiating an end to the crisis. Half a million dollars were to be paid and a long list of prisoners freed.

Guardias were visible along the route as the busses full of hostages headed for the airport and there was the chance that the busses would be attacked. "Ah, but that trip was the reward the people gave us for our stand, for our behavior, for our struggle," Pastora remembered. "The road was overflowing with people along those eleven kilometers. They cheered us. 'Viva! Viva!' they shouted."

At the airport waited a Venezuelan airplane sent to pick up the hostages and their captors and fly them to Panama. The busses rolled through the gates. The prisoners from Somoza's jails had already been brought there and Pastora began to read down the list of those who were supposed to have been released. The first name was Tomás Borge. Pastora called it out. There was no answer. "Tomás Borge Martínez," he repeated. Borge looked at him coolly. "Present," he said. Pastora smiled. "Tomasito. My little Tomás, is that you? You are here, Tomasito?" Pastora continued to read off the names of the other prisoners. When all had answered they turned, almost in unison, to

Borge. "Who is that?" they asked him. "He is Edén Pastora," Borge said contemptuously. "A *tercerista*." It was August 24, 1978.

On July 20, 1979, when the Sandinistas had triumphed, when the Directorate and the new junta had finally appeared before the crowd in the Plaza de la República (now the Plaza de la Revolución), there was chanting for Pastora. Louder than the name of anyone else, one heard his name and his pseudonym. "Zero. Zero. Zero," they called as they saw him up on the platform. He arrived in Managua with his hair long, almost down to his shoulders. His beard was weeks old, his fatigues covered with dirt. Pastora stood there as a revolutionary—*the* revolutionary; a Nicaraguan man—*the* Nicaraguan man. With his coarse language, his bragging, his bravery and his womanizing, his kindness and his many, many children, he was everything Nicaraguan men grew up laughing about and loving in themselves. And since the day eleven months before when he had stretched out his arms, raising his gun in front of him in a gesture that was both embrace and an act of defiance, then boarded the plane for Panama with the released prisoners and the hostages and the money he had wrested from the dictator, Pastora had been The Commander. Commander Zero. But he was not the commander of the revolution. He was only its star.

IV.

OFF NICARAGUA'S COAST

The sergeant called Suicida groped slowly through his pack. Was it two days since San Juan del Sur? The sun had been up for hours and was bright and hot and penetrating as it shone off the low swell of the sea around them. He kept his eyes closed and felt through his few belongings as if he were blind. His lips were open slightly. When, gingerly, he pressed them together he could feel the dried and cracked skin moving across his teeth. His stomach seemed to have moved up to the base of his throat. The sergeant's fingers felt the cool, wrinkled metal of the tube. He pulled it out and slowly twisted off the top. He put it to his lips and squeezed the toothpaste slowly onto his swollen tongue, then shut his white teeth over it. The taste of mint covered the taste of rot in his mouth, but the acid began to churn in his stomach.

They had run out of water and food on the first day, and now, halfway into the second, the suffering had become serious. There was no fuel left and there was no way to put in to shore without being captured and, they were certain, being killed.

Suicida passed the tube to Julio César, who bit off a bit of paste and pushed it around his mouth with his tongue.

Another soldier took the bandana off his head, unrolled it and dropped it over the edge into the seawater. He wrung it out and pushed the cool cloth against his forehead, but there was no relief.

In the last days of the war, the ranks of the Guardia had been bloated to almost fourteen thousand men. But the fighters had always been few: never more than four thousand who really knew what they were doing. The rest were clerks, secretaries, drivers, traffic police. It had been, the soldiers on the barges thought in those long, deadly hours beneath the sun, an uneven fight from the start. So many people against them, so many guns going to their enemies. And yet it was just—what, five weeks ago?—that they had been winning the war, clearly winning the war, when they forced Pastora back into Costa Rica. The Americans had cut off their guns a long time ago, but they had found other sources. Israel had come through for them and the *guardias* on the barges looked like nothing so much as Israeli soldiers, with their Israeli Galil rifles and, for those who had not thrown them away, their Israeli paratrooper helmets. Then the Americans had pulled some strings with the Israelis just as a ship was due with crucial supplies and ammunition. The ship had turned away. The supplies never arrived.

Yet, still, they had not thought they would be defeated. Those who were at the front truly never thought they would fall and kept the faith that they would eventually, somehow, get the people behind them. They had seen that the Communists were gaining ever more territory, especially in the north, but for some reason that they could not explain, even to themselves, the soldiers had kept their spirit, never thinking of defeat until, finally, it had come and they found themselves alone on this wide sea.

Somebody tried to shout, but the sound emerged as a groan. The man twisted his body to the side and stared out toward where the land should be. There was a boat coming. Suicida squinted. It could be a patrol boat. The Communists. "The bazooka," he said. His voice came out as a whisper. The boat was rising high above its wake as it approached, and the men on it were armed. Everyone was aware of it now and those who still had their guns pushed them up onto the edge of the barge and along the railing of the tug. Some looked about them for the other boats and barges that had come up from San Juán del Sur, but since they had run out of fuel the night before they had been drifting apart and now they were lost to each other.

The makeshift patrol boat, a cabin cruiser commandeered by the Communists, was bearing down. Suicida hoisted the recoilless rifle onto his shoulder. There was almost no ammunition for it; perhaps one or two shells.

The men on the approaching boat made out the form of Suicida and as the significance of the long, highly machined tube propped on his shoulder dawned on them they quickly decelerated. Suicida never took his eyes or the barrel of his recoilless rifle off them.

How long, exactly, this confrontation lasted, or what exactly persuaded the young representatives of the new government of Nicaragua that this floating collection of half-dead *guardias* was not worth a fight or even a serious risk, is not certain. But as Suicida told the story they turned tail when they thought he would blow them out of the water and they left him and his men alone.

Alone with their thirst and their hunger. And with no fuel for the tug.

Suicida had taken a course at the U.S. Army School of the Americas in Panama. For days he had marched through the jungles there, living on reptiles and beetles, listening to instructors talk about edible plants, hiding in the mud in imaginary ambushes. They had taught him how to stay alive and to fight in the jungle. But they had taught him nothing about how to stay alive in defeat.

What would happen now? If they made it to La Unión, if others made it to La Unión, then maybe there was hope. If they moved quickly, they would have much of their fighting force left intact. Of the total number of real combat troops in the Guardia maybe a third had been pulled out of San Juan. If they regrouped, and if they could win the support of some other country to re-arm them, then there was a chance. The Communists were not such fighters after all. They had won only because of the treachery of the United States. If this journey, this sun, this thirst, could only be brought to an end, maybe there was a fight still to be fought.

Later on the second day those *guardias* whose eyes were still open watched as Antonio Calderón, the pilot of the tug, searched for and, finally, found an old bucket. He rubbed his hand around the inside of it to clean away some of the oil and other refuse that stuck to it. The *guardias* watched passively as Calderón unfastened his pants and began to piss into the bucket. It must have seemed a curious bit of fastidiousness. And then the tugboat captain sat with the bucket in front of him, staring at his urine.

"The seawater will kill you," he explained to those close enough to hear him. Calderón raised the bucket to his lips and drank. When the bucket was empty he passed it to the *guardias*. They did not follow his example.

V.

MANAGUA, NICARAGUA

The United States embassy in Managua was housed in a prefabricated building on the South Highway that looked like nothing so much as a collection of trailer homes. As makeshift and impermanent as everything in Managua, including this new peace, it was a "temporary" structure that had been around since the aftermath of the 1972 earthquake, and it was not an agreeable place to work or to think or to have to sort out the records of disaster which now began piling up on everyone's desk, including the new ambassador's. Now that the dictator was gone and the new junta in place—a government with an anthem that called the United States the enemy of humanity—there was little left to do for the moment but to try to cut losses and build, from less than nothing, new relationships.

Lawrence Pezzullo had arrived in Managua for the first time on June 27, 1979, at the height of the Sandinista offensive. Over almost twenty years he had built his career in the foreign service on his wits, his intensity and his expertise on Latin America. A tall man with rough but distinguished features, Pezzullo had joined the foreign service as a boy from the Bronx vying with ambitious aristocrats, and he had developed into a diplomat with something of the streetfighter about him.

His first job upon his arrival as ambassador to Nicaragua had been to get Somoza out.

For almost a year a formula had been sought that would persuade the dictator to leave. Delegations had been sent from Washington and from the Dominican Republic and even Guatemala. Their hope had been to derail, if not the growing momentum of the revolution, then the burgeoning strength of the Sandinistas within it. The tactic of the United States was to build the center, to reenforce the position of businessmen and other moderates who mistrusted and hated Somoza but who also hated and mistrusted the Sandinistas. But the center, in the face of the Sandinistas' maneuvering and Somoza's intransigence, had never been able to hold. And the tactic of the Ortegas and others of courting the moderate opposition and playing down their Marxist rhetoric and views had pulled the center steadily toward the Sandinista camp. It was as if, after a forty-five-year gestation, the people of Nicaragua were about to be delivered into the light, and the country was bursting with hope and expectations and all that stood in the way was Somoza.

But when the United States had come down to deliver the baby it could not do it. Despite entreaties and maneuvers and threats by Washington in the months after the taking of the National Palace, Somoza would not budge. He stalled, agreeing to a plebiscite and then announcing that a plebiscite was no good because the Liberal party—the party he controlled—would not go along. As the Nicaraguan people gradually saw that the great United States could not deliver the dictator's resignation, much less the revolution, the talks broke down and the strength of the Sandinistas grew still more. They had presented themselves as the only force capable of actually bringing the dictator down. And they were proved right.

Pezzullo's boss, Assistant Secretary of State Viron Vaky, came to the conclusion that "Somoza was quite prepared through all of this to see the center disintegrate and get chewed up because he wanted it to polarize. I think he felt that if he could polarize it and make it a situation of Somoza versus Marxists that the United States and everybody else would rally to him. And he always used the argument of '*après moi le déluge*' and I think he was perfectly prepared to let that happen. It was a measure of the contempt that he had for the moderate opposition."

As the Sandinistas' final offensive gathered momentum in June the United States scrambled to gain control of the situation. It was trying to maneuver into a position where it could shape the new regime, getting guarantees that at least part of the Guardia Nacional would be preserved, that there would be something like conventional American-style political pluralism, and that the Nicaraguan revolution would not prove too contagious. Certainly there was concern that the new Nicaragua would become a staging area for all the other revolutionary movements in the region that were chafing to break loose.

But the dictator whose family dynasty was built on its ability to manipulate the prejudices and needs of the United States understood the American democratic system far better than Washington's Democrats understood him. He had made himself part of an influential old-boy network of ultra-conservatives in the United States who admired his tough talk and his steadfast hatred of communism so utterly devoid of self-doubt.

One of Somoza's best friends was Congressman John Murphy. They went to LaSalle Military Academy together in Oakdale, Long Island, back in the thirties and forties, and after Somoza graduated from West Point they continued their friendship in New York. After Murphy went to the Congress with many Central American responsibilities and Somoza inherited his dictatorship, they continued in close contact.

"Tacho was a man's man—the kind of a man you like to have a drink with, to go fishing with, and the type of person everyone respected, not only for his strong personality but also for a very keen intellect," Murphy said.

There were many other conservatives as well who, if not so personally close to the dictator, supported his stand against communism at any cost. Ronald Reagan, a kind of pre-candidate for U.S president at the time, surrounded himself with such thinkers. They were convinced that Carter's talk of morality in international affairs was a delusion; that the greatest immorality in the world was the immorality of communism and anything that seemed in the least to give in to the Communists was dangerous and unacceptable. In the end, it did not matter how the Nicaraguan people felt about Somoza; what mattered was that his position was one of maintaining the dignity of the United States. That was what Somoza stood for and why he should be supported.

"It was quite obvious to knowledgeable people in Central America that Nicaragua was America's closest and strongest ally," Murphy said. "Nicaragua was a blocking position in Central America in that it extended from the Pacific Coast to the Atlantic Coast and nothing could move up or down the Americas without being monitored or going through Nicaragua on land, without being exposed to Nicaragua's territorial seas, or flying over Nicaragua's air space. And therefore its strategic importance was very vital to American interests. As is all of Central America."

Somoza, and his brother who was president before him, and his father, who was president before them, "were absolute allies to the United States," Murphy said. But the Carter administration had come into office preoccupied with the aftermath of Watergate and the revelations by congressional investigations of massive immorality and, often, conspicuous ineffectiveness in the United States' dealings with the world. Carter was elected amid hopes that, somehow, the goals and designs of U.S. foreign policy could be brought into conformity with the values that most Americans still believed they held, and held firmly, "human rights" among them. Anticommunism was not considered sufficient justification for barbarity.

On June 20, a week before Pezzullo's first meeting with Somoza, an American television correspondent was videotaped walking up to a Guardia roadblock in Managua. His name was Bill Stewart. He was taped as a young, red-eyed *guardia* ordered him to his knees and then to his belly. The *guardia* looked at him and calmly blasted a rifle bullet into his head. Such support for Somoza as had been mustered in the United States was, suddenly, muted.

On June 23, the Organization of American States, which had begun to fear both Somoza's endurance and U.S. impotence to deal with it, called unequivocally for the replacement of his regime. It also demanded a new government representing all the forces that opposed the dictatorship—conservatives, centrists and Sandinistas—full guarantees of human rights for Nicaragua's citizens and "free elections as early as possible." But point number one was that the *Somocista* government must go. And still, Somoza did not resign.

Pezzullo met the dictator at 4:30 on the afternoon of the twenty-seventh. Congressman Murphy was there and at each of the three crucial meetings that followed. (At one point, taking note of this, Pezzullo warned Somoza to stay away from U.S. politicians, especially Ronald Reagan, if he went into exile in the United States. Somoza secretly taped the conversations and later published them as part of a vitriolic attack on the Carter administration accusing it of conspiring consciously to impose a Communist government on Nicaragua.)

Somoza suggested they talk in English. "Me being a Latin from Manhattan, I had rather listen to the things in your language because I can understand them just as well as in Spanish."

Pezzullo, who would not formally submit his credentials, was cordial but blunt: "We don't see a solution without your departure; we don't see the beginning of a solution without your departure."

Pezzullo watched the dictator carefully. He was dressed in a very formal business suit and looked more like a banker than a leader of a nation and the leader of its military in the middle of a war. His nerves seemed taut, but he was also businesslike. He clearly understood what was going on and was concerned about protecting whatever was left of his image and his dynasty, however problematic such ambitions might have been.

Somoza wanted guarantees for himself and his family and his party and even his country, and he talked about these questions in very personal and emotional terms. "Let's not bullshit ourselves, Mr. Ambassador, I am talking to a professional. You have to do your dirty work and I have to do mine." There was always something reminiscent of pulp-fiction melodrama in the dictator's voice. "Let's get down to the hard fact, Ambassador," he said. "If you don't give me an alternative to go where I think my country is, the U.S., my alternative is to resign and go to the bush. And then you have Sandino again, all over again, and this poor goddamn country will never have peace. So I need guarantees for the people that are close with me." He reminded Pezzullo about the services he had performed for the United States, helping to overthrow the leftist government of Guatemala and providing a staging area for the Bay of Pigs invasion. "I am practically in your hands, so now administer your puritan justice on this matter."

But when the dictator spoke of the Guard itself he took a strangely distant approach.

The army that had been created by the United States as an apolitical peacekeeping force in the 1920s, and had been subverted almost instantly by the Somozas to become the rock on which they built their dynasty, was now, once again, nothing but an extension of the United States. And it was Jimmy Carter's responsibility, not Somoza's.

"After you have spent thirty years educating all of these officers I don't think it is fair for them to be thrown to the wolves," said Somoza. "Mr. Ambassador, these men who are actually fighting today are not babies. They are people that you brought from common houses of Managua, Nicaragua, and made them gentlemen and good people through the education of the United States—right now the United States is going against these people! . . .

"These people have felt themselves alienated because they have been fighting communism, just like you taught them at Fort Gulick and Fort Benning and Leavenworth."

Several times the dictator came back to the same point. "Out of some nine hundred officers we have, eight hundred or so belong to your schools." Ironically, it was much the same point made in the Sandinistas' anti-American propaganda.

Pezzullo was quick to reassure the dictator. "We are not abandoning the Guard,'' he said. The U.S. had indeed been training them and it merely wanted to see them as ''a professional guard that could serve this country loyally and patriotically under any circumstances. It's the political issues that . . .'' But Pezzullo stopped short. He had not been looking for a debate. And it should have been clear to everyone in the room that the Carter administration, while it had cut off the weapons supplied to the Guard in order to pressure Somoza, wanted to preserve the institution as the only measure that could forestall a complete San-dinista victory. The whole idea was to save the Guard by separating it from Somoza.

The dictator suddenly offered to leave the next day, without any further preparation.

''Please don't move too precipitously,'' Pezzullo cautioned. He had visions of Samson trying to bring down the temple.

''I am not going to move without having my back well protected,'' Somoza said. ''So you are my protection.''

''Let's do it with grace,'' said Pezzullo.

''Right,'' said the dictator.

But when Somoza finally did leave, when it appeared that a deal had been struck and the Sandinistas and their new government junta had agreed to several conditions—most importantly of all the preser-vation of most of the National Guard under a newly selected leadership —when, after three more bloody weeks, the dictator finally did depart, it was utterly without grace.

The arrangement, reiterated countless times in what had seemed endless meetings, was for Somoza to leave the country at about four in the morning on the seventeenth. He would hand over power to the Congress. Francisco Urcuyo Maliaño, a little man with a fat face and a toothbrush mustache that made him look like a waiter at a stuffy restau-rant, would then be elected briefly to the position of constitutional president. The junta—Daniel Ortega and Sergio Ramírez and Moisés Hassan for the Sandinistas, Alfonso Robelo and Violetta, the widow of Pedro Joaquín Chamorro, for the non-Marxist opposition—would fly in from Costa Rica the same day and they would all sit down and sort out the details of the thoroughly prearranged transfer of power. It was a deal as tenuous as it was elaborate, but it was all there was and Pezzullo had taken several steps to make sure there was no confusion. In case Somoza had not bothered to let Urcuyo know what was ex-pected, and lest there be any misunderstanding on that score, Pezzullo

arranged two meetings in which the whole deal was explained to Urcuyo in front of Somoza. It was the only way left at this point to end
the war while still saving the Guardia.

But as the countdown proceeded toward the resignation and departure of the dictator, signs of trouble began to develop that, in retrospect, Pezzullo felt he might have seen.

On the fifteenth, two representatives of the junta were in Managua
secretly to work out the arrangements. Pezzullo suggested they talk to
Urcuyo directly, but the next day they called back and said they could
not make contact with him. Pezzullo thought it was a problem, but a
minor one, and plans went ahead for the revolutionary government to
arrive at the Managua airport at eight the following morning, four hours
after Somoza was scheduled to leave. The junta would talk to Urcuyo
about the political issues that had to be sorted out and members of the
Sandinista Directorate would talk to the new commander of the
Guardia.

Then Pezzullo got a call from Somoza himself. If the Directorate
came in to the main airport there might be trouble, Somoza said. Some
of them would probably be in uniform. Some would be armed and there
might be some sort of, well, some sort of scuffle. This is a war; somebody would get trigger-happy. Pezzullo thought about this for a moment. "What's the alternative?" he asked Somoza. The dictator
suggested that the new Guardia commander meet separately with the
Directorate in some neutral location. Pezzullo started trying to make
arrangements. But when he called Somoza back, Somoza was not
available. And Urcuyo was not coming to the phone. Finally the ambassador got a line through to the new commander of the Guardia,
Colonel Federico Mejía. Pezzullo had never spoken to him before, but
he told him that a U.S. plane with adequate security precautions would
be at the airport at seven in the morning, an hour before the junta
arrived, to take Mejía to Costa Rica for a meeting with members of the
Directorate in a neutral location. Mejía listened and agreed.

At about three in the morning busses began rolling up to the por-
tico of the Intercontinental Hotel, where many of Somoza's friends and
much of his government had gathered. They had run up enormous bills
and, in many cases, had been drunk for days in boredom and fear in
this building that looked like an odd, modern Mayan pyramid or tomb.
The now-retired zone commanders, members of the general staff and
the cabinet spilled nervously out of the building, their faces unshaven,
their *guayabera* shirts damp in Managua's heavy air. By three they

were on their way to the airport through the dead black of the city's vast, vacant center.

At 4 A.M. the dictator, tears streaming down his cheeks, had flown by helicopter to the airport. Within an hour he and his son and the other leaders of his government were on their way to Homestead Air Force Base in Florida, where they had been promised hospitable treatment as part of the agreement for his resignation. Their passports said they were businessmen.

At 7 A.M. the plane arrived from Costa Rica to pick up Mejía. It waited. But Mejía never showed. Pezzullo was being apprised of this as Urcuyo appeared on nationwide television. He was ludicrous in the blue-and-white sash, but what he was saying was serious, and disastrous. Urcuyo announced that, not only was he the duly elected president, he would finish out Somoza's term. Two years.

All bets were off; all the guarantees so carefully prepared were now voided, especially those concerning the Guard.

Pezzullo notified Washington and Washington got Somoza on the phone at his house in Miami to see if the deal could be salvaged. He was not welcome in the United States, he was told, because he had not lived up to the agreement. Somoza said he couldn't do anything. After all, he was no longer president. Why didn't they just order out Urcuyo the way they had ordered him out?

The ambassador was trying to do just that, but Urcuyo was acting as if he never heard of any agreement. And by the evening of the seventeenth the reports began to come in of the Guardia's complete disintegration.

Pezzullo left on the eighteenth rather than appear to be cooperating with Urcuyo's government.

After the final victory of the Sandinistas, Pezzullo was back in days to try to pick up the pieces. The junta was in command of the country. Urcuyo was gone. The Guardia was no more, and there was no basis on which to reconstruct it.

Hundreds of *guardias* already were being rounded up. Others, the officers mainly, had sought asylum in embassies. There were sporadic reports of summary executions. And the damnable thing was that, in the end, the dictator had made this mopping up so easy for the new regime. He had left almost all of his army's files intact: the personnel files, with their data on families; the intelligence files, with the contacts and sources and informers, were all there in black and white for the

Sandinistas to find. Several of the Guardia's people had also worked with the Agency, the CIA, so the intelligence disaster was contagious. For the next six months one of the biggest problems Pezzullo's embassy would face was the business of tying off the past so it would not affect operations in the present. Whole new networks had to be created from the ground up, and all loyalties had to be newly considered, or newly formed.

As Pezzullo looked over reports that indicated the extent of the damage, and as he thought back on Somoza's behavior, he could not escape the idea that the Guardia's intelligence files had been left behind on purpose; the dictator's last act of spite, a final gesture to guarantee that after him would come the deluge.

VI.

MANAGUA, NICARAGUA

Bill, the American, landed in Managua on July 19 in a phony Red Cross plane.

A couple of Somoza's *guardias* had made a pass before. But when they asked permission to land and the tower welcomed them to "Sandino Airport," they turned back to San Salvador. Bill took charge there. He painted the DC-8 he had brought down from Miami with the insignia of the Red Cross and flew back for Managua. Somoza's men stayed behind this time. Only Bill and the pilot, copilot and flight engineer touched down.

Bill was good at this sort of thing. An Italian-American from north of New York City, he did not talk much about whom he worked for. Most people who met him thought maybe he was being paid by the Somozas. But in any case his mission was clear. He was to rescue Colonel Justiniano Pérez, the second in command of the EEBI. He and his unit were favorites of Somoza's son. They were the core of the fighting force. If there was going to be any effort to win Nicaragua back, it would need them and their commander.

The airport was chaos. No one knew what anyone else was doing there. It was full of children carrying guns as tall as they were and claiming to represent the new regime. Here and there were young men wearing the tunics of the Red Cross. Somehow Bill found a taxi and a few minutes after he landed he was headed toward the city.

*   *   *

Most news about what was happening in Nicaragua in the days after the Sandinista triumph emphasized the joy of the victors and the problems of getting a new government organized. The focus was on the politics in the capital, and on the personalities of the new junta and the new *comandantes*. The picture that emerged was of a revolution that looked mainly to the future, one that was hopeful, not vengeful. There was no capital punishment. *Guardias* were told they could surrender to the Red Cross in the city and they would not be hurt and they would not be arrested. Even when, a few days later, the Sandinistas announced that all the *guardias* at the Red Cross center would be detained, tried and sentenced for their "crimes," there was little international protest. After all, they might have been shot in the streets.

But in the countryside and the provincial cities where the fighting had been heaviest the environment was more hateful, less controlled.

In León, Nicaragua's second largest city, "bodies were everywhere and the smell of death was penetrating." León had seen some of the fiercest fighting of the war. Virtually the entire center of the city was leveled. The market, with its elegant colonial arches, looked like a ruin from another century. The main public buildings, including the hospital, were destroyed. Of perhaps 100,000 inhabitants, more than 5,000 were believed dead. Many had been killed as they hid in their homes under the bombardment of Somoza's makeshift air force.

All the dictator had had were a few little Cessna-built O-2s with propellers fore and aft—"push-and-pulls" they were called—and a handful of other light military aircraft. But Somoza's men used them with deadly, indiscriminate effect.

"The bombs that Somoza was using at the EEBI were CIA bombs from the Bay of Pigs," said one of several Latin mercenaries who advised the dictator's men behind the scenes. "They were so old, and they was no delivery system; they just rolled them out of the backs of the planes.

"Then there were no more bombs, so we concocted giant Molotov cocktails from fifty-five-gallon drums of gasoline. At first we made them like napalm with trip flares. Then we discovered they were more effective if exploded at about a hundred feet, which would create an igneous cloud that would burn the people below to a crisp." The bombs ultimately had little impact on the combatants, but the impact on civilians was devastating. When word spread that the fighting was over, many people emerged into the light as if rising from the grave after a burial of weeks.

Neighborhoods were cordoned off with barbed wire and signs were posted at the entrances to many streets warning that the area was "contaminated." But the stench was enough to tell you that.

A Costa Rican reporter wrote from León that the victorious Sandinista rebels had "prisoners in practically every command post in the city." The Sandinista commander there was Dora María Téllez, who had been with Pastora in the taking of the National Palace. She told the reporter that more than a thousand prisoners had been taken in this one province. "We're looking for more," she said. "We know they are armed and in the mountains and that they come down at night to the cities and kill our people."

But stories also abounded of how the *guardias* and, especially, those who helped them—their informers, or their "ears," the *orejas*—were ferreted out and killed.

From talks with townspeople the Costa Rican reported that the first *guardias* who surrendered were paraded through the streets by Sandinista combatants asking people, "What do you want us to do with these beasts?" One older resident was quoted saying the scene was like something from a Roman circus, only the lions had been replaced by humans. In some places where the *guardias* refused to surrender the Sandinistas were reported to use firehoses to spray gasoline on their hideouts and threatened to burn them out. When the *guardias* tried to cut and run the "boys" chased after them as if they were dogs, shooting them down one by one.

"A woman who had been raped by a military officer was told that the guilty party had been captured. She then decided to identify him in the people's jail and asked the commanders if she could display him in the streets. She and the military officer and the other Sandinistas paraded throughout the morning, from corner to corner in León, asking people how the *guardia* ought to die. At the end of the day a long parade of the curious and *milicianos* had formed, and the woman took a bayonet and slit the throat of the supposed rapist."

Bill, the American, rode toward the low hills outside Managua where wealthy diplomats made their homes. The embassies there had filled up quickly with refugees, most of them members of the Somoza government, *guardias* and their families.

On the highway to Masaya the Guatemalan embassy took in almost four hundred people. One was eighteen-year-old Pedro Núñez Cabezas, who had had no direct part in the war. Sallow, acned, slow-talking and sleepy-eyed, he had been a high school student who tried to mind his own business, but he was now a refugee at the embassy with twenty members of his family because some of his uncles were *guardias* and his mother had worked with Somoza's Liberal party. One of the Somoza men who had made the initial pass at the airport was a relative and might have rescued him. But not now.

As Bill waded into the throng of refugees he was looking for only one man. "Who is Tino Pérez?" Bill had brought a pair of Red Cross vests and helmets "recuperated on the way," according to one account. Pérez came forward and Bill gave him one. They headed back toward the airport.

Mercenaries and agents of all descriptions were fleeing Managua any way they could for several days. Some went out with a bang, like the German who rampaged through the Intercontinental Hotel holding up reporters at gunpoint.

Some never made it. Cuban exiles, several of them veterans of the Bay of Pigs, had helped train the Guardia's paratroops, their armored corps, their intelligence service, and some worked with the *guardias* in the field. At least two of the Cubans were killed in action.

Other foreign advisors left more quietly. For several months a team of Argentines reportedly under the command of a young man named Carlos Durich had worked with Somoza's secret police. There were about half a dozen of them, from several different branches of the Argentine military, they said. They were not there in any "official" capacity, they told the Guardia commanders.

"Really, they didn't know shit from Shinola," said another of Somoza's foreign consultants who had frequent contact with them. "They didn't know much about organization. Their methods of interrogation were very primitive. But they were anticommunist from conviction."

They were hunting for the *montoneros* and ERP guerrillas who had joined up with the Sandinistas. They provided files showing the structures of the subversive organizations that had operated in Argentina, personality profiles of the various members of the guerrilla groups, the methods of operation used by the Argentine terrorists who had made it to Central America.

"The objective was a one-to-one exchange. They would send us any Nicaraguans in Argentina and we would send them any Argentines who turned up in Nicaragua."

They also proposed to supply Argentine passports for Nicaraguan agents and expected Nicaraguan passports in return. It was, said the consultant, "pretty standard stuff."

But when the Argentines saw that the Somozas had ordered their private jets to Managua, they assumed it was time to go themselves. They left on one of the last commercial flights, under assumed names.

Nicaraguans who worked with them had to fend for themselves.

Guardia Major Emilio Echaverry had gone to military school in Argentina from 1958 to 1961. He had married the daughter of an Argentine officer and, in the eyes of fellow officers, had picked up a considerable dose of Argentine arrogance. He served as a special assistant to Somoza starting in 1979 and he had helped the Argentine team try to track its enemies in Central America. But when Managua fell, all he could do was scramble for asylum in the Argentine embassy and stay there for the next six months.

Bill had smuggled Colonel Pérez onto the plane, but the Sandinistas were insisting now on searching it. No *guardias* were to get out. Before they came aboard Pérez managed to get up to the cockpit and put on the helmet of the flight engineer, whom nobody would have mistaken for a Nicaraguan. The disguise seemed sufficient and the boys cleared them and they started to taxi toward the runway. But now the tower ordered them to stop.

This search looked to be more thorough. If there were questions, the whole thing could come apart. Bill looked at the roof of the cabin. There were panels there that could be removed and he prized one open. Pérez crawled into the ceiling. The second Sandinista search team found no sign of the *guardia*. The plane was allowed to leave.

Over the next few days, Bill went about the business of pulling together remnants of the Guardia officer corps and their families from Guatemala and El Salvador. By the time the DC-8 set down in Miami again there were about 130 people on board. Survivors of the old Guardia, they had the potential, they hoped, to build a new one with a little help from friends like Bill and Congressman Murphy.

VII.

Off Nicaragua's Coast

At 10:30 on the morning of July 23 the *Don Gerardo,* a commercial fishing boat out of Corinto, Nicaragua, approached what appeared to

be a tug and barge full of corpses. A makeshift sail had been jury-rigged
above the tug's cabin, but the wind did not fill it. Men in ragged clothes
of olive green lay in what shade the sheet provided as if they had been
stacked there. When the *Don Gerardo* drew near, one or two of them
rose to their elbows and a few tried to stand, bending joints that had
been unmoved, now, for hours; flinching as their sun-blistered skin
cracked and stretched. They must have looked utterly helpless as the
Don Gerardo pulled alongside the barge. One of the fishing boat's crew
had a rifle which he trained on the men—hundreds of them—who lay
in the barge, but they seemed to be without the energy even to raise
their hands in surrender.

One of the *guardias* shouted to the fishermen with whatever
strength he could muster that they were bound for El Salvador, just a
few hours away now, if they could get some provisions. They had been
adrift now for four days and wanted no trouble. The fishermen were
dubious. They might pull the barge and tug into Corinto, or they could
leave these men completely, or they could help them. The officers
asked to talk and, with a few of their men, they boarded the *Don
Gerardo*.

Antonio Calderón, watching from the bridge of the tug, could not
be sure exactly what happened after that except that there was a scuffle
on board the *Don Gerardo* and the man with the rifle and the captain of
the boat were overpowered. The *guardias* trained their guns on them
and on the rest of the fishermen, and, like drunken pirates, the half-
dead soldiers on the barge and the tug began clambering onto the fishing
boat. They were, none of them, used to moving in ships. Many were
terribly weak. One of them, groping for the rail of the fishing boat, lost
his grip. He fell into the sea and sank out of sight. Scores of the men
were trying to board the boat at once and they spilled over the gunwales
like fish slithering over the edge of an overfull bait-bucket. At least five
of the *guardias* died like that, disappearing into the blue-green depths
of the Pacific. They did not even struggle, it seemed, but sank as if they
were weighted, twirling downward, even gripping their guns.

Calderón thought that, if only he could get some fuel, just a small
amount, he could get the tug back to Corinto and then take it back
down the coast and, so, return home again. It was the first moment of
hope he had. He approached a *guardia* and began trying to explain.
The captain of the fishing boat could take them to La Unión. He could
go home, now. He had done what they asked him. He could go to
Corinto, now.

The *guardia* put the muzzle of his Galil against Calderón's throat. "No, old man, you are coming with us."

It was perhaps two hours before all the men had abandoned the tug and others had been persuaded to stay in the barge and the barge had been tied to the *Don Gerardo*. By late afternoon they were headed across the Gulf of Fonseca making good time. Occasionally they thought they saw or heard other boats in the darkness around them, but there was nothing that brought them new problems and, at some hour after midnight and before dawn, they saw the lights of La Unión.

The barge was made fast to the pier and the *guardias* began crawling off. Officers, both Salvadoran and Nicaraguan, were waiting for them. There was Briceño, the lieutenant from the garrison at San Juan del Sur. There was Bravo, his teeth showing in a faint smile under his heavy mustache. He had trained in Italy and he liked to show a little style in whatever he did. When things were going well he would speak Italian. "*Molto bene,*" he would say. Things were going as well, now, as could be expected. "*Molto bene.*"

Some of the *guardias* still tried to maintain order and discipline. A few stood unsteadily at attention, their knees uncertain on the solid ground, and they saluted.

Antonio Calderón thought that he was forgotten and that he might now be safe. But a *guardia* private, perhaps twenty-four years old, with dark skin and blank eyes and a wisp of beard, the face of someone stoned or crazy, threw the bolt on his Galil and pointed it into his face. "Old man," said the private, "son of a bitch," he said, "we're going to kill you."

The private sprang a bullet into the chamber of his rifle.

"All right," said Calderón, "kill me. What else is there I can do?"

But the private did not fire. He turned away. He threw his rifle onto the truck the Salvadorans had brought. Other rifles clattered down on top of it, loaded like sugar cane to be taken away.

And the Salvadoran officers stood by watching, closely.

VIII.

SAN SALVADOR, EL SALVADOR

In El Salvador the summer that Somoza fell in Nicaragua, soldiers no longer felt safe in uniform on streets they once dominated with unchallenged authority. Embassies were occupied by the left, ministries were occupied by the left, farms were occupied by the left. Parades were held through the middle of the capital that taunted the armed forces, challenged them, humiliated them. They struck back furiously, finding enemies everywhere, from the streets to the pulpits. Demonstrations were fired on and scores of people slaughtered. Priests who organized their rural congregations for political action were ambushed and murdered or beaten and driven from their parishes. International opinion, to the extent it took note, was outraged. El Salvador was ever more isolated in the world, and the army was ever more isolated in El Salvador.

The institution of the armed forces was decayed and disintegrating. The greed of some officers led to unprecedented corruption. At least one took a page from the guerrillas. He ran a security service for members of the oligarchy and wealthy businessmen, and he also kidnapped them. When a human rights mission from the Organization of American States discovered secret cells in the National Guard headquarters in 1978, it also found a room with a camera and a rebel flag that looked as if it might be used for photos sent to victims' families to extort ransoms.

El Salvador's young officers felt the pressure for change and saw that the regime of General Carlos Humberto Romero would not deliver it. He was a hard-liner named to the post by his predecessor and ratified in it in 1977 by a fraudulent election. The consensus for a coup to replace him began to grow.

By 1978 the question among many Central Americans was simply which government would fall first, Somoza's in Nicaragua or Romero's in El Salvador. When the Guardia collapsed and the Sandinistas triumphed, it seemed obvious that El Salvador would soon follow, and the fear among the Salvadoran officer corps was that a tide of real revolution would sweep the region and they would have no place in it. Nicaragua's Communists would now have "breakfast in El Salvador, lunch in Guatemala, and dinner in Honduras," Central American military men warned each other.

If El Salvador's young officers wanted to avoid being served up to the Communists, many of them felt, they had to change the way they had been operating.

Colonel Jaime Abdul Gutiérrez was one of the plotters. A basically conservative man, he came late and reluctantly to the conspiracy. But the fall of Somoza, and the spectacle that followed it, gave the coup the momentum it needed to roll forward to its conclusion, pulling him and others forward with a force that seemed unstoppable.

The young Salvadoran officers saw Nicaragua's Guardia routed.

They saw the older officers, the big fish, escape to luxury while their own contemporaries suffered.

"Really all the highest levels of the Nicaraguan army, which were the ones that did not fight, came out in helicopters and airplanes of the armed forces or on whatever they were able to find to leave the country," said Gutiérrez, "while those who really defended the Somoza regime, those who were in command positions, had to come out in a very pitiful way. They came in barges to the port of La Unión. And they brought neither money nor anything with which to feed themselves. Some had to sell their equipment and guns and things like that. They lived for some days out of charity. Some had their families, too. And the whole families of these military men were in a bad situation. Little by little they were receiving some help so they could get out of the country, but that was very costly, and there was no one that wanted to give them a cent to help them. And, really, it is very pitiful to see a defeated army. We saw in them a mirror of what could happen to the Salvadoran army."

In Washington, after Somoza's fall, "there was great concern about El Salvador and Guatemala in part because we didn't know what to do," said Bob Pastor, who was then the senior staffer on Central America at the National Security Council. There was worry about Cuban involvement in Nicaragua and the self-proclaimed Marxism of many figures in the Salvadoran opposition. But U.S. military links and assistance to both countries had been cut two years before because of their governments' notorious policies of repression. If there were no changes *in* El Salvador and Guatemala, it was thought, there could be no changes *toward* El Salvador and Guatemala. And there had not been many positive signs.

In El Salvador in May more than twenty protestors had been slaughtered on the steps of the Metropolitan Cathedral in full view of television cameras. It was a grotesque scene: men and women scrambling over each other to get through the cathedral's doors as National Police fired into them, the guns on full automatic. Stains, like red flowers on Hawaiian shirts, spread across their backs as they died. And Walter Cronkite showed it all.

Guatemala had also opted for full-scale repression and as death squads ran wild in the city those few Guatemalan politicians who had seemed to offer a moderate alternative to the extremes of left and right were blown away on the streets.

"We had," said Pastor, "two governments that saw the world in such different terms from us and were not going to be persuaded of our approach, and we were not going to be persuaded of their approach. It was an impasse, and when you have an impasse, it leads to frustration.''

Shortly after Somoza fell, Assistant Secretary Vaky went to the Casa Presidencial in El Salvador to make one more try at persuading the government there to reform. His excellency the president of El Salvador, General Romero, was unsure what to expect as Vaky mounted the stairs past the large painting of the Salvadoran army's founder. (''The Republic shall live as long as the Army shall live,'' read the slip of paper in his hand.) Romero could not have anticipated an agreeable encounter, but certainly he did not imagine it would be as sharp as it was.

What Mr. Vaky wanted to suggest to the president was that, perhaps, there were a few things to be learned from the Nicaraguan experience.

''I had the feeling,'' Vaky said later, ''that when I arrived what the Salvadoran high command expected was that we were going to come down and say, 'All right, fellahs, it's on our doorstep now; circle the wagons and let's dig in and hold the fort.' And that they were a little surprised that what we were saying to them was 'Start to reform so you don't get into the same box.' ''

Washington was indeed concerned, Vaky told the general. It was clear that polarization in El Salvador had reached new and dangerous levels. A threatening head of steam seemed to be building and something had to be done to let the pressure off. His excellency's government had what would be called in Washington a ''credibility gap.'' It was important that his government move to establish more credibility, establish its desire and its real intention to undertake basic reforms, open up the political system so the alienation and dissension that were building could be vented.

''I was saying that he really needed to do something very dramatic to establish that credibility and I made the suggestion that, for example, wouldn't it be interesting if his regime decided to announce that they were going to call elections early and have free democratic elections? He said he simply couldn't do that and I guess that in retrospect he assumed more to my point than was intended. I did not, as some people have said, demand that he quit or leave office.''

* * *

The Salvadoran coup came in October, promising sweeping reform and gaining the instant approbation of the United States. Its leaders hoped to co-opt or undermine the rising insurgency. But while the coup ended the old regime, neither the violence of the revolution nor the repression was over. In fact, they were just beginning.

IX.

MIAMI, FLORIDA, JULY 1979

The handful of Guardia officers who went to the United States with Bill, the American, saw their first days as exiles filled with disappointments, big and small.

They had arrived with Bill at about seven in the evening on July 27 and there was not much of a welcome. Their American friends even had trouble getting them in at the Miami airport. They had no papers, and immigration authorities threatened to fine Bill a thousand dollars apiece for bringing them there. He made some calls. He got them in. But they were not treated well, they thought.

At Danker's Motel, a run-down pink-and-green inn built on Miami's Southwest Eighth Street before it was called Calle Ocho, television crews besieged them, demanding interviews of the officers, of the motel owner, of anyone who would say anything.

Cuban exiles who had arrived under similar conditions twenty years before collected clothes for them, and workers at the Jesus Foundation down the street whipped together peanut butter and jelly sandwiches. But the women and the kids started complaining. Here it was hot as hell and the hotel management told them not to swim in the pool without proper bathing suits. Who the hell had bathing suits? Have a little humanity, Bill told the hotel manager. But the hotel people had their backs up. "It was like they were political refugees but they wanted to be treated better than anyone else," remembered Betty Castillo, who worked there. The owner's nephew was the maintenance man and "he took pride in his pool and didn't want people in dirty pants in it." The Nicaraguans wanted their rice and their beans and their meat as they used to get them in Managua, Castillo recalled. The maids found piles of food from the Jesus Foundation thrown in the trash. And soon the management was complaining about the long-distance phone calls, and wondering who was going to pay.

They were calling all over the States and they were calling Nicaragua, trying to stay in touch with old lives while piecing together new ones.

Then somebody who said he was from the Nicaraguan embassy and represented the new Nicaraguan government came by and ordered everybody to go back to Nicaragua. The men were meeting upstairs, and some of them came down angry. People said it was lucky there was not more violence.

On August 1, a select group went to Washington. Several were well known among the ranks of the Guardia, if not to the general public. Congressman Murphy presented them at a Capitol Hill press conference.

One was Tino Pérez, whom Bill had rescued from the Guatemalan embassy.

One was Noel Ortiz, who had left the Guardia years before to make a small fortune as a pilot, then went back into the ranks during the insurrection. He led patrols near Chinandega that the Sandinistas would later say had slaughtered some of their people. He would say it was all done in a fair fight. He also flew bombing missions tossing dynamite out of crop dusters. Finally he was forced to fly out at gunpoint by his old commander, even though he wanted to stay and fight, he said. ("Deserters Arrive in El Salvador" is how the little item in the San Salvador press on July 19 heralded his landing.)

With Ortiz in Washington was his woman, Laura. She was sexy, aggressive and self-confident. She spoke English well, interpreted for the *guardias* who didn't and watched over them like a mother.

Another officer at the conference was a lieutenant who survived the voyage from San Juan del Sur. His lips were still cracked and blistered, now more than a week after he landed at La Unión.

Colonel Enrique Bermúdez was already in Washington when the others arrived. He had been posted there throughout the war, in fact, and was regarded with a certain suspicion because of that.

Bermúdez had an interesting record. He served with the Nicaraguan contingent that stood alongside the U.S. occupation force in the Dominican Republic in 1965. He was defense attaché in Washington and he had been chief of the Nicaraguan delegation to the Inter-American Defense Board. His contacts with the American military's old-boy network were many, and there were many in it, like retired Lieutenant General Gordon Sumner, who were already looking for some way to help Nicaraguans who wanted to fight back against the Communist menace.

But Bermúdez was, as Laura Ortiz put it, "kind of an office officer." And if that were not enough to raise suspicions, he had been on the list the Americans made up of men they would like to see take over the Guardia when Somoza left. Bermúdez was a symbol, of sorts, of the senior officers the junior ones felt had abandoned them.

The hero of that moment was still the commander called Bravo, Major Pablo Emilio Salazar.

He put himself across as the man with a plan. He had the combat record to show his capability, and from the beginning of the end, through the defense of the Southern Front, the evacuation from San Juan, now this trip to Washington, he was staking out his claims to leadership of this vestigial, withered army.

His admirers saw a man who was tough beyond description. He had held Pastora to a standstill, he "never gave an inch," they told each other proudly.

"Gallant" was the word Somoza himself used for him. "No one could ask for a better combat leader than Bravo. He was fearless, but he knew how to exercise caution. To him, his men always came first and his combat troops would have followed him to the end of the earth."

Those who respected Bravo less among Somoza's coterie would say privately he was "not very bright. He was a creation. We came up with his name to sort of balance Commander Zero, you know."

The reaction to the press conference "was negative," as one of the participants recalled. Military men rarely know how to dress when they are not in uniform, and in such clothes as they had thrown together for this conference they looked ludicrous, some of them like thugs, others like busboys on a day off. Appearing with Murphy before the reporters, they tried to tell what they knew about the Communists. They tried to explain about Soviet designs to build a new canal across the isthmus through Nicaragua, and how Nicaragua was the breadbasket of the region and could be made to feed its Cuban masters, and about its coveted gold mines and about how the Soviets were going to expand their doctrine in Latin America now that they had this beachhead. It sounded like hysterical talk.

"Most, if not all of us, were trained directly or indirectly by the U.S. Armed Forces. Our noble military friends have now turned their backs on us. We defended our government with the same high ideals of duty, honor and country taught by your American trainers," said Bravo. "All of us here today feel betrayed, not by our American comrades but by Jimmy Carter's policy."

It was a confused presentation, convincing no one but the converted in its small audience. And it was made more confusing still because as many Washington partisans of the Sandinistas showed up to heckle, it seemed, as there were reporters there to write.

Bravo was supposed to be presented as a hero and a symbol. He would focus attention on the plight of those *guardias* who had been left behind, and the people linked to Somoza who were being persecuted. But only the most devoted followers of the news in Washington had any idea who this mustached, swaggering and apparently not very smart member of the old Somoza National Guard might be.

"We are not asking for compassion," Bravo concluded, "but an opportunity to help you understand that destruction of our democracy is in the hands of the Siberian Bear dressed in colorful Latin clothes."

The left-wing activists waved photographs showing the kinds of carnage the Guardia had left in its wake as it defended the dictator.

Bravo seemed distracted. In fact, he had other things on his mind. He was worried about his girlfriend, Barbara, in Managua. And when he could he caught the eye of Ortiz's woman, Laura, and he asked her to put calls through to Barbara. He was calling her twice a day.

"Please, please come on," Laura remembered him saying. "I need to talk to her."

He was crazy about that woman, Laura remembered.

MANAGUA, NICARAGUA, SEPTEMBER 1979

It was one of Comandante Tomás Borge's many talents that he appreciated the nuances, even the beauty of pain. In wood and in metal, in stone and in straw, figures of Christ on the cross covered the walls of his office in Managua's ministry of the interior. He could speak of suffering with the empathy of experience, artfully and persuasively, and that is what he is said to have done with Barbara.

She was still young, with a peculiar ability to challenge and seduce a man at the same moment which is common among Nicaragua's women, and she had worked for several years at Somoza's housing institute in one of the jobs that women were given to use up their time in the day and keep them available at night. She had been the lover of Somoza's Comandante Bravo, and their relationship, indeed everything about Bravo, had been of much interest and occasionally even amusement to Sandinista intelligence. On the Southern Front Pastora's radio operators often listened to Bravo's intercepted conversations with Managua as he talked to his wife one moment and to Barbara the next. But when Bravo had fled to El Salvador, he had not been able to take both women, and, choosing one, he had picked his wife. When Borge learned of this he had Barbara found and brought to him and he began to work on her.

He could play on her anger and her jealousies and her fears. The *guardias'* women could not expect much mercy from the mobs and the *muchachos* and they had not been shown much. When she was singled out and brought to Borge she might have expected more brutal treatment than he gave her. But the threat of suffering always lingered in the background with Borge, this little man with the voice of a poet, the eyes of a zealot, the collected icons of pain. He could strike chords of abandonment, tune her passion for revenge. The fear could remain unvoiced.

Borge is said to have told Barbara that Bravo left his troops behind just as he had left her. Did she know that he had taken his wife and his three children to live in Miami? He told Barbara that the war had stopped, but that Bravo wanted to keep it going and, from the safety of Miami, continue the suffering of the Nicaraguan people. He had announced in Miami that he would organize a force of seven thousand men to attack the new government—the people's government. Bravo was visiting El Salvador and Guatemala and Honduras to build his new army. If he succeeded, thousands more people might die, and the new deaths would be as pointless as those that had gone before. The revolution was not going to be defeated. There had been so much killing already, why would he want more? Barbara could help stop a new bloodbath. She might be able to keep those thousands of people from dying. . . . And Barbara had listened and finally agreed.

The operation came under the general direction of a Cuban who had worked for many years and very closely with Borge. He held the rank of commander and was effectively in charge of intelligence at the interior ministry from the beginning. Another key figure in the operation was Lenin Cerna, who had spent most of the war in Cuernavaca, Mexico, working in intelligence. By September of 1979 he had been named head of state security, but this was not yet widely known. He was officially a diplomat at the Nicaraguan embassy in the Honduran capital.

At eleven o'clock on the morning of October 10, 1979, a private airplane flying in from El Salvador arrived at Tegucigalpa's Toncontin airport in Honduras. For weeks, Bravo had been promoting his Aid Committee for Nicaraguan Refugees. Now a shipment of twenty tons of supplies for his men had arrived at a Honduran port but was being held up for bureaucratic reasons, or a bribe, or both. At five in the afternoon Bravo was supposed to meet with other exiled commanders of the Guardia Nacional to discuss the matter.

Shortly after noon, Bravo checked into the little Hotel Istmania in a neighborhood near the center of Tegucigalpa called Los Dolores. The sorrows. Shortly before, the Honduran National Directorate for Investigations, the closest thing Honduras had to secret police, had moved into its offices across the street. Bravo would have reason to believe that he was safe. He arrived accompanied by four other men, signed the register and went straight to the long Formica and Naugahyde bar where he made a phone call.

The woman who arrived a few minutes later was a dyed blonde, the hotel manager remembered. When Bravo left the hotel with Barbara, they left alone.

Four days later, the neighbors around an empty little stucco house in the neighborhood called Miradores de Loarques called the police to complain of the stench there. It was another three days before the Hondurans felt confident enough of their identification to say it was Bravo's body. A portion of the Honduran security forces' report on their findings concluded that "the body shows undeniable evidence that he was subjected to brutal torture prior to dying." The face was badly mangled and one report suggested he was shot while kneeling on the floor. There was one bullet below the ear and another in the upper part of the cranium. He had apparently been burned as well, and portions of his skin peeled off. Somoza, in his book, published a pair of grotesque photographs of a face from which most of the skin was peeled. By several accounts the genitals had been cut off.

In Managua, Edén Pastora was told that his old enemy had been eliminated personally by Lenin Cerna, with two shots from a .22-caliber pistol.

A message had been sent to anyone thinking of organizing against the Sandinista revolution about the strength and the penetration already possessed by its clandestine services.

"The head of that sector of the counterrevolution has been cut off," Borge said on Radio Sandino the day that Bravo's body was identified in wire service reports. "The enemies of our people will fall one by one, and sooner or later the assassin Anastasio Somoza's turn will come."

By some accounts Barbara eventually went to live in the United States, possibly in Los Angeles. But others place her in Nicaragua, still.

"She was a *morena,* dark-skinned with long hair, sympathetic. But since then she has become an alcoholic. She began to drink and now she lives there in Managua as a drunk," Pastora said later. "But she was darling, that *morena*. I knew her."

X.

La Unión, El Salvador, July 1979

"Commander Zero's coming to get you," taunted the Salvadoran children as they peered at the Nicaraguans in makeshift camps on the waterfront.

Hundreds of the defeated enlisted men waited there on such charity as the Salvadoran Red Cross and the Salvadoran government could find for them. Some of the gunmen were recruited quietly by Salvadoran officers and civilians for work in private security services, informally added to the roles of "supernumerary" ex-enlisted men in El Salvador's own armed forces who could guard the wealthy residents of the capital or carry out special errands for them with whatever degree of violence was required.

But Suicida and the men closest to him in the Rattlesnakes seem not to have been interested in that route. It meant being, in effect, servants. And there were none of them who wanted that. They had had enough humiliations at the hands of their own officers. But if they looked coldly at their prospects at that moment they were few indeed: living as unwanted refugees in Central America, hiring themselves out as gunmen, maybe, or truck drivers, or laborers in the streets. They had no money to buy a *milpa* and, anyway, no desire to farm the land of another country. If they had wanted to be farmers, after all, they would not have gone into the Guardia. Some might go to the United States and try to make some sort of life there as refugees or as *mojados,* wetbacks. But who had any real idea what that world was like? And who had the money to get there? Some of the *guardias* began plotting robberies. Some thought of banks. Some knew their way around the

Honduran-Nicaraguan border regions where cattle could be moved easily and sold profitably. But some, like Suicida, began thinking almost immediately of how they were going to get back to Nicaragua itself.

All they really knew how to do was fight, and the territory they knew how to fight in was Nicaragua. From the guerrillas they had fought for a decade they thought they had learned a few things about survival.

As Suicida later told the story, he was not in El Salvador very long —a few weeks, no more—before he and about 140 other men made their way to Honduras. He got to know a Honduran army captain who was the head of the local police unit, the FUSEP, at one of the border crossings. In those days these were sleepy places, where people moved slowly, especially the soldiers, and talked a lot, sitting in cots or lounging in dirt-colored hammocks drinking Coca-Cola and dirty ice from little plastic bags. Suicida had an easy manner, and probably the Hondurans found it easy to relax with him. He told stories well and Honduran soldiers are often as fascinated as they are envious when men from other armies tell them about real fights against real enemies.

How long he stayed there at the border crossing and exactly how he won them over, Suicida did not say. But when he left he had convinced them that his fight would eventually be their fight. The captain and the police chief gave him a hunting rifle and a shotgun and a pistol.

Suicida and his men and a few friends with contacts in Guatemala meanwhile contrived a name for themselves. In the annals of the counterrevolution it is little remembered. It was only this handful of combatants. But it suggested how they saw themselves: the Anti-Sandinista Guerrilla Special Forces. In a few days they made their way down to the border, just north of the Segovias in Nicaragua. They had waited for their old officers to come to their aid, but none had. No one had. Now they were their own men. They were beginning their own war.

BEGINNINGS—1980

I.

DETROIT, MICHIGAN, JULY 1980
On July 17, 1980—a year to the day, as it happened, after Somoza fled Nicaragua—Ronald Reagan accepted the Republican party's nomination for president of the United States.

The former cowboy star was riding a strong current of frustration and anger building up in the middle-class mainstream of American society. Who was not sick of what Jimmy Carter called "malaise"? The course of foreign affairs, especially, had led from one humiliation to another. Americans were filled with impotent rage by the seizure of the U.S. embassy in Iran, then emasculated by the disastrous failure of the military mission to rescue the hostages. They were angered and appalled at Russia's occupation of Afghanistan and surprised by Carter's apparent surprise that Moscow should make such a move. They felt overwhelmed by the flood of refugees that sailed to Key West from Cuba in the Mariel boatlift.

For the Republicans, Nicaragua was an outstanding symbol of these humiliations brought on by "a foreign policy not of constancy and credibility, but of chaos, confusion, and failure."

It did not matter that Nicaragua was small and backward, with its population only 2.5 million, its economy all but destroyed by the war, its army a motley array of militias, its air force a collection of captured Cessnas. It was cast as a major part of the Soviet threat.

The Republican platform claimed there were "clear danger signals indicating that the Soviet Union was using Cuban, East German, and now Nicaraguan, as well as its own, military forces to extend its power to Africa, Asia and the Western Hemisphere."

There was no evidence to support a charge about Nicaraguan troops, but the Reagan platform pursued the Sandinistas nonetheless. It echoed the arguments of Murphy and Somoza the year before. The Carter administration "often undermined the very governments under attack. As a result, a clear and present danger threatens the energy and raw material lifelines of the Western world."

"We deplore the Marxist Sandinista takeover of Nicaragua and the Marxist attempts to destabilize El Salvador, Guatemala and Honduras," said the platform. "We will return to the fundamental principle of treating a friend as a friend and self-proclaimed enemies as enemies, without apology."

The Republicans were also clear about the means to be used against America's enemies. Almost enviously, it seemed, they concluded that "the Soviet Union and its surrogates operate by a far different set of rules than does the United States." By definition, in this year of the hostages, these included collusion with "terrorists" who "reject the rule of law, civil order, and the sanctity of individual human rights."

"We do not favor countering their efforts by mirroring their tactics," the Republicans said, but a Republican administration would certainly put a high priority on improving intelligence capabilities, including covert action.

"We will provide our government with the capability to help influence international events vital to our national security interests, a capability which only the United States among the major powers has denied itself."

In this context the Sandinistas read closely the Republican vow to cut off aid to their regime but "support the efforts of the Nicaraguan people to establish a free and independent government."

MANAGUA, NICARAGUA

Fidel Castro was in Managua the week Ronald Reagan was nominated in Detroit. He was the grand man of the celebration. He was holding court, it seemed as you watched him, among his children.

There he stood at the big reception in the Casa de Gobierno, his trademark cigar in his hand, an ever-shifting circle of the curious and the admiring from the diplomatic corps and the government moving in and out of the smoke. For Pastora, for Humberto Ortega, Castro seemed to be the mythical father. Their every move around him suggested filial devotion; Humberto grinning as he waited for some sign of approval, Pastora puffing himself up under Castro's gaze. Although in Pastora's case as he sometimes left the crowds of dignitaries to wander among buddies from lower ranks—there was a suggestion of rebellion, too.

In the grandstands on July 19 it was hard to escape the notion that the celebration was meant as much for Fidel as for anyone else there. The sun was bright and hot as the crowds packed densely into the July 19 Plaza. For days the radios had chanted to a salsa rhythm: "*Vamos todos a la plaza con el Frente Sandinista.*" Masses of people came by bus and on foot, swarming like pilgrim insects down the hillsides into the vast vacant lot that had become the site of celebration. People swayed to the music as they arrived. An American photographer in the press gallery made contact with a militia girl across the parade route through his 200-mm lens. She saw he was looking at her. He started to move in rhythm. She started to move with him and the wave of contagious rhythm caught on all over the crowd. Then the parade started and the tanks began to roll: the old Shermans captured from Somoza. And then the four-mouthed anti-aircraft guns. The handful of leftover planes zoomed low overhead. Humberto and Edén descended the grandstand and got into jeeps to review the troops, the two *comandantes* rigid at attention as they rolled along, Pastora's jeep always just a bit behind Humberto's. Rank upon rank of militiamen marched by in the high-kicking, stiff-legged step of the Eastern Bloc, eyes right to their *comandantes* and to Fidel. And Fidel smiled benignly.

Yet Fidel in Managua appeared older than the world was accustomed to see him. He was tall and powerfully built. He has no neck to speak of, so not only his head but his shoulders rise above those of other men, bearlike. But his face was flushed and mottled. His arms and legs seemed thin beneath his tailored uniform, the eyes tired as he joked with his retinue. The beard had grown scruffy, heavily threaded with gray.

Anastasio Somoza once gave facilities to the CIA for training the men who carried out the disaster at the Bay of Pigs. As they left Nicaragua Somoza told them, it was said, to bring him back a hair from Fidel's beard.

It was a story Castro enjoyed telling that week in Managua.

He liked to talk, as well, about the Republican platform. He had, after all, long experience with Washington's efforts to "influence international events."

Fidel's people in the Americas Bureau also had looked very carefully at the other writings of the Republicans' ideologues. They came across a document issued by a conference in Santa Fe, New Mexico. Among its several authors were Georgetown academic Roger Fontaine and General Gordon Sumner, whose strategic views Somoza had often quoted. Its premise was that the norm of international affairs was war and not peace, and that in a real sense, the Third World War already was under way against the Soviets. Containing them was no longer enough. And Latin America was a key battleground. Castro was the major enemy, and any friend of his was an enemy: in Grenada, in Nicaragua, in Panama, even in Ecuador.

Since before the days of the revolution when Fidel helped pull together the Sandinistas' three factions, he had counseled the Ortegas and Borge and Wheelock to be careful with the United States, not to make the mistakes he had made in provoking Washington. The money of the United States was good money and if you were smart, and the right administration was in power, you could get it to underwrite the rebuilding of the country.

But this Republican candidate, Fidel said, he is something else. If he and these men should come in, calculations will have to change.

Military leaders of the Salvadoran guerrilla movement were in Managua, too, that week, closed up in one of the confiscated mansions and told not to come out.

They had helped the Sandinistas during the Nicaraguan insurrection. They had supplied money gained through spectacular kidnappings, and they had supplied men to fight in the field. Now the Sandinistas seemed to have forgotten.

The Salvadorans had arrived on the thirteenth, but no one important would see them. They were told to stay indoors, a phone call could come at any minute. But it didn't. The Sandinistas were busy with the celebration.

"The Front was very conservative," the guerrillas' local representatives complained, "and it had a tendency to look down on the situation" in El Salvador "and to protect the Nicaraguan revolution."

It was in the context of defending the Nicaraguan revolution that the Sandinista leadership argued the question of supporting the rebels in El Salvador. If the Salvadorans could seize the momentum begun by the Sandinista triumph in Nicaragua and win in their own country, then the United States would be hard pressed to roll back either revolution. Even if the Salvadorans did not win quickly, a second front would distract the United States from its counterrevolutionary designs, some Sandinistas contended.

There was, however, a countervailing argument. If material support for the Salvadoran rebels were delivered in substantial quantities, the Americans would certainly find out and would almost as certainly cut off their much-needed economic assistance. They might also do worse. There was no reason to believe that if the Carter administration won a second term the United States would inevitably attack the revolution in Nicaragua, especially if it followed the course of modified socialism that the Frente had long proclaimed. The first loyalty of Nicaragua's revolutionaries should be to Nicaragua's revolution. Its greatest contribution to the international cause would be to survive and to succeed.

As this debate went on, thousands of people were butchered in El Salvador by the security forces and the death squads, and hundreds of those people were the grass-roots organizers of the guerrilla movement. By midsummer the strength of the Salvadoran Left began to ebb. Strikes that froze the country in its tracks in May hardly slowed it to a crawl in August. They could put 150,000 people in the streets in January; they couldn't put 1,500 in the streets in December. But the guerrilla leaders convinced themselves, first, that their waning support was not waning. And second, that if they had problems it was only because they lacked the guns to protect their people and to mount their insurrection. If they had guns, they said, then they could put them in the hands of the people who marched in January 1980 and have them fighting before January 1981.

Still the Sandinistas balked.

"Gentlemen, all right," one of the Salvadoran guerrillas pleaded with the Sandinistas, "we understand that Nicaragua must be protected, but for that there is an art and a science which is called '*conspiracy.*' Let us conspire together."

Ten days after their arrival, the Salvadoran guerrilla delegation was allowed to meet with Sandinista Commander Bayardo Arce, a member of the National Directorate. He gave them the good news that they would get some of the arms and ammunition they requested. But they might also have to share some with guerrillas in Guatemala. Arce was curt and critical. He doubted the Salvadorans' numbers were as high as they claimed, he said, and their propaganda was bad: it looked to the world as though they were being massacred.

Nicaragua's businessmen were waiting, too, that week of the celebration. They had supported the fight against Somoza a year before. Their economic clout was vital to it internally; their political moderation was essential externally. And they had been promised a mixed economy and pluralism and something like a regular Western democracy, they thought, with elections and a free press and all the other rights one associated with such a government.

Disillusionment had come early and then the sense of betrayal. By July 1980 as the crowds of dignitaries were scheduled to arrive at Augusto César Sandino Airport a handful of ambitious anticommunist businessmen had already plotted to rain bombs on the parade.

The plan, devised in the well-appointed rooms of Guatemala City's Camino Real, called for some former Guardia pilots to steal a couple of small American A-37 fighter planes from the little Colombian island of San Andrés. As the Sandinistas paraded their new army before the grandstand with Fidel Castro and the whole Nicaraguan National Directorate looking on, the airplanes would open up with their mini-guns and level the area with their fiery ordnance. It could all be done so quickly, from the time of the theft to the time of the bombing, that the Sandinistas would have no chance to react.

The plotters calculated that the whole operation would cost at most fifteen thousand dollars. You had to rent the plane to get the people to San Andrés, take over the little airport there, take the jets and get out to Managua, bomb the hell out of the celebration, then land in El Salvador or Guatemala to make the getaway.

"We were going to kill Fidel Castro and all the people who were there."

It would have been messy, of course. Castro was not the only dignitary in the grandstands. The U.S. ambassador to the United Nations led the American delegation. There was the former president of Venezuela. There were distinguished representatives from Europe. There were many reporters. But the political rewards would have been, well, potentially decisive.

It came to nothing.

"Unfortunately, we couldn't get that quantity of money," one of the plotters said later. "At the beginning"—in 1980—"it was very difficult."

On November 4, 1980, by a margin of 51 to 41 percent, Ronald Reagan was elected president of the United States.

Once again, Central America's world was turned around and once more, as often happened in the region's history, the hard-liners on the left and right began to fulfill each other's prophecies.

Despite their secret pledges of support to the Salvadoran rebels, up until the American election the Sandinistas were stalling. Other revolutionary countries—Ethiopia, Vietnam—agreed to supply the Salvadorans with more arms. But the Nicaraguans restricted the flow.

U.S. intelligence learned very quickly about the shipments that were made, and Ambassador Pezzullo warned the Sandinistas to quit. Congress required certification from President Carter that the Nicaraguans were not exporting "terrorism" if they were going to continue receiving U.S. economic aid. Seventy-five million dollars was at stake. The Sandinistas backed off still further from the Salvadorans. By the end of September 1980, Nicaragua had stockpiled as many as 130 tons of arms for the Salvadoran rebels. But only four tons had made it to El Salvador. Through the month of October, the Sandinistas were still stalling. Carter certified.

But as the election results came in, with Reagan and his Republican platform the obvious winners, the Sandinistas opened the floodgates for the Salvadoran rebels. By the middle of November the Salvadorans were complaining they couldn't distribute so much matériel.

You couldn't hide that many arms. Some were caught. Others were tracked through radio intercepts. And from that point on, the new Reagan administration could present proof that the judgment of its ideologues had been right, the battle for El Salvador and the battle for Nicaragua were one and the same.

Before the Republicans even took office, there was talk about giving the Sandinistas a dose of their own medicine. A notion began to take shape that was as fearful as it was neat: "symmetry," it came to be called, "trading one little war for another little war."

But the planners stumbled again and again on a basic problem. Who would fight it?

At the end of 1980, working mostly on their own, some of Nicaragua's businessmen still thought they were the ones, and that they were ready.

II.

MANAGUA, NICARAGUA, NOVEMBER 1980

"Look, Jorge, if you're not happy—" Pastora paused. He was looking for the right words. He glanced around the other tables in the shaded patio outside Los Antojitos in Managua. He changed his tack with his old friend. "You know what the Defense and Security Commission is?"

"Yes," said Jorge, his gaze direct through his Porsche-style glasses. "It's like the National Security Council"—he said National Security Council in English—"in the United States."

"Right," said Pastora. "Well, you know what they talk about there? What they know there?"

Jorge nodded, perhaps imagining.

"Then look, Jorge, if you're not happy with the revolution, then I'd advise you to get out of Nicaragua."

What Pastora knew was that Jorge Salazar, his old schoolmate from the Colegio, was plotting against the Front, and that the Front knew it and Jorge was going to die. The sentence was handed down by Borge and Humberto Ortega from the National Directorate. The decision had been announced to the Defense and Security Commission, and Pastora, as a member, was informed. But Pastora played this child's game with his old friend: he had this thing to tell that he could not bring himself to say.

"Look, Jorge, conspiring is a science. And you don't have a command of this science. You learn it the hard way. You could go on conspiring against these conspirators all your life."

Salazar did not seem to get the message. Jorge Salazar had listened too much to the people who called him "The Magician."

Jorge had a way with people. He was old enough, at forty-one, to have authority, young enough to have energy; he exuded confidence and evoked it. He was forever organizing: head of the cotton growers' cooperative; a founder of the national union for farmers and cattlemen; a member of the national development institute. People came from all over to see him at his family estate, Santa Maria de Ostuma in Matagalpa. When the war was over he organized the coffee growers around him in northern Matagalpa and kept the Sandinista cooperatives out. He made them angry. But that, by itself, was not why they wanted to kill him.

A new opposition to the Sandinistas was taking shape among their old allies in the fight against Somoza; a "clean" collection of businessmen and landowners, some members of the old Conservative party and some leaders of the Catholic Church untainted by the reputation of the dictator. They were lovers of democracy, enemies of communism. They were readers of the Venezuelan Carlos Rangel and the French *nouveau philosophe* Jean-François Revel. You bumped into them at the airport waiting for flights to Miami or Caracas and copies of *The Totalitarian Temptation* were tucked into their flight bags. Some of the most important of them were old high school classmates of Pastora and Salazar. By November 1980 members of the drum corps from the band of war were working night and day against the members of the National Directorate.

Alfonso Robelo, the snare drummer, was the most prominent. In the elaborate, contrapuntal politics preceding Somoza's fall he was an oft-quoted voice of the moderate opposition to the dictator. Finally he was made the example of pluralistic representation on the junta installed in July 1979. When, just after the triumph, the junta went to Havana to appear with Fidel, it was Alfonso who embraced him, Alfonso who spoke for the new Nicaragua. But nine months later, Alfonso resigned from the junta to set up an opposition party. The Sandinistas were stacking the deck against democracy, he said. It was a matter of the totalitarian temptation.

Chicano Cardenal, the bass drummer, was a construction contractor, an alumnus of Catholic University in Washington, D.C., and a rather portly pillar of the business community in Managua by the time the final rebellions against Somoza began in 1978. But twenty years before, fresh out of high school and full of adolescent ideals, he had gone to Cuba for three months after Fidel's triumph and now in middle age he would say he knew a thing or two about revolutions. He was flamboyant and passionate. When he talked politics he often shouted, a shock of his white-blazed hair would descend limply on his forehead and his cheeks, beset by nineteenth-century mutton chops, would burn with a pink flush.

But Jorge was the man with the magic. He would always say that he was not a politician, but he was more than that. He was a *patron* who spoke the language of the Americans and of the peasants, of money and the land. He was a natural to lead the struggle against the Sandinistas, with all the style and all the credibility that the others lacked. Only, he didn't know the science of conspiracy.

"Do I tell him or don't I tell him?" Pastora is thinking. Or, at least, that is what he said he was thinking. "Damn! You see how different it was. I'm a conspirator. I've conspired all my life. Of course in the United States people damn conspiracies, they look down on them. But for us the conspirator is an honorable man. So I, who know all the rules and everything, do I tell him or don't I? If I do, it condemns *me* to death. Because Security has it all under control," Pastora thought, "and this boob is going to go on talking, and conspiring, and it's me they're going to kill."

Jorge Salazar and Chicano Cardenal had been plotting secretly for eight months. There were public trips to the United States to seek aid for Nicaragua's reconstruction. But there were also more private purposes.

The Carter administration had decided late in its term that some sort of covert action was needed in Nicaragua, and in Central America generally, to fight the Communist ploys there: nothing paramilitary, nothing too broad or sophisticated; a matter of a few dollars to a politician here, a few planted stories there in the local press. It was a precedent that the agency cited later, but it did not amount to much at the time. The Carter administration's main effort was the $75 million in overt money battered out of Congress and disbursed as much as possible to the "private sector" instead of the revolutionary government of Nicaragua.

Jorge and Chicano were major figures in the private sector. Whether they received some of the covert money is not clear. But Chicano subsequently said that Jorge was looking for money from the Americans as early as February 1980 to start a clandestine radio station broadcasting against the Sandinistas.

Then in April 1980 came the council of state affair. In their talks before Somoza fell, the Sandinistas had agreed with their allies, and tacitly with their backers in Costa Rica and Panama and with the United States, that they would create a legislature made up from all the various unions and interest groups that had made the revolution possible. But when this council of state was about to be installed in April, the Directorate changed its composition and gave the Sandinista Front and its unions and organizations a solid majority.

Robelo, on the junta, fought against this, and in the fight discovered something of his own impotence. He resigned in protest. His move was backed by the other non-Sandinista on the five-person junta, Violetta Chamorro. She resigned as well but claimed that her poor health was the cause. The leaders of the business community—Jorge and Chicano among them—threatened not to participate in the council at all. It could meet without them, but it could not be credible without them, they thought.

Chicano was hoping a mass resignation would strike a major blow to the Sandinista regime.

But then, partly patronized by Ambassador Pezzullo, negotiations began between the business leaders and the Sandinistas. Chicano watched as, slowly, the Sandinistas persuaded the businessmen to lend their presence to the council's installation. Most of the persuasion was based on resurrected promises. There would be a mixed economy, allowing the businessmen to keep their property and their profits. Most importantly, they had said that sometime before the first anniversary of the revolution on July 19, 1980, they would announce a date for national elections.

Chicano was disgruntled and, as usual, he showed it. But the Sandinistas, full of confidence, toyed with him. In one meeting Sergio Ramírez looked at him and said "Chicano, if you're mixed up in something conspiratorial, we'll kill you." No warning could be blunter. But when Chicano reluctantly took his seat in the council, the Sandinistas named him its vice-president.

The formal installation of the council was a gala affair by Managua standards. It was held in the Rubén Darío theater, which Somoza had built as his own down-sized version of the Kennedy Center. Sergio Ramírez read out a state of the union address dense with soporific statistics that defied any literary pretension. It was an interminable evening of high-minded speeches. Then Pastora came onstage.

His part of the ceremony was simple. He didn't say a word to the audience. He carried the folded blue-and-white Nicaraguan flag that he had taken from the National Palace when he captured and ransomed Somoza's Congress. He spread it over a box so it could be seen, and he snapped to attention, his heel pounding a sharp note into the stage as he saluted. The audience was on its feet exploding into applause that endured for minutes after Pastora marched off. There were tears of happiness and triumph. Pastora had brought back the spirit of liberation. He was still the star.

At the reception afterward, the *comandantes* appeared in their best-creased uniforms. Their women were turned out in Miami fashions. A small crowd followed Pastora around the theater lobby like iron filings following a magnet. Formally attired waiters and waitresses served the revolutionaries and their guests.

Chicano moved through these celebrations furious and feeling isolated. He had made his decision to lead the resignations, but it was clear by that night that no one was going to follow. "No one would even look me in the face."

A few days later his resignation was public, along with his vow to fight the Sandinistas. But his voice seemed hollow and alone.

Only a little later did Chicano and Jorge get together again, outside the country, and resume their plotting.

The tale of Chicano's wanderings in 1980 trying to build an opposition to the Sandinistas is a story of ephemeral plots that came to nothing and ringing statements that went unheard, but it is also a chronicle of contacts.

A week after he left Nicaragua, Chicano had a brief meeting at the airport in Washington with Colonel Enrique Bermúdez, Somoza's former military attaché, who seemed always to be keeping in touch with the different threads of opposition to the Sandinistas. Bermúdez was beginning to emerge as a man who could take charge. He was the man with the connections among veterans of the army and the Agency who might be helpful—if anything serious got started.

There was a trip to Venezuela, looking for support. There were talks with all sorts of American "friends." But nothing seemed to come into focus for Chicano's conspirators.

It was the problem all the exile groups faced as they orbited around each other, formed and re-formed alliances, plotted and conspired, conjuring names and acronyms but little that was more substantial.

Then Jorge and Chicano turned for help to El Salvador. "The Salvadorans were going to give us territory for training," Chicano recalled, "and arms, and they were going to give us money, too."

"The insurrection would begin as not such a big thing, but would get bigger afterwards with the participation of the Nicaraguan people."

Jorge, the Magician, was still in Nicaragua. He had the people and the organization, inside Nicaragua through his coffee growers' unions and his cotton growers' unions in Matagalpa and Boaco and Chontales and León, to make things work.

By early fall, Salazar was moving so quickly that communications were becoming confused. Jorge had developed a prize contact—Alvaro Baltodano, a guerrilla commander known as Polo who was related to Jorge's wife. Salazar was convinced that Baltodano was working with him as an agent against the Sandinistas, helping him to plot. But that was Jorge's mistake.

"Look, man—Jorge—you're not in agreement with the revolution. But *why* don't you go along with it, brother, if it hasn't touched even a single coffee bush of yours? It hasn't touched a single teat of a single one of your cows. Brother, I'm asking you to work *with* the revolution," Pastora pleaded at lunch. "We want you. Think of it, man. Get in line. Help. The more there are like you who are involved, the stronger we'll be in the democratic line."

Jorge had heard all this before. Jorge knew about the broken promises. He had waited in vain for the date of elections to be announced in July. And all the Sandinistas said was wait five more years.

"All right, you're not happy with the revolution," Pastora remembered saying, "You're not satisfied. Get out, then." Pastora claims he even went so far as to tell Salazar, "You've got friends who are going to screw you—who are screwing you.

"To conspire is a science," said Pastora. "And you don't have a command of this science."

"A crisis can be a cancer or a common cold," Comandante Tomás Borge told the reporters hanging on his words in the Intercontinental Hotel's coffee shop one night in November 1980. "A crisis can be"— he drew out each syllable; he had been talking earlier about the revolutionary as poet, and even now that the politics of the moment had come up he kept on in a lyrical vein—"the sting of a wasp, or a case of pneumonia."

The death of Jorge Salazar, he said, was not a crisis.

Jorge had been gunned down in a filling station parking lot. A man with him supposedly fired on police coming to arrest them. A duffel bag full of rifles supposedly was found in the back of his car, but Jorge himself was unarmed. And he was the one riddled with bullets.

"These reactionary bourgeois—primitive, stupid, ignorant," Borge said, dismissing the bitter mood that had settled over the business community and what had been the loyal opposition. "They could not manage to understand that we managed to pull this country out of savagery.

"They want everything for themselves. That's why they conspire," he said. Salazar's death, he insisted, was unintentional, but it was inevitable.

"He who makes himself a warrior can get killed in the war. He wanted to be a warrior and he died in the war."

Borge's face took on a deep-lined frown, theatrical and confident. His bodyguard smiled from the door of the kitchen. "We're not afraid of war," Borge said. "We don't want war, but we don't have any fear of war. War, for us, is a sport. Because we got used to it over eighteen years, running around in the mountains, running around dirty, sweaty and surrounded by fear in the mountains and in hiding. What demons are they going to threaten us with in a war? How are *they* going to make war if they don't have any calluses on their hands? How are they going to make war against us if they have to rub lotion on them when they go to the beach so the sun doesn't burn them? How are they going to make war against us if they use a raincoat and an umbrella when they go out in the street in the winter? We're used to sleeping on the ground and being in the rain, bitten by mosquitoes, dead from hunger. That doesn't mean a thing to us. We almost feel a kind of nostalgia for that lovely past in which we fought. If that's what's going to happen, let it come."

III.

GUATEMALA, NOVEMBER 1980

The little farm in Guatemala was called Detachment 101 as if it belonged to an army. But the Nicaraguan exiles who trained there in 1980, who tried to think of themselves as soldiers and who called themselves the September 15 Legion, were becoming just another bunch of hired guns in Guatemala's bloody underworld of politics and crime. They sweated through pushups and wind sprints, getting fit for a fight that seemed never to begin. Then they would be called on for "special operations." There were robberies and kidnappings, threats and extortions. There were murders. Market vendors at the bus terminal in Guatemala City's fourth zone were prey to the operations described as "recuperating funds." Many of the men found this business petty and demoralizing, but they kept on. It was a matter of survival, they said. And other actions were more political. There were jobs for the Guatemalan police and for certain Salvadoran exiles.

Most often, the veterans of Detachment 101 would remember later, the orders came through one man—Colonel Ricardo Lau.

"He's very cold," one of the exiles said of him. "Let's say he was very oriental. He didn't laugh, and only with difficulty would you make him smile. He was a serious type. Serious serious. Fairly thin, with a look that made you afraid. A real cold oriental." They called him "El Chino" Lau.

He had spent much of his career connected to Somoza's Office of National Security, the OSN, a service better known for brutality than effectiveness with its narrow cells full of prisoners and its card files full of cockroach shit. A top official at the CIA who knew his record called Lau a "Somoza hatchet man." A *guardia* who worked with him called him "a torturer."

"He operated where they put on the hood and the 220 current," the *guardia* officer said.

So many people hated Lau with such intensity, so many came to fear him, that he was later described among the veterans of Detachment 101 as something like evil incarnate, not only brutal but cowardly, not only violent but venal. He had trouble shooting men who could shoot back, combat officers would say. And in the war he stayed in his clandestine work until it got so bad that "everyone, even Somoza's bodyguards, had to fight." During the insurrection Lau served as second-in-command of Carazo province, then head of the Model Jail in Managua. He is said to have run a checkpoint near the airport where young men were stopped and their knees checked for scrapes and bruises. Those who had them were assumed to have been behind the barricades and were shot.

When Lau left Nicaragua, he went to a second home in Guatemala.

Ricardo Lau was not the most senior of the former Guardia officers to settle there and link himself to the fledgling Legion. Officially, Lau was only one member of what passed for a general staff, and by the middle of 1980 another colonel, Enrique Bermúdez, had arrived from Washington to take over the general direction of the group.

Bermúdez, forty-eight years old at the time, still was not popular with some of the young officers. Their dreams of regaining and rebuilding their country had grown in direct proportion to their helplessness. Theirs would be a fight for a new Nicaragua, not a resurrection of the old one. But they began to recognize, as they sought support and funds from what they had expected to be friendly Latin governments and businessmen, that someone more senior and better connected than they would have to be at the head of their organization. There were talks with Bermúdez in Washington and he was persuaded to move down to Miami, then to Guatemala. His broad face and stern features gave him some air of authority; his reported differences with Somoza over the years took away some of the taint of the old dictatorship. Most important, his long service in Washington, the young officers thought, would give him the keys to the doors they had not been able to open.

But Lau was the G-2 responsible for intelligence. The Guatemalan underworld was dominated by members of old intelligence networks: Salvadorans exiled by the 1979 coup, Nicaraguans who fled the revolution, veterans of Washington's agencies and Guatemala's own operatives. It was a kind of a duty-free zone for right-wing conspirators and free-lance murderers. And Lau appears to have had the talent for operating in it. He worked closely with Bermúdez, each protecting the other in the small, jealous and violent organization they were shaping.

Bermúdez and Lau provided a kind of nucleus around which the *guardias* could begin to coalesce. First there were five of them, then fifteen, then thirty at Detachment 101. In addition to Lau's own house a few blocks from the airport, there were three safe houses scattered around the city.

By the middle of the year, some of the men who had taken asylum in the embassies in Managua began to appear. Captain Hugo Villagra had escaped from the Argentine embassy during the Christmas holidays, then made his way down across the border with a compass through the rough mountains around Peñas Blancas. Others were released on amnesties. The boy Pedro Núñez Cabezas got out of his captivity at the Guatemalan embassy with his family and joined one of the other Guardia gangs in Guatemala until it was folded into the ranks of the Legion.

The biggest single group was the Miami crowd that had been with Comandante Bravo. They considered themselves the actual founders of the Legion—people like Justiniano Pérez and Noel Ortiz, along with Colonel Guillermo Mendietta and Dr. Eduardo Román, who managed the boxer Alexis Argüello. Suspicion, frustration and fear had torn apart their organization after Bravo's murder, but the core group had recuperated enough to decide, finally, to leave Miami for Guatemala City.

Their arrival was a measure of their haplessness. They came with their pistols in pieces in their luggage and a clip dropped out of someone's sleeve, clattering across the polished airport floor, instantly attracting the Ray-Ban eyes of the Guatemalan security police. They were all arrested before they ever cleared customs. But they had a phone number for a member of the old right-wing web of contacts. They were released after a couple of hours. And Lau soon had the new men under his protection and into his network.

"You put a lot of time and investment into training; developing relationships, of course," said one of the CIA's old Latin Americanists. In a region where the occupants of the presidential palace sometimes change from week to week, in the police and security forces "you try to get somebody in charge who will stay in no matter how many times the governments may change. It gives you continuity."

What the CIA had built in Latin America since the early 1950s was a lot of continuity. In 1954 it had put together a small army and a large propaganda operation that ousted the left-leaning president of Guatemala. In 1961 came the fiasco at the Bay of Pigs, where the CIA created a secret army that wound up in Castro's jails after a brief fight, then on the streets of Miami looking for revenge. There was Operation Mongoose, meant to humiliate or eliminate the Cuban dictator, and there were all the long, mysterious and fruitless links between the Agency and the Mafia trying to do something, anything to get rid of Castro.

There was the "public safety program" that trained Latin American policemen to meet the threat of Communist subversion with the best basic political, propaganda and intelligence tools the CIA could provide.

Special teams of the U.S. Army Special Forces helped track down and kill Castro's friend, the adventurous Argentine Ché Guevara and his small, incompetent band of guerrillas in the mountains of Bolivia. There were the operations in Venezuela, building an underground network that, for once, helped protect a democracy instead of destroying it. In 1968 U.S. advisors were back in Guatemala to work with military and paramilitary forces to design the effective, bloody repression of a Marxist-led insurgency.

Each one of these operations left its legacy of operatives, even little armies, trained by the Agency.

In 1965 in a meeting of Central America's interior ministers, formal links were established among the secret services of the five republics. Information was to be exchanged on Communist subversion; cooperation encouraged. The war between Honduras and El Salvador that came four years later ended a lot of the formal ties, but informal contacts kept up, as ever.

In 1973 there was Chile; the downfall of an elected Communist president, the rise of a brutal right-wing general, all aided and abetted by Washington.

Then there was Watergate.

In the tide of guilt and recriminations that swept the country after the revelations that began with the break-in at Democratic headquarters, distasteful stories from the Agency's past floated belly-up into the public consciousness. The Watergate break-in was staged by Howard Hunt, a veteran of the Guatemalan and Cuban operations who employed Cuban exiles originally trained for the Bay of Pigs. The agency was put under a microscope. Questions were raised about the tortures inflicted by U.S.–trained police and about plots to kill foreign leaders.

The time had come for the Agency to pull back from some of the old networks, officially close out its relations with others. The public safety program and the International Police Academy in Washington were shut down for political reasons and the CIA station in San Salvador was closed for economic ones. But the network had been set up for continuity, formal or informal, and that survived.

By the late 1970s, Latin America's right-wing intelligence circles had taken on a life, a direction, a continuity of their own, in some areas directly challenging the United States' public policy: blowing up a Chilean exile in the middle of Washington's embassy row; engineering a Fascist military coup in Bolivia against the bitter opposition of the U.S. ambassador there. The network bore the liberal administration of Jimmy Carter no loyalty at all.

When Bill, the American, ran over the limits on his credit cards in 1979 and went back to his job in Irvington, New York, other newfound friends of the *guardias* helped keep them alive, and members of the old networks came forward as well. Veterans of the old Bay of Pigs Brigade 2506 found them a place to train in Miami, first in back of a hospital and then, less conspicuously, in the Everglades. In Guatemala the *guardias* found support from the men who carried off the little war of 1954.

Mario Sandoval Alarcón and Lionel Sisniega Otero were well-established and still-feared figures on the Guatemalan political scene twenty-five years after they helped the CIA bring down the government of Jacobo Arbenz and helped themselves to a share of power. Their party had as its official emblem a crusader's crosslike sword. Their colors were red, white and blue. Their totem was the Black Christ of Esquipulas. But the white handprint of *la mano blanca,* the most famous of Guatemala's death squads, was the symbol with which they were associated by the relatives of their murdered rivals.

Sandoval made himself the godfather of the crowd coming out of the broken Salvadoran and Nicaraguan intelligence networks in 1980. He put several of them up in an apartment hotel behind his home and found houses for others to share. He gave them advice on how to fight the Communists with politics—by building a party to carry their message, as well as underground groups to enforce it. But he was the first to admit, publicly and without reserve, that "of course we understand that this is a dirty war."

One of Sandoval's protégés was a young exiled Salvadoran major.

"I know the moral qualities of Major Roberto d'Aubuisson," Sandoval vouched for him one day. "He is my friend, and even though he is younger than me I respect him."

The front line of the underground war in those days was in El Salvador, and d'Aubuisson was running it. Nineteen eighty was the year the death squads of El Salvador became famous. The left was carved out of the cities with midnight murders, torture and disappearances that the Salvadoran government never began to control. Other exiles living near Guatemala City's Aurora airport at the time remember the light planes flown by d'Aubuisson's dashing young men, many of them rich kids who had gotten their pilots' licenses out of boredom, bringing the hit teams back from their missions in San Salvador with businesslike regularity.

Theirs was an enterprise that dealt in quality, not quantity. They were not the men who slaughtered people by the tens of thousands in El Salvador during the worst days of the underground war there. The government's own security forces, sometimes in civilian clothes, sometimes in uniform, were the ones who carried out that wholesale carnage and built up the anonymous statistics. The group that operated out of Guatemala went after names, people whose faces everyone knew, the sensational cases of people they thought were Communists at the top of Salvadoran society: a Christian Democratic cabinet member; an Archbishop of San Salvador.

They worked with the intelligence branches of the black-helmeted Salvadoran National Guard and the infamous Treasury Police. By one account, many of their murders were coordinated by the Salvadoran high command. They drew their killers mostly from the ranks of soldiers who wanted extra pay, showed special talents and had the right sadistic flair. But for the biggest operations, it seems, they also contracted outside talent—specialists—and there were plenty of them to be found in Guatemala's right-wing underworld. The man to contact, it appears from such evidence as is available, was El Chino Lau.

When d'Aubuisson was captured briefly by his political enemies in El Salvador in May 1980 an appointment book and other papers were found on one of his aides. There were records of payments and there were organizational diagrams. There were shopping lists and checklists of tools for assassination: a G-2 rifle with a silencer, a .257 Roberts with a starlight scope, Guatemalan license plates for undercover operations, payoffs to right-wing officers and the telephone numbers of wealthy Salvadorans reputed to fund the death squad operations. There were also itineraries for the pilots who ferried the hit teams back and forth to Guatemala.

Although the CIA took more than two years to begin seriously analyzing these papers, they eventually were recognized as a kind of Rosetta stone for deciphering the Salvadoran death squads.

In the middle of the appointment book there is an entry under the date March 27, 1980. That was three days after the politically powerful yet almost saintly Archbishop of San Salvador, Oscar A. Romero, took a bullet through the heart as he raised the chalice in the middle of a memorial mass. The seized notes record a contact with Orlando De Sola, one of the richest and most radical of El Salvador's rightists, in room 305 of the El Dorado American, a luxury high-rise hotel in Guatemala City. Then there is the name of Juan Wright, another wealthy Salvadoran. Then two notes: "Contributions to Nicaraguans $40,000" and "Contributions to Nica—$80,000."

An exiled Salvadoran colonel and head of intelligence who had been d'Aubuisson's boss before the October coup knew several of the people involved. He has said since that these notes recorded the payoff for the murder of the Archbishop, and that there is no doubt of that. He also said, much later, that the next annotation is the most significant of all since it is the name of the Nicaraguan who contracted out his men to do the job.

"Col. Ricardo Lao tel. 67-475" is the way the entry reads.

Salvadorans, Nicaraguans, Guatemalans—there was also one other major element in Central America's terrorist equation in 1980.

The Argentine killers of the left and the right, of the revolution and the government, who had stalked each other for so long, now began to strike the enemies of their friends and the friends of their enemies.

On September 17, 1980, a hit team commanded by a leader of Argentina's ERP guerrillas blew apart Anastasio Somoza Debayle with a rocket-propelled grenade as he drove through the streets of Asunción, Paraguay. The Mercedes-Benz and the dictator lay in pieces all over the road in that out-of-the-way fiefdom of another dictator-general where he had finally found asylum. Managua, when the news arrived, erupted in celebration.

On the other side of the fight the moves of the Argentine army were less noisy. But they were better funded, more ambitious, more methodical.

At least 8,960 people had disappeared in Argentina at the hands of the Argentine armed forces and police after they seized power openly in March 1976. Probably there were many more who were never accounted for, never even mentioned by their families for fear of reprisal. They were workers and professionals, students and clerks, housewives, journalists, actors, and artists. Some were members of the underground terrorist organization of the left. Many were simply political opponents of the regime or voices raised in protest against what was happening, or persons unlucky enough to have their numbers in the address books of other suspects. Thrown facedown on the floors of little Ford Falcons or sealed vans, they were taken to secret detention centers. In all there were more than three hundred of these centers. "There were no excesses," it would be said. But "atrocities were a commonplace, daily practice." Tortures were varied, sadistic, imaginative. "Children and old people were tortured next to a relative in order to force the latter to give information." Corpses were often mutilated or destroyed.

By 1980 the masters of these techniques had won in Argentina. But the men who waged this war were ambitious. They acted as if they had discovered a great truth, the final solution for communism, and they wanted to apply it beyond their borders. It was no longer just a question of chasing old enemies. They saw themselves filling the strategic gap left by Carter. They saw themselves rolling back the advances of the Soviets in the new world war that was already begun; a war without frontiers.

The Argentines sent new military attachés and officials to the countries that surrounded Nicaragua, and they sent free-lancers and men whose talents were partly criminal to advise the fighters of the underground wars—the men with Sandoval and with d'Aubuisson and Lau.

November and December 1980 erupted with incredible violence. The terrorists of the Right thought they could do no wrong in the eyes of the newly elected American president, so whatever constraints they might have felt before now slipped away. The revolutionaries of the Left were building toward their ill-starred all-out offensive in El Salvador, and to stop that from happening, no actions were barred.

The Salvadoran slaughter reached new, ever more grotesque levels, and no one was immune from the fury of the death squads—not the civilian leaders of the left, who were murdered en masse on Thanksgiving Day; not even Americans. Four churchwomen from the United States were abducted, raped, tortured and murdered, then buried in a shallow grave by a squad of Salvadoran soldiers. An American journalist was kidnapped, then his hands and face were blown off with a grenade. In January 1981 two American labor advisors and the director of El Salvador's agrarian reform program were gunned down in the Sheraton restaurant.

And all the while the Argentines lingered in the background, working with the right's killers, grooming them, testing them to see if they were suitable as shock troops for their secret battles.

IV.

COSTA RICA, DECEMBER 1980

Captain Hugo Villagra, known as Visage, and his team from Detachment 101 pulled into a restaurant not far from Liberia, Costa Rica, and bought some empty whiskey and rum bottles. Closer to San José, they bought gasoline and oil. Visage ordered one of his men to tear some strips off his shirt and they started making the Molotov cocktails.

Visage was worried that there hadn't been a chance to test the guns. But he told his team they had to move quickly—that same night. He'd been warned that the Argentines were anxious. They wanted the radio taken out immediately and if the Nicaraguans stalled or failed, there was a Salvadoran team waiting to do the job instead.

Visage wanted this done right. This was, at last, an operation for real men. It was not a matter of knocking over the market stalls of old women, or killing a gambler who tried to welsh on his debts, the kinds of operations Lau had gotten his people into before. This was a chance to get the Argentines firmly behind the Legion and then to begin in earnest the war to regain Nicaragua.

The Argentines had wanted for a year to eliminate a powerful shortwave radio station in the village of Grecia on the outskirts of San José which was broadcasting reports and propaganda about the atrocities of the generals' war, promoting the revolution and subverting their control on the flow of information.

Radio Noticias del Continente, Argentine President Roberto Viola had warned, was broadcasting the message of the *montonero* leaders who had escaped the army's wrath. It was the voice of communism couched in the rhetoric of human rights. But the Costa Rican government would not lift a finger to shut it down.

A Salvadoran team commissioned by the Argentines tried rolling makeshift bombs out the door of an airplane. In another incident the building was sprayed with machine-gun fire. But those attacks achieved nothing. Radio Noticias del Continente was still on the air and the Argentine generals were apoplectic. Argentina's government, Viola told Buenos Aires reporters in stiff military jargon, "has developed and will develop permanent activities with the aim of annulling the action of these elements who attempt to destroy our traditional national values."

The struggle against terrorist criminals, Viola said, "offers difficulties that many times are not understood, as a result of the atypical aspects of this phenomenon which does not stop short of any methods to achieve its ends." Argentina's armed forces, Viola wanted the reporters to know, "adapt to the circumstances as these elements present them."

In December 1980, Visage's hit team from Detachment 101 was the adaptation.

They arrived near the transmitter in the village of Grecia at about two in the morning on the thirteenth, thinking that there would be few people around. Wearing dark sweatshirts over their clothes, they crept toward the little building through a light mist. But this was not like most Central American radio stations, a shack next to an antenna. It was not like the church station that had been blown up so many times in San Salvador. This was concrete. The windows were as small as gun ports. There was a barbed wire fence and then a wall. Now dogs were barking all over the place. High-powered floodlights went on. There was a watchman—a sentry—and he began to shoot.

Visage's men fired frantically at the floodlights, putting them out one by one, then tried to move forward in the darkness. But the firing was intensifying from inside the building and they were pinned down. A couple of the Molotovs were hurled into a shed off the side of the building where there seemed to be some generators. But the damage was not significant. One of the boys, Benavides, went down with seven bullets in him. His arm was shattered and his leg shot up. But there was no way to get to him to take him away. The second-in-command of the operation, "25," was shot as well.

Visage ordered a retreat and they fell back to the jeeps to discover that one was riddled with bullets. It would barely run. Oil dripped out of it like life's blood as they tried to get away. Finally they had to abandon it and cram as best they could into the one jeep that remained. Hurting, exhausted and failed, they arrived back at their little base near Liberia at about five in the morning. Visage called the commanders in Guatemala, Mendietta and Pérez. The news was already out in the region and time was running out for Visage's team. The airplane to pick him up, he was told, would be at the strip by six, at the latest 6:30.

They waited. They waited all day. And the next. The plane never came.

Visage was sleeping when his lookout brought word that a force of Costa Rican policemen were moving in on them. They scrambled into a pickup truck and tried to make one more getaway. The road was blocked. They threw down their guns.

The first major operation by the September 15 Legion ended in humiliating failure.

V.

MANAGUA, LATE 1979

La Negra came to Suicida early in 1980. There was no other place for her.

The anger of Managua's barrios against the *guardias* and their people was slow to die. Little monuments were built to the boys and girls killed fighting or, more often, simply murdered in the streets by Somoza's men. In some neighborhoods almost every corner had its little brick or cinderblock shrine painted red and black with the name —or maybe a small framed photograph—of a teenager who was killed and burned and buried on the spot.

A few *guardias* found family and friends to protect them. In a few barrios they even tried, in the late nights, to walk the streets once again with their guns and grenades, firing in frustration and fear in the dark. But one by one, week after week, they were arrested and taken away.

Life in the poor barrios of Central America is one of forced intimacy with hundreds of people. You dress in public, bathe in public, as often as not you make love in public, and you prosper or fail in public. It is a life with only shreds of privacy or modesty, and pride is forced. Each morning you wake to the grit of dust on your body that seeps into your bed through the wide cracks between the rough boards that make your walls. Sweat turns the dust to rivulets. Sex turns the dust to mud. The men who live in the slums are used up by their work and if they don't work, they're used up by the bottle. And the women are used up by the men. Sex begins most often as rape, and it begins young. A woman looks for a protector. Relations are informal, brutal and one-sided. Marriage is rare and largely irrelevant. Children are everywhere.

But La Negra had no sense of herself as victim. She thought she was smarter than most of the men she knew, and probably she was right, and she was nearly a physical match for many of them. Her shoulders were broad, her grip was firm. She liked tests. When the Sandinistas decided to pick her up in late 1979 they found someone who was difficult to handle.

When La Negra talked about her month in the Sandinistas' prison she sometimes mentioned thinking of the children she left behind, but more often she told of the torture she suffered. It was a dramatic story that changed from telling to telling. How much of it is true is difficult to say. The Sandinistas had made her eat her own feces, she told a woman who knew her in Honduras. December seventh was the day of the worst torture, she told a reporter. They wanted to make her turn in Suicida. "They said I had him hidden."

She said her feet were smashed with rifle butts by the Sandinistas and her toenails pulled out. She told a story of being stripped and forced into a room with a wet floor and an exposed electric wire strung across it. She was made to touch it, she said, and the third time she passed out.

La Negra escaped when she was moved to a new cell. She spent all night sawing through the bars with some implement she had found, and she and two other women and three men were able to get away.

Her children, she said, were taken by the Sandinstas, and she did not see them again. She said she later heard that one of them, the boy who was eight when she left him, became a member of the Sandinista Youth and was sent to school in Cuba.

La Negra made her way to her man.

NUEVA SEGOVIA PROVINCE, NICARAGUA, 1980

When Suicida and La Negra and Julio César talked about their first camps along the Honduran-Nicaraguan border and their first actions inside the Segovias they talked about the days when they ate monkey meat and palm shoots to survive; when they marched with .22s and trained with crossed sticks and selected enemies one by one to kill with a knife across the throat or a bullet through the heart. And in their tone was unmistakable nostalgia. There is no indication that they were very effective at what they did. Available records do not confirm the particular assassinations they said they carried out at this time, although much is suggestive. But they were proud and sentimental about the days with .22s, when they could make their own rules, administer their own justice, fight their own fight in the savage mountains of the Segovias.

And in odd, incongruous ways they identified with the war Sandino waged over the same trails fifty years before against the United States Marines. Julio César claimed that his grandfather was killed by Sandino for refusing to fight among his forces, and Julio César Herrera cursed Augusto César Sandino for that and seemed to cultivate the memory for some added margin of hate to keep him going. But Suicida talked of Sandino almost as a man with a kindred cause. And La Negra may have liked the idea of Sandino the hero as well: Sandino's woman had also been a famous ally in his fight, a telegraph operator who taught the men to communicate in Morse code with drums and whistles. She married Sandino one day in the jungles of Nueva Segovia among trees that almost obscured the sun.

This old history was alive more than ever in the Segovias when Suicida arrived there. The Sandinistas of 1980 painted stylized versions of Sandino's Stetson on the roads, traced out his silhouette in white rocks on the mountainsides. They cherished his legend and claimed it as the foundation for their politics. But if Sandino's memory was invested with a great deal of ideology by Marxist revolutionaries who made themselves first his political allies, and then his political heirs, the ideology, as such, never held much resonance for the people of the Segovias. They identified with the man. Their tradition of accounting to no one but themselves was not changed in fifty years. It was the same tradition the Sandinistas of the 1970s exploited to mount their campaign to overthrow Somoza. Now Suicida and his men exploited it to keep alive.

The affinity with Sandino, such as it was, was their hatred of authority, so that even men whose lives now revolved around killing the people who called themselves Sandinistas, could believe they and Augusto César Sandino had something in common: the raising of a tough little army; the fight against all odds, alone and defiant and vengeful.

What is known about Suicida's activities in 1980, the setbacks he suffered and the slow progress he made, must be gleaned from the Sandinistas' propaganda, reports in the Honduran press, and the bits and pieces of information recalled by the combatants themselves.

We know, for instance, that most of his group were from the Rattlesnakes, or *Cascabeles,* and that they often traveled to Danlí in southern Honduras. And we also know that in April 1980 Borge's troops and State Security arrested twenty men infiltrated into northern Nicaragua from Honduras. Some of them were made to talk very quickly, and State Security was able to outline in detail a picture of small bands organized under "boards of directors" that included presidents, vice-presidents, treasurers and members. The group that was captured operated out of San Marcos de Colón. Another worked out of Choluteca, and a third operated out of Danlí, not far from the area where Suicida set up shop. On the board of directors of that little group was a former Guardia colonel who had specialized in counterinsurgency, and another officer who had been with the Rattlesnakes. Probably Suicida had ties to them.

There is also Suicida's story that he received some of his best advice and training from a Cuban-American with a withered hand in the Honduran commercial city of San Pedro Sula. Suicida said this man was a Bay of Pigs veteran originally trained by the CIA, and that he became mentor to him in his own fight against the Sandinistas. To put alongside this bit of information is the report in May 1980 that a clandestine radio station broadcasting anti-Sandinista propaganda in the name of the Anti-Sandinista Guerrilla Special Forces—the group with which Suicida identified—was shut down near San Pedro Sula by Honduran authorities. The man running it, according to these reports, was a Cuban-American with a long history of anticommunist activities.

Whenever Suicida and his people joined other organizations, it seemed, those organizations were either crushed or fell apart for lack of interest. Finally they linked up with the men of the September 15

Legion. "But many of them," remembered one member of the Suicida gang, "instead of going to the mountains, they went to Honduras and had their little bit of liquor and created problems."

So the forces commanded by Suicida remained, month after month in 1980, as few as six or eight or twelve men. Perhaps sometimes there were as many as twenty people in the band.

For most of those first two years Suicida's people were trying to prove themselves, if not as leaders, then as killers.

"At first," explained Julio César, "people couldn't put up with the regime, but didn't give us support because they didn't think we were competent."

The gang eliminated anyone it thought the mountain people might resent. And Julio César especially seemed to enjoy the work. He dressed as a peasant or farmer or as a member of the Sandinista militia, and went into a village to find his target, standing on a corner or strolling down the dirt street looking for his victim, then making his move. That is what he did, he claimed, with a Cuban schoolteacher in the town of San Francisco del Norte.

"The people told us to get rid of him," said Julio César.

The people of the mountains often said that they like their priests to be priests, their teachers to be teachers. They did not like them coming to teach politics, especially not Communist politics, and they did not like them to come from some other country.

"The majority of the people of San Francisco del Norte were with us," said Julio César.

So he shot the Cuban in the chest, he boasted.

The killer in disguise was a common technique. In one incident reported in October 1981 two Cuban teachers and two militiamen were killed in Nicaragua's northeastern jungles by unidentified men. The killers dressed as members of the militia. The murders were an embarrassment to the Sandinista government. Borge himself raged at the actions, and Sandinista zealots vowed to retaliate. Even as the killing of the Cubans was made public, Radio Sandino announced that a local commander had begun "to settle accounts with the murderers."

"The band is made up by members of several families who live in various areas of the mountains," said the radio. "For this reason, it is difficult to locate them after they commit their crimes. The militias have already made contact with them and already have begun to apply revolutionary justice."

Suicida could tune in to such reports with considerable pleasure.

Revolutionary justice was rarely meted out to those who actually committed counterrevolutionary crimes. Those who did suffer, however, both the innocent and the complicit, built up a reserve of resentment that would help in the fight against the Sandinistas later on. On top of that, Suicida and his people loved any attention that Radio Sandino—that anybody—gave them. They listened intently to Borge's speeches and his rages. One night Julio César heard Borge vow on the radio to catch him alive and eat him for dinner. And Julio César thought that was funny.

In those days Julio César was using the pseudonym William. Later he decided to change it in honor of Borge's remark. Someone, probably an Argentine, told him that in the waters off Patagonia huge whales ate millions of tiny bits of sealife called krill. But no matter how much krill the whales ate, there was always more. This image of the whales and the krill was an odd one for a Nicaraguan. Julio César liked it. And there was something that seemed ominous, menacing about the sound of the word. Julio César took it as his new nom de guerre. He would be Krill. Let Borge try to catch him. There would always be more of him.

Julio César ventured away on his own from time to time, out to the coast, doing bloody bits of business. On February 13, 1981 (a firm date Julio César attached to one event above all others in his mind), he tracked down a man who had insulted his mother. She was a Honduran and she often carried minor contraband back and forth across the Rio Negro near Guasaule in the flat lands of northern Chinandega. It was the kind of thing that the Guardia had rarely noticed when it ran the border, and to Julio César's way of thinking it should have been a matter of a little payoff if she was caught. But a local Sandinista official, a militia commander, jailed her for seventeen days. Julio César heard of this. He hunted the man. He waited, watching in the little village. He found his moment and he murdered him. And then Julio César—Krill—disappeared once again into his wild mountains.

FINDINGS—1981

I.

Washington, D.C.

By way of a discreet little elevator in the Capitol basement near the bust of Susan B. Anthony, witnesses rode to a hallway near the dome and the windowless chambers of the congressional intelligence committees. The door behind the security guard opened onto a hearing room paneled in dark wood where the congressmen sat in green leather chairs behind a long table that wrapped in a horseshoe around the witnesses. There was a sense of hermetic isolation; a low, Strangelovian light. The room had first been used by the Joint Committee on Atomic Energy, when the men who discussed the bomb wanted a great sense of security and secrecy to imbue their deliberations. That committee's seal, carved in marble behind the congressmen, was now covered with an American flag. The plaster seals of agencies concerned with intelligence lined another wall: fifteen in all, ranging from the National Security Agency to the Defense Mapping Agency to the profiled eagle of the CIA. Opposite them was a map of the world they watched.

The House and Senate Permanent Select Committees on Intelligence were formed in the aftermath of Watergate and the revelations about dirty dealings in the Central Intelligence Agency that erupted in the early 1970s. There was, in those days, general amazement and a fair amount of revulsion at stories of plots to kill Castro (or to make his beard fall out), CIA complicity in attempts to murder the Congolese leader Patrice Lumumba (with the agency saved from guilt only by the fact that someone else did it first), and other numerous infractions, inspirations and debacles. Worse still in the context of Watergate break-ins, plumbers, mail reading, telephone tapping and drug testing was the growing fear that the intelligence agencies were spying on the people of the United States as much as for them. The hearings held by Senator Frank Church in 1975 and 1976 exposed much that was bizarre and disconcerting, and the posturing and pronouncements of politicians raised ever higher the specter of a secret state within a state account-able to no one and capable of just about anything.

Liberals, then in ascendance, rumbled about the impossibility of having secret agencies inside an open society, and the rationale behind the creation of the committees was that, somehow, they might help the intelligence agencies to survive—save them from themselves, if you will, work with them and watch over them so that America could be sure they were staying in line with the Constitution even as they pro-vided the government with the vital information needed to protect the nation. "Oversight committees," they were called: a curious locution that meant they oversaw intelligence activities but seemed to imply they overlooked them.

The committees were created when there was still some notion that foreign policy could be run on the basis of consensus, even a secret foreign policy. There might be little problems here and there, but every-one would be part of the same Establishment. By the time Ronald Reagan took over the presidency and William Casey seized the reins at the CIA, however, nobody in charge saw things that way.

Casey was a man with a mission that he seemed to have felt in his blood since he served with Wild Bill Donovan in the Office of Strategic Services' London office during World War II. He was a rich man, a shrewd dealer in securities. He was a powerful man who had made more than one politician with his organizational skills and his connec-tions. But the most important politican he had made was Ronald Rea-gan, whose election he managed in 1980.

Casey was a brilliant man; yet he mumbled almost unintelligibly when he spoke in public. He was old and his face was deeply lined. His wisps of gray hair blew erratically around the bald top of his head and sometimes curled around his collar. His shoulders were hunched and in photographs he looked to be of small or average build. But he stood over six feet in person. He was a man of unexpected aspects.

Casey had asked for the Agency position, and even in 1981 he was ready to run with it. He seemed to thrive on his job, to be rejuvenated by it. "It was like he was hydroplaning on the way to the nursing home," as one of his colleagues at the Agency put it.

He put a major emphasis on action, almost for its own sake. "He distrusts analysts and prefers operations officers who've seen the world."

Casey's mandate was to resurrect and rebuild. If the oversight committees wanted to help, then fine, his attitude suggested to committee staffers. If not, then they could stay out of his way. He was as leery of Congress as he was of the press.

"He started out deciding there would be no relations with the press and no relations with Congress and discovered it wasn't very smart," said a senior intelligence official.

According to some of his colleagues in the intelligence community, Casey saw the House committee, dominated by Democrats, as hostile, posturing, and porous. Many people at the agency viewed its chairman, Edward P. Boland, as a tool of the Democratic Speaker Tip O'Neill.

On the Senate side, at the other end of the hall, the new administration had hoped for more support. The chairman, after all, was Mr. Conservative, Barry Goldwater. But only a few weeks into Reagan's first term, stories broke in the newspapers suggesting that the man William Casey had put in charge of his Directorate for Operations, Max Hugel, was involved in questionable business dealings. Hugel was not an intelligence professional but a businessman picked by Casey for political reasons to run the most sensitive division of the Agency, the one that runs agents, the one that runs little wars. Goldwater suggested that Casey might think about resigning. Casey did not, but the remark was not soon forgotten. The bond of trust that might have been there was gone. So it was in an environment of cool, mutual suspicion that Casey presented the president's decision that a major covert action program was warranted in Central America in December 1981.

The Reagan administration had been in office for almost a year. By the time it told Congress what was happening, all the actors were in place and it was just a matter of pulling the curtain aside for a glimpse of the set.

*　*　*

The shaping of what came to be called the Secret War was taken in hand by a small collection of men whose names for the most part were buried at the second or third levels of their bureaucracies: an assistant secretary of state; a deputy assistant secretary of defense; a division chief of the CIA's Directorate for Operations; a Marine Corps colonel on the staff of the National Security Council.

They called themselves the Core Group, or the Restricted Interdepartmental Group (RIG) or the Thursday Afternoon Club, although they never met on Thursday afternoons. They got together on the sixth floor of the State Department "as often as necessary" to manage the developing policy toward Central America.

Thomas O. Enders presided. Tall—about six feet six inches—imposing and aristocratic, the assistant secretary of state for inter-American affairs was a master of bureaucratic maneuver. Ambitious, experienced, relentlessly tough, he was part of that small, patrician club of "five percenters," what were once called "the best and the brightest" at the State Department, who run their offices with all the self-assurance of men who have known since they walked the snow-covered paths of their prep schools that they were meant to dominate the world around them. But Enders knew one thing more. He knew how to survive.

When the United States began secretly bombing Cambodia in the early 1970s, Enders was the number two man at the embassy in Phnom Penh. It was he, not the ambassador, who directed the controversial strikes. And it was Enders who was accused afterward by congressmen of having lied about them. But Enders had done what he did on orders from Henry Kissinger, and Enders, his influential friends argued, should not see his "brilliant career" spoiled by this single mistake. He soon became the assistant secretary of state for economic and business affairs, and then ambassador to Canada.

When Ronald Reagan became president, he made another Kissinger man, General Alexander Haig, his secretary of state. And Haig picked Enders to take on Latin America. It was one part of the world in which Enders had no experience at all. But in the context of the new administration, that was considered something of a virtue.

"The administration came in convinced that the problem in Central America was that Carter was soft," said one member of the Core Group. Despite years of experience and seniority in the foreign service, most of the veterans associated with the Carter policy were fired, forced out or moved to obscure and distant posts. Carter's last assistant secretary was sacked. His principal deputy for Central America was transferred to Katmandu.

Enders and the men he brought in to replace them were, as one put it, "action-oriented." And cutting across bureaucratic lines to "get things done" was the raison d'être of the Core Group.

It was, one member said admiringly, "a constantly evolving organizational framework" that became the "principal decision-making body.

"Often it was not what it seemed," he said. "When it got too big there would be a steering group."

The idea was to keep control.

At higher levels of the administration all hell was breaking loose. Two days after Reagan's inauguration, El Salvador and Nicaragua were discussed in what Haig found "an anguishing series of meetings in the National Security Council." Haig was trying to make himself the vicar of U.S. foreign policy and succeeding mainly in starting pitched battles with other members of the cabinet and advisors to the president.

Reagan's new secretary of state knew nothing about Latin America and generally couldn't care less. His main interest was the North Atlantic, not the banana republics. The ideologues obsessed with the region, the old friends of Somoza, the people around owlish and ultra-rightist North Carolina Senator Jesse Helms, had found in Haig not an ally but an adversary. When they made their bid for control of policy Haig stopped them.

But in the new Reagan administration, its bright young men liked to say, there were in fact no moderates and no liberals. "The only division," as one of them put it, "is between the hard-liners and the ideologues."

"There was," said one of the Core Group's veterans, "a kind of tendency to want to prove your manhood."

The Salvadoran rebels had challenged the new administration. They had launched their general offensive—they had called it their "final offensive"—on January 10, promising they would present Reagan with "an irreversible military situation" by the time he took office. They failed miserably after three days. They took not a single government garrison in combat, and they limped into the mountains to regroup their shattered forces. By the end of the month their challenge seemed a bitter joke and their destruction rather than their strength was what looked irreversible. But in the course of their humiliation they had also allowed their Nicaraguan and Cuban support to be fully exposed. Many of their documents were captured. Trucks full of munitions were uncovered. The hand of the Soviets in this was evident, even if all the implications were less than clear.

Haig took an interest.

"Al Haig came in with Nicaragua having, in his view, gone. Salvador was next. And if that went, God knows," said a member of the Core Group.

Haig began talking about Central America but thinking about Korea in 1950 and Cuba in 1962. A line had to be drawn, a statement made. He saw himself eyeball-to-eyeball with the Soviets in El Salvador, but when he tried to make his point he felt his turf being chipped away from beneath him in his continuing bureaucratic battles.

As his position grew weaker, his rhetoric got stronger. Haig began talking publicly about "going to the source." Cuba. But the president's other advisors were not going along. El Salvador was a local issue that could be handled in low-key ways, a little money here, a little military training there. The president's main men were interested in the economy, not El Salvador.

It was up to the Core Group to try to sort this out.

"Haig had this real hard-on for Castro. He kept saying, 'Give me a Cuban policy!' Which was really looking for some way to knock off Castro. He wanted to 'defang' him. But there wasn't really any way we could do that.

"We were under a hell of a lot of pressure to come up with a policy," said one of the Core Group's people. "Haig had told everybody the fate of the Western world depended on El Salvador—and we weren't able to do anything about it."

Enders saw that direct military action against Cuba "clearly was not possible." Its armed forces numbered in the hundreds of thousands. The risk of direct and very dangerous confrontation with the Soviets was too great. The public had no interest or will for such a fight. Instead, as the Core Group shaped the policy, the decision was made "that we had to compete with Cuba at all levels." Part of the competition would be with economic development and military support for the region's non-Marxist governments. The other part, building on the principles of the Republican platform, would be covert action against Cuba, its surrogates and its allies in the hemisphere.

On March 9, 1981, six weeks after Reagan took office, he issued a "finding" for stepped-up covert action in Central America. A finding is a written statement by the president, required by a 1974 law, outlining a given CIA operation in general terms and establishing that in the president's judgment it is important to national security.

Carter had made his own very general finding for covert action toward the end of his term. But the new administration saw it as toothless. Reagan's was more specific and ambitious, focused on protecting the Salvadoran government from the insurgency there. The emphasis was on undercover political and propaganda work and improved intelligence gathering on outside support for the rebels. There was also mention of efforts to "interdict" the weapons supplied to the rebels.

At about the same time, the decision was made to cut off all U.S. assistance to Nicaragua, including the PL-480 food program. The Carter administration, in the last days of its term, had suspended what was left of the the $75 million in aid it won for the Sandinistas a year before. There had been little choice. Certainly there would have been no way to certify, after the Salvadoran "final offensive," that the Sandinistas were not abetting other rebel movements. The Nicaraguans had acted with incredible indiscretion. Years later Salvadoran dissidents and rebel leaders who were in Managua and Havana at the time would shake their heads when they recalled how they even trained acrobats for the victory parade through San Salvador. Edén Pastora would remember the Salvadoran guerrilla commanders decked out in well-pressed uniforms directing their triumph—then watching their defeat—from a command center at the house of Somoza's mistress. By January 14, U.S. intelligence had picked up an avalanche of incriminating evidence, including a truck with a roof full of M-16s rolling through Honduras. The game was over and the chits were being called in. "You people are just irresponsible," Ambassador Pezzullo told Borge and Daniel Ortega when he saw them at a cocktail party. "We've got you red-handed." And the Sandinistas knew it. They began taking measures to recoup. By March they had shut down the airfield at Pamplona that had been used to supply the Salvadorans. The airplanes were decommissioned, the pilots dispersed.

But that was not enough. The Reagan administration was intent on sending signals to Moscow, and Nicaragua was one medium for the message. At a "Washington soirée," Haig told the Nicaraguan ambassador that "while the Sandinistas betrayed their neighbors there would be no business as usual. America was prepared not only to cut off all aid, but to do other things as well."

Pezzullo, as best he could, argued against the cutoff. Obviously the Sandinistas had supplied the Salvadorans, but just as obviously they had stopped. If they had been reluctant to support the Salvadoran rebels in the first place, they would be more so now. The existing suspension of U.S. aid was enough to demonstrate anger. If there was a complete and highly publicized cut it would likely prove to be permanent. The Congress had only barely passed the aid when Carter was president and pushing for it. It would never pass again under Reagan. But without the aid to offer, the only alternative way to influence the Sandinistas would be by force. "You're throwing away your chips, man," Pezzullo warned Haig.

The members of the Core Group discussed the matter. But they concluded that the Sandinistas had cut off the Salvadorans only temporarily. It was a seasonal ebb and flow, they would argue later, although only one season had passed when they made their recommendations.

The announcement was made on April 1. "We have no hard evidence of arms movements through Nicaragua during the past few weeks, and propaganda and some other support activities have been curtailed," it said. If this "favorable trend" continued someday there might be new U.S. assistance for Nicaragua. Certainly the United States wanted to continue "to assist moderate forces in Nicaragua which are resisting Marxist domination, working toward a democratic alternative, and keeping alive the private sector." And the United States was not going to demand that its loans be paid back immediately. But the aid was cut off, including shipments of wheat. That much was clear.

Nicaragua started getting its wheat from the Soviet Union (which was getting its wheat from the United States since Reagan had lifted that embargo). It also got Soviet tanks, imported through Algeria. It got its cash from Libya, which offered to deposit $100 million in its Central Bank. By the end of the year Managua residents could buy copies of Colonel Muammar Qaddafi's little green book at the Intercontinental Hotel in Managua, or spend a week celebrating the thirteen-hundredth anniversary of Bulgarian statehood in public ceremonies. And soon, of course, the Salvadorans were once more being helped by propaganda and volunteers from Managua. But as Pezzullo had predicted, the United States had thrown away its carrot, all that was left was the stick, and the question, as the Salvadoran rebels launched new attacks at the end of the summer, was how large that stick needed to be.

Haig ordered a report prepared by his state department counselor, Robert C. MacFarlane. Titled "Taking the War to Nicaragua," it ran down the options for putting pressure on Managua and Havana. Haig still favored open measures that could range from downing Cuban aircraft and sinking smugglers' boats to a full-scale naval blockade. But Haig was still alone. The president's personal advisors and the Core Group were leaning heavily now toward stepping up the covert action with "paramilitary operations" that might include commando raids, or something like secret war.

The key vote on this was going to belong to Director of Central Intelligence William Casey. It was his agency that would carry it out. And he, as much as any man, had the president's confidence. But his agency was divided. Its veterans had seen firsthand the kind of bureaucratic carnage wrought on the intelligence apparatus by paramilitary projects that fell apart. They remembered the Bay of Pigs and its internal aftermath. They remembered, quite vividly, the purges and the revelations of the Church committee hearings when their most closely held and embarrassing secrets—their "family jewels" as some called them—had been laid bare and the agency, as a result, had been laid low. Some were opposed to paramilitary operations on principle. Such actions tended to interfere with careful intelligence gathering, creating blind spots, diverting resources. Others objected to the kind of scale that was being proposed, and the obvious vagueness of the goals that were being discussed.

"If you're going to overthrow anybody you have to do it pretty quickly," said one CIA veteran. "These operations always unravel—unless they take over the country—and they always make a mess."

And when Casey first took over, that was the voice he heard the most of, and the kind he seemed to respect. In the cabinet he appeared, without ever making himself perfectly clear, to be the one figure leaning toward Haig's arguments for overt rather than covert action.

But there was also another current in the Agency, what more cautious men called "cowboyism": a go-get-'em, can-do attitude that said now was the time for the agency to win some certifiable victories against the Communists. For Casey, the old disciple of Wild Bill Donovan, this faction certainly had a visceral appeal. And in the summer of 1981, Casey found its perfect voice.

At a meeting of his Western European station chiefs, Casey came away very impressed with the man who ran the Rome operation. Duane

R. Clarridge, known universally as Dewey, was "a real doer, a real take-charge guy," Casey reportedly told his associates. No one who knew Dewey would dispute that. He was famous in the world of the agency for his enthusiasm and his flamboyance.

"Dewey was a very 'spiv' dresser," said one of the agency's old hands. "Pastel jackets. White shoes. Kerchief in the pocket." The veteran, one of the classic gray men of the CIA, shook his head when he recalled. "I don't know where he got all his clothes. But everybody was quite amused by Dewey."

Clarridge was forty-nine and still a jock. "His barbells served Dewey well," his yearbook from the Peddie School in New Jersey had put it. At Brown University and at the Russian Institute at Columbia he was remembered for his gregariousness. His master's thesis on the World Federation of Trade Unions in Asia concluded "with admittedly inadequate evidence" that Moscow directed its activities to subvert newly independent nations. The self-assured conclusion was typical Dewey. He was, one woman who knew him said flatly, "a climber." For a while he lived in Loudoun County, Virginia, in the Hunt Country, where a number of the old hands of the CIA have retired to comfortable views of the Appalachians or invested in real estate on the flourishing fringes of the outer Washington metropolitan area. His retreat, said the woman, "was, well, pretentious. You know, sort of a log cabin with a bidet."

Clarridge had served with the Agency in Nepal and in India and in Turkey and in Rome. His background in Latin America was nil. But, as was becoming the rule in the Reagan administration, that was seen as an advantage.

Nestor Sanchez, the Latin America division chief at the Directorate for Operations at the time, had a lot of experience in the region and a lot of contacts. Born in New Mexico in 1927, he was slight and short and dressed very neatly and correctly. He spoke fluent Spanish and had spent most of his almost thirty years in the Agency serving in the region. He knew all the figures who counted, he was plugged in to the old networks and he knew the way they thought. In 1967 and 1968, Sanchez had served in Guatemala at the height of *la mano blanca,* the fight for the city, the extermination of the Communists. Sanchez had served in Venezuela, where the agency had long, deep ties with the local services. Sanchez knew how to talk to the Argentines.

But there seems to have been something about Sanchez that Casey didn't like. (At least, that was what Dewey told people later.) Sanchez appeared to be less than enthusiastic about some of the grander schemes being hatched for the region, always talking about repercussions, bringing up problems of local sensibilities. And in early August, Sanchez was retired from the Agency and moved to the Department of Defense as a deputy assistant secretary for international security affairs. From that position he could stay in touch with the operations. He would stay in the Core Group. But Dewey, as the new division chief at the Directorate for Operations, would take the point. And Casey would listen, increasingly, to what Dewey had to say.

Managua, Nicaragua

There is a fork in the road, Thomas Enders told the Nicaraguan foreign minister in Managua one afternoon in August 1981. One way leads to accommodation, the other to separation. We are afraid you may be too far advanced on the wrong road.

Enders had come to Managua for only one day, and his trip went largely unnoticed in the United States. But he was big news to the local reporters who staked out his entrances and exits from the ministry behind a steak house on the South Highway. At last a senior Reagan administration official had come to see the country for himself. The Nicaraguan reporters were pleased. And he was so tall! They were amused. He loomed head, shoulders and torso above the rotund Maryknoll priest who served as minister, Father Miguel D'Escoto.

But there was not much amusement in the meetings themselves. Enders wanted things to be quite clear for the Ortegas and Borge and the rest of the Directorate. The United States wanted Nicaraguan aid to the Salvadoran rebels stopped. The Nicaraguans could say, as they always did, "Show us the proof," but while that went over well with the public it was a sterile point with Enders. He knew the support was there and he knew, from the cutoffs a year before and in the spring, that it could be stopped. If it were not, he wanted the Nicaraguans to know there would be serious problems.

Through the previous seven months of debate inside the administration the focus on El Salvador had steadily narrowed. Any suggestion that its war was primarily an internal struggle was overwhelmed by the talk of going to the source, the insistence on seeing it as a confrontation with Moscow. But outside the administration, few people were convinced by the East-West rhetoric. Many Democrats, as well as leaders of the Roman Catholic Church, and the skilled coterie of human rights lobbyists on Capitol Hill, flatly rejected the administration's claims about El Salvador. Its history of oppression and poverty bred its revolution; made rebellion, indeed, necessary and inevitable. The Soviets had little or nothing to do with it.

The blundering brutality of the Salvadoran government itself meanwhile consistently undermined the administration's efforts on its behalf. The murders of December 1980 could not be lived down. And as one Carter envoy asked toward the end of his stay there, who wanted to support "a genocidal nun-killing regime"?

Some of the U.S. military advisors who began arriving in February privately marveled at the incompetence of the Salvadoran army and wondered if all the talk of Nicaragua and Cuba and the Soviet Union did not just offer an excuse for the officer corps to do nothing. The government forces were fighting a nine-to-five war, while the rebels worked round the clock.

Yet the more the administration was challenged about El Salvador, the more fixated it seemed to become on Nicaragua's role there. In the Core Group it was said that it might be impossible to sustain the Salvadoran regime if Nicaragua "could continue with impunity to support the insurgency there."

Enders's August 11 visit to Managua was a way of testing what it might take to get the Sandinistas to back off; specifically he wanted to see "if you could use the threat of confrontation rather than confrontation itself" to make them cease and desist.

"The Enders visit," as one of his associates put it, "was very confrontational."

The Sandinistas complained about reports that Nicaraguan exiles were training to overthrow them at camps in the Florida Everglades. They told Enders they wanted this stopped. They demanded it be stopped. They complained bitterly about the aid cutoff. They brought up, as they were wont to do, the long history of U.S. intervention.

Enders came back with cool reiterations of his position, making subtle but clear distinctions between U.S. concerns and U.S. demands. Washington did not like the direction the Nicaraguan revolution had taken internally. It did not like the harassment of the opposition press, the increasingly circumscribed role of the private sector, the failure to hold elections. All these were concerns. The buildup of the Sandinista armed forces was a major concern. The Soviet tanks. The pilots sent to Bulgaria to train in MIGs. The talk of putting more than fifty thousand men and women under arms. The Cuban advisors were a concern as well as the East German and Soviet involvement with the State Security apparatus.

It was all for self-defense, D'Escoto would explain. The revolution
had to be ready to defend itself from any outside aggression, including
and especially the aggression of the United States.

Enders treated that kind of reasoning with contempt. The United
States was two hundred times as big as Nicaragua. It was much more
than two hundred times as powerful. If Nicaragua was building its
army, sending shivers of fear through its neighbors, with the idea that
it could take on the United States, then the effort was silly and futile.

D'Escoto's line was that the United States thought the same in the
time of Sandino, and Vietnam.

Enders listened coldly. He reiterated his original position. Aid to
the Salvadorans had to be stopped. That was a demand.

When Enders left, an exchange of letters began and for a few
weeks the rhetoric died away on both sides. But the Salvadoran insurgents continued building their forces. On October 15 they blew up the
biggest bridge in El Salvador. They were destroying hundreds of electrical pylons, blacking out the capital and large portions of the country.
They began to cripple the economy. They opened a diplomatic offensive with cooperation from Mexico and the new Socialist government
of France, which recognized them as a representative political force in
El Salvador that had to be taken into account by any peace settlement.
And Daniel Ortega, appearing before the United Nations, presented the
Salvadoran rebels' peace plan. He acted as if he were their patron,
their friend and their spokesman. For good measure, it seemed, he
excoriated the United States with a long litany of all the interventions,
big and small, that he counted over the previous 125 years.

The Core Group was not really surprised. A veteran said later,
"Few people thought that the Sandinistas would talk to us seriously.
But we had to try." The administration could not go to Congress with
word of its new plans until it had an answer to the question "Have
diplomatic means been tried?" Now the answer could come: "They
haven't worked."

The planning for the paramilitary option was well under way. Haig
finally signed on, as he later told a reporter, "almost by default."
Bureaucratically, politically, there seemed no other options available.

The Core Group, now with Clarridge sitting in, prepared its proposals for the National Security Council. Clarridge wanted an all-out
strategy to overthrow the Sandinistas. He wanted, one member of the
group suggested, "a cause." But Enders was still in control, and all he
was looking for was a tool, a lever. The ten-point program that Ronald

Reagan approved on November 16 as National Security Decision Directive 17 did not sound so ambitious.

It included open military and economic aid to friendly nations in Central America and U.S. contingency planning in the case of "unacceptable military actions" by Cuba. U.S. military maneuvers and deployments would be a visible public aspect of the policy. U.S. military action, however, would be covert. The hand of the United States was not, itself, supposed to touch the gun. It would "work with foreign governments as appropriate" to conduct operations "against the Cuban presence and Cuban Sandinista support infrastructure in Nicaragua and elsewhere in Central America." About $19 million would be needed to build the five-hundred-man force to carry out this program.

Casey went to Capitol Hill, to the somber hearing rooms of the intelligence committees, to lay out the plan.

WASHINGTON, D.C.

As the Director of Central Intelligence spoke, committee members sat forward in their green leather chairs, at first simply to make out what he was saying in his usual mumbled phrases, and then with intense attention.

November's NSC document gives a good idea of the CIA program he presented. It was intended to:

"Build popular support in Central America and Nicaragua for an opposition front that would be nationalistic, anti-Cuban and anti-Somoza. . . .

"Support the opposition front through formation and training of action teams to collect intelligence and engage in paramilitary and political operations in Nicaragua and elsewhere.

"Work primarily through non-Americans to achieve the foregoing, but in some circumstances CIA might (possibly using U.S. personnel) take unilateral paramilitary action against special Cuban targets."

The committee's questions were sharp. What happens if your commandos get caught? What if the Nicaraguans cross the Honduran border in hot pursuit? Couldn't they provoke a war? The congressmen were worried about the size of the force. They wondered about the kinds of tactics it would employ.

Casey's tone was matter-of-fact. The operation was well under way already, he said. In fact the Argentines had already set up training camps in Honduras. In effect, the United States was just "buying in" on a program that they had started.

A platoon of Suicida's men marching toward a camp overlooking the destroyed Sandinista outposts at La Pampa and Zacateras. The soldier in the foreground carries a Belgian-made FAL assault rifle.

Christopher Dickey/The Washington Post

A company of contras from Pino Uno base as they presented themselves for review by Sonia Zapata Reyes, "La Negra," on March 23, 1983, at a camp on the Nicaraguan-Honduran border.

"Cascabel," one of the platoon leaders from Krill's company, adjusts a brand-new American field radio before setting out from the border base camp for the march into the interior the morning of March 24, 1983. La Negra had just distributed new equipment to several of the troops and commanders, including new digital watches for radio operators.

Christopher Dickey/The Washington Post

Christopher Dickey/*The Washington Post*

Members of Krill's patrol marching toward a rendezvous with Suicida in March 1983. The man in the foreground is armed with an American Light Anti-tank Weapon or LAW, a disposable one-shot bazooka, and with a Soviet-style AK-47 assault rifle.

Krill, seated, talks with one of the farmers who sold the troops a steer for slaughter. Wearing the beret in the background is Josué, one of Krill's platoon commanders and by some accounts one of his cousins.

"Coyote," one of Suicida's most skilled machine-gunners, rests along the trail on the morning of March 25, 1983.

Pedro Pablo Ortiz Centeno, "Suicida," outside a farmhouse outpost near Arenales in Nicaragua, March 26, 1983. Fighting was raging with Sandinista units on the ridges behind him.

Christopher Dickey/The Washington Post

Having fallen back from his initial position on March 26, Suicida consulted with Krill, on the left, and with Eco, another of his commanders, on a hillside at the center of his troops. Sandinista mortars soon bracketed this position. Suicida carries an AR-15, the same Colt-manufactured gun favored by Edén Pastora four years before.

Christopher Dickey/*The Washington Post*

Suicida and some of his field commanders pose for a picture at his temporary headquarters near Arenales. They include Eco, Krill, Suicida, Josué (beardless in beret), and, crouched, Delta (looking vaguely like Omar Sharif).

Suicida presents his assembled troops near Arenales on the morning of March 27, 1983. As this picture was taken, shooting broke out along the other side of the hill.

Salvador Icaza, bareheaded at the center, surrounded by contra pupils proudly holding up copies of the CIA-prepared manual on psychological operations in guerrilla warfare. This picture was taken in late 1983 or early 1984 by a friend of Icaza's after the disintegration of Suicida's forces. By that time Icaza was training small squads of psychological warfare specialists in an effort to clean up field operations.

II.

GUATEMALA

In a Guatemala City safe house, Suicida puzzled over the sheet of paper the Argentines gave him. This test was made for other kinds of men.

During January 1981, almost a year before Ronald Reagan signed off on major paramilitary operations against the Sandinistas, word went out among the Nicaraguan exile groups that the Argentine army was ready to support them and train them (the fiasco at Radio Noticias notwithstanding). Lists of candidates were drawn up from members of the September 15 Legion and the Nicaraguan Democratic Union–Nicaraguan Revolutionary Armed Forces (UDN-FARN) and the other little collections of would-be freedom fighters. Among them was Suicida.

When he went to Guatemala this seemed a great opportunity. But when he got there it was clear that most of the other candidates were from backgrounds very different from his. They were middle class, some of them with the old names of the old aristocracy, from the old ranks of Somoza politicos, the old ranks of the Guardia officer corps.

Suicida was ill at ease. Waiting with the others in a room of the safe house, he looked around absently. A dark-haired, fair-skinned man caught his eye. He seemed as middle class as the rest, maybe more, but they struck up a conversation about nothing in particular: the weather, the test. Suicida asked him his name. "Mark" was his nom de guerre, he said, but his real name was Noel Ortiz. Suicida volunteered that his real name was Ortiz as well, Pedro Pablo Ortiz. He said he had heard of Mark and his exploits flying during the war. Everybody had.

The pilot responded easily to the flattery. He liked this sergeant's quiet manner. Parientito, he called Suicida, because their last names were the same. "Little relative." They became friends almost instantly, and later Ortiz the pilot would say with something like awe, and more than a little defensiveness, that Ortiz "El Suicida" was "a born guerrilla," even if he did not have much learning from books.

But Ortiz the Pilot and Ortiz the Sergeant did not see each other again for a while. Suicida "failed to fulfill the requisites" on the Argentine exam. He went back to Danlí and to the mountains to wait and see what would happen next. Ortiz the Pilot went to Buenos Aires.

* * *

BUENOS AIRES, ARGENTINA

At the beginning of March 1981, the first twenty Nicaraguans arrived in the Argentine capital on a flight from Miami. Their army hosts loaded them into sealed vans. No one seeing them pass would ask where they were going or what they were doing. The city was numbed by five years of the Dirty War that had brought it constant fear and gradual peace. For the month that each group of Nicaraguans trained in Buenos Aires there was no contact with the city. They were kept in a barracks behind a high stone wall and stands of trees. Each day began before dawn with a run and exercises in the compound's yard. The rest of the time was spent indoors in classes. The only respite was the occasional volleyball game in the yard by the wall. Sometimes the ball would go flying over into the unseen street. Someone, perhaps a child, would throw it back without hellos or thank-yous.

The *guardias,* Ortiz and "El Chino" Lau among them, found little that was new in the Argentine courses. But some of the civilians, like the young Pedro Núñez Cabezas, discovered much to learn.

The pimply high school student who had never fired a gun during the revolution watched closely as the Argentines in blue jeans and sport shirts explained the basics of commando raids, explosives, demolition; the rudiments of moving with stealth. There was even a lecture on how to jimmy open a locked car door. There were basic principles of intelligence and counterintelligence, interrogation and counterinterrogation.

"Mostly it was psychological: how to put pressure on an individual. Techniques like the good guy and the bad guy." There were lectures on what to do if you were captured, how to protect your urban cells and buy time for your comrades to get away before you broke.

For young Núñez Cabezas, who had spent months locked up in the asylum of the Guatemalan embassy, then more months selling dishes door to door in Guatemala City, the training was the beginning of a new identity. Like everyone else, he took a pseudonym. He decided to call himself "El Muerto." It was the same name his uncles used in the Guardia. The Dead One. You might say it was a family tradition.

Others of the trainees, however, felt from the beginning like prisoners in their Argentine school. They could not even learn the real names of their instructors: "Pérez" and "Pirulo" and "Mora." The one time they went to a firing range they were taken, once again, in a windowless van. The weight of boredom grew heavier every day. The thrill of mystery and secrecy, of conspiracy, quickly palled. Some recruits began to harbor private doubts about the whole undertaking. If a few were impressed with the Argentines' pontifications, others were resentful of their arrogance. The focus of the Argentines was always on their own great accomplishments eliminating Communists in their cities. Nicaragua does not have any real cities. The lessons learned seemed hardly adequate, in the end, to the conduct of the war the Nicaraguans would have to fight. The training seemed hardly worth the tedium.

TEGUCIGALPA, HONDURAS

The yearbook of the Argentine Military Academy, class of 1961, was a prized bit of memorabilia in the private office of Colonel Gustavo Alvarez, the head of the public security forces in Honduras. There was his picture in the long, upright rows of cadets, stern-faced and martial. When he showed the book to friends and acquaintances he would point out his buddies. This one here, he was Guatemalan. This one, he was Nicaraguan. There were not many Central Americans at the academy. The Argentines had made them all feel lucky to be there.

Gustavo Alvarez came from Tela, a pretty little town on a sleepy beach on the north coast of Honduras, the sleepiest of Central America's republics. It is hard to say where he got his transcendental ambition. But certainly it was finely honed by the time he graduated in Buenos Aires after three years at the academy. Gustavo Alvarez returned to Tegucigalpa in 1961 as a man of grand designs, and in two decades working his way toward the top of his institution they had only grown greater. But he was born to lead in a country that seemed born to follow. He always chafed for more than Honduras could offer.

The fall of Somoza, the triumph of the Sandinistas, the panic that spread through the region in the following months were the liberation of Gustavo Alvarez. The threat of Communists just across his country's southern border gave him a cause. More than that, it was a kind of license to greatness.

"Everything you do to destroy a Marxist regime," he once said, "is moral."

In 1981 his old friends from Argentina gave him a framework for his cause. At its heart, their war without frontiers was structured like a club dominated by old, close friendships. In it Alvarez could move easily, and in it Alvarez was key.

The man the Argentines chose to run their program on the ground was Colonel Osvaldo Ribeiro, who had known Alvarez since he was at the academy twenty years before. Short and husky, balding in front, with a sharp, some might say aristocratic nose, and teeth stained dark by nicotine, Ribeiro was "very imperative," said one Nicaraguan acquaintance. His pseudonym was "Balita," or "Little Bullet."

The ex-Guardia the Argentines eventually decided on to oversee the troops in the field was Emilio Echaverry, who called himself Fiero. He was a handsome Nicaraguan, fine-featured and commanding in appearance. He was the son-in-law of an Argentine officer and he was the Nicaraguan cadet in the yearbook picture that Alvarez showed to friends.

Most of Honduras is a nation of empty forests, swampy coasts and sieve-like borders. It is a land made for smugglers and conspirators, and they have always found havens there, from pirates in the coves of the Mosquito Coast to O. Henry escaping embezzlement charges in Tegucigalpa, to the Sandinistas arming their troops in the fight against Somoza and cocaine traffickers heading north to Miami. But the security forces can make things easy or difficult for any organization that wants to operate underground, and in January 1981, Alvarez started winning points with the Americans by making things difficult for Salvadoran rebels smuggling arms.

He picked up ten of them at once. But he presented only nine of them to the press. The other, a rebel leader, was kept incommunicado and his presence in the country was denied until an airline hijacking two months later forced Alvarez to free him along with the rest.

Alvarez, as head of the security forces, had command of the blue-uniformed police in baseball-style caps who patrolled the streets of the capital and ran the life of many little villages. His were the agents of the National Directorate for Investigations, the DNI, which was always ready to function as a political force. His were the men under a bright young captain named Alex Hernandez in "Special Investigations," a squad he personally organized on the Argentine model to take care of suspected subversives. By April 1981 outright political "disappearances" began for the first time in Honduran history. There were the first reports of secret cells; arrests made by police in plain clothes, then denied by the authorities.

Hondurans were long used to corruption but not to brutality. They were long accustomed to think that their society, for all its weaknesses and poverty, had a certain gentleness not found among their more aggressive neighbors. Alvarez was changing that. People began to talk of the "Argentine method."

Hondurans were also brought up to view as their most likely and constant enemy their neighbor to the west—El Salvador. It was small and tough and very overpopulated. Honduras was big and easygoing and almost empty. The Salvadorans were always moving in on the Hondurans, always treating them with contempt. The war they had fought in 1969 was waged, as many saw it, to keep the Salvadorans from simply taking over.

But by the middle of 1981, after a handful of border incidents with Nicaragua, and some prompting by Washington and some pushing by Alvarez, that focus began to change. More and more the enemy was Nicaragua. More and more the preparations that the Honduran army made for open war, it made with the Sandinistas in mind. The secret war, meanwhile, was scheduled to begin right away.

In the spring of 1981, under the direction of the Argentines, and with Alvarez running interference for them, Bermúdez and Lau moved the base of operations for the September 15 Legion from Guatemala City to Tegucigalpa. The idea was to get closer to the scene of the fight against the Sandinistas. But almost as soon as they arrived a major failing in their organization began to be apparent. These leaders of the Legion and their advisors, the Argentine masters of urban warfare, were firmly committed anticommunists, and they vowed to do whatever was necessary to win back their country—except, it now seemed, to leave the city.

The Argentine planning and preparation had gone on for months. There had been endless contacts, and a fair amount of money spent. (One of the exile leaders reportedly got $50,000 in Buenos Aires in five neat stacks of hundred-dollar bills.) And now it was apparent there was next to nothing practical to show for it.

There were three self-proclaimed anti-Sandinista armies: the Legion, the National Liberation Army led by a Spaniard who had owned the Managua match factory before the war, and the UDN-FARN led by Chicano Cardenal and hard-drinking, hell-raising Fernando "El Negro" Chamorro, a bourgeois revolutionary whose greatest claim to fame was an attempt against Somoza before the war where he rigged up a mosquito coil to a rocket launcher and lobbed a shell from a balcony of the Intercontinental into Somoza's conference room at the EEBI. But neither the Legion nor the army nor the armed forces had any troops to speak of. They were conspirators and talkers who never seemed, quite, to go to war.

Sixty men had been sent to Buenos Aires for training in March and April and May, and all but a handful got off the plane when it got back to Miami and stayed there. Of the group of twenty that Lau took down to Argentina, only three came back to Central America to carry on. In all, perhaps a dozen actually found the will to fight in a war that now, obviously, had no hope of a quick victory, no guarantees of a long-term one, and, as soon became apparent, nothing like the resources in men and matériel needed to wage one.

In the early summer of 1981 the Argentine operation was desperate for volunteers who would actually go to the border, start recruiting and start fighting.

El Suicida, who had not fulfilled the requisites on the Argentine exam, offered to go on doing what he had been doing all along. Suicida, now, was acceptable.

For those willing to lead troops in the field, there was still the problem of where to find the troops to lead. And for those who found troops, there was the problem of arms. To build the ranks, cattle rustlers, fugitive criminals and ex-*guardias* on the edges of survival were the easiest recruits to come by.

Noel Ortiz was assigned to set up a base in the hot, low hills of Choluteca in Honduras, just north of the western Nicaraguan province where he lived and fought before the fall of Somoza. His first volunteer was an escaped prisoner named Villalta. The Espinoza brothers had a gang of eight rustlers, part of a thriving business stealing cattle from Nicaragua and selling them in Honduras. They joined Ortiz, bringing their own guns, attracted by the promise of more. Over the next two or three months, slowly, others showed up at the "training camp" called Sagitario base to run makeshift obstacle courses and fumble through drill, waiting for weapons. There may have been as many as two hundred of them there by the fall, waiting for action and waiting, still, for weapons.

Suicida scavenged some old shotguns for his "base" near Las Trojes, but they had no firing pins. Nails were used to improvise. There was contact with a member of the Sandinista militia who was bribed into giving him ten old American M-1 rifles. There was still a collection of battered .22s and pistols, but Suicida told anyone and everyone who would listen that it was getting to be a humiliation to fire such guns. When his men had to engage the Sandinistas, usually running away from them, their Soviet Bloc AK-47s would rattle out repeated blasts against him, and his .22s would answer "pee-pee-pee." The Sandinis-

tas would shout insults at them. "Guardia sons of bitches!" And Suicida would answer back with the .22s. Pee-pee. The Sandinistas would
fire BRRRAAAAP. How could you fight a war like that?

MIAMI, FLORIDA

The Argentine called Villegas met Chicano Cardenal in the lobby
of the hotel at the Miami airport one afternoon in August, at about the
same time that Thomas O. Enders was visiting Managua. They walked
along the cool, cavernous concourse to the coffee shop to talk. Villegas, who was now second-in-command to Ribeiro, laid out the plan.

Support for the fight against the Sandinistas was going to be "tripartite," Villegas said. The United States was going to give the money.
Argentina was going to provide the training. Honduras was going to
provide the base of operations.

Chicano was weak from some minor surgery, and probably weak,
too, from a certain sense of futility. For almost two years he had been
trying to build a political organization, talking to exile groups, meeting
with friends in Venezuela and Guatemala. Groups had come together
and then split apart. There had been a link with the September 15
Legion, Bermúdez and Lau. That had disintegrated a year before. But
now, sitting in front of him in casual civilian clothes was this gray-
haired, soft-spoken gentleman. About fifty years old, convincing and
smooth, he was talking about new unity.

"We're ready to help you with your problems," Villegas said. But
the groups had to get together. He had just come from Guatemala, and
the members of the legion there and the members of the UDN, Chicano's own group, said they were ready to sign. There would be a new
organization called the Nicaraguan Democratic Force (FDN).

"We're aware," Villegas assured him, "of the importance of the
civilian part of this organization. It's going to be the predominant part
of the movement."

That was just what Chicano wanted to hear.

In fact, Villegas said, Chicano had done so much good political
work that the goal of the movement should be to try to get the military
part up to the standards of the civilian side. Villegas said he was in
charge of that. He would be preparing the armed forces of the new
unified FDN. It wasn't necessary yet, he added, but Chicano and the
other political leaders should think about moving to Honduras by the
end of the year. Villegas claimed the Americans had promised equipment for ten thousand men by then.

Meanwhile, Chicano and the other political leaders could continue working with regional support committees among the exiles in the United States, building up the name of the new FDN, in Miami and Los Angeles, Houston and San Francisco, still biding time.

Meanwhile, the character of the revolution itself was changing.

III.

MANAGUA, NICARAGUA

Commander Zero had begun to wake up in the mornings, his friends would say, and see in the mirror not the revolutionary with a gun who captured the imagination of his nation and the world, but a revolutionary bureaucrat unsure what desk he was supposed to occupy.

He had come, for a while, under Borge's wing at the interior ministry. Borge had wanted to keep an eye on him. Then he was picked up by Ortega at Defense and put in charge of the militiamen. But when the ranks of the revolution had been handed out, he was made only a Guerrilla Commander. The members of the Directorate were Commanders of the Revolution.

And as Pastora was neglected, his doubts about the revolution began to grow. Socialism seemed to be on the wane, communism on the rise. He was bothered by the pretensions of the other commanders. Their arrogance.

He had been disturbed by the killing of Jorge Salazar, the jailing of Bernardino Larios, who had been a vital collaborator in the National Guard, even if they had been plotting against the revolution.

Pastora had argued against the Salvadorans' final offensive. He had thought they weren't ready. You couldn't just take a crowd carrying placards and hand them guns instead and expect that they would be an army. The Salvadorans had suckered themselves and the Sandinistas.

Then the plans had started for nationalizing more of the factories and businesses. Some of them were justifiable, the owners having been using them to channel money out of the country. But many of them weren't.

The Cubans, it seemed, were not just helping out, they were taking over the army and police.

"This country's turning into shit," Pastora decided.

*   *   *

The dictator of Panama was the idol of Edén Pastora. Conservatives in the United States, including Ronald Reagan, cast General Omar Torrijos as corrupt and unscrupulous, a "tinhorn," a friend of Fidel Castro. There was some truth in all of it. Photographed in his bush hat with the brim snapped up on one side, a cigar in his teeth, his eyes underlined by heavy bags from his legendary drinking bouts, Torrijos seemed to relish the role.

But the United States, even the United States of President Reagan, knew how useful and how capable this "tinhorn dictator" could be. "He had style, but he was ruthless," said a grudging admirer in the State Department. Torrijos had helped Jimmy Carter by giving the Shah of Iran a place to stay when the world had rejected him. He helped the Reagan administration by giving it lines of communication all over the ideological map.

"He'd been around so long and survived so long," said one member of the Core Group, "he had credibility on all sides." He talked to the Sandinistas and to the Hondurans. "We were using him to talk to the Salvadoran left and to the Salvadoran generals."

Edén Pastora had admired Torrijos, and worked with him for a long time to help make the revolution in Nicaragua. Torrijos had been an essential conduit for arms on the Southern Front during the war. They had talked often since. And when Pastora's disillusionment began to grow, they talked still more.

In the spring of 1981, Commander Zero was thinking maybe there were other revolutions that needed him more than Nicaragua's. In Guatemala there was a movement that hadn't gone completely Communist. It was being butchered by the repression there and needed help. He could make the Guatemalans' fight his own.

Come to Panama, Torrijos said.

Pastora collected people who had been with him on the Southern Front. José Valdivia, frail and intellectual and intense; burly Lionel Poveda. And he collected three Mercedes-Benzes and a Fiat.

When everything was organized, he put guns under the seats and behind them, and got his bags ready to leave Managua between two and three in the afternoon. He figured he would arrive at the border at Peñas Blancas just before it closed for the night.

Until then, he wanted everything to look normal, so he went to his early morning command and general staff course with the Cubans at the defense ministry.

"I was attentive, asking questions, answering them, just as interested as could be in the tactics of war, the movement of battalions."

Lunch was with Chief of Staff Joaquin Cuadra and some other officers: It sure is nice to be having lunch with you here at the bunker. Who would have thought during the war that we would all be sitting here like this someday? I hope we have a chance to do this again sometime soon.

"Well, friends," said Pastora, "I've got to excuse myself, if you don't mind. I've got an important trip I've got to make."

"Hey, where are you going?" asked Cuadra.

Some of the officers exchanged glances and smiles, as if Pastora were planning to take off for a while with one of his girls in uniform.

"Well, comrades of the general staff, it's been good to see you, now if you don't mind . . ." Pastora excused himself again, his heart pounding in his chest as he walked away.

He stopped. "Son of a bitch." He ducked back in. If anyone wanted him, he said, he would be on the firing range at target practice. (There was no communication with the firing range. If they wanted him they'd have to send somebody, but in the meanwhile he would be long gone.)

Pastora left behind a public letter that talked in romantic terms of his need to continue the struggle elsewhere, and a letter that was not published criticizing the way the revolution was developing and the mistakes he thought the Front had made, jeopardizing revolutions in the rest of the region by making its own Communist leanings so obvious.

His car peeled away on the South Highway. The other Mercedes-Benzes linked up with him and they sped toward Peñas Blancas. They passed the checkpoints there without problems and drove straight through to Panama.

"We started talking as soon as we got there," said Pastora. He and Torrijos "talked all those thirty days." They drank together. They traveled together. Torrijos had a passion for flying to remote corners of Panama, visiting small villages, holding court. Hiking in the mountains was a favorite sport. Most often, Pastora went along.

On the morning of July 31, Pastora put on his boots for a long walk with the general at Coquelecito, a little village on the far side of the mountain range from Panama City. He waited for the general to send for him.

"Nine o'clock. Ten. Eleven and they hadn't sent for me."

A light plane, an inexperienced pilot and a sudden storm. The general had crashed and burned in the mountains.

"Everyone thought I was on the plane with him," said Pastora. "The Directorate, I knew, celebrated."

Feeling lost suddenly without his chosen patron and protector, Pastora could only think to make his way to another idol. With the idea of contacting the Guatemalan guerrilla leadership there, he went to Havana.

IV.

WASHINGTON, D.C.

The November 1 meeting between General Leopoldo Galtieri and Director of Central Intelligence William Casey went well, by all accounts. It was essentially a formality, and afterward the Argentines settled comfortably into their suites at the Watergate to enjoy their new status in Washington and the rest of their stay in the United States.

A year before, they were pariahs in the eyes of the American administration. The Congress passed a law against selling them arms, the State Department regularly condemned them for atrocities and interfered with credits from international organizations. But now, in 1981, they were the best of friends. And Chief of Staff Galtieri could say that he, more than anyone else, had made that possible.

In March, President Roberto Viola visited Washington and opened some of the doors. But since April, Galtieri and his American counterpart, General Edwin Meyer, the chairman of the Joint Chiefs of Staff, had carefully cultivated each other with reciprocal visits, dinners, apparently enjoying each other's company as military men with similar interests. On his visit in August, Galtieri had flown to military bases all over the United States in a jet supplied by his American friends.

Now Congress authorized the president to suspend the legal provision prohibiting arms for Argentina. There was talk—detailed talk—about a role for Argentine forces in a regional alliance against the Communists, there were joint maneuvers, there were consultations with the Reagan administration's top emissaries. Jeane Kirkpatrick had come to Buenos Aires. So had Vernon Walters, the linguist, ambassador at large and former deputy director of the CIA. The Caribbean basin, the South Atlantic, these seemed the new strategic focus of the United States—

as they always were for Argentina. There was talk of a South Atlantic Treaty Organization in which, of course, Argentina would be the major partner. There was every sign of approval and mutual admiration. Galtieri, in November, even went so far as to offer his men for the Sinai Peacekeeping Force, half the world away, which was a project dear to the Reagan administration's collective heart at the time.

But none of those public projects and pronouncements seemed to bear as much fruit as the one that was secret: this war against Nicaragua.

Now all the pieces were put meticulously in place thanks to the Argentine army's Battalion 601. Ribeiro was in place in Tegucigalpa. Front organizations were established. The camps were set up along the Nicaraguan border.

Now when Galtieri lunched with the Secretary of Defense, or met with Mr. Enders or General Meyer, he could relax and look, with some real anticipation, to a future of warm relations. He could expect the resolution, with the support of the United States, of issues that had long preoccupied him and his people.

There was, for instance, the especially difficult question of some windblown islands several hundred miles off the Argentine coast. The Malvinas, they were called by the Argentines, who claimed them. The Falklands, they were called by the British, who kept them.

TEGUCIGALPA, HONDURAS

The new American ambassador to Honduras looked slightly awkward in a *guayabera*, the loose white shirt with four pockets on the front that Central Americans consider adequate as semi-formal attire. John D. Negroponte was the tall, bald son of a Greek shipping agent. Born in London, educated at Exeter and Yale in the United States, he was one of the bright young men at the Saigon embassy before Henry Kissinger tapped him to be a special assistant during the Paris peace talks.

His career had had some ups and downs since then. There had been that long stretch as a consul in Salonika after his falling out with Kissinger over the terms of the peace. (Negroponte thought them too soft.) And on its face it was rather difficult to say in December of 1981 whether the capital of Honduras was an up or a down. Until Negroponte got there it had been a nowhere in the eyes of the ambitious.

Defensively, he wrote to the Exeter alumni bulletin, "There is much more at stake in Central America than seems to come through in our media. . . . It's a helluva lot closer to home than Saigon."

Beside the ambassador was his wife, Diana, the daughter of an English lord, greeting the guests with that self-assurance that made the British such consummate colonizers. She was a strikingly handsome blonde, but she wore a modest, rather dowdy full-length hostess skirt of the kind that ladies' magazines used to recommend for entertaining at home. Perhaps the dowdiness was meant to make the locals feel comfortable.

Members of the new government filed in; members of the press corps. There was a crowd of hacks in Tegucigalpa to record the outcome of the first elections for a civilian president in Honduras since the early 1960s. Another crew of visitors down from Washington to mark the occasion showed up at the party as well. There was John Carbaugh, the ubiquitous aide to right-wing Senator Jesse Helms, and there were a collection of ideologues from the militantly conservative American Security Council. They were all interested, it seemed at the time, in this burgeoning experiment with democracy.

That disappearances had steadily increased in Honduras, and that the man responsible now seemed on the verge of becoming the new commander of the Honduran armed forces after cutting a deal with the winning candidate, was a topic of conversation among some of the press that night. But that did not keep Colonel Gustavo Alvarez from being the star of the party. The new ambassador circulated, chatting blandly. Alvarez stood squarely in place, holding forth as men and women watched as if enthralled, sipping their scotches. Alvarez was drawing a little diagram in the air: a pyramid with more little pyramids beneath it—an organizational chart. This is how the subversives work, he was saying. They are divided into cells and each one only knows three others below him, and one above him. To get to the top of the pyramid is very difficult. When you capture one subversive you must find out from him quickly where his comrades are, before they have time to escape. The colonel did not say exactly how one did this. A couple of journalists in his audience took deep sips of their drinks and said nothing. Alvarez was playing to a woman, the wife of a businessman, who was terribly impressed with the depth of his knowledge about Communists. Alvarez was at his best when he talked about Communists.

What he knew, and what Negroponte knew, and perhaps Carbaugh and the men from the American Security Council knew as well, but what was secret to the rest of the people that night at the ambassador's residence, was that democracy was not the only new phenomenon to be getting under way that month in Honduras.

Negroponte. Alvarez. They could as easily have been celebrating the beginning of a war.

Negroponte's job was to keep the Hondurans happy and help manage their protection as the fighting escalated. The Sandinistas had to be discouraged from any attempts at retaliation. An American military presence in Honduras could guarantee that, if necessary. Negroponte would have a lot of input on such questions. It was less his business to manage the war, as later reported, than to manage its side effects.

Mike, the new station chief, would keep an eye on things and direct them from a distance. He had found a nice house near the airport for himself and his staff.

The director, Bill Casey, came down to check out the scene firsthand. Clarridge already was talking enthusiastically about the insurrection that could be sparked against the Communists by this operation.

Ribeiro and the Argentines had set themselves up at the Honduras Maya Hotel overlooking the swimming pool and patios and beyond them the quaint tiled roofs of the city. They liked the Monte Carlo Casino there, the steak house downstairs, the bar and the disco full of young fawn-eyed and willing women every Friday night.

Enrique Bermúdez had a comfortable safe house, and Lau was well established in one of the city's wealthier suburbs. As the United States began to take over the operation, Bermúdez later told a reporter, "I could feel the steps of a giant animal."

As far as the people in Tegucigalpa were concerned, as far as the people in Washington and in Buenos Aires were concerned, everything was ready to go.

Except, of course, they still needed someone to fight the war.

THE HONDURAN-NICARAGUAN BORDER

The men in the border camps of the new Nicaraguan Democratic Force were tired of waiting. At least, those who were left. Whatever faith commanders like Suicida had had in the promises of old officers in Tegucigalpa, it was fading now as their men once again began to drift away from this army built on broken promises. They had done about as many push-ups as they intended to do, and they were in rebellious moods. The Americans were supposed to have made their decision. There was supposed to be money coming in now, and supplies. Everyone had heard about that promise of equipment for ten thousand men. And some of the men had stayed on in hopes that those would reach their hands soon. Members of the general staff would drop in on them, down from Tegucigalpa for the day, and present them with tantalizing menus: powdered milk, cheese, meat at least a couple of times a month. But the milk and the meat never came. And the sense grew that the men in the capital had no idea what the men here on the border were suffering.

Suicida had built enough loyalty among his few-score troops to keep many of them in line. But he had to watch them closely. He enhanced their loyalty with a heavy dose of fear. The consequences of desertion were severe, he warned.

The seed was there already among Suicida and La Negra and their men of a belief that the officers in the capital were no good; that they were hindering the war as much as they furthered it, and if he were to follow their orders, nothing would ever come of the risks Suicida took, or the deaths his men suffered. It was probably in this period that the belief became a conviction. But as yet the most serious problems were still to be found in other camps.

One day in late 1981, Noel Ortiz was down in the zone where operations were supposed to take place, reconnoitering as best he could along the border for an attack to be carried out if the promised weapons ever came through.

As Ortiz returned to camp he saw a former Guardia colonel and several members of the FDN general staff from Tegucigalpa standing around with the Argentine Villegas. Most of the men in the camp ran around the well-worn course at Sagitario base, sweating and stumbling as the visiting commanders looked on.

Ortiz almost fell across one of his recruits, hiding on the edge of the camp. The man's bitterness was undisguised as he pulled Ortiz aside. "We're going to kill these people," he said, looking in the direction of the general staff.

"What's happening?"

"These men are punishing us," said the recruit. "They want to make us exercise and they don't want to give us anything to eat. We're hungry already. If we can't eat the little there is, we're going to die."

"Why aren't *you* running?"

"Because my leg is hurt."

Ortiz took the recruit to the camp's medic. He walked him directly past the officers from Tegucigalpa. The medic confirmed that the recruit could not run.

Ortiz turned around. "Give this man something to eat," he said.

The Guardia colonel was embarrassed in front of the Argentines who had come to inspect the camps, and he was furious with Ortiz. He turned on him. They had come to find soldiers, he said, and what they found was this collection of criminals and ragged recruits full of insult and insubordination. There was no discipline here, and Ortiz seemed to be provoking even more chaos, he said.

"Why are you raising these people's hopes?" Ortiz shouted, the frustration of all these pointless months in the hills spilling out.

Ortiz's people looked like shit, said the colonel, and Ortiz was filling their heads with shit.

"No," said Ortiz, whose anger came as easily as his smiles, "these people can't look like shit. These are the people who are doing the fighting. Without these men we're nothing. If anyone is guilty because these men are upset, the guilty ones are you people who've brought this menu a couple of months ago and haven't kept up your end of the bargain. These people are complaining because you are always coming here and saying you're going to bring rifles and you haven't brought a single rifle."

A few days later, Ortiz was ordered to report to Villegas at the Hotel Maya in Tegucigalpa. Lau, the internal policeman, took him there.

"Where's the money you've received? Where are the arms you've gotten?" Villegas demanded of Ortiz.

Ortiz was taken by surprise. "I've never gotten a penny," he said. "And I haven't gotten arms from anybody. The guns we have were captured from the enemy or loaned to us by neighbors in the zone."

Villegas was skeptical. He had personally disbursed the money for the maintenance budget of the Sagitario base to a member of the general staff and he wanted to know where the hell that money was now. Ortiz said he had no idea.

The interview was part of a larger investigation. FDN funds seemed to be evaporating. An accounting was demanded. Tempers rose. Bermúdez and Lau and the general staff in Tegucigalpa said the money had been used to buy the guns, but the guns had not yet been turned over. That was all there was to this problem, they said. If Ortiz complained, if others said differently, then Ortiz and the rest were just troublemakers. That was what the general staff had to say about it.

From Villegas's perspective, they all looked like troublemakers.

This kind of mutual suspicion, this graft, would be disastrous if the forces began to grow.

"Ortiz, tell me what you think of the general staff."

"I don't think they're doing a damned thing," said Ortiz, recounting the long months of broken promises and apparently embezzled money. "And I have problems with this one," motioning in the direction of Lau. "In Guatemala he was a criminal."

Villegas cleaned house—up to a point. It was the first of many housecleanings over the next two years. Of the six members of the general staff, four were let go. Tino Pérez was flatly accused of stealing. His wife had been taking expensive trips while the men in the field were starving, Villegas noted.

Only Bermúdez stayed. And Lau.

Ortiz meanwhile was removed from his command and put in charge of the clandestine radio near Tegucigalpa. He took the transfer well. The former pilot and makeshift bombardier liked the work of propagandizing the revolution. His woman, Laura, could come from Miami to join him at the station. But first he had to raise some quick cash to buy tubes for the transmitter. It had ceased to function since its previous manager absconded with most of the station's budget, even selling off parts of the equipment. Graft did more to silence the voice of the new Nicaraguan revolution, Radio 15 de Septiembre, than anything the Sandinistas could have hoped to do through sabotage. Ortiz needed money for parts. In the time-honored tradition of his country's exiles, Ortiz sold his watch.

Then the money started to arrive by the box, and the guns by the crate.

THE SECRET WAR— 1982

I.

GUASAULE, NICARAGUA

The detonations rumbled like Armageddon along the rocky course of the Rio Negro in Nicaragua on the night of March 14, 1982. Cattle began lowing and roosters crowing as if dawn had come. The concrete bridge groaned suddenly under its own weight, crashing down in an avalanche of dust that was black in the lightless landscape seen through night-vision goggles.

A hundred or so miles to the east on the Rio Coco the scene was repeated. The bridge crumbled. The commando team moved quickly, quietly away along the cow paths and through the scrub brush and pines on the hillsides above Ocotal.

The CIA's new people had trained these men under a Comandante "Richard" at El Anillo on the way to the Valley of the Angels outside the Honduran capital. They carried knapsacks full of C-4 explosives; claymore mines that they set up as a perimeter around their camps when they slept. The Agency wanted this operation to be an inspiration and a provocation.

Still farther east, along the Atlantic Coast, Miskito Indians trained on the little island of Vivorillo off Honduras were in action among their

131

old communities. They had never liked the Sandinistas—never thought much of any of the Latins on the opposite side of the country. Cut off by hundreds of miles of jungle, they felt themselves a different people and, in their crude huts and primitive settlements, speaking their own language or English before Spanish, they felt themselves a separate nation. Their resentments were enhanced by the clumsy ignorance and arrogance of the first Sandinista officials assigned to integrate them into the life of the nation. They were natural assets for the Agency.

"Up to March 1982 you could change your policy," recalled a member of the Core Group. The issue, after all, was still the question of support for El Salvador's rebels, and if that ended, so could pressure on Managua. But once the Miskitos and the first forces of Nicaraguan exiles were trained under U.S. patronage and their war set in motion, their cause had to be accommodated. Any real negotiating posture would have to be much more ambitious, much harder in order to take them into account. The blowing of the bridges was an announcement that the scale of things was changing. Accommodation with Washington would not be so easy. "To step back after that would have been a much more fundamental change in policy."

A couple of weeks later, the Reagan administration put forth a negotiating proposal, but it went nowhere and nobody in Washington seemed to expect that it would. As a summary paper of the National Security Planning Group put it, the tactic at the time was one of "co-opting cut-and-run negotiating strategies by demonstrating a reasonable but firm approach." The Argentine–CIA operation was just beginning to gather momentum. This was not a time to turn it around.

For Clarridge and Casey, the bridge operation was something to be proud of. It overcame last-minute problems. (One of the squad leaders suddenly said he couldn't go because of a stomachache, and Villegas had to lock him up incommunicado until the mission was over.) And it had a nice symmetry to it. Exactly five months before in El Salvador the rebels there had brought the Golden Bridge crashing down into the Rio Lempa with what the Agency assumed was the benefit of Cuban and Nicaraguan training. This was a two-for-one reply. It was a nice example of "trading one little war for another little war."

In El Salvador the leftist guerrillas prodded a repressive right-wing government into something like genocidal frenzy. In Nicaragua, if the CIA's operations meant the Sandinistas became more radical, more repressive and more Soviet-allied, that was all to the good. It would increase their isolation from Europe and the rest of Latin America.

They were being forced to show their true colors. It was a strategy the Marxists called "exacerbating the contradictions."

Then somebody began talking in Washington. Word leaked to *The Washington Post* that Reagan had approved the covert action campaign in December. In public, a debate began about the "Secret War."

Agency officials maintain that Casey was furious, that this is just what he had worried about when the question of a major paramilitary program first came up. There were tirades against the sieve-like congressional committees. But the leaks that began to expose general details of the operation served his purposes well in Central America, and some administration officials would say later, privately, that as the war dragged on, Casey himself was the source of many of the leaks. As an American military officer involved with the program suggested later, the public side of the Secret War gave the rebels the most important asset of all, "the mantle of inevitable victory." With the United States behind them, how could they lose? And the Sandinistas, their fears confirmed about who their enemies were, would act more hostile still to the United States.

"The Sandinistas are under increased pressure as a result of our covert efforts and because of the poor state of their economy. For the first time the Sandinistas have cause to doubt whether they can export subversion with impunity," gloated the National Security group's summary paper (which was leaked to *The New York Times* a year later).

In fact arms to the Salvadorans, such as they were, had not stopped. They had increased. El Salvador's government, despite the propaganda triumph of its March elections, was more fragile than ever. So was that of Guatemala, where an evangelical born-again general had just seized power.

There was nothing to suggest that the CIA program did anything concrete to stabilize the region.

But the day after the bridges were blown, the Sandinistas declared a state of emergency. Direct censorship of the press began for the first time. Surveillance of the population increased. Sandinista mobs went into action with a vengeance against suspected counterrevolutionaries.

Some members of the government said later that the National Directorate had been waiting for just such an opportunity. Only through greater control could they effectively clear a path toward socialism.

The Sandinista response to the first Miskito operations was the forced relocation of more than ten thousand Indians from the border regions to camps deeper inside the country. Thousands more fled into

Honduras, their fears fueled by rumor and propaganda that turned the real brutality of the relocation into mythical atrocity.

Six weeks after the bridges were blown, Daniel Ortega was in Moscow. And in Managua, at a May 1 rally in the Plaza de la Revolución, Tomás Borge stood before a forest of banners bearing the hammer and sickle.

II.

NUEVA SEGOVIA PROVINCE, NICARAGUA

"The end of the line," thought Sister Lisa Fitzgerald of Troy, New York, as she arrived for the first time in Jalapa, Nicaragua. "Another world." It was February 1982. The dry season. Heat and dust and horses and dented jeeps. Other sisters of the Sacred Heart had come here before her, of course, and she was not exactly a pioneer. But still, as she might put it, this place was pretty primitive stuff.

On a rutted side street behind a metal door and a wall of rotting stucco indistinguishable from all the rest was her new home. Still enthusiastic, smiling easily, she introduced herself to the little religious community that lived there. There were three Spanish priests and the two Mexican nuns. Lisa Fitzgerald was thirty-eight, but her voice was full of golly-gee excitement, her language leavened with phrases from the sheltered life of a dormitory. She talked about "the guys," meaning anyone from the priests to the Sandinista soldiers and the rebels fighting against them.

Lisa had been working as a lawyer in the cause of the poor and of the Church in Boston until she came to Jalapa. Before that she had never thought much about going to Central America.

But Lisa had a quiet—that is, usually quiet—rebellious streak in her. She was restless and her work at the National Consumer Law Center, dealing with insurance and public utility cases, had quit bringing her satisfaction. When the opening came in the Sacred Heart mission in Jalapa in 1982 it was just as she was deciding there was more to life, more to her calling than she had found in Boston; more to being a woman religious than what she was. Lisa Fitzgerald wanted an opportunity to get close to people and to relate to them in a different way, not just across a desk working over briefs. And she wanted to be in a place where she could learn.

In the time before she had taken her final vows she had lived several months in the Philippines near the U.S. military base at Subic

Bay. She had spent time with a family of scavengers. "It was hard, but I learned a lot," she would say. The family used to go out at night to comb through the garbage of the base. "They had Marines guarding the dump with dogs. I went with them more out of a sense of courtesy than courage." Lisa would remember the women, too, the prostitutes who visited the base every Monday and would be seen beforehand lining up outside the municipal building with their panties in their hands waiting to be certified. "For people who'd never experienced anything in the third world it was upsetting. It was shocking," Lisa said. "I didn't see the best side of the United States in the Philippines." But what she did see was a side of the religious life that appealed to her enormously. In the new world of Catholicism since Vatican II, many nuns had abandoned their habits for blue jeans and bandanas and found new ways to work with the poor. But in the Philippines, "it was the first time I'd had contact with a church that was courageous. . . . I felt I was living my vocation more truly than before. That's why I went to Nicaragua. I knew I could give something. I knew I could learn a lot."

To be in the middle of a revolution that was real, that was happening, changed one's sense of familiar words: "the people," "the army," "the bourgeoisie." Here, when you said people died for their ideals, there was nothing abstract about the concept. But now, she thought when she arrived, the need for bloodshed was past. Now was a time for building, and that would be the role she could play.

Less than two weeks after Lisa Fitzgerald arrived in Jalapa, the bridge south of Ocotal was blown to bits by the contras.

"Not exactly what I expected," she said later.

She had come there to build. But as the terror around her grew, she would stay there to bear witness.

TEGUCIGALPA, HONDURAS

Chicano Cardenal and his friend Mariano Mendoza arrived in Tegucigalpa in March 1982 with high expectations and rattled nerves. They were the first of the Miami civilians in the Nicaraguan Democratic Force to relocate to Honduras and they had doubts about the whole operation, about their security, their position, and the goals of the people working with them. Chicano had the distinct feeling that the other members of the Miami group were letting him stick his neck out and were waiting up in Key Biscayne, still, to see if it got cut off. "Cowards," thought Chicano, but somebody had to be on the scene to manage the political side of the war, he thought. And then he got there.

From the moment that Chicano and Mariano checked into the

Hotel La Ronda on a noisy downtown street they began to feel like bystanders in the war they were supposed to lead. Nothing was ready for them. Their rooms were supposed to have been paid for, but weren't. And they could see they were watched by the hotel staff when they went out. No doubt the hands of the Argentines were in this.

They complained to Bermúdez and the other members of the general staff. "We can't be pawns for all these other people," said Chicano. But even as he spoke he had the feeling that five minutes after the meeting was over, the chief of operations, Echaverry, or this man El Chino Lau would be telling the Argentines everything.

Every day brought new irritations. Ribeiro and Villegas—"our brothers in the struggle," Chicano would say with undisguised irony— had not bothered to rent a livable house for the supposed civilian and military juntas of the Nicaraguan Democratic Force. While the Argentines ran around in grand cars, Chicano had to take taxis and busses, or walk. Once or twice, "just by chance," he and Mariano went to the discotheque at the Hotel Maya overlooking the city. And there were Argentine trainers and administrators, decked out for the evening like playboys.

At Radio 15 Noel and Laura Ortiz were going twenty hours a day, part of the time on the radio, the rest of the time trying to inventory all the rifles, mortars and explosives—dynamite, C-4 plastic—coming through the warehousing operation set up there.

"The trucks arrived at night," said one of the people who worked with them. "We received the guns and accounted for them and then according to requirements we distributed them.

"We'd have to unload the boxes into the house. Then we'd type the serial number of each gun—V-Zs, and AKs and some FALs—then get up in the night and give it to them. The house was so full of C-4 and dynamite, if one grenade had gone off, I mean, we would have disappeared."

It was Villegas who decided who would get what. "The Americans were nowhere to be seen anywhere in this," remembered one of his cohorts. And as serious encounters began along the border and the pace of the fighting picked up, Villegas was increasingly inclined to put his faith in Suicida.

"All of the best that arrived was for Suicida," said one of the Nicaraguan exiles. "Suicida was Villegas's favorite"—because Suicida was mixing it up with the Sandinistas, Suicida was pushing himself and his men into Nicaragua's own mountains. "The others were practically border patrols."

The United States was re-arming the Honduran forces of Gustavo Alvarez, and as the Hondurans got their new American M-16s, they passed along their old rifles to the men of the FDN in lots of half a dozen.

When the first six Belgian-made FAL light automatic rifles and three machine guns arrived in the spring of 1982, it was party time on patrol out of Suicida's camp, Pino Uno. Krill and Suicida waited in ambush now with more to rely on than machismo and the pee-pee of the .22s to get them through a fight.

"It was exciting like—shit, with six FALs we were going to take the capital," laughed Krill when he looked back.

Suicida shook his head. "When they gave me the first guns I was a fanatic."

Now when a militia patrol came down the trail, boys in light-brown shirts looking every way but toward the barrels of their attackers. The firing started with a rattle and built to thunder. No more "pee-pee."

"Guardia sons of bitches!" shouted a *miliciano* hidden in the forest. "Animals!" Underlining the insults with a burst of fire.

"Piricuacos! Jodidos!" Suicida's men yelled back. Beggar dogs. Fuckers. Sandinista sons of bitches. Suicida had a little surprise for the bastards. "Listen to this band!" he shouted as the FALs opened up around him in the forest. "Listen to this!"

Suicida would remember with a smile, "We attacked *comandos,* we attacked everything."

"Comandos" were little groups of half-trained militiamen deployed in log shacks at irregular intervals along the border. They were not well armed and their best defenses were usually a deep zigzag trench or their position on barren hilltops. But they dominated Suicida's best infiltration routes to the Segovias, and even with the FALs they were hell to take. Suicida said later of his days as a "fanatic" with his new guns that those first attacks on the *comandos* cost him too much in men.

But as the guns kept coming, so did new recruits. Not thousands, certainly. Not an army yet, but something that was more than a gang. And the guns got bigger, and more varied, and more sophisticated. And then there were the mortars. They worked better on the border posts.

"Hear this, you son-of-a-bitch *piricuacos?*" Krill and Suicida shouted. "We've got a fucking orchestra here!"

* * *

It was Easter week that Lisa Fitzgerald learned about mortars.

She and one of the Mexican sisters shared a single mule on the mountain trail that led toward the border. One rode, one walked and it took them almost two days, but at the beginning of Holy Week they arrived at Tererios, a settlement near the Honduran frontier that could be reached no other way.

"A number of guys who had been in the Guardia lived there," she recalled. "They had gone to Honduras, but they came back periodically, at night for example, because their families were still there."

War nerves were already building again among the people of these mountains. For weeks since the bombing of the bridges and the beginning of the state of emergency, old hostilities had been renewed and allegiances questioned. The nuns were there as agents of the faith, not of the government, but whatever their intentions, Sister Lisa and Sister Marimer were suspect in this village that lived half its life in hiding. The American and Mexican nuns decided to leave on Ash Wednesday for San Pablo, a town identified with the Frente.

They were welcomed by Pedro Carazo, the delegate of the word, and by his family.

On Maundy Thursday the sound of cocks in the early light was mixed with the rumble of distant explosions. Lisa could not, in her early morning grogginess, tell exactly what they were.

Closer at hand she heard the farmers of the village moving out on their horses and mules. They were armed with machetes. No guns. And their women had cooked them food to see them through the battle. More than a dozen were riding up across the little mountain range to the outpost called Las Pampas in a broad valley overlooked by Honduran mountains.

Lisa and Marimer followed them up the hillside to see what was happening. Las Pampas was under attack, Pedro Carazo explained. Deep, echoing explosions reverberated through the valley. Blossoms of smoke and dust appeared around the little command post.

"Mortars," someone said. Lisa had never seen or heard anything like this before. She was stunned, fascinated by the randomness and violence of the scene.

The explosions suddenly were much closer. Everyone was running for cover. Animals scattered before the multiplying concussions. San Pablo itself was under attack.

"The first time you hear mortars you're not scared," Lisa Fitzgerald said later.

"It's not just the sound of an explosion, it's more like the sound of a VW door shutting, the feeling of the air being compacted. There's a distinct sound to it as it pounds the air into the earth.

"The more times you hear them the more frightened you are. Because you know."

When she worked in Boston's South End she had heard guns fired in anger and seen the damage worked by Saturday night specials, but there was nothing ever to suggest the scale of this violence erupting all around her. "I'd never pulled shrapnel out of a woman's back. I'd never seen kids full of shrapnel."

III.

MANAGUA, NICARAGUA

Humberto Ortega, Tomás Borge, the defense ministry and the security apparatus respectively, knew quite well what was happening in the mountains of the Segovias and the forests of Jinotega. In the first two years of the counterrevolution they had penetrated its ranks from the highest commanders to the lowliest recruits. In 1981 some of their men had been weeded out, some had been killed. But Nicaraguans are not careful people, and as much as they are inclined to conspire they are not good at keeping secrets. A brother talks to a brother, your child's godfather talks to you, your old schoolmate decides there is something you had better know even though you are on opposite sides of a war. Covers are blown. Conspiracies unravel.

In December 1981 an Argentine-trained Nicaraguan saboteur was captured in Managua and exposed countless details of his connections. He talked about the training in Buenos Aires, the money given to El Negro Chamorro by the Argentines, the tripartite concept. Borge presented him to the public and he claimed he had plotted his sabotage in Costa Rica with the aid of Venezuelans and the Salvadoran Captain Eduardo Avila, a key figure in the death squads and in the murder a year before of two American labor advisors, although this could have been a bit of Sandinista misinformation.

Humberto Ortega, in the bunker, had a map that covered an entire wall of Somoza's old conference room. Black lines around its edges traced the flight paths of American spy planes and the courses charted by ships equipped with sophisticated electronic intelligence-gathering equipment. But those were not Ortega's greatest concern. His problem was with the areas along the Honduran border marked in blue circles and the patches of territory lined off in the mountains of Jinotega, the forests of the Atlantic coast and the jungles along the Rio San Juan. His concern was how to fight a silent invasion launched from bases protected by the Honduran army without, in fact, engaging the Honduran army and causing a provocation.

He had 25,000 men under arms now in his regular forces, plus Borge's special operations units. He had tens of thousands more in training as militiamen. He had a handful of Soviet tanks and Soviet Sam-7 rockets and he was thinking about getting some Soviet MIG fighter planes if the Soviets would give them to him. But this was not enough to take on the United States and if he attacked Honduras, he knew, that is what he would have to be ready to do.

"When your patience runs out you have to look for more patience," a founder of the Sandinista Front used to tell Humberto. Now he scanned the map as if searching there for patience.

In the last six months the contra bases had grown steadily stronger. They had all kinds of arms: M-79 grenade launchers and light antitank weapons and FAL rifles. They even had C rations. And they had succeeded in penetrating deep into Nicaraguan territory. From their Honduran bases they had detachments of eighty or a hundred men at a time inside northern Jinotega. On the Atlantic Coast Ortega's forces had had to fight a running battle of twelve days before finally wiping out a group of 120 fighters near the settlement of Seven Benk. When Ortega put pressure on them they would retreat back to their bases and the defenses supplied by Gustavo Alvarez's army.

"Patience and more patience," thought the young defense minister.

The blue circles looked as dense as filling stations on the map of the Honduran border. There were more than a dozen of them, their total forces perhaps four thousand men. There was Ruz Ruz in the Mosquitia in the east, Cacamulla in Choluteca in the west. Las Tunas. Las Dificultades. Baldoqui.

"Here we have Las Trojes," Ortega told a visitor. He was tapping the circle on the map with his good hand, his shriveled arm with the old wound hanging limply at his side as he studied the ink-line undulations of the terrain. "This is important. From here we've had a lot of attacks inside. There are about four hundred contras operating out of here."

Las Trojes. Ortega did not mention the name of the contra commander there, but already it was well known to his troops.

*   *   *

LAS TROJES, HONDURAS

El Suicida's Pino Uno base near Las Trojes was an old farm and the headquarters a little barn with a big antenna protruding at a slightly awkward angle. Pup tents were scattered around in the little pastures and paddocks that led up toward stands of high, hardwood trees. It was always, it seemed, a little more than the men there could manage to keep it looking as martial as it was meant to be. But in the summer of 1982 it took on more the look of a refugee camp than a military one.

Men were coming out of the Segovias with their wives, their babies, their daughters and their sons. And a lot of them were coming to find the wherewithal to fight. Since the state of emergency was begun, they had found the Sandinistas interfering in what seemed every aspect of their lives. They were told where they could sell their cattle and their crops, where they could buy their sugar.

The Managua regime built its internal surveillance network on local defense committees, modeled on the neighborhood organizations of Cuba. They took the busybodies and the zealots in each community and neighborhood and imbued them with the authority of the state. Suddenly mountain men who had never been accountable to anybody found themselves answerable to neighbors who wanted to know whom they had talked to, whom they had seen; officials who told them when they had to get inoculations and when they had to march with the militia. They were warned about what they said, and they were warned about where they worshipped. Protestant Evangelicals, followers of born-again cults, and Catholics in the congregations of priests not committed to the revolution found themselves suspect.

One of Suicida's toughest recruits was Curo, who was forty-six years old but looked older still. He was an evangelical and his congregation had been pressured and persecuted by local officials. "When we couldn't stand the Sandinistas any more some of us took this decision," he explained one day in the field, glancing at the rifle in his hand. "They jailed me in Ocotal and accused me of helping the people in the mountains, even though I didn't know them. They had me locked up for seventy days before they decided that I wasn't involved in anything. Then I was at home for three months. But a friend told me State Security was looking for me and so I went with a group of seven, all of us evangelicals. And then my family left.

"I have two sons in the struggle and other kids in a refugee camp in Honduras," he said. "My wife died when I was jailed."

El León was sixty years old, his face still handsome and sharp-eyed and unforgiving. Around his neck he wore a large crucifix and on his hat were a pair of crossed safety pins as a second talisman. El León had owned property around the town of Jícaro in the southern reaches of the Segovias. In all he had about six hundred acres and a hundred cattle. It was all taken from him. He and his two sons had taken up arms.

The National Directorate's most citified commander, Jaime Wheelock, was the man the Sandinistas chose to head the agrarian reform. Handsome in a pretty way, he had little popular appeal even in the cities; he had none in the countryside, and next to no credibility. The Front's plans for agrarian reform called, at first, only for the seizure of land that had belonged to Somoza and the *Somocistas*. Then fallow lands were included. Then lands were taken from people said to be conspiring with the counterrevolutionaries. And the credit to keep the land from becoming fallow kept drying up, and the definitions of counterrevolutionary activity kept changing.

Even the smallest landowners, who had not the slightest prospect of seeing their farms confiscated under the Sandinistas' stated programs, began to fear that the lands in which their lives were sown would be taken suddenly away from them. It was better, some decided, to abandon them and to fight.

Fernando, a twenty-three-year-old kid with long black hair, sharp, handsome features, and eyes full of lively intelligence, was the son of a man who owned two thousand acres in Jinotega. Sandinista officials took it away, and his father had fought in the courts to get it back, but the lawyers did nothing for them. So Fernando and his brother took up arms to win back the land while their parents moved into exile in Honduras.

These were the kinds of men that Dewey and Nestor liked to talk about at the Core Group in 1982. These were the small landholders, the salt of the earth, the freedom fighters. But few of them, not even those with thousands of acres, had thought of going to war before the spring of 1982. Many of them said that they had little to complain about from the Sandinistas until the March 14 blowing of the bridges provoked the state of emergency. Before March 14, whatever the Sandinistas' real intentions, their real presence in these wild mountains was token. Only afterward was it oppressive enough to make such men want to fight and to kill.

That was when and why they came to Pino Uno. Because they had heard of Caramalo, who could murder Sandinistas like a cat destroying mice. And Suicida himself, who took his men into the valley of death and brought them back out again alive, as long as they didn't cross him.

TEGUCIGALPA, HONDURAS

El Suicida sat stolidly on a chair outside Radio 15 near Tegucigalpa as his *parientito* Noel Ortiz scissored away his shoulder-length hair. He was thin and looked more than ever the inscrutable Indian. Except that he was laughing with Laura and Noel about what La Negra would think when she saw him. He liked to look good for her. He liked it when they looked good together.

In July 1982, El Suicida and La Negra made regular trips to the capital and the Ortizes' operation at Radio 15 to pick up the now plentiful supplies paid for by the United States. There were mortars and grenades big and small—round like olive-drab apples or cherry tomatoes. Suicida kept several on his new web belt and shoulder straps. The one-shot disposable bazookas called LAWs were prizes. There were the heavy-bladed knives that replaced machetes in the soldiers' belts. And there were field radios as effective, sometimes, as telephones. When Suicida was in the mountains he and La Negra sometimes talked over them like teenagers in love over long distance. The Sandinistas monitoring their frequencies listened in wonder as they discussed every homely detail of their daily lives and needs. Suicida had a problem with his teeth? La Negra would say she had found a dentist who might be good. They talked about their friends and their boys.

When Suicida was inside Nicaragua, La Negra ran everything for him. The ranks of the counterrevolution were growing more quickly now that the Sandinistas had declared their state of emergency. As the recruits came in, La Negra picked their pseudonyms for them. Peasant, Deer, Goose 1 and Goose 2. Whatever came to mind.

When Suicida came out they might drive to Danlí for a dinner at Pepy-Lou's restaurant, tortillas and rice and chicken smothered in tomatoes and onions, bottles of beer and *guaro*.

On trips to the capital they went to the American-style supermarket at the edge of the city and bought all the food they couldn't find in Danlí. La Negra, who knew more about these things than Suicida, was the kind of woman to talk about champagne and caviar, even though they didn't buy any. Someday they could have champagne and caviar. But she knew what Suicida liked to eat and drink. Educating him to other tastes that she thought might be more sophisticated was a long, slow process. His strength was in his simplicity.

And when they were in Tegucigalpa they could see Villegas. Villegas was liked by most of the combatants who knew him. He often visited the camps along the border. He was "such a sweet person," said one of the women of the camps. "Everybody loved him. People respected him, and he put order to things."

But Osvaldo Ribeiro outranked Villegas and with Ribeiro had come the whole crowd from Miami. Calculating businessman Aristides Sanchez, and fat Frank Arana the politician, stuck to him like disciples. The worst was this Guardia Major Emilio Echaverry—Fiero—the old schoolmate of General Alvarez and the new chief of operations, with his Argentine airs. Ribeiro's friends and partisans had little room for Suicida and La Negra. They did not like it that a woman had so much power in one of the task forces. She was effectively his whole staff. She handled all the logistics. He consulted with her, and sometimes only with her, about every move he made. Echaverry and the rest in Tegucigalpa saw all sorts of problems with this. Suicida might be fighting, but he had no sense of organization. He was only a sergeant, with nothing of an officer's administrative skills, and he depended on this woman to take up the slack.

The problems between Suicida and his commanders in Tegucigalpa only got worse in August when the Tegucigalpa general staff appointed José Ignacio Ramírez Zelaya to Suicida's staff and made the boy Pedro Núñez Cabezas, El Muerto, his chief of intelligence. Ramírez Zelaya, known as B-1, was an Argentine-trained protégé of Echaverry's. El Muerto had never marched in the mountains and never fired a gun at anybody who could fire back. But of course he trained in Argentina, too, and he reported faithfully to Lau.

IV.

WASHINGTON, D.C.

There were a lot of questions the congressmen hadn't asked, and a lot of answers Dewey wasn't going to give. In the summer of 1982, in retrospect, it was amazing how some things had slipped by. Six months into the program, it seemed to be out of control.

Dewey sat before the committee like a rich boy whose father owns the county being brought up before a local traffic court. His contempt was transparent. He was Casey's man, he knew. They talked to each other for hours about "The Project," Casey bypassing his more senior deputies in order to work directly with Clarridge. In six months "The Project" had become "Casey's War" and Casey had the wealth of Ronald Reagan's trust and friendship. Against that, the reservations of the Hill and the dangerous political games of the Democrats stood for very little. If the congressmen did not understand what they had signed on to in December 1981, then it was because they hadn't paid attention.

For the gravest misunderstanding of all, it might be said that everyone shared the blame. No one—not Enders' Core Group, not Casey or Clarridge and certainly not the congressmen—foresaw that the Argentines believed their services were so valuable to Washington that they could occupy the British-held Falkland Islands and count on United States neutrality.

On April 2, only five months after General Leopoldo Galtieri was feted in Washington and returned to Buenos Aires to make himself president; and only two and a half weeks after the first major attacks of the Secret War against Nicaragua—the ones so hard to step back from—the Argentines announced their capture of the Falkland Islands in the South Atlantic.

No explicit quid pro quo has ever been proved. None of the American officials who had warmed relations with the Argentines was ever established to have given them a bright-green light. The Argentines seem rather to have made a colossal miscalculation. The generals did not seem to think that Britain would fight. But it had. They had thought Washington owed them a great debt. But of course when Washington had to choose sides, it chose London.

The generals had spent a decade talking of "war without frontiers" and imagining themselves the paladins of the West in the great Third World War against the invisible threats of godless communism. They believed, truly believed, that they were indispensable to the defense of the West. All their contacts with Ronald Reagan and his people reassured them of that. But now the generals who had killed so many people in their beds and the streets and their cells to win their battles, found themselves exposed to an open fight against the British navy. A very conservative woman prime minister beat the pride of their armed forces to a pulp in less than a month of combat. By June, President Leopoldo Galtieri had resigned in humiliation. The regime of the generals came apart. From the fissures that opened, the rot became evident. Within another three months the graves of the dead from their Dirty War began to be found, and to be opened.

The congressmen had not asked many questions about these Argentines when they were told by Casey that the paramilitary operation against Nicaragua was just a question of "buying into" a going concern. Certainly no one had talked about, or expected, a price like this. Everyone had been thinking and talking about El Salvador.

But even before the Falklands, they began to worry about just what it was that was bought from the boys in Buenos Aires. What exactly was the Secret War supposed to be doing? Was it supposed to be a war at all?

"In December '81 when the finding came in, they told us there would be five hundred people in four-man patrols to do this interdicting of arms supply lines on the Nicaraguan side of the border and the training was going to be done by the Argentines," recalled one intelligence committee member. Then "we found out in February '82 that they [the Argentines] had already been training some seventeen hundred Miskito Indians," this congressman recalled. "We didn't know about that before February '82!"

At each briefing the numbers of all the forces seemed to grow. What did a force of five thousand men have to do with interdicting arms? This sounded as though it might be another kind of force altogether.

"It was a trumped-up misunderstanding," said a member of the Core Group, dismissing the complaints. "It would have defied logic for anyone to think that the sole purpose of an anti-Sandinista soldier was to intercept arms traveling down a trail."

But the misunderstanding was there nonetheless. And there was a question of the targets. The congressmen made it clear they did not want economic targets hit. That was not the idea. The Agency agreed. Then the press would report that an oil storage tank had been blown or a coffee mill burned. Who the hell did that?

"Not ours," Dewey would say. "Checked it. Not ours."

But by the summer there was no hiding the fact that the program was fraying at the edges. The "commando teams" had become something like an army of refugees and bandits, farmers and cutthroats, all mixed together with no one clearly in charge. The program's goals had become increasingly confused and confusing. And the question of who was giving the orders and who would follow them was, at best, vague.

After the break between Buenos Aires and Washington over the Falklands, what was left was a secret war waged by a rabble and run for the United States by men who felt, quite strongly, that the United States had betrayed them.

So, Dewey, how would you describe the command and control of the anti-Sandinista forces? the congressmen and senators would ask.

"We've got good command and control," Dewey would respond sharply.

Dewey never apologized, of course. But Dewey, always on the move, already was working on another, much more attractive, angle.

SAN JOSÉ, COSTA RICA

Pastora came late to his own press conference. It was a strange spectacle of public secrecy. The location was supposed to be unknown, but the press was brought in tourist busses from the main hotel in the center of the Costa Rican capital to a country club conference room in the hills. They waited with coffee and cookies for his arrival. And waited. (It seemed some of his neighbors in the suburb of Escazú had grown suspicious of all the mysterious-looking men hanging around his house. They called the police. That had taken a while to sort out.)

It was Pastora's first public appearance since his mysterious departure from Managua. The first thing people noticed as he arrived— backed up by his lieutenant Lionel Poveda in dark glasses, the Panamanian Spadáfora hanging around in the background—was that Commander Zero had put on weight, and he looked uncomfortable wearing a leisure suit instead of fatigues.

He was there to announce that he was the watchdog of the revolution. He was there to decry the degeneration of Sandinista ideals at the hands of the nine *comandantes* in the Directorate. He was there, he said, not to take up arms but to try through moral suasion to win the Sandinistas back to the path they had set for themselves during the insurrection, the moderate, social democratic path of Tercerismo.

On his wrist was the gold Rolex President watch he had captured for himself at the National Palace in 1979 and a diamond ring that Torrijos had given him.

He quoted Torrijos a lot that day.

Torrijos had told him the United States was like a vicious monkey sitting tethered to a limb in a roadside menagerie. You could play with the chain and make him jump, but you better not play with the monkey.

The reporters goaded Pastora. What was he going to do if the Sandinistas ignored him? Because it was obvious they would. Everybody had waited for so long to see what he was up to, and now that they saw it, it looked like hot air.

He wasn't sure, he said, and launched into anecdotes about all the decadence of the nine *comandantes,* their flashy cars and their houses in Las Colinas.

But what would he do if they ignored him? He had no troops. He had, as far as anyone could tell, no anything.

He would see, he said.

But . . .

Pastora was getting worked up. All right, he said, if they don't come around, "I'll take them out at gunpoint from their mansions and their Mercedes-Benzes."

Dewey had liked Pastora from the start, it seems, or at least had liked the idea of Pastora. An old case officer like Dewey would see that there never was a man more obviously made to be recruited than Edén. For at least a year he had been a walking, breathing target of opportunity. Slighted by the National Directorate, bored with the life of the revolutionary bureaucrat, he had left Managua to make himself the hero of another war and been thwarted at every turn by his old enemies, and some of his old friends in the Directorate.

"Edén wanted to be like a Ché," one of the Sandinistas' strategists would say later, "and he came back a traitor."

Pastora had traveled back and forth from Panama to Cuba, then secretly to Nicaragua at the insistence of the Cubans. Did he disagree with something about the revolution? a member of the Directorate wanted to know. "No, *hombre,*" he said. He went back to Cuba with his buddy Valdivia, thinking that from there he could continue building his ties to the Guatemalans. But he was beginning to discover that the Guatemalans did not want him. The Cubans, the Directorate, had talked to them about him.

Did Edén think he could go to Guatemala and get a lot of support with his name? said one of the Directorate's political operatives. Then he did not understand what he was doing. The fact is that Edén was made famous by the Frente Sandinista, not the other way around. He was "a famous Zero." That should tell you something. He was "an idol of clay," "his fame was the stuff of old newspapers, old magazines." He was never anything more than a combatant. And the fact is, the revolutionary struggle is very complicated. What would the presence of a Sandinista commander in Guatemala do to the Front's argument that it was not supplying troops or guns to other revolutionaries? This plan of his was madness and the Directorate had told him as much.

The Guatemalans backed off from Edén, and the Cubans who had been his hosts, he found, soon turned into his keepers.

Fidel appears to have humored Pastora. "You've got to be more intelligent than ever. You have to be more politic than ever. Don't pull away from the Directorate. Don't fight with the Directorate. You've always shown discipline and great maturity. Now more than ever you need to show these qualities." But when Pastora wanted to leave, he could not. For four and a half months, until January 1982, he had been kept in Havana until, finally, some Panamanians interceded on his behalf. But when he was free, no one seemed to want him anymore.

"When we went back to Panama we had no one to help us. We had to sell the Mercedes-Benzes. I pawned my watch. I pawned my ring. Son of a bitch, I almost sold it!"

Pastora went to Mexico and made contact with the Guatemalans there. He went to Los Angeles secretly and he may have bought them a few guns from an old connection there. But everything was coming apart. Valdivia decided to go back to Nicaragua and try to put his life together again there.

It may have been just about then, perhaps on the trip to Los Angeles—the sources are vague about this, but certainly it was early in the year—that Dewey caught up to Pastora and put a proposition to him. No one would know what was involved. Only Dewey and three or four others would be aware, directly, of the contact. Pastora would be able to get what he needed to fight—but not in Guatemala. He would fight in Nicaragua, against the Directorate. There were farmers and former Sandinistas joining the ranks of the Nicaraguan Democratic Force already in Honduras. There was a front to be opened in Costa Rica, Pastora's old territory. Dewey could help make Pastora the star of the second revolution as he had been the star of the first. And Pastora, who loved conspiracy, was willing to conspire in that. He was willing to take the money, certainly, if it came without strings and if he did not have to know, exactly, where it came from and would not be in any way identified with the Agency. Pastora knew his credibility was in his independence. And so did Dewey.

But knowing what was needed and knowing how to get it, as things turned out, were problems the Agency could not quite resolve in Pastora's case.

Pastora's coming-out party at the country club in San José brought a new element to the project, but it was not an element that anyone could control.

TEGUCIGALPA, HONDURAS

Commander Zero came on the scene in the Secret War just as the last vestiges of organization and control under the Argentines were beginning to disintegrate. Political credibility, never high, was at an all-time low. Jealousies were rampant. Resentments had degenerated to the point of rage between the Argentines and Americans. And Pastora's presence made everything worse.

Pastora was there to divide them, the Argentines and FDN leaders said. Pastora was a spy of the Sandinistas, a double agent, they said. And if he was not, then the people who surrounded him were.

Pastora had been joined by his old friend, the Sandinista plotter and strategist Carlos Coronel. Former schoolmate and junta member Alfonso Robelo brought the support of his party to Pastora's side. Behind the scenes Edén was advised by Arturo Cruz, who had also served on the junta for a time and had been the Sandinista ambassador to Washington. Cruz's son, a professed Marxist, worked on the staff of the Sandinista Directorate before he, too, took up Pastora's banner. These were the kinds of people that more sophisticated thinkers in Washington wanted to see around Pastora. Their departure from Nicaragua was a signal that some of the country's best intellects and most loyal patriots felt betrayed by the Sandinistas. These were the men who would give Pastora political credibility, it was thought. But the Argentines and FDN leaders were not comfortable with them. Some had been genuine revolutionaries. Some still claimed to be genuine revolutionaries. How could such men be trusted?

And Pastora did crazy things. He went up to the Costa Rican border to receive publicly a group of Nicaraguan deserters coming over to his side, and got himself kicked out of Costa Rica as a result.

Pastora went to Europe to lobby for support from the Socialists, then came back to Honduras to talk to Alvarez and the Agency about joining the FDN. But he demanded that all the *guardias* be gotten rid of before he would sign on. What he wanted, it seemed, was to take over.

Then something happened. Pastora was getting ready to leave Honduras and found out, suddenly, he couldn't. He was "under the protection of General Alvarez," the Hondurans told him. But "I saw the handiwork of the CIA," he said.

"Argentines and the CIA!" Pastora shouted in mock consternation as he told the story. "The CIA had the FDN set up already and it was starting to work. And they want me to be in Honduras to legitimize the FDN. They want to hold me in Honduras!

"So at a meeting I'm telling them I want to get out of Honduras and I say to Alvarez, 'Look, General, you can't conquer me. These people of yours have cannons, airplanes and tanks and an army, but you can't defeat me. You know why? Because I'm invincible. I'll tell you why. Because the man who is determined to die is invincible.'

"So while I'm saying this they are coming around me slowly, this Alvarez and . . . this guy from the CIA, a big blond guy I didn't know. They're coming around me and just at that moment I whip out my pistol and I say, 'I'm determined to die.' Everyone backed off—but right away!—when they realized I had the pistol up against my head. I said, 'Would you like me to demonstrate?' " He tilted his head slightly to one side against the pressure of the gun barrel. "They're saying, 'Calm down, Pastora, calm down.' And this son of a bitch falls on top of me."

Pastora wrestled with his captors for a few seconds and the meeting broke up with a lot of sweat and a little blood flowing off several participants. But Pastora, finally, was allowed to leave.

Bermúdez and Lau used to talk after that, none too discreetly, about how they wanted to kill Pastora and Alfonso Robelo. "Not just once, not just once," did they talk of using Pastora and killing him, said veterans of the Nicaraguan Democratic Force.

But the Agency still wanted Pastora. It was still willing to fund him; to mollify him.

FDN leaders "repeatedly asked to open a front in the South"—in Costa Rica—according to one of the CIA men running the operation. But they were stopped by the United States, which was keeping the South for Pastora.

By late summer, frictions were getting dangerous. It was clear that an alternative to the Argentines, and some potential alternative to Pastora as well, would have to be found. Congress was growing increasingly restive once again about the project. At one point Dewey and Casey had to admit they had lost a little control, but they vowed to the congressmen they would get it back. A new organization, or at least a new image, was an urgent necessity.

The business of putting a new face on the FDN and, by extension, on the whole Secret War, was conducted by a man who sometimes called himself Tony Feldman and sometimes Philip Mason but was best remembered for his three-piece suits.

"He has the face of a young man and wears thin little glasses. He looks like an executive," said one of the Nicaraguans he controlled.

"But what does an executive have to do with a war? He looks like he is managing a business. That's one of the errors they've committed, the CIA. They think they are managing a business."

Several of the senior political figures in the FDN were flown to Washington for talks. Chicano Cardenal was put up at the Key Bridge Marriott and interviewed for hours by Feldman/Mason. Chicano complained about the Argentines, especially about Ribeiro. He complained about Bermúdez and about Lau, "nefarious criminals who ought not to be in those positions."

Feldman/Mason and Monica, a woman consistently described by those who know her as both smart and unattractive, spent long hours with Chicano going over all these problems in a restaurant overlooking Washington. They sent Chicano back down to Tegucigalpa with the advice that he should be careful.

V.

TEGUCIGALPA, HONDURAS
A new station chief took over in Tegucigalpa in September. Tall and muscular and blond, he made some of the Nicaraguans envision the athlete Carl Lewis in whiteface. Others recalled Robert Shaw in the James Bond movie *From Russia with Love*. He was confident but cool, affable, a good man to have a beer with and a good man to work with. His colleagues remember his enthusiasm for his job and for women, including the young woman who used to be his secretary and was now his wife.

Shaw, as we will call him, had the job on the ground of getting the Argentines out and getting the war back under control. The Argentines, he would say, started out as a "fig leaf" and had wound up as "a pain in the ass."

Shaw, who had some experience with people like the Argentines, inherited contacts with what amounted to four different rebel organizations full of mutual jealousies and hostilities. There was the FDN itself. There was the small group under Fernando El Negro Chamorro, who divided his time, it was said by his enemies, between the bottle and the press, and who, they said, could fit all his troops in a microbus if he had to. There were the Miskito Indians under the self-important and unpredictable former agent of Somoza, Steadman Fagoth. And there was Pastora, who, as yet, had no real military force of his own.

Shaw's mission was to keep his eye on the bottom line. El Negro was always claiming great popular support and strong anti-Somoza as well as anti-Sandinista credentials, but he never seemed to deliver. The Miskitos were, as Shaw once told an acquaintance, "not a central element in Nicaraguan life."

The war was supposed to be run by a "unified general staff." At the top were Shaw and the officer who headed up special U.S. training and paramilitary activities; Ribeiro and Villegas represented the Argentines; General Alvarez and his man Colonel Calderini represented the Hondurans, and Bermúdez and Echaverry represented the FDN.

Below this was a complicated and often uncoordinated arrangement. A joint staff including Shaw and Ribeiro and Bermúdez and Echaverry was supposed to take basic operational decisions. But the Hondurans meanwhile had an extensive liaison setup with all levels of the operation.

Alvarez's right-hand man in charge of his "special operations" was Captain Alexander Hernandez, and Hernandez was a key liaison between Alvarez and the day-to-day operations of the Secret War with Lau and his contract men.

Shaw told acquaintances that he "knew all about Lau," and demanded his official removal from the FDN general staff almost as soon as he arrived. But while Lau's title changed, his role as the judge and sometime executioner of those he deemed dangerous to the cause remained the same. He kept his house in Tegucigalpa. He kept his men.

The showdown had been building between the Agency and the Argentines now for five months. At the end of September a series of meetings took place in Buenos Aires and Washington to try to sort out the new relationship or at least end the old one.

Chicano, Mariano Mendoza and Aristides Sanchez, the three members of the "old" FDN Directorate put together a year before, were now caught in the middle. The Americans seemed to want to keep Chicano and Mariano but had no use for Sanchez. The Argentines felt exactly the opposite way about them.

October 7 was a bad day for making secret war. It was the day that the Argentine connection broke wide open, and it was the day that Chicano Cardenal panicked and went into hiding. The Sandinistas were the authors of the first disaster, but Lau and Bermúdez brought on the second.

One of the Argentine operatives in Honduras and Costa Rica was a slight, wiry intelligence officer from Battalion 601 who went by the name Hector Francés. "Even though he was a young military man," Chicano said, "he had a completely criminal gorilla mentality." Most of Francés's work was in San José organizing cells for the Argentine operation which the Agency, at this point, was beginning to frustrate. Francés commuted back and forth to see Ribeiro and Villegas in Honduras and on October 7 he had just returned to Costa Rica with his paycheck. A group of armed men snatched him in the street not far from his house, and the next time he surfaced he was on a videotape released by members of the Frente Sandinista de Liberación Nacional. Obviously nervous, seeming to recite his lines, he claimed to be a defector. But he exposed much less than a man who wanted to break the network would have been willing to divulge. Francés talked a little about Ribeiro's role and Villegas. He named other agents who worked with him. He talked about the war without frontiers and the men who waged it. From what he told them, the Sandinistas—who had had their eyes and ears inside the FDN steadily cut off by the Agency, the Argentines and Lau—now once again had a detailed and mostly accurate picture of their enemies' operations. What happened to Francés after he talked remains a matter of conjecture.

What happened to Chicano on October 7 was more complicated, and it is hard to say, even now, how much of it was paranoid fantasy and how much fact. Paranoid fantasies often came true in Central America in 1982.

Chicano, on the advice of the Agency, stayed out of Honduras as long as he felt he could. He traveled in the United States. He met with Mason/Feldman again in San Francisco to talk to a former Guardia officer who might serve as a replacement for Bermúdez. Chicano believed, or was led to believe, that he would be the central figure in the new organization taking shape.

Soon after he finally returned to Honduras he decided he wanted to go to Costa Rica, where an influential churchman seemed ready to give his support to the fight against the Sandinistas. In Costa Rica, of course, he could make contact with Pastora's people as well. Chicano was thinking about making some public statements about the way this war was going.

But he was stopped at Tegucigalpa's Toncontin airport.

First there was the problem of the documents. It was a classic little screwup in an operation that was running on the margins of control.

Chicano had an Argentine passport, a Nicaraguan passport and an Ecuadoran passport that John Perham, Chicano's CIA case officer, had given him and had then told him a little later not to use because there were some problems with it. But Chicano was so nervous that day, so much was going on, that he handed the immigration officer the Ecuadoran documents.

"What idiocy from the CIA! They just put any old numbers on it, and it was obvious that the numbers weren't the ones that are used." That took a while to straighten out for Chicano and Mariano.

Then as they were waiting in the departure lounge, Chicano saw one of Lau's assistants a few yards away, looking them over. A few minutes later airport security picked them up, demanding they go through all their baggage. Chicano tried to explain. They demanded both the Ecuadoran and the Argentine documents. And Chicano began to think of disappearances, how easy it would be, now that technically they had left the country, for these men to take them away and turn them into people who never existed. Once they handed over their papers, however, they were allowed to go back to the safe house where they had been living.

Another surprise awaited them there. For months they had had the same bodyguards. But now those guards were being changed. A couple of members of the general staff were there to oversee the job.

"One of the new guards is an operative we know Lau has used to disappear people."

Chicano was furious and frightened. One of the members of the general staff called Villegas to see what to do. Villegas insisted the guards should be changed. The Argentines were setting up a new operation called the Quinta Escuela on an old chicken farm not far from Tegucigalpa and they wanted these men for that job.

But the old guards said they wanted to stay with Chicano. There was shouting, screaming and accusations and in a matter of a few minutes Chicano and the guards and Mariano took off for a friend's house. Soon they were followed, or thought they were.

"Mariano," said Chicano, "this isn't a game. This is serious."

John Perham, his CIA case officer, was on vacation. Chicano had lost the alternate contact's phone number. He made his way to San Pedro Sula in the north and from the house of a friend called David, the station chief in Miami. David wasn't there.

For more than a week Chicano and Mariano hid out in San Pedro Sula. One night, Chicano went to see a movie at the local theater:

Missing, with Jack Lemmon and Sissy Spacek, about the search for a young American who disappeared in Chile after the coup against Allende. He watched the bad excuses unraveling, the stories that the boy is hiding or out of the country, the string of lies abetted by the Americans to explain why he has ceased to exist.

"Son of a bitch," thought Chicano, "that's what's happening here."

VI.

MIAMI, FLORIDA

When all was said and done in the meeting at the end of September, the Argentines stayed. By some accounts, the Argentine government was in such chaos in the aftermath of the Falklands that it did not want to have its men back lest they complicate things even more. There were some reports that their official status had changed as well and they were now strictly "private" employees. The agency made it clear it still wanted to phase them out. But it still left Ribeiro in Tegucigalpa holding court at his room in the Maya. And Villegas was still the man in the field most seen by the fighters.

The biggest changes would come, instead, in the face the FDN put forward to the public. When Bermúdez returned to Tegucigalpa from consultations in Washington he told his men there was going to be a new directorate. Whom does it represent? one of them asked. Bermúdez just looked at him. Bermúdez was on the new directorate to keep the *guardias* in line. But the new names that were floated were of people closely tied to the old Conservative party opposition to Somoza and, directly or indirectly, might provide the bridge that the Agency still wanted for bringing Pastora openly into the project.

In Miami, one by one, the CIA approached its potential candidates for the new leadership. Most often David, the station chief in Miami, would make the first contacts. Then that would be followed up by sessions with Feldman/Mason in the cool, sand-colored rooms of the Brickell Point Holiday Inn looking out on the speedboats and windsurfers of Biscayne Bay.

One of the new members of the FDN directorate was Lucia Cardenal de Salazar, the aristocratic widow of Jorge, the martyr of the private sector. One was a former Somoza vice president, another was an industrialist, one was a veterinarian.

Adolfo Calero, a stalwart of the Conservative party, was the manager of the Coca Cola bottling plant in Managua.

Another new member, Edgar Chamorro, had spent most of his life as a Jesuit before getting married and going into advertising.

"Ron Plata para hombres muy hombres," was the slogan of his that people remembered, "A rum for men who are very manly," and they always smiled when they said it. Chamorro seemed so unlike that.

Edgar was part of the old, aristocratic crowd in Managua and Granada, and as such he had certain ties to Pastora. Carlos Coronel, one of Edén's most trusted friends and closest advisors in the war against Somoza and now in the fight against the Sandinistas, was Chamorro's cousin. Yet Edgar was, you might say, on the opposite rim of Pastora's circle. When Edén and Chicano were marching in the band of war and breaking legs on the soccer field at the Colegio Centroamerica, Edgar was one of the Jesuits' seminarians there. For twenty years, until 1970, Edgar was on his way to becoming a priest without ever quite making a wholehearted commitment. And then he spent three years at Harvard and he gave it up.

He went into public relations. *Ron Plata para hombres muy hombres.*

Edgar was in his office when the Americans gave him a call. The man on the phone said his name was David and that he would wait downstairs. He never identified himself directly, but you get to where you think you can spot a man from the government the way you can spot a bill collector or a man selling life insurance. Tall and strong, about six feet two inches, he had the athletic look that came to seem to Edgar the trademark of the Agency. Later there would be Pancho, "a roughneck, very vulgar," and Mike, "a very good guy" from the local station in Miami. But that first day it was just David, and then an invitation to another meeting at the Holiday Inn on Brickell Point.

The man in the three-piece suit had a suite overlooking Biscayne Bay. It was a cool, comfortable setting. The man, who was calling himself Tony Feldman at the time, exuded confidence.

Chamorro was flattered at the attention he was receiving but a little cautious. "What is our purpose?" he asked the man in the three-piece suit.

The goal, the expectation, said the man, was to be in Managua by July, eight months away, or at the latest by the end of 1983.

"He insisted," Chamorro recalled. "He assured us that this was a commitment from the United States government to overthrow the Sandinistas. I said, 'I've got to give up my job to do this, so I think I have some interest in knowing if the U.S. is really committed.' "

"Yes," said Feldman. "The president of the United States is very concerned with Nicaragua's direction and the militarization there. We will not allow another Cuba."

"He reassured me," Chamorro said. "that this time we were going all the way."

Of course, that was not what Congress was told at all.

In October a new rash of leaks about the project, including a cover story in *Newsweek* about the Secret War, made the undertaking a public issue once again. The photographs of airplanes, the image of a secret army at work, played havoc with the pretense that this was merely an effort to stop the underground export of arms to El Salvador's insurgents. The leadership of the Secret War seemed to be, as indeed it was, tied up with thugs from Argentina and former soldiers of the Somoza dictatorship. By early December a new bill was before the House that would prohibit any form of aid whatsoever for the anti-Sandinista rebels. To keep this from happening the administration had to accept publicly restrictions on the project that were proposed by House Intelligence Committee chairman Boland. By a vote of 411 to 0, the House prohibited support "for the purpose of overthrowing the government of Nicaragua." But for the purposes of "interdiction" the money could continue to flow.

It was to mollify Congress that the man in the three-piece suit had been working. That was why the new face of the FDN he pieced together had to be as clean as possible of *Somocista* features. Once the new Directorate was presented to the public it was at least marginally easier to claim that the "new" Nicaraguan Democratic Force had some sense of what democracy actually meant. And it was for the benefit of Congress that the new directors were coached for more than a week at the Four Ambassadors Hotel on how to avoid saying, quite, that their aim was to throw the Sandinistas out.

If, privately, the man in the three-piece suit and the boys from the local station were saying otherwise, and indeed were effervescent with expectations that the Sandinistas would fall in less than a year, that was not really Washington's concern.

A member of the Core Group, asked afterward about the discrepancy between what the Agency's people told Congress and what they told the contras, said drily, "I can imagine that they would tell them what was necessary to get them mobilized." The Core Group was clear enough about what it wanted, after all. Its purpose was still merely to squeeze the Sandinistas, using the new Directorate and the men of the FDN fighting in the field as "instruments of pressure."

"If there was some American somewhere who was telling them they were going to be in Managua in six months I would say he was either self-deceived or deceiving them. Certainly I never heard anyone say that it would be in Managua in six months."

The money continued. And so did the war.

VII.

Las Trojes, Honduras

In November 1982, Suicida had his men, he had his guns and he felt ready for his old kind of war: big attacks looking for big wins. In the chill mountain evenings he and La Negra talked often about strategy. First they would eliminate the Sandinista outposts along the border, then they would push their forces deep inside the narrow northern tip of Nueva Segovia. They would attack Jalapa itself. If they could take it, they would call in support on the airstrips around the town, and reenforcements overland from Honduras. They would declare a liberated territory. Then the war to oust the Communists could get serious.

But in Tegucigalpa there did not seem to be much enthusiasm for this idea. The general staff toyed with it. It sounded good. But the Americans, the Argentines, Bermúdez and his officers were cautious. The men at the other bases were still in training, and they did not want to act until everyone was ready—if then. They did not want to give the resources. They did not seem to trust Suicida.

So Suicida continued to make his plan and to make his preparations, but he told less and less about it to the spies El Muerto and B-1, sent down to work on his staff by the men in Tegucigalpa. He gave them no idea of his objectives or designs. He rarely even met with them if he could avoid it at the camp. He asked of El Muerto, his supposed chief of intelligence, no information at all. Then in the middle of November, without orders from Tegucigalpa, and on his own account, Suicida began his infiltration and his offensive in the Segovias.

Squads of twenty men were sent across the border under his lieutenants Krill and Cancer and others; about two hundred men in all moving down through the area around Providencia while Caramalo operated in the zone around Chachagua and Quilalí. Suicida set up his command post on the mountain called Chachagua to direct the operation and finally, several days after he began, allowed El Muerto and the others to join him.

The initial attacks were small. Most of Suicida's new recruits were raw; many could not be relied on to fight. But the Sandinista forces they were up against were often half-trained militiamen as raw as anyone in their own ranks. As Suicida's people gained experience in little ambushes and engagements the scope of the fighting grew. Krill and Cancer were spearheading the operation and well past Providencia they had yet to encounter major resistance. The only problem was ammunition. The new recruits wasted a lot and they were running out quickly. Suicida started calling to the other bases asking for support, trying to draw them into the fight. But one by one the responses came back over the radio. "Negative." Now he called Tegucigalpa. He had an offensive going. He was giving hell to the Sandinistas, couldn't they tell that? And, however reluctantly, they began diverting supplies to his camp to try to sustain him.

The general staff in Tegucigalpa, muddled by all the reorganization going on in Miami, had not known what to do about Suicida's offensive when it began. But they soon saw that, at least in the short term, it could give them the credibility they wanted as a fighting force. He was inside Nicaragua, he was fighting, and he was holding his own. Some of his squad commanders captured and recruited dozens of new men. While most of the FDN bases could count only two or three hundred potential combatants among their ranks, Suicida's force looked as if it could swell to eight hundred or more.

Now a broader offensive was begun to coincide with the announcement of a new Directorate for the FDN. Other commanders were moving their forces into Nicaragua, clearing out of their bases and looking for combat. But Suicida had made a jump on the rest. His men were more numerous and seasoned now than anyone else's. His reputation grew steadily as Krill and Cancer pushed through the pine groves of the Segovias toward the valley of Jalapa itself.

Jalapa, Nicaragua

Over the icy trickle of the shower, Lisa could hear the other nuns and priests talking away the night around the dinner table in the next room. Just the sound of their voices was reassuring.

For two days refugees had been pouring into Jalapa from the mountain villages to the north and west. They came with their children and anything else they could carry in their arms or on their backs over the ground trail through San Juan: a few ragged blankets, a bag or two of food; sometimes a radio. There was not much. There had not been much to begin with, except the animals and the land they left behind.

They came both night and day, and in the mornings you could see them making their way in long lines down the mountain trails. They were all over the streets. Whole families sat on the irregular curbs, waiting, many of them too tired even to talk. They had no place to go, so they came to see the priests and the nuns.

"And they'd tell you, 'Oh, I'm from Providencia,' and they'd tell you, 'Oh, we left and I don't know where my son and daughter are. They went out into the hills and I don't know if the contras got them. . . .' "

Some were wounded, mainly from shrapnel, and they were taken to the hospital. Lucinio, one of the priests, and Marimer had both spent much of the day there.

The rainy season lasts late into November and December in Jalapa and most of the shutters in the house were closed against the weather, except for the bathroom, which opened onto a covered porch.

"I started hearing shots," Lisa remembered. "You hear them frequently enough in that area. Even the kids can tell the difference between shots: if somebody is just drunk for instance, or somebody sees a cow and thinks it's a person and shoots it. (I don't want to think about how many livestock have been killed at night in Jalapa by the *vigilancia*.) But you can tell the difference between that kind of shooting and where two sides are responding to each other. And by that time I could tell. And I was beginning to hear mortars. But I mean *close!* And it was about nine or ten at night. And I finished up my shower and I came back out and I said, 'Do you guys hear that?' And they said, 'Hear what?' I said, 'Open the shutters. Listen to this.'

"It was the first time we had heard that kind of raid really on Jalapa's doorstep."

If the town were to fall, Lisa was sure that she and the rest of the nuns and priests would be singled out for killing. The contras hated them with a special intensity, it seemed. The contras saw them as "internationalists." In their radio broadcasts, people told her, they named everyone in Lisa's religious household, the Spanish priests, the Mexican sisters and herself, as agents of communism. The contras had accused every Maryknoll missionary in the country of teaching communism. But if you were identified with a Cuban doctor or Spanish priests or the American Capuchins in Jícaro, what could you do about it?

The danger was mounting and had become ever more specific. People who worked with the priests began to be contra targets, the terror seeking them out even as they slept in their beds. At the settlement called La Fragua near Jícaro at the end of October seven men from the same family were killed. All were delegates of the word who also worked with the Frente. Their mother and two of their babies were left alive, after they were allowed to watch their people die. In another village three farmers who worked as Sandinista militia were murdered and the blood of one was used to write, "God Yes, Communism No."

Pedro Carazo, the delegate of the word who had welcomed Lisa and Marimer to San Pablo and then watched over them in the grim days of bombardment during Holy Week, was dragged from his isolated house one night in November. His corpse showed up on the outskirts of town a day later, on the path to Jalapa, his throat cut and his body half eaten by dogs.

Lisa Fitzgerald listened as the shelling grew nearer. Some of the townspeople moved reluctantly, most of them dutifully to the trenches that circled Jalapa. They had worked long and hard to dig them, only to have Sandinista officials examine them and declare them insufficient, and they had had to dig them again. But now they crouched down in the pale dirt waiting for morning, waiting for blue-green uniforms to appear from the night, gun muzzles blazing in front of them. In the streets of the town people stood anxiously in their doorways. Those not armed with guns had penny whistles in their hands ready to sound an alert if the contras slipped through the line.

In the long-shadowed light of morning you began to see in the distance the figures of the enemy moving along the mountain trails. The troops defending Jalapa were falling back. They had set up staggered rows of mortars near the outer perimeter of defenses. But contra units were so close now that they could not angle the barrels down to hit them. They broke down the heavy metal tubes and pulled them to the edge of the town, into the cemetery, to make the range. Lisa watched, wondering at what moment the war would erupt into the streets around her.

"I can remember," she said, "that there was a difference in my kind of gut feeling—that, first of all, I wasn't looking for a way out. Whereas the other times it was 'how are we gonna get out of here?' I mean that I had become enough of a part of that town that I didn't feel it personally. I was afraid for all of us in the town. Scared, yes. But that dissipates fear a lot when there are a lot of people in the same situation."

Jalapa had the lure of vulnerability. It lay before Krill and Cancer like a target in the middle of its flat little valley of tobacco fields. But its exposure there was also its protection. With artillery, with a few airplanes, it could be taken apart. But with nothing but a handful of light mortars, the wide stretches of flat open land were a shooting gallery for the Sandinistas defending the town. Krill would have known this. So would Cancer. They were veterans of the war of '79, veterans of the Guardia. But they were also competitors.

Krill had been away for months on the coast pursuing his little vendettas, looking for the odd dollar, sulking and drinking and screwing. And then he had shown up again in the camp at Pino Uno and taken over again as the intimate of Suicida and of La Negra. Krill was a survivor and a killer to be reckoned with. No one could deny his skills in the field. But he brought with him his mix of sullen passions and childish glee at the prospect of slaughter. And he took what he wanted from the men and their women. He was an agent of bitterness that spread like a stain on the morale of the camp.

"Cancer was not like Krill," commandos from Pino Uno would say later, as if that were Cancer's most important quality. Short and dark, with clear brown eyes and the regular, high-cheekboned features left by a lot of Indian blood, he had a quiet nature, but not a sullen one. And he showed considerations that the men and his women appreciated. He was a fighter but not a killer and at least one of the girls who went with him remembered him for his gentleness.

The tensions between Krill and Cancer were palpable and the attack on Jalapa became a contest not just against the Sandinistas but between the two commanders. It picked up momentum, carrying itself forward ever more recklessly as they vied against each other. They came onto the rises above Jalapa with their troops like huntsmen slipping hounds from the leash to see which would be first to take the quarry. Commandos were scrambling down the hills toward the line of fire only to throw themselves prone in the dust of the fields, wriggling, running, crawling again to the cover of long tobacco barns. Soon the thin, slatted walls were perforated like paper by the exchanges of fire. The mortars were playing hell with what passed for discipline among the recruits. Each thudded launch sent them flat again and successive concussions left some of the young commandos frozen in place, disoriented, their heads emptied by the noise. They fired wildly. The nearer they got to the Sandinista perimeters, the more of their rifles fell silent. The push was slowing down. It was crawling. It was stopped. And now some of the men began slowly to pull back. The low, rolling skirts of the hillsides that had launched them began to be seen as a refuge. The stall became a withdrawal, the withdrawal a retreat.

When it was over it was impossible to piece together exactly what happened between Krill and Cancer in those moments when their offensive died before them, in those hours when they fought to keep the march back to Honduras from turning into a rout. They had to thread their way through ambushes, trying to avoid them rather than breaking them the way they were accustomed to do. Maybe it was during one of these that a debt was incurred. In the mountain trails, with ammunition low, survival in an ambush depended on the ability to call in reenforcement, to hit the back of the attackers even as you were pinned down in front. One can only speculate that this is what happened with Krill and Cancer. Having fallen into the S-shaped snare of an ambush, Krill must have been badly pinned, and Cancer, his rival for the love of women and of Suicida, may have been the agent of his salvation one late, bloody afternoon in December.

Whatever happened in fact, what was apparent later, is that Krill seemed to feel there was a debt there. And it was a debt he would come to both honor and resent.

San José, Costa Rica

"Get these pirates out of here!" shouted the president's security man. He was talking about reporters. Ronald Reagan had come to Central America, to the Cariari Country Club on the outskirts of San José, Costa Rica. Believing their own message about the danger of terrorists in the region, his men had insisted on turning the golf course and its grounds into a temporary extension of the United States embassy—a bit of U.S. territory, as it were, where they could run every aspect of the program without having to depend on Costa Rica's hapless police for protection. But the journalists, expecially the American journalists who had showed up from the local press corps to cover the event, were something less than cooperative, attempting to walk past barriers and through back doors to get to Central American presidents and ministers they knew and talked to all the time.

Control. The Reagan people insisted on control. And it was slipping away all around them. They were coming in off a faux pas of small but humiliating proportions. On his visit to Brazil Reagan had said his next stop was Bolivia when in fact it was Colombia. His audience had the sense he wasn't sure of the difference. Now there were jokes circulating about his confusing San José, Costa Rica, with San Juan, Puerto Rico. "It doesn't matter," was the ritual response. "They're both American territory now." And now there was this problem with the pirates of the press trying to infiltrate suites where they were not supposed to be. They were screwing around with everything. Because of one of their reports a whole vast series of military exercises along the Honduran-Nicaraguan border had to be postponed so they wouldn't clash with the president's message. Then there were some brusque words from Colombia's president about U.S. interference in the region that were played up by all the American correspondents, much to the embarrassment of the winged White House. "Pirates," said the security man. "Let's get these pirates out of here."

But for all the fumbling and faux pas, the president went down well in his meetings with the presidents at the Cariari. El Salvador's Alvaro Magaña felt bolstered by his encounter with the smiling Californian; Costa Rica's President Monge was encouraged. A day later at the airport in San Pedro Sula, Honduran President Suazo Cordova pronounced himself satisfied, and even the Guatemalan dictator seemed very pleased. There had been a lot of reports that the born-again general was waging something like a genocidal campaign in the Indian highlands. But he hit it off well with the president. And the president declared he had been given "a bum rap."

The government of Nicaragua found no place on the president's schedule. The trip, it was said, was designed to encourage the proponents of democracy in the region, not Marxist Sandinistas. Democracy, as always, was the goal. That much had come clear in two years of Ronald Reagan's administration. But if the message was now apparent, the medium was still a problem.

VIII.

THE NICARAGUAN-HONDURAN BORDER

Krill's men moved only as quietly as they had to along the sharp edges of the mountains above the government cooperative at Wuambuco. The rows of dark-green bushes up and down the steep hillsides showed the red berries of ripe coffee, and Krill knew the Sandinistas would send somebody to try to pick it. They needed the money too much to leave the coffee on the trees even this close—three hundred yards—to the border. All Krill had to do was wait for word that the pickers were arriving and then deploy his men for the attack.

Krill's commandos talked with contempt, sometimes pity about the enemy they were up against in these engagements. The local people and migrant workers who usually picked the delicate berries now refused to go to the coffee estates near the combat zones, especially those run by the government, so militiamen and students, government employees and members of the Sandinista Front's political apparatus were sent instead. Most had had a little rudimentary military training and about half of them had been handed guns along with their harvest baskets when they went into the groves in the morning. But they did not really know how to fight, and Krill's fighters who killed them and terrorized them and captured them talked about them as the Sandinistas' cannon fodder.

At Wuambuco men and women in thrown-together work clothes, bandanas and baseball hats, several of them obviously townspeople, stumbled and sweated on the rough paths along the hillsides. Some were old and fat and gulped air every few paces. They worked slowly among the bushes trying to identify the ripe berries and remove them without damaging those still growing.

Krill's attack began clumsily. A lookout spotted some of his men and ran shouting down the hillside. "Get down, get down! The contras are coming there!" The workers, even most of those with guns, scattered and scrambled through the bushes. An M-60 went into action, raking back and forth near the harvesters; then Krill's men began to follow them along the peaks, dogging the prey from the high slopes, knowing they would try to make it back to the farmhouse. A heavy-set, middle-aged man reached a jeep and was using the radio to call for help. One of Krill's men raked him with a burst of fire and ran on.

Occasional shooting continued for a couple of hours, but Krill's men were soon rounding up prisoners. Near the bullet-riddled jeep they looked for the man wounded in the initial encounter. They found him in a ditch with a middle-aged woman beside him looking as weak and as bloody as he.

By some accounts the woman had a gun in her hand but was so

afraid that she did not know what to do and had forgotten to drop it as members of the patrol surrounded her and her husband. Another story suggests that the husband's efforts to call for help over the radio singled him out for abuse. But however that may have been, Krill began to work on them as soon as they were captured. They were weak already, they were old and soft for this kind of action. Apparently they were vulnerable to each other's pain and could be made to talk to protect each other. It was not difficult to beat some information out of them. Whether in the long night of marching the woman was raped and just how badly they both suffered in their first interrogations is not a matter of any certainty. Some interviews suggest she was hemorrhaging before she was captured, others that she was left at the mercy of Honduran and contra troops at the border for three days. But by the time Krill got them back to Pino Uno—the man wounded and half-crawling, the woman doubled over in pain, drying blood smeared along the insides of her legs—Krill probably knew he was bringing Suicida a pair of prizes.

Their names were Felipe and María Eugenia Barreda. He was fifty-one years old, she was forty-nine and people called her Mary. They were from Estelí and they had been Sandinista partisans for a long time. They were the kind of people who had made the revolution possible in the first place: middle middle-class; he was a self-made man, a jeweler and onetime member of the Lions Club, a bit of a drinker and gambler and then a committed Christian; she was an activist who first worked with the Sandinistas because her son worked with them and was jailed, then went on to lead groups of mothers on hunger strikes, fighting for human rights and against Somoza. During the war, their home was a headquarters and safe house for Sandinista leaders, including a member of the National Directorate. They stored an arsenal of three hundred guns there. After the war she was an indefatigable member of Estelí's reconstruction junta. "We won the revolution, but I lost my wife," her husband used to say, only half joking. They were active in the party, active in the left wing of the Church, proselytizers of the revolution. "You're an egotist," Mary would chastise guests who complained about the shortages and the bureaucracy of the Sandinistas, "your fellow being doesn't matter to you." Her last months were spent working with the poorest of the poor of Estelí in the neighborhood of shacks called Barrio Omar Torrijos.

The Barredas went to the coffee plantations to make a political example of commitment to the revolution. Mary wrote to the destitute workers of the government tobacco factory in Estelí, in the Barrio

Omar Torrijos, that she was missing Christmas dinner with them in order to do this work because this work, itself, was like a gift for them. "The little that I can pick will be translated, or rather converted into *health,* clothing, housing, roads, schooling, food, etc. And it's for that that I'm going to pick coffee with all the love and enthusiasm of which I'm capable."

Later, a Sandinista volume of interviews and propaganda about the Barredas declared that "if they had been born in Italy, they would have made them saints."

When Suicida had got hold of them he had called them "*los meros meros,*" the essence of the essence.

Suicida was famous but frustrated in his limited world. In the mountains of the Segovias everyone knew his name. And in Tegucigalpa and Danlí he was feared as well as admired. He was the object of pride, envy and anger among the other task force commanders and the general staff in Tegucigalpa. With his reputation, resentments grew around him, and within him. He had been fighting, he said. He had only needed more ammunition to take his objective, he said. And there were those who believed him. Krill's capture of the Barredas could only build Suicida's reputation more and he called his *parientito* Ortiz at Radio 15 to come down and interview them.

Meanwhile, Suicida had handed the Barredas over to El Muerto, the sallow twenty-two-year-old boy with a gaunt face and heavy lids whom he saw as Tegucigalpa's spy. Maybe he thought he would be flaunting his prize this way, or perhaps he simply wanted the dirtiest jobs under his command to be carried out by his most hated subordinate.

Prisoners were chained to trees at Pino Uno. They were left to sleep half naked and sometimes unable to lie down in the rains that fell in the evening and the bitter chill that settled into the mountain forests. What beatings did not do at first, exposure was left to accomplish for a night or two. And the noise of other beatings, screams that could not be identified, worked on the mind as well. Nearby was the graveyard of Pino Uno, with scores of mounds visible.

Not all prisoners were treated harshly. Any man captured, especially if he surrendered his weapon, was likely to be encouraged to join the ranks of the FDN. Some did so thinking they would escape later, and some out of conviction, and some because they thought they were going to be on the winning side. Suicida and Krill and the rest, and everyone above them up to the level of the Directorate, were certain this war would be won by the summer at the latest. After all, that was what the Americans told them.

There was, then, only a vague distinction between prisoners and recruits. But the vagueness of the distinction was its danger.

Several young *milicianos* were caught at Wuambuco with the Barredas and, after interrogation, briefly joined the ranks of the FDN. But when they were taken to an old Masonic lodge in Danlí where refugees were housed, they managed to call the Nicaraguan consul from a telephone nearby. He picked them up and they returned to Managua, where they told vivid horror stories published by the Barredas' Sandinista hagiographers months afterward. If it were not for what happened later, their stories might be discounted. But as it is, given the events of the spring and summer, their observations at Pino Uno have a certain grim credibility.

One of the *milicianos,* for instance, said he was present when "the greens," as the Honduran soldiers were called, turned over three FDN deserters, one of them thirteen, another seventeen and one twenty years old. "They had tried to escape to Nicaragua. They were all torn up, naked, their bodies black and blue all over from the blows, as if from whips. You saw the blows on their chests and their arms. When they were going to be executed the thirteen-year-old kid screamed to El Muerto, 'Boss, I won't do it again. Don't kill me boss.' El Muerto shut him up and kicked him. And he cut his throat there." He used one of the heavy combat knives the FDN troops usually carried. "You felt that the screams were escaping from the wound, from the throat. And the others who were tied up to some stakes then also had their throats cut."

El Muerto did most of his work in a little house set a short distance from the rest of the camp. His room, as described by some of his prisoners, had a military cot, an electric generator, even a coffee maker. He had a little television and a big tape recorder on which he used to listen to "that music from Manhattan Island, modern music from New York" to drown out the screams.

The Barredas were kept apart in the open and interrogated individually. By some accounts El Muerto beat Felipe Barreda with the butt of his pistol, reopening Barreda's wounds. A former member of the Guardia's intelligence unit named Tijerino is said to have come from Tegucigalpa to help in the interrogation, and El Muerto's assistants Juan and Tapir went to work on them while he and Tijerino rested. There were differences in the stories the Barredas told about who they were and what they did. Then El Muerto brought them together and confronted each with the other's "lies," his voice and the beatings and the threats of death growing more savage as the interrogation went on. And to contrast with El Muerto's threats, others would play the part of "good guys." It was a technique the Argentines taught.

Ortiz arrived from Radio 15 four days after the Barredas were captured. With him was Edgar Hernandez, Colonel Lau's official replacement as the new head of FDN intelligence. Suicida took them proudly to where the Barredas were being held. They looked weak, in pain, as they lay bound, filthy and exhausted on the ground.

"Why are they like that?" Ortiz asked Suicida.

"They're *los meros meros,*" said Suicida, smiling. There was that coarseness, that combination of naivete and brutality that made Suicida both appealing and dangerous and for certain things so effective.

Ortiz wanted to talk to the Barredas for the radio and he had brought a television camera to make a propaganda film. These prisoners, it was hoped, could be made defectors. But they were not presentable. The Barredas had pissed on themselves from fear. Ortiz asked La Negra for some clean underwear and clothes for Mary Barreda.

Mary Barreda spoke to Ortiz as someone who might, at last, bring relief. Could she have something, she asked, to help the pain? Ortiz ordered an injection for her. Mary and Felipe Barreda were taken to a stream to bathe, and they washed the blood and dirt from each other, delicately, painfully.

"Excuse the abuses of the war," Ortiz said lamely as he took the woman aside. "We understand you're directors of the Sandinistas. We don't want to commit abuses." He asked Mary Barreda what she did, exactly, and he understood her to say she was the political chief of Estelí. As Ortiz saw things, that made her Tomás Borge's personal representative.

"Look," she said, "really we were fooled into coming to this area. I thought we were going to pick coffee. I got people together to do this." But they were moved from one farm to another, ever closer to the border and combat, and they were getting rifles and training and when she asked about this the *responsables* had said only that "the dogs were near." She was fooled, she said, until she and her husband were in the middle of combat. She was fooled, she repeated. She was fooled.

She was taped for Radio 15 the next day, saying that she was tired, naturally, but not mistreated and that she had a bad conscience for bringing people to pick coffee when really they were taken into combat. But she did not denounce the revolution. She did not turn against it.

It may be that Ortiz told Suicida he did not want the Barredas hurt, and that when he went back to Tegucigalpa he met with a representative of the International Red Cross at the Hotel Maya to try to arrange a prisoner exchange. That is what he claimed later. But there never was an exchange. It may be that Ortiz did not know what had happened to the Barredas when, more than a month after he had seen them, Radio 15 announced they would be saying something about the forthcoming visit of Pope John Paul II to Central America. As late as May, the fate of the Barredas was one of Pino Uno's unspoken secrets.

Ortiz said afterward that they were left in the hands of El Muerto and he was responsible for what happened to them.

But who actually gave the order and why is still not certain.

In the summer of 1983, after El Muerto was a prisoner of the Sandinistas, he first denied that he was responsible, then said that the order came from Suicida, then that it came from Tegucigalpa.

The hagiography of the Barredas maintains that they were killed because they would not betray the revolution.

But one of the FDN officers who looked into the case later said that Suicida had been ordered to turn the Barredas over to the commanders in Tegucigalpa. What could Suicida have thought but that Fiero and Bermúdez wanted to claim these prizes as their own? And Suicida refused. "Screw those sons of bitches, I am going to do what I please" is how the officer described Suicida's attitude. Instead of being taken to Tegucigalpa, Felipe and Mary Barreda were executed, the officer said.

In El Muerto's words, always in the passive voice, "They were eliminated."

"You buried them there?"

"Correct. They made a hole. They lay down. And they were killed there."

TEGUCIGALPA, HONDURAS

"My house is your house," said the station chief, smiling.

The new directors of the Nicaraguan Democratic Force filed in for their first meeting with Shaw, the man who would work with them, guide them and, though he never said it to them, was supposed to control them in the coming months. Everyone wanted to appear businesslike and relaxed in the airy living room. But it was difficult to avoid looking at the big, blond American without a little curiosity. No one was quite comfortable. And Edgar—Edgar was still worried a little about what he was doing there. And finally he said something.

It was this question of goals again. He started laying them out the way he used to do with his students, talking about organizing one's material and knowing about one's objective. And he was wondering, well, about this matter of being in Managua by July.

"Pressure," that was what Shaw talked about. Maybe there was a victory to be had somewhere down the line. But let's not talk about dates. Let's talk about "pressure."

"Pressure?"

Shaw saw his mandate in two parts, as he had discussed it with headquarters at Langley. Part of it was to try to stem the arms flow to El Salvador's rebels. But he did not put much emphasis on that with the FDN directors. The other part of his brief was to "put pressure" on the Sandinistas. He agreed with Ambassador Negroponte that they needed "a threat at their door" to "make them change their ways." From the United States point of view the important thing was to show resolve. From the point of view of Washington's Nicaraguan friends, this could be a means to build a force capable of pushing the Sandinistas out. They should take advantage of this. But they had to understand that while their goals might coincide, they were slightly different.

Chamorro had the unsettling feeling he had signed a contract printed in invisible ink. He was here. He was committed. But before his eyes the terms were changing, the guarantees evaporating. The man in the three-piece suit had talked of victory. This man who worked with him talked of pressure.

Where was the man in the three-piece suit? Chamorro began asking. He was gone, he found out later, assigned to Switzerland, off to another kind of business.

FIGHTING—SPRING 1983

I.

THE HONDURAN-NICARAGUAN BORDER

I drifted in and out of sleep, buffeted against the door of the Toyota jeep, jolted by bursts of apprehension and adrenaline any time we braked quickly. Each return of consciousness flashed an eerie and unexpected scene: a nighthawk swooped up from the dust of the road; the jeep slowed behind huge yellow earth-moving machines building a highway at night in the middle of the wilderness; another nighthawk, heavy-winged and batlike in the headlights; then we were stopped again. We were in a mountain pine forest, and men with Kalashnikov rifles emerged from the shadows to talk in whispers with the man and woman who were taking us to the Nicaraguan border.

James LeMoyne of *Newsweek* and I had arrived in Honduras less than two days before, never believing, really, that the elaborately laid plans for a journey into combat with the Central Intelligence Agency's secret army would work out. But with what seemed extraordinary ease we had made our prearranged contacts, the word had been go and on the afternoon of March 22 in Tegucigalpa we had been turned over to a woman who called herself La Negra and a man who was called Krill. She was the woman, we were told, of Commander Suicida, the man we were supposed to meet and interview as he fought his war. She was in her early thirties, with clear, dark skin and wavy black hair drawn back in a tight ponytail. She was muscular in her T-shirt, Windbreaker and blue jeans. She was aggressive and sensual and she rode with a Browning 9mm pistol beside her in the jeep. Krill did whatever she asked of him, talking little, moving slowly. His eyes were blank and he wore an adjustable baseball cap that sat high on his long, stiff hair.

In the pine forest at night, I could not hear what the men with the Kalashnikovs said to Krill and La Negra, nor could James, and we were not meant to. But of the three armies around us somewhere in the dark—the Honduran and the Nicaraguan and the Agency's—these could only be the Agency's. We drove on again and again I slept only to be awakened by another stop, this time on a long, straight stretch of road in a narrow valley, and there were more boys with Kalashnikovs, more consultations. In the silver-green landscape lit by the moon a ridge of low hills stood a few hundred yards to our right: Nicaragua.

We sat there in the open as La Negra laughed and talked with the boys who carried Kalashnikovs. I huddled against the door of the car, closing my eyes.

At one point we passed on the right a low building near a roped-off side road. It was little more than a house and it looked abandoned. "The customs shed," La Negra said as we drove by. "That's the road to Jalapa." Minutes or hours later—I was not sure through the haze of sleep—we were driving up a road suddenly rougher and deeper even than the one on which we had come. Through a crude fence the road cut sharply downward to a hollow among the steep-sided hills where a farmer's hut showed in our lights and cattle lowed in surprise at the sound of our arrival. La Negra and Krill and others who had suddenly appeared around us began unloading the truck. My body trembled from the chill in the air and from excitement and from fear.

La Negra and Krill pulled U.S.–army specification backpacks and web belts and harnesses from the back of the truck. "You can leave this here," La Negra said when she saw the little knapsack I'd picked up in the capital. She unrolled U.S.–made jungle hammocks for James and for me and we strung them under a shed near a cattle manger. She handed us camouflaged poncho liners to keep us warm. The hammocks and all the other pieces of equipment were brand-new.

For the rest of the night the jeep shuttled supplies. At dawn, as I crawled out of my hammock to the sound of a horn calling cattle in from the hillsides, it was returning with six more men. Its back was full, now, of Kalashnikovs and these new arrivals were uniformed in dark-green work clothes and matching, baseball-style caps. Their boots were army-issue black or jungle boots. Some had hand-embroidered patches on their shoulders: FDN; or crudely stitched triple lightning bolts—homemade versions of the U.S. special forces insignia.

A farmer emerged from the one-room house and stood watching all these preparations passively, his hand resting on a six-shooter in a leather holster. His young son was saddling three battered old horses for us.

The morning was clear and bright and I could not understand how we planned to move across the mountains undetected by Sandinista patrols. Why didn't we move at night, when there was better conceal-ment?

Krill looked at me as if he found this idea vaguely surprising. "The *piricuacos* still fight like guerrillas," he said. "At night there are am-bushes. But in the day, we see them and they see us and our patrols are big, so they run away."

La Negra mounted one horse, James and I climbed on the others and at 8:30 we moved out on the trail. There are few more vulnerable feelings in a war fought with high-powered rifles than the sensation of riding horseback. "Sitting ducks" is the impression I scrawled in my notebook as we came, again, to a sudden stop. A peasant up ahead had discovered a pit viper on the trail and decapitated it with one swift swing of his machete. Our horses and the men with us moved slowly past the still-twisting body of the snake.

TEGUCIGALPA, HONDURAS

When the list of the reporters' names was submitted to "the Phan-tom," the contract agent who kept an eye on the public affairs opera-tion, he was skeptical. But he was careful not to veto anyone. The Americans, in the early spring of 1983, were still trying to feel their way through the transition from Argentine control and the Argentine front, to direct contact with the FDN leadership and field operations on a day-to-day basis. The Argentines had kept a tight leash on everyone in Tegucigalpa and wanted every move approved. The Americans had the idea that the Nicaraguans should take the lead as much as they could. And that was especially true of dealings with the press. Any question of direct Agency contact with American reporters in the field was more of a headache than it was worth. So when fat Frank Arana asked the

Agency man what to do with the journalists clamoring to go to the war zone, the agent had chosen his words very carefully.

"It is not up to me to say whether you can let them in or not," said the Phantom according to one of the people in the FDN office that day. "But I could counsel you a bit about the papers you're dealing with." One of the names on the list was Christopher Dickey, for instance, from *The Washington Post*. And *The Washington Post* was not much in favor of this operation. Neither was *The New York Times*. *Newsweek* had run the big cover story about the Secret War.

Frank and Edgar figured that it was so much the better if they could get something good reported in those papers. The Agency's man knew that, of course. And everyone seemed to agree that some coverage was necessary. It was time to make it clear that this was not a war that would stop. This was not a Bay of Pigs that would fold up and be over after a single battle. By publicizing it, showing how strong the rebel forces were and how deeply they operated inside Nicaragua, the Congress and the American people might be pulled along behind them. The point must be made again and again that this was a real revolution against Communist oppression, and you could not just do that with Miami press conferences. The war needed credibility.

It was also time to put faces on the fighters. Everyone in Tegucigalpa read and talked about other guerrilla groups and tried to learn from the Communists. It was important, it seemed, to have some heroes and some martyrs. And no one would know about your heroes and martyrs if you did not allow the press to meet them. The Salvadoran guerrillas had taken all sorts of reporters into the mountains with them, and the Salvadoran guerrillas had been made to look like heroes. Castro himself had gotten his greatest boost in the Sierra Maestra when *The New York Times* wrote glowing profiles of his rebel band. Taking reporters to the front with the FDN would be another good little bit of symmetry.

When Edgar talked to reporters who might go in with the FDN troops he talked about the need for new heroes. Pastora was grown overcautious, he said, like a bullfighter who still loves to talk about blood and sand but is afraid to go into the ring. Pastora had gotten soft, was the way Edgar had put it to Dickey. But there was this new man, Suicida. Everyone was talking about him. He was a real peasant, and a natural leader. He was the man who could take the place of Pastora in the hearts and minds of the Nicaraguan people.

Actually, Edgar did not know very much about Suicida.

II.

THE HONDURAN-NICARAGUAN BORDER

In a shadowed gully near a stream, a peasant house served the mountains around it as a general store. Its inventory was soft drinks and cigarettes and a few small plastic sacks of fried banana chips, all of it hauled there on mules. James treated the squad to as many Coca-Colas as there were, but El Pollo, a young boy no more than fifteen with a festering shrapnel wound in his head, was not much interested. James peeled back the boy's bandage to look at the wound. With the gauze came flesh and hair and scab and dirt. James spread some Neosporine over it, and El Pollo looked at him with less thanks than humiliation. This was unwanted care, unmasculine concern.

"Take this," La Negra said, holding out an Israeli Uzi submachine gun. "No," I said, "it's against the rules." That sounded foolish here in this gully on the edge of a secret war.

What did she think the possibility was of an ambush on these narrow trails? There was always a possibility, she said, but we are always ready. "I've been ambushed a lot," she said. "I think probably they'd like to kill me because I'd be difficult to replace." She looked at my expression and laughed. "If there is an ambush we'll turn back."

Krill and La Negra rode through several stretches on the same horse. It would soon be the planting season and the farmers from whom horses were normally borrowed wanted them back, she said. There was seed to be bought and carried, so there was less transportation available for what they called "the logistics." Where the trail narrowed in low-lying land, deep ruts and holes had been worn in the mud by other horses. Now the mud had dried hard and the footing was treacherous. Krill would sit behind La Negra, half on the saddle pad and half on the rump of the horse. He clung to her, but often let his body shift and slip loosely from side to side, always seeming on the verge of falling off.

Above our heads a large jaybird peered down from a branch and I could see Krill's curls flop back as he stared up at it, studying. He slipped off the back of the horse, pulled his Browning from the belt of his blue jeans and squeezed off a shot. The explosion of the bullet echoed through the forest. The bird flew away unharmed.

Even though I had seen what was coming I was startled. The noise could have been heard for miles.

"Those birds tell people where you are." He grinned and jumped back onto the horse's rump.

Three hours after we set out from the little farm where we had spent the night La Negra pointed out a break in the foliage about two feet wide on each side of the trail. The border, she said. An hour later we descended to a rough dirt road that wound along the mountainside above a little valley. In it, in the distance, Krill pointed to two dark stains on the pale green fields of the valley beneath us. They were structures of some sort that looked deserted and dark in the distance even under the hard light of noon. Krill said they were the Sandinistas' command posts at Zacateras and La Pampa that had been captured and burned in the fighting in the previous six months. All this territory we saw, La Negra said, was under the control of "our" forces.

A peasant family watched passively as we approached their house on a small promontory beside the road and drew up our horses. Above us was a hill that dominated all the surrounding terrain and La Negra led us on foot to its top. Reclining along the path, cleaning their rifles in the shadows of the young trees, eating beans and tortillas, talking with each other and studying us as we passed were a couple of dozen uniformed men.

A few steps along the ridge and I turned slowly to take in the scene around me. A few steps more and I turned again. The hills of Nueva Segovia were there stretching miles away below us, a palette of greens and browns, forests and fields animated by the shadows of the slow-moving clouds that drifted above them. At eye level a bird of prey, a kite, with a white head and black body and long swallow-like tail, soared along a current of air moving up the mountainside. We were all in the middle of a gorgeous wilderness. And James and I were in the middle of a story that our colleagues had touched only on its edges.

We interrogated the soldiers, we inventoried their weapons: two M-60 machine guns, a 60mm mortar, two M-79 grenade launchers, eight disposable light antitank weapons, one RPG-7. The older soldiers and the youngest ones carried battered Kalashnikovs. The better troops were armed with FALs.

There were basic questions still to be answered in those days about who the contras were, the involvement of ex-*guardias,* the extent to which they had popular support, what kind of arms and training they were getting, and there on the hilltop James and I came back again and again to those questions. It soon was obvious that, as we had expected, there were certain things they were not supposed to tell us.

But where did they get all these guns? None of the men were sure. They were given them by La Negra, or they captured them in battle. Krill, where do these guns come from? "Recuperated from the enemy," he said. What kind of machine gun is that, an M-60? "Recuperated," he said. What kind of bazooka is . . . "Recuperated," he said.

Some said they were ex-*guardias*; some, we discovered later, lied when they said they weren't. But most appeared to have been small landowners whose property had been taken from them by the Sandinistas or were told it would be or just believed that it would be. There were evangelicals who believed they could not worship under the Sandinista government. There were several sons with their fathers.

La Negra ordered the troops to assemble on the hilltop. Sixty of them stood before us in four neat rows and she addressed them with the authority of a commander, attempting to inspire them but also coaching them. She surveyed their ranks like a sergeant.

"You are ninety-nine percent peasants," La Negra coached them. "A lot depends on this visit," she warned her men. She was talking about us. "Be sure you are careful, but tell the truth one hundred percent," she told the patrol. Take care of these reporters, she said, "we don't want any martyred journalists."

The meeting broke up and La Negra watched her men disperse.

"It won't be much longer," she said. "Not much longer until we take Jalapa." Her eyes scanned the mountains below us. "Then we are going to declare a liberated zone that the real nonaligned countries can recognize, and aid will start coming in to us. . . ." She went down the hill to take care of some business.

I looked around for the face of a man who looked as though he liked to talk and hit on a commando who called himself Cascabel. Rattlesnake. He had a few days' growth of beard and a disturbing fervor in his eyes as he spoke about the *piricuacos,* beggar dogs, the Sandinistas. He was twenty-eight years old, he said, and he came from Estelí.

"I never got on with the *piris,*" he said. "It was enough to watch them to know that I didn't like them. I watched and I was convinced that really they were Communists. Then they told me that I would have to go into the army and when I said no they wanted to put me in jail. So I went out in '81 looking for connections when this thing was just beginning. That was in the time of the September 15 Legion. We had heard of Suicida and we've been with him ever since then."

What is so special about him?

"He has a good record with our soldiers, the way he operates, and, well, he's just good."

You have camps in Nicaragua? How do you get supplies?

"We manage inside Nicaragua and they send us what we need."

Do you take prisoners?

"We get information from them and then we pass it along to the *comandante*."

Then what happens?

"You have to eliminate them." An uncomfortable moment. "Only those that are legitimate Sandinistas have to be eliminated," he said quickly. "The others are just indoctrinated. They don't know what they're doing. We let them go.

"They're afraid when they fight," he said, nodding his head slightly in affirmation of his own statement. "We're moving ahead triumphantly. Why, now we have to go to the edges of the villages to ambush them. Because now in the mountains it's very difficult to find them."

I nodded and scribbled.

"In other words," said Cascabel. "They don't come looking for us. We have to go looking for them."

JALAPA, NICARAGUA

At the time that James and I were making our way into the mountains above her valley, Lisa Fitzgerald had lived in Jalapa for a year and a month. She went down to Managua in March 1983 to pick up her friend the directress of novices visiting from the United States, and as they traveled back up the long, narrow highway through Estelí toward Ocotal and the turnoff for Jalapa, Lisa Fitzgerald could say, now, that she was going home. But she dreaded those last twenty miles of dirt road. The very last stretch ran flat and straight through the floor of the valley flanked by tobacco fields and drying barns. "You're really alone, even if you're with other people in a jeep or something; really exposed." There had been several ambushes. It was, she said, "a real adventure to travel between Ocotal and Jalapa."

In September, a veterinarian and an accountant from the Agrarian Reform Ministry were captured on that stretch and their throats were cut. A second vehicle was ambushed minutes later and five farm workers were wounded. The farm workers were shown the two corpses and told they were a message. In October a couple of store owners were murdered by contras in the village just south of Jalapa on the Ocotal road. The same group accosted a tractor driver and for some reason demanded he turn over his machine. When he refused, they cut off his hand. Sometimes busses were stopped and all the men on them marched away. There was one case, Lisa remembered, when a couple of young teachers she knew were riding back from a workshop in Estelí. On the road from Ocotal to Jalapa, the contras stopped the bus and took off all the men. They divided them into three groups and marched them away in different directions so that nobody from one group would know what happened to those in the other groups.

"One was an English teacher. They gave him a gun, a uniform and boots. He was with them a couple of days and then the first opportunity he had he threw down the gun, took the uniform off, took the boots off, all of which are immediately recognizable in this area as contra clothes, and ran all the way with his bare feet, in his boxer shorts, to Ocotal. He's from Estelí. He's twenty years old. His mother has never let him out of Estelí since." Lisa smiled and shook her head. "And Jalapa is still without an English teacher."

Lisa herself had come close to being killed on that road. Traveling at dawn with one of the priests to a meeting in Estelí, they had caught a ride with some senior Sandinista officials in a two-jeep caravan: official cars and all the officials in them were armed with AKs and pistols. "One way that people defend themselves on the road is to go like speedballs, like sixty-five miles an hour over this stupid little road—how they make the bridges I don't know—but they do it on the assumption that you avoid an ambush if you're going fast." There were other cars behind them. Occasionally, through the billowing dust thrown up by their own caravan, they could make out another jeep and a truck loaded down with coffee beans trailing in their wake.

It was only moments after their little group arrived safely in Ocotal that they heard the explosions in the distance and, minutes later, ambulances coming through. The truck and the jeep behind them had been ambushed; everyone in them killed.

A ride on the road to Jalapa became a game of Russian roulette or, as someone joked, Reagan roulette. Busses were harder and harder to come by. And when Lisa and the directress of novices arrived in Ocotal on March 22, with fighting reported nearby, they thought they might have to stay there the night and take the early-morning bus. At last, after much cajoling, a lone driver decided to make the afternoon run. Lisa spent most of the trip wondering why she had tried so hard to get back that day, why she dared take this road at all, and on the final stretch leading into Jalapa her mouth was as dry as the tobacco in the barns. But they made it, finally, without incident.

It was the early-morning bus that got hit.

It was a patrol led by Cancer that did it.

III.

NUEVA SEGOVIA PROVINCE, NICARAGUA

All through the night we listened to La Negra's laugh. She was sitting up with her boys telling jokes and war stories. The stars, when the bright moon descended, were spread like sugar across the sky. In the dark hours of the morning the dew came down like rain. And always there was the laughter.

The movement in the camp began before light. The commandos were rolling up their belongings, throwing their gunstraps over their shoulders, pissing in the bushes, assembling at the base of the little hill near a meat-drying rack and a little shed where a sign read "*prohibido a particulares,*" which translates roughly as "employees only."

From the shed La Negra took new harnesses and web belts for James and me. We already carried the U.S. army packs she had issued us and the baseball caps of the contras. Cascabel helped another commando hoist a brand-new military field radio onto his back. Krill no longer wore blue jeans and a T-shirt but an American green-and-brown camouflage "tiger suit."

La Negra was at the door of the supply shed handing out bits and pieces of equipment. She had a wad of money so fat that her hand could not span it and she gave it to Krill. He folded it into his pocket and surveyed the assembled commandos. Walking down the line he checked their equipment. Cascabel was fumbling with the antenna of the field radio. Krill looked at it and folded it neatly.

Krill was showing authority we hadn't seen before. Then La Negra told us she was leaving us here. This was Krill's patrol. She would pick us up in a week when we got out, she said. But in the company of Krill, this killer of jaybirds, there seemed no assurance that we would get out.

At 6:30 we were on the march through the dew-damp grasses, moving among the last, skeletal trees of what had once been cloud forest, then along the floor of the valley, wading through a fast-running creek. A couple of the commandos stripped off their packs and dove beneath the water. The mountain that rose above us was covered with dense forest that could have provided perfect cover for an attack, but they splashed and shouted, playing in the water, bathing on the march, apparently secure in their control of the area, or its isolation.

Ten minutes climbing that first mountain with a full pack and my knees were burning, my lungs gasping. Each step was a work of concentration and will and I watched, fascinated, to see how effortlessly these peasant soldiers moved over the terrain. Some stretches of the narrow trail were so steep that the boots of the man in front of me, usually Krill's, were at the level of my eyes. Shallow steps, one after another. I copied them, studied them, contemplated them. Short and measured steps, never misplaced, a gait different from the bounding stride of North Americans who hike for recreation or climb only in the stairwells of their office buildings. The Nicaraguan takes small steps that continue on and on; the American takes great ones that exhaust him. At least, that is what I had done. By the time we reached the top of the mountain, Krill had ordered a couple of the commandos to carry James's pack and mine. Even as we shed our burdens and they doubled theirs, they moved more easily and efficiently than we did.

The abandoned farm on this mountain had an orange grove, and the fruit was heavy and ripe on the branches. The commandos went to work harvesting for their packs with festive abandon. Among our patrol were a couple of girls, carrying their own Kalashnikovs, dressed in the same dark-green work clothes of the FDN. One of them, Aurora, was perhaps eighteen years old, quiet and uncomplaining, as unheeding of the rigors of the march as the men. She picked oranges for Krill, who cut them open with his heavy black-bladed survival knife and handed them to James and me. The juice poured down my throat and chin and hands and I lay back on an old board along the ground to rest.

Aurora turned on me suddenly and picked up a heavy stick. She thrust it like a dagger into the dirt inches from my head. *"Alacrán,"* she said as I jumped to my feet. I couldn't remember what it meant. Krill grinned and pointed with his knife. A scorpion the size of a field mouse and covered with a crowd of smaller scorpions writhed under the point of the stick.

By midmorning the land opened up before us. The mountains were bare of forest. Our column continued to travel single-file along the narrow cattle-paths that laced the mountainsides. There were basically three squads in our patrol, each with about twenty men. When the middle squad topped a rise, the lead unit could be seen moving up the side of the next mountain or hill in the range. There was no cover from attack.

Any little stand of trees or bushes was like an oasis of shade and the commandos would bunch up there as they could. Krill shouted at them, ordering them to spread out. When they were allowed to stop in some small glen that neither cattle nor men had defoliated the men dropped their packs, drank from their canteens. In the barely cool shade they would, many of them, take out worn Bibles to read, word by word, to themselves. They would lie back among the weeds and sleep. Some sucked on bits of sugar cane hacked from a little deserted grove. Some pulled oil-covered toothbrushes from their breast pockets to clean their rifles.

Krill pulled a bottle of pills from his pack. Vitamins, he said, to give him energy. He still wore his cap awkwardly perched on his thick hair. Yet he was not the same stoned street kid of Tegucigalpa or the fool who had shot at the jay on the trail to the first camp. His FAL automatic rifle was always at hand. He was alert, a small predator ready to attack or be attacked.

I asked him what we were going to do if we were ambushed.

Well, he said, what we did not want to do was fall back. What he would do, and what his men would do, would be to hit the ground and then, when the enemy fired, rise up and fire back at the sound, moving into the attackers and through them. They expect you to fall back, and there is usually a trap behind you, he said, drawing in the dirt to show the S-pattern of a standard ambush. So the only way out is to rise and fire and move forward into the sound of the attackers.

Krill looked at James and at me seriously. It was obvious that in such a case we would be helpless. "We say we came from the earth and we'll go back to the earth." Krill paused. Ashes to ashes, dust to dust. "But the earth saves you too." He smiled. Our best bet would be to hit the dirt and stay there.

"New Dawn," said the cover of the little notebook. It was left over from the national literacy campaign of three years before when thousands of schoolchildren were mobilized by the Sandinista government to go out into the countryside and teach the people of places like Nueva Segovia to read. It was supposed to be an expression of the hope of the moment, the new dawn that the revolution was to bring to the people of Nicaragua. Probably the young radio operator who wrote down laborious letter after letter the codes for communication with the base camp did not see any great irony in the fact that he used a notebook left over from the old literacy campaign, the new dawn. I never asked him about it. "Sierra 1, this is Sierra 5, do you read me?" There was nothing to report.

We had seen houses built crudely of rough boards or logs, but there was no one in them. No cattle wandered the cowpaths, no pigs wallowed in the mud of the sties, no cur dogs barked warnings at this group of strange men. The *piricuacos* had ordered everyone out of the area, the commandos said, and those who had refused to leave their land were considered contras. One house near us had been bombed, the commandos said.

Not until midday did we reach a small home that was still inhabited, but it was without men. Some of the commandos from the lead squad were already butchering a pig and smoke billowed from a room at the back of the house where two women tended a pot full of meat, preparing to feed our patrol. Blood slicked the long grass that sloped to a stream below the house. James wandered off to fill his water bottle and mine. At the door of the kitchen two barefoot young girls just on the verge of adolescence, their faces streaked with the dirt of play and the stove, flirted shyly with some of the young commandos.

"Where are we?" I asked one of the little girls. She looked at me as if my question were incomprehensible. I wanted to be as sure as possible that we were where we were told we were, doing what we were told we were doing, and children often forget what they are told to say, and not say. "Where are we? What country?" The little girl looked at me vacantly. Maybe she didn't know. One of the women looked out the door. "Are we in Nicaragua?" I asked. The woman said yes. The little girl smiled, black edges of decay showing on her teeth.

We ate the pork beneath a tree as the commandos told stories that they said were their own true stories. There was something of the theater about their chronicles, like tales told around a campfire.

El Campesino was thirty-two years old, he said, and had been the driver of a Toyota jitney in Chontales. He had joined the ranks of the FDN as a combatant only a month before. He claimed to have been sent to Cuba for Sandinista indoctrination and to have come back "with a lot of haughtiness."

"I didn't believe in anything, not even in God. 'I shit on God,' I said." But then somehow he came to his senses and for a year before he joined the ranks of the FDN combatants he had been collaborating as an informer, he said. He said this with little flair for storytelling and left me with little conviction that it was true. He knew little about Cuba and seemed uncertain of where he had been when he was there.

Krill wanted to make the point that La Negra had told everyone to remember: most of these troops were peasants. "Of all the personnel that you are going to see, there are only about ten ex-military men among them," he said.

But Krill was talking more and more and the phrases that sounded as though they were learned by rote began to break down. There was less talk about recuperated arms, less special pleading, more pride evident in having been a member of the Guardia Nacional and in the days after the fall of Nicaragua that he had spent living and killing in the mountains before this new army was formed. He talked about his escape with Suicida from San Juan del Sur, about the days spent at sea without food or water. He talked about the Rattlesnakes and their reputation in the Guardia. "The way Somoza figured, we were the most capable of all." He talked about the days when he and Suicida had nothing, and about when Tomás Borge had sworn to capture him. And in the present, with some coaxing, he talked about how he handled his own prisoners, when he took them: it was difficult to shoot someone who had been captured and who had no defense, he said, always difficult. "But some of them don't deserve to live," he said.

I lay on the dirt, feeling the cool grit against my back, drinking water that tasted of iodine pills and smelled like a swimming pool, watching Krill as he surveyed the scene around him. His men were spread out on the hillsides eating their meals, and the women and girls emerged from the house. "I took it hard, going into exile," he said. "You suffer when you're a soldier. I want to come back here some day in peace, have a farm. I want to work on making some children."

He was looking at the little girls as they talked to some of his men. They were pretty, I said. He looked at me. "Do you want one of them?" he asked, and grinned. He was being hospitable and I couldn't tell if he might be serious. No, I said.

Krill wandered off toward the house with a hand full of money: eight hundred *córdobas*, he wanted us to know, to pay for the pig.

"Blood," said Krill, pointing to a splatter of dark red and brown glistening on the mulch of the trail. "Maybe vomited blood."

We had emerged from a forest onto a thinly wooded hillside near a settlement called El Mapa. There had been an engagement here eight days before and Krill guessed that the blood came from a wounded Sandinista soldier. But one of the men from a small patrol that had waited to meet us here said no, the blood was from an injured bull that had charged blindly along the trail a short time before.

The march, by its discipline and rhythm, had begun to seem routine. And the routine had begun to lull the fear. But this sign of a wounded soldier or a wounded beast—the blood itself—made danger tangible again.

On a mountaintop a mile away I spotted soldiers moving along a ridge. "They're ours," said Krill. On another mountain at least as far away, more men. "Ours." But somewhere in the distance beyond the line of sight there was an explosion. A few seconds later another and another, rumbling along the hillsides like a wave over rocks. That would be Coral with his supply train headed in by a separate route, the commandos said. Must have made contact, they said. But here, they assured us, we were safe.

We stopped at last to sleep on top of a mountain beneath a lone, lightning-blasted tree. Some of the men pulled wild yucca roots from the ground, peeling them and gnawing them as they moved out to a ragged, distant perimeter. James and I made our bed of poncho liners and settled down to eat peaches and Vienna sausages from the Tegucigalpa supermarket.

In the valley below us smoke poured from the cooking fire in a little farmhouse and a man could be seen working among his handful of cattle, apparently oblivious to this force of men above his home. Almost eighty heavily armed men were bedding down here. If Sandinistas appeared there would be a fight, and this man's farm would be, as likely as not, in the middle of it. And he has no idea, I thought, that we are here. What could he do if he did know? Would he find a way to inform the Sandinistas?

Krill walked out along the perimeter in the dusk and, just before all daylight was lost, satisfied of our safety, he returned to the rugged bed Aurora had made for them both a few feet away from our own. We were exposed but protected. Lying on the mountaintop, dressed and ready to run if a Sandinista patrol should slip through the perimeter, James and I talked until we fell asleep, about our wives, our fathers, our mothers, loves remembered, losses mourned.

In the morning, the farmer from the valley brought us coffee.

IV.

JALAPA, NICARAGUA

As James and I had begun our second day with the contras, word spread quickly in Jalapa of a major battle going on along the road to the south. Trucks full of troops went barreling through the town early in the morning, and hours later they had not come back. Word on the street said the contras had hit the morning bus from Ocotal.

When Lisa Fitzgerald heard the news, she felt the blood drain from her face. Her first thought was how lucky she had been to make it back to Jalapa the night before, and then she realized how frightened she was.

It seemed that a group of contras had stopped the bus near the town of San Nicolás and taken everyone off, but one man had escaped. He was able to flag down a car and get a ride back to a command post, which sent out a contingent of soldiers and radioed to Jalapa to send a force from the other direction. They caught the contras in a vise.

Throughout the morning the sounds of fighting echoed among the hills in the distance. There was no way to know if the town might be cut off again for days or become the object of another offensive like the one in December. No one knew how big the contra unit was, or whether it had reenforcements nearby.

Lisa Fitzgerald stepped out of the street to let one of the *compañeros'* pickup trucks rattle past her, headed back toward its headquarters north of town. Something was piled high in the back. From a distance it might have been a ton of rags and old clothes except for the bits of flesh and the faces that showed among the filthy blood-wet cloth. Boys and men—contras—were piled one on top of another. Gore dripped in a thin trickle from the rear edge of the truck bed. Dead eyes stared toward the sky, toward the street, toward Lisa Fitzgerald. There were, altogether, more than a dozen corpses "stacked, literally stacked, like a mountain of bodies in the back of this pickup truck," she remembered.

Later, when she talked about what she saw in Jalapa and what affected her, she would remember this day and one other in the hospital where corpses were piled like cordwood in the halls, as the moments that "did it to me."

"The sheer number. . . ." She paused. "I felt it more at these times, more than like seeing a dead body, a victim with eyes gouged out or something, although some of the doctors in the hospital in Jalapa say they've never seen some of the stuff that they've encountered as far as bodies being mutilated, and they've seen everything. But it didn't do that to me except the times that I've seen bodies just stacked.''

The battle ended in the afternoon. With what seemed great good luck, the passengers on the bus had escaped uninjured. The Sandinista militia, it was reported, lost only four killed and one wounded. Seventeen contras from Cancer's patrol were killed.

V.

Nueva Segovia Province, Nicaragua

The radio was set up on a narrow stretch of trail protected by heavy foliage. The literacy notebook came out, the code sheets were studied, the antenna strung and the dials adjusted on the Patrolfine Model SC-130. Another message was already on the frequency.

"Sierra 7," the voice said through the static crackle. "Sierra 7." The message was hard to make out. The caller was another commander named Cancer, someone said, and it was an emergency. He talked about being in the same hacienda as always, waiting for a vehicle. He had some sick people because he had had "a crash." The radio operator explained the transparent code. Cancer's crash was an engagement with enemy forces on the Ocotal–Jalapa road. He had taken some casualties.

Krill was excited and intense as he listened to the message. James and I did not know then of any special link between him and Cancer, but something clearly was upsetting him. He looked at us as if we were keeping him from this fight miles away. He wanted to go there and he shouted over the radio with the home base trying to decide if he would head toward the fighting anyway. Maps were consulted and distances calculated. No. His orders were to link up with Suicida the next day. Suicida was moving in from the west. Krill had to keep on course with the reporters. Cancer would have to fend for himself or find another unit to help him. For a few moments Krill was silent. Then his face relaxed. Someone had brought him a bag of cookies. He offered them to us.

We moved on through country that was no longer empty. Itinerant merchants made their way along the logging trails carrying cookies and candies, elixirs and pills in bags on the backs of mules. We emerged from forests haunted by the cries of howler monkeys to find farms where people still lived and worked. But while it was inhabited country, it was also contested country, and it, too, was emptying slowly.

In the first minutes after dawn the man who brought us coffee had been pleading his case to Krill. He wanted to be taken out to exile in Honduras, he said, because the Sandinistas suspected him of collaborating and had brought charges of some sort against him three days before. He seemed uncertain and befuddled about his situation. He wanted to get out, he said, but he had these cattle, he said, and he did not want to leave them behind. Krill said another patrol, coming from somewhere else, would help him.

At another house on a small, barren hill an entire family watched our approach: the man in torn trousers, boots, his shirt misbuttoned, the woman in a dirty shift, a baby playing at her feet. Other children peered from the door of the house or lay in hammocks made of corn sacks. A mangled dog showed only a dull curiosity. We were welcomed passively, without fear or pleasure, it seemed.

This family, too, wanted to be taken to Honduras. The woman said her husband's father and two uncles were prisoners in Ocotal. They had been there almost five months, and every passing patrol of the Sandinistas seemed to bring new trouble to the family now. "When the *compas* come and ask for food and we don't give it, they say we're saving it for the contra," said the woman, brushing a limp strand of hair off her face.

Tell me about the Sandinistas, I said when Krill and the others were not listening.

"Some are angry, some are happy, but some, especially the leaders . . ." She shook her head. "Now they are worse than before, because at the beginning they were friendly people." When did they change? "About a year ago." That was about the time the bridges were blown up near Ocotal and Chinandega, I said.

The husband was listening now. "It must be because of the fighting," he said.

"They accuse you of things," the woman said. "They said I went to Honduras and came back. Now, if you don't have a position with them in the militias or the CDS [Sandinista Defense Committee] you are nothing."

So, you are on the side of the contras?

She answered, "One has to be. All of my family is in Honduras and his father is in jail." She glanced at my face, over my shoulder, and away. "If they come tomorrow and know you've been here they'll tie us up and—"

Krill was beside us. He had five hundred *córdobas* in his hand. "Feed your people in jail," he said.

The patrol fanned out to enter a new wall of forest. Along its dark trails each man walked with his gun at the ready, and if he did not, if he seemed to slouch, Krill spoke sharply to him, warning him to stay alert. A soldier who fell out to the side of the trail to relieve himself got a sharp reprimand. Only James and I were indulged in our constant, stumbling weariness. When we found a road, we no longer walked it, but moved into the foliage beside it.

The honey-eyed, sweet and slow-witted man called Jesús, who had made it his job to carry my pack as well as his, moved cautiously a few strides in front of me. "Sometimes," he said, "the *piris* just grow up out of the ground." We were in the land of the enemy, but the enemy was a ghost. There were signs of him. You imagined him in front of you, behind you, watching and waiting for you.

At a twist in the trail one of the commandos found a piece of paper. "Ambush," it said. But the paper looked battered and the message faded, as if it had been through a rain. The danger it warned of might have passed; probably had passed. Ghosts.

The trail pushed steadily up the mountain and the footing on the steeper grades gave way again and again beneath my strides. Each boot seemed weighted. My feet ached and my knees and thighs had begun to cramp from the constant climbing. One foot after the other I watched the stride of Jesús and of Krill. Short and economical. One foot after the other.

As we emerged atop the ridge Krill saw something along an embankment that made him freeze. I don't know what it was—a footprint, perhaps, a broken opening in the brush where there should not have been one—but he moved toward it listening and watching and ready for sudden movement. He boosted himself up into the bushes, then reappeared and called to us showing us a clearing, almost a nest in the middle of a thicket. It looked like a place where deer might bed down except for a couple of torn plastic wrappers from the cheap crackers sold by the mule merchants.

They were waiting for us here, Krill said. Maybe yesterday, maybe the day before. They have people who spend weeks out in the field waiting in ambush for us.

The troops spread out along the road below us to rest. Coyote, bearded and filthy with his hat on backward and bandoliers for his M-60 machine gun crisscrossing his chest, leaned on the barrel of his weapon like a staff. León and one of his sons dropped off their packs nearby. Platoon leaders Eco and Josué took detachments farther down the road looking for food and provisions. Krill sat out in the open near a crude barbed wire fence, looking past it at the view that stretched away toward Jalapa and Ocotal.

A farmer sold us a steer and came up the hill to talk. He was forty-six years old, he said, but he looked like a tough sixty. His skin was leather dark and covered with gray stubble. His hands were as tough as rope and he seemed unconcerned about blood seeping from a slash across several fingers made while butchering the steer.

About a hundred Sandinistas had passed this same place yesterday on the way from Murra to El Doradito, the farmer said. The day before he had been there and seen more soldiers than civilians. Twenty-five IFAs, the East German troop trucks, had arrived, full of men, and seven others had been there the day before that.

He wanted us to know he hated the Sandinistas and he wanted us to know why.

The Sandinistas, he said, "ride roughshod over us" and "they pay me the price for my cattle they want to and say I can't say anything about it. And another thing that I don't like is that they sell us things with rationing. You have to walk twenty kilometers to some official's house to buy two pounds of sugar. Last year all they would sell us was two pounds for six people for eight days. It's only thanks to my having some poultry that I'm here telling you this.

"When we complain, they say we just have to put up with it, that it's a problem of foreign exchange, and this and that and I don't know what. I tell you, we're living in the middle of calamities.

"During the Sandinista revolution I was working with the priests in Jícaro. They're Americans." The farmer looked at James and at me. "Are you Americans?"

Well, we said, we're. . . . This question had come up before. We did not want to advertise the fact that we were American journalists traveling with this group lest the Sandinistas get wind of our presence and make a special effort to come after us.

Krill said we were from a part of Nicaragua known for its fair-haired inhabitants.

The farmer looked at us. He had already heard our non-Nicaraguan accents.

Well, he said, the Sandinistas had thrown him in prison for twenty-three days in March the year before and twenty-four days in November. "And when I was in jail, the gringo priests never showed up," he said. "And I saw that they had fooled me in those times. I'll tell you something. I believe in God, but those men, I don't believe in them."

The Sandinistas had taken many prisoners from the area, he said. There had been two hundred families around here before, but now only five were left.

"I'm going to stay here." He closed his mouth tightly for a moment, looking for the way to say this to strangers. "And another reason I'm going to stay here is because this is the land where I was born, and fucking Fidel Castro himself is not going to get me out of here.

"We're using technique," he said, "to defend ourselves. They come talk to us and we tell them a great quantity of armed men have gone by and they get all excited and take off."

It was technique that could work—or fail—with either camp, I thought. But this old man did not seem to be a natural liar. He seemed not to give a damn, in fact, what anybody thought of him as long as they didn't mess with him.

Was it always so bad here under the Sandinistas? I wanted to know.

"No, no," he said flatly as Krill and Josué listened. "A year and a half and everything was all right, no big problems. It was when the contras began that things started to go bad with us. It was about a year or a year and a half ago that we started to get massacred."

The old farmer turned his hard eyes from us to Krill and the other commandos.

"I saw," he said, "seven people with their throats cut in La Fragua and they say that was done by the contra. They were *milicianos* that were killed, maybe, but it was bad. I saw them with my own eyes, and I can tell you this is ugly work."

"The *piris* do these things and blame them on us," said Krill.

"People say they were the contras that did it," said the farmer. "A whole pile of country people were saying that."

Krill was about to say something but didn't. Josué listened closely, his grin easy and enigmatic.

"We're with you," said the farmer. "But when we see something like that we say it's better to stay away, because that sows terror."

"It wasn't us," said Krill.

"They were dressed in olive green like this," said the farmer, gesturing with his head toward Coyote.

"Look, you," the farmer said suddenly to Krill, "we're secret democrats now. We've got to be. But if we are going to win this fight we have to be real democrats. With that kind of screw-up we can wind up with nothing, we can lose everything. And another thing, you have to respect the country people."

Where he got his ideas of democracy, I don't know. The word seemed to be religious for him. It meant, I think, that nobody messed with him; perhaps nothing more, nothing less.

We made camp and slaughtered the steer at an empty house nearby. Long strips of beef garlanded the fence line. The commandos cooked over an open fire.

We ate with Krill and with Eco, who said he was an electrician from Chinandega who had taken up arms only six months before. He was made a field officer, he said, "because of what I showed in the combat zone and my discipline." And maybe he had known Krill before in their home town.

In one corner of the yard a commando was propped up under a tree looking at a little religious pamphlet he had found tossed in a corner of the deserted house. "The Great Questions in Life." The kites were back in the distance, circling on a thermal, their black-and-white bodies floating incandescent above the landscape in the afternoon sun.

Krill chewed on a chunk of half-burned beef with canine enthusiasm.

"Will you be able to go back home soon? When the war's over?" I asked.

He shrugged as his teeth sank deep into the meat.

"How long do you think the war is going to go on?"

"That depends on the aid that's provided us in the future," said Krill. "If the civilian population wants to help us and we want to give them arms but don't have them, then that is trouble."

"Yeah, well, where is it exactly that the arms come from? They're from the United States, aren't they?"

He looked at me from under the brim of his cap. "We are not informed what country is helping us. Those of us down at the lowest levels are not informed." He was getting tired of the questions.

"What do you think happened with the people who were killed at La Fragua?"

Krill didn't know. Maybe it was some other group. There were problems with bandits, common criminals, who called themselves the

FDN and did things for which his men were blamed, even though it wasn't true. "Do you want some more meat?" he said, and wandered off to get some.

Eco sucked on a string of gristle stuck in his teeth.

What do you do with prisoners, Eco? Some of the men say that some of the tough ones get killed, but most of them get taken back to the base camps. I guess that's not always easy to do, is it?

"The ones who beg and say that they were only in it because they were obliged to be in it, we let them go," said Eco. "And then when they go back to the other side they say that they hid or that they were captured but escaped."

And the ones who don't beg, who say they fight because they believe in what they're doing?

Eco looked into the middle distance without hearing me. He had things to attend to.

One of Curo's sons, Paladino, had taken a special interest in James and in me. He was a bright kid in his early twenties and he wanted to find out from us if some of the things he had heard were true. He waited until we were bedded down; then late into the night he sat beside us under a little stand of fruit trees, oblivious to the mosquitoes that harassed us or to our Spanish slurred with sleep or to the shooting stars that showered across the sky behind his head. He had heard that the United States was the country that had given so much support to the Nicaraguan Democratic Force and he wondered if that might be true?

Yes, that was true, as far as we knew.

Paladino was full of excitement and expectation. He was just out of school, he said: sixty-five days studying under six Argentine officers at a place just outside Tegucigalpa.

Oh yeah, Argentines. I thought they left after the problem with the Malvinas war.

No, said Paladino, they were still teaching, although he thought maybe they were going to be replaced soon by Nicaraguans.

Do you get your supplies from the Argentines?

Paladino thought that the uniforms came from the Argentines and that maybe the LAWs, the lightweight one-shot bazookas, did, too. But probably the best things came from the United States. That was why the support of the United States was so important. "The Sandinistas have to know that the United States is the most powerful nation in the world. With the United States behind us we can't lose. It must demoralize the Sandinistas."

I thought of Krill and his lie about the men at the lower levels not knowing where their supplies came from. I was not surprised that he had lied, of course, but as the chance increased each day that we would enter combat I could wish that I could trust the man who was leading us there. Visions came back to me of the stoned-out street kid. Street smart, jungle smart. Who knew where his loyalties, his duty, might lie? We were so goddamn naive.

"The minute we need arms, they come," Paladino said. "We have equipment. But getting it in here is a problem. We have to bring supplies in on our shoulders." A landing strip for airplanes would be good. "That is the objective in taking Jalapa," he said, "so we can get supplies from other countries. Right now we can't get helicopters in here because Nicaragua will say that Honduras is mixed up in all this.

"The United States is the greatest country," said Paladino, excited to be talking to two Americans about their wonderful land. "If the United States takes its support away from us, then if we lose a FAL, it's lost. But we know that the United States has promised to help us until the bitter end."

VI.

Clouds moved along the tops of the mountains, feeding the tall, gray-trunked trees, hiding whatever moved among them. In a clearing near a windblown grove of lemons Krill pointed to a pile of branches laid over a slight indentation in the ground. A grave, he said. A friend had been killed fighting here two weeks before with Sandinistas from the post at El Doradito.

Jesús and other members of our patrol had been in that engagement, which began with an ambush and went on for hours. Many of them were moving now not just with caution but with fear. Up ahead of us somewhere was a road often traveled by Sandinista troops in their IFAs. If contact were made it was easy for them to get reenforcements, and easy for us to be outnumbered. But somewhere on the other side of the road, Suicida was supposed to be waiting.

A farmer on a cadaverous white horse came down the trail and the commandos questioned him with growing hostility. Josué and Krill took over the interrogation as James and I listened. The man watched the ground or the back of his horse's neck, answering in a low voice, glancing only occasionally at James or at me. The way up ahead was clear. No problem, he said. Other farmers and their families had been friendly or argumentative or, most often, passive. But this man was afraid. Krill did not like his fear. James did not like it either. The man was lying, said James, and he wanted to know if they were going to let him go. Neither of us thought they should. If the farmer believed the road was clear, then he should come with us. That was Krill's order. A member of Josué's squad took the reins of the horse and led it behind him.

Down into a heavy stand of trees again. The sides of the trail are strewn with rotting logs, the remains of timbering that has cut back the cloud forest to these last vestigial stands of trees. The smell of rotting wood and earth is heavy in the air and the wet leaves slip under our feet. The forest grows denser and the trail narrows. Several members of the squad are spreading out among the trees where there are no trails at all, sweeping our flanks in search of whatever ambush might be there.

Jesús, the soldier in front of me, seems barely to breathe as he walks ahead. I look at the logs beside the trail wondering how long it will take me to get to them and behind them, hell, under them, if something happens. Krill is attentive to every stirring in the brush around us.

"James," I said in a voice so low it seemed barely to pass my lips, "what the fuck are we going to do if we get hit?"

"Get down," he said, shaking his head.

"I don't think we've got much choice if something happens. I think we've got to do whatever Krill says to do." I had thought about this a long time. We had touched on it before. It seemed, now, incredible that our lives should come down to such utter dependence on this one man, but he had changed so much over the three days of marching that to stay with him, do exactly what he said, seemed not only the only alternative, but also the best.

James nodded.

Every log fallen across the path was a potential trap as it slowed the column. James had twisted his knee somehow and was leaning heavily on a stick. I had begun to carry the dime-store canteen I brought from Tegucigalpa in my left hand since its strap broke. I sipped it like a bum knocking back Night Train, hoping that each new draft might give me the courage and the little increment of energy needed to go on. But the canteen interfered with my movement any time I needed to use my hands to balance or climb.

The shooting broke out up ahead with the kind of rhythm that says in seconds this is no accident. First a rattling burst of one or two guns. Then a pause. Then short bursts from guns with a different timbre, angry and erratic and building. Then the throaty sound of a machine gun and the blasts of grenades.

"Behind here," Krill said, pulling us to the massive stump of an ancient tree. "Down," he said. Leaves began to fall, severed by the bullets clipping a few feet above us. I studied James's face, his eyes darting about us, then looked at the mulch and insects at the base of the tree an inch or so from my eyes, thinking what an asshole I was to be here.

Krill crouched and gave orders. The radio operator had gotten to us and he was trying to make contact with his other units. I saw Josué coming up behind us. I do not know what happened to the farmer who had been with him, but Josué's face was full of excitement. His enigmatic grin was a full-fledged smile as Krill ordered him to take his squad with their LAWs up the hill and get behind the ambushers who seemed to have hit the forward unit. "Right," said Josué. He was off like a boy let out of school.

Krill listened to the sounds of the fighting. He picked out the throaty M-60, probably Coyote's. "Ours," he said. The rushing blast of a LAW. "Ours." The tinny rattle of many AK-47s. "Theirs." Detonations in the treetops of RPGs and M-79 grenades. And always moving closer, louder.

"We've got to get out of here," said Krill. "When I say so, we head this way." He started a count to get us ready.

"Where?" I wanted to know.

"Down there," he said, pointing along the trail toward what I thought must be the middle of the combat.

Krill started to count.

"Wait a minute!" It was James. "Are you sure this is the best way to go?"

Krill looked at him.

Krill finished his count and we broke onto the trail running. James was directly in front of me and now that he had to muster speed it wasn't there. His limp was getting more pronounced with every pace and as we scrambled half doubled-over, staying low and moving down and down toward the road where most of the fighting was taking place, he winced constantly with pain and the stick he had cut himself seemed no support at all. My own legs ached with exhaustion, but at least the pain was distributed evenly. We fell over logs and roots, slid on inclines like slides, stopped for a second or two as Krill seemed to scent the scene around us, listen to the movement of fighting. "If I didn't have to take care of you," he said, "I'd be up there fighting. Those are my brothers. But my orders are to keep you alive."

There was the dirt road and it was covered with soldiers. Contras in green uniforms. But they were strange faces from another patrol, one we hadn't seen before. Just below us was a thick knot of about a dozen who looked as confused and frightened as I was. Their commander was herding them past us to some new position. Krill started shouting for them to move, to hurry. They were looking over their shoulders toward something coming at us down the road.

"Go!" Krill shouted, and I ran across, scrambling up the opposite bank and about fifteen yards into the cover of the forest there, sliding into a hollow in the ground for whatever protection I could get, waiting for James. And waiting. James was hesitating at the edge of the road, looking at whatever was coming down it. Finally he sprinted in his half-limping stride and dove over the bank, hitting his head against a log in the dirt and leaves, then scuttling down to where I was. Krill got to us and ordered us to follow another soldier from the patrol we had not seen before, a bearded commando with an RPG slung over his shoulder who seemed not to know, quite, why we were suddenly in his charge, but we kept moving until we broke out onto open ground once again and sprinted down to a little house.

There was coffee waiting.

The farmer who lived there was preserving something of the routine of hospitality even as the war approached him. Now one unit after another of the commandos came through his little broken gate and marched on its way to the next range of hills and he stood watching, holding a chicken by the feet at his side, perhaps ready to pluck it and cook it if they wanted.

Fighting was still audible on the far side of the hill. I watched a logging cut at its summit that provided good cover and looked down directly on the house where we had taken refuge, and I could not bring myself to stand up straight. I imagined any soldier with a rifle or a mortar or LAW dropping one into the little building and I did not want to be there. Both James and I lay mostly prone outside the house making notes. But I drank the coffee greedily, sweet and strong and full of caffeine.

Eco and Krill had both arrived and they sat talking to each other as they waited for more of their units to appear. One after another they did. The sound of firing was dying away and James and I finally stood up. Every movement hurt.

There was a rush of noise like a rainstorm among leaves as the fighting broke out again on the far side of the hill. We could see soldiers now, suddenly moving down through the littered tree trunks of the logging cut.

"Let's go," said Krill.

One foot after another along the cow path behind the house, down into a deep ravine and then up out of it again into heavy forest. As soon as we were under the cover of the trees we paused so I could breathe. My body felt as if it had quit on me, but after two or three minutes we moved on. I doubted I could keep this up much longer. Adrenaline had quit sustaining me even with the Sandinistas in hot pursuit.

As we reached the top of the forest-covered mountain we heard detonations below us, the continuous rush and blast of the LAWs. They were incoming, hitting near the cover where we had stopped only a few minutes before.

In the open again, Krill told us to run. Somewhere ahead in the distance was the low thud of a mortar leaving the tube. We threw ourselves on the ground. I put my arms on each side of my face and my hands on the back of my head waiting for the impact. The explosion was close enough to send a shock wave across my body but not so near as to hurt any of the people with us. We got up and we began to run again, but each step was leaden. Another low thud in the distance. We were down again and, even waiting for the blast, I was glad for the rest. The impact came, more distant this time. Running again. Another thud and another impact. This time closer. We were running on a little logging trail and a fork came into it from the side. Krill jumped into the middle of the fork and started firing up the road. "They're coming," he said. "Move! Move!"

A few hundred yards later our pace slowed and Krill caught up to us. Where is the mortar? I asked him. He pointed to the right, toward some bare hillsides. But I saw nothing. The shells were landing farther from us, behind us now. Our pace slowed some more. And then the bushes to our left came alive with men shouting, and among the leaves were faces, smiling faces. Jesús pointed to one young man with his same honey eyes poised behind an M-60. "My brother," he said, saluting with his fist and a smile, but we kept moving.

These were Suicida's men and this was an ambush he had laid for the Sandinistas if they got this far. These men were safety.

Surviving left me oddly silly. I began wondering what we were going to say to Suicida when we saw him: the first words.

It was another half-hour before we topped a rise to look down on his command post around a little farm at a place called Arenales, and the machine guns were still rattling in the near distance. I think it would be fair to say we staggered down the hill. There were a handful of commandos, but only one of them wore a tiger suit. His long black hair was held in place by an olive-green web strap. He carried an AR-15 rifle. His beard was wispy and a two-inch scar sat on his dark cheek like a badge of honor. Beneath his camouflage bush jacket was a green U.S. Army Special Forces T-shirt. He wore a gold chain with a tiny gold calendar around his neck, a gold Omega watch on his wrist.

"Comandante Suicida, I presume" was all I could think to say.

VII.

The farmer whose house Suicida had taken for a command post begged us to leave. His woman was old and fat and sick, he said, and couldn't walk, much less run if the Sandinistas came. Many of the commandos were getting nervous, too. There was talk of hundreds, maybe thousands of Sandinistas surrounding us; talk of the IFA trucks full of troops that we had heard of the day before. Caramalo was moving among the men, reassuring them, checking on them, trying to keep them in order and calm. But Suicida and Krill were busy going through the Marlboro bag brought all the way from the Miami airport duty-free shop: a microcassette recorder, some digital watches, a canvas holster. Caramalo was back at Suicida's side, impatient but respectful. Something had to be done, he said. Suicida looked at him absently, then casually ordered his people to relocate while Caramalo and another commander, Pájaro, took their squads into action.

At the fallback position on an open hillside Suicida and Krill and Eco stood watching the perimeter on the mountains around us. One of the Sandinistas' 82mm mortar rounds landed a few hundred yards to our left. A couple of minutes later, another round landed about a quarter of a mile to our right. We were in range and being bracketed.

"Mortars are nothing," said Suicida. "All noise," he said. He remembered one of his soldiers eating a tortilla and a mortar blowing the tortilla right out of his hands, but not hurting the soldier at all. Did Krill remember that? Sure. Mortars were nothing. But this time it was

Eco who became nervous, who consulted with Suicida, suggesting that we relocate. A few minutes later we marched to the next hill.

Hour after hour the fighting continued. Suicida checked on its progress over the radio, confident and unconcerned, sometimes chiding his troops like a coach with a team of delinquents, sometimes posturing self-consciously for us. "As some general said, without communications I'm nothing," he said. Most of the Sandinistas did not know how to fight, he said, and certainly not against a soldier such as he, who knew both conventional and guerrilla warfare. *"Guerrilla convencional,"* he called his troops.

Most of the men arrayed against him were untrained militiamen who were forced to fight. "In reality, they're terribly afraid," he said. They would run when they could.

"We walk as lords of this land," he said. The thunder of still another firefight broke out in the treeline about half a mile away. Suicida shrugged. "You have to fight the ones who want to fight," he said, picking up the radio.

He made contact with Pájaro, who said he was hit by another ambush but had repositioned his men and raked the enemy with his M-60s. Caramalo was on the radio now, and angry. Pájaro had abandoned his position, he said. Suicida was amused by his temperamental boys.

Our whole situation seemed in some way to amuse him. There was this insouciant daring about Suicida, sometimes ludicrous, other times incongruous and terrifying. Suicida wasn't sure when we would be able to get out, he said, since we were surrounded. Probably we would have to blast our way through one section of the perimeter. We might do that tomorrow, he said. Couldn't just sit here, after all. His business was to fight. But in the middle of the fighting he was finding time to play. There was a card game with Krill and Eco, five hundred *córdobas* apiece anted into the pot. They laughed like family and with Krill, especially, Suicida showed affection and delight. Krill was his boy, I thought, wondering how best to describe them, as father and son, or as lovers. Someone turned up a bag of miniature marshmallows, more bounty bought off the mule merchants. Suicida made a show eating a handful himself, savoring them, examining the bag, determining that they met his standards, then walking around the camp portioning them out to his men.

We were settled now at a farm only recently abandoned. Its hedgerow of maguey cactus was well tended. The roof had no holes, the fences were mended and in the paddocks the straw was still fresh. And the handful of women and girls in the patrol worked to make this, for the night, their own home. A young woman who called herself Joanna or Jamilet, depending on her mood, made it her business to find a bed appropriate for Suicida. They built a fire in the kitchen for cooking, and Aurora, Krill's woman, scavenged through the house. As I strung my hammock between two uprights in the narrow porch (stringing it low in case we were fired on in the night) Aurora emerged holding a wedding bouquet of artificial flowers. Where normally she wore the green cap of her uniform there was now the white headpiece of a bride's ensemble. She smiled uneasily.

The level of fighting slowly dropped away. Bursts of machine-gun fire no longer provoked rising crescendos of response. The shooting was intermittent, in short, precise bursts. The commandos, we were told, had staked out positions near the Sandinista dead and wounded and they were shooting anyone who tried to get to them.

In a paddock beside the house Suicida spread out minutely detailed topographic maps covered in protective plastic to show us the path we had taken to this place, and to give us an idea of the territory he covered.

We traced our trail past Zacateras and La Mapa moving south and east, always, I saw now, in a path nearly parallel with the border that only gradually brought us deeper into Nicaragua itself. Suicida pointed to the towns of Wiwilí in the south, Quilalí on the east and Santa Clara on the west. "All of this is mine," said the sergeant-turned-general. "Territory something like the size of all of El Salvador falls to me." He looked at the twisted lines of the maps. "Ah! Here is El Chipote," Sandino's old hideout only a few kilometers away from us. Suicida swept his hand over the areas where he felt strongest. In this town there were Sandinista garrisons, but in that, his people were in control. "Every day I am breaking ground. They're not going to get me out of here now."

In some areas, said Suicida, he had put booby traps. In the area of Providencia, northwest of Jalapa, he had put some mines. "Nobody enters there," he said. One of the commandos glanced at him, his expression sharp. But the commando said nothing. Mines. Booby traps. Dangerous games.

An M-60 machine gun barked in the distance, answered by desultory mortar rounds.

At the center of Zone 2, Suicida's territory, there was Jalapa. "The next step," he said, "is to take population centers. Our intelligence tells us the populations are waiting for us to come."

JALAPA, NICARAGUA

Lisa Fitzgerald remembered, much later, how people in Jalapa felt about Suicida and La Negra and their men. It was interesting, she said, how little intelligence they showed. And how much they came to be hated. Everybody knew what they were doing, she said. "A lot of these people knew the members of Suicida's band by sight. A lot of them came from this area." And that fact made the way they made their war all the more inexplicable:

"People in this area, especially *campesinos,* really didn't know what the revolution was about. Most of them had not had that much experience with the Guardia, let alone Somoza, or never knew what was going on. They could have been persuaded to do anything. Instead, they're run from their homes, they're terrorized. The few good things they are experiencing in recent years, like medicine, a free clinic, et cetera, the people who work in these places are being targeted. It turned the whole area against them."

ARENALES, NICARAGUA

José Ernesto Cuadra Orozco stared blankly from the photograph on his Sandinista union identity card, which said he was a truck driver and a volunteer policeman.

Suicida was riffling through a loose stack of papers and cards. He handed me Orozco's. "Dead," he said, and sorted through a few more; men killed when Suicida ambushed a truck on the road to Murra. Most were in their twenties. One was responsible for an army unit's "political-military capacitation." Another was a driver for the construction ministry. "Dead." He carried these papers like trophies, and wanted them appreciated that way.

Silhouetted against the early morning sky, long lines of commandos were descending from the mountaintops around us. We had moved back to the house of the farmer who had begged us to leave the day before. Another cow had been butchered and the meat roasted in a greasy cloud of wood smoke. Krill was getting his boys ready for the trip back. Cartridges for the FALs were divided up like poker chips on a tarp. The men stripped their packs, sharing or throwing away any extra weight, readying their equipment for a day of heavy fighting and long marches.

Reports had come in at dawn of more Sandinista trucks on the move.

Suicida decided to take his main contingent, what looked like about three hundred men assembling nearby, in a head-on run against the Sandinista lines, drawing fire and pulling the bulk of the Sandinista force against him as Krill tried to get James and me back out to Honduras. We would be breaking trail through the mountains toward the Poteca River, avoiding combat if possible.

Suicida was relaxed. He had talked late into the night and was ready to talk some more in whatever time was left. He had a vision he wanted to share, a life he wanted recorded.

"The Sandinistas don't know what we're all about," he had told us sitting on a bench in the dark as Jamilet waited patiently for him to come to bed in the little house with the maguey hedge.

He talked of the future he wanted, when the men who fought alongside him could return, each one, to his farm in these mountains; when the Communists would be gone and free elections could be held. It would be no more than six months, maybe less before he was in Managua, he said. And it would be no more than six or eight months after that that the people would vote for their leaders.

But mostly this man wanted to talk about himself. He told of his exploits in the escape from San Juan del Sur in 1979 and the long years living and killing in the mountains with little real support from outside. He talked about Pastora, and even a possible alliance with this old enemy who had never known him. "He's never fought very well. But he really has support among the people, in the militias and all." Suicida spoke with contempt of the old officer corps of the Guardia Nacional. "They haven't shown up much." Why not? "Partly cowardice," he said.

Suicida showed us a diary full of terse entries. Most recorded engagements of an hour or less, ambushed IFAs where weapons were captured and every occupant killed. Some were curious. On February 22 a "recuperation patrol" picks up a car battery at Mocoron "without prejudicing said owner." On February 28 at a place called La Morena there was supposed to have been twenty minutes of fighting against six hundred men. "I was in the middle of the Sandinistas with only twenty men," Suicida interjected. "But the next day I got out." The eight-hour fight on March 14 that had left at least one of his men dead in a lemon grove not far away from where we were was described simply as "satisfactory on our part."

Suicida had a little display of captured arms for us to see, although whether they were really captured was impossible to say. One odd-looking projectile he showed as a kind of Russian mortar was in fact the rocket from an American LAW. He wanted to make sure we talked to as many of his people as we could. He and his patrol leaders were only sixteen *guardias* among almost two thousand troops, he told us many times. In fact 30 percent of his forces had been Sandinistas, Suicida claimed. And 90 percent had had some sort of training by the militias.

The men were assembling in long rows near the dilapidated barn below us, about 150 squaring up their ranks, tidying their uniforms as best they could, when firing broke out on the far side of the hill behind them. A commando came sprinting toward the group. The *piris* were attacking, he yelled.

Suicida shouted to the men in parade formation below to stay in place. "Take a picture," Suicida told us. Other commandos were scrambling to take up combat positions. "Take another," he said. "Is that all you want to take?"

Krill stood by, waiting but not impatient.

We shook hands with Suicida and quickly said goodbye. "We'll see you," said James.

"In Managua," said Suicida.

For fourteen hours we marched up and down the mountains of Nueva Segovia. We waded along the middle of stream beds to cover our tracks. We followed slowly as point men of the patrols hacked trails out of the forest. The paths were slippery and uncertain, and often a step forward was matched by slides that pushed us several steps backward. The commandos tired quickly, James more quickly, and I more quickly still, but still we kept marching. And every so often I sipped from my canteen. Again. Again. Krill warned me not to, but the dryness in my throat turned it to sand in the noon sun. Small sips of the iodine water, it seemed they could not do that much harm. We stopped at the house of a farmer and I fell asleep instantly on the ground. But a few minutes later we had to move on. The commandos began to tell me that our destination was over the next mountain. And we would cross that mountain, and they would say, no, it was the next one. And then the next one. We reached a hill that had been heavily logged, its face nearly vertical and, now, there was simply no way for me to climb it. One foot would not follow the other. My throat screamed. The commandos rigged a rope for me to hold on to as I stumbled forward and upward, half-crawling over the logs that littered the slope. And there was another mountain, still, to cross.

We came to a road that was flat and easy to walk. Jesús smiled encouragement. But then we spotted footprints. He called Krill and Krill identified them as the tracks of Sandinista boots. We began, again, to break trail to avoid the ambush Krill guessed was up ahead. We were moving very slowly now, but there was no rest. My tongue began to swell in my mouth, filling my throat, cutting off my breath. James poured water over a kerchief and held it to my head. "A little further," he said. I couldn't speak. Always a little further. Just five more minutes. Just one more mountain. A cool blanket of dusk settled over the forest, but there was no relief now. The dark was coming and I was slowing the whole column. Each step was driven by the fear of ambush and the knowledge that I was putting all these lives at risk. Not only my own and James's, but all of them. Jesús. Krill. Aurora. Paladino.

A farmer who said he was a collaborator intercepted us to guide us. There had been an ambush laid. There was indeed a Sandinista patrol nearby. Krill halted the column in a dense stand of trees and we sat on the hillside as dark enveloped us completely. He spoke softly on the radio with Suicida. The main unit had been in combat most of the day. Suicida had lost one man dead and another wounded. He said he had killed perhaps fourteen of the enemy, but there was no way he could help us if we had to fight. Krill put down the radio.

"If we have to," he said quietly, gravely, "we can stay with you here." He paused. There was no need to say how much risk lay in such a decision. "But it would be better if you can go on. It is only one more mountain. Truly, this time."

I looked at James, who was in bad shape, but not nearly so bad as I. And I knew I couldn't go on. My body had betrayed me. No adrenaline, no fear could push me on. I put my head to my knees between my knees and closed my eyes, praying, searching for the energy, the life, to push myself farther. The ghosts were all around us in the forest night. James and Krill helped me to my feet and supported me as we slid down one more hill and I struggled up what was, now, indeed, the last one. The farmer opened his doors to us. James fed me, wrapped me in a poncho liner, helped me into the hammock he had strung.

All this comes back to me now as the most disturbing sort of dream. When we were safe at the house on a bare hilltop Krill disappeared into the dark, coming back hours later after checking the perimeter. Krill, I thought again and again—Krill and James—had saved my life.

In the morning, as rested as we were going to get, we marched three hours more before, finally, a couple of the commandos turned up with a battered old horse commandeered from a nearby farm. Now I rode among them, only vaguely disturbed by my conspicuousness as they warned that the Sandinistas often set up ambushes near the crossing into Honduras.

Somewhere in the distance I heard the low hum of a small airplane engine, but nothing appeared. And then, just below us down a steep grade, there was the Poteca River. The border itself.

I slipped off the horse and slogged toward the water. Wading into the river, having emptied my pockets but kept on my shirt, pants, boots —to my knees, to my groin in the cold mountain water. My body had betrayed me badly and I knew by now it could do worse. I'd warned Krill and the rest, warned myself that if we came under fire the adrenaline might not suffice. But here we were at the river, the border, safety. The men were splashing and laughing. The girls in their bras bathed and giggled. Krill's wiry body was stripped and he was playing like some crazy Huck Finn, naked in the river. And I was in the middle of the stream letting the water rush over me—my chest now, my shoulders, my head down into the water and holding onto the bottom against the current. My pores were drinking. It was the most sensual experience.

And then the fighting started. There was a burst from one of the FALs. A pause. The clatter of fire from behind. An M-60 answered. The Sandinistas had followed us. I remember glimpsing Krill with a FAL he had grabbed up, standing naked spraying bullets across the hillside as I tried desperately to make it up the mountain into Honduras. I couldn't do it. Halfway up, everything quit. I had found a refuge behind a little dip in the ground near a deserted shack, but James tried to get me up farther into the cover of the trees. I couldn't make it. The shooting was still going on and I lay down totally exposed, unable to go farther, in the ash of a burned garden plot. My only thought was the rhythm of my labored breathing and the expectation of the shot that would kill me.

No shot came. The Sandinistas never crossed the border. They fell back and stopped firing and when Paladino appeared with the horse I was able to crawl onto it and ride to the top of the hill and finally to safety, to the little settlement where La Negra did indeed pick us up and drive us through one more long night to our beds in Tegucigalpa.

The next morning at the Maya Hotel other journalists looked at us as if we had returned from the dead. I did nothing to disabuse them of the notion as I limped up the stairs, moving each limb with visible fragility. James, more reserved in his ostentation than I, did not shave for several more days.

VIII.

WASHINGTON, D.C.

At the center of the House Intelligence Committee's green-leather arena sat the usual witnesses with their back-up staff, their overhead projectors, their maps and diagrams.

In the late spring of 1983 the controversy generated by rapidly escalating press coverage of the covert war on the ground in Central America and the administration's ever more overt acknowledgment of support for it in Washington charged the atmosphere in the committee room with hostilities only thinly disguised by customary gentilities.

Basic goals were as unclear as ever, and a series of power plays between the administration's ideologues and its hard-liners made matters worse. The Core Group had been reduced to chaos. Enders was being ousted in a slow-motion bureaucratic coup. The towering assistant secretary had been clear from the start on one point. The strategy of pressuring the Sandinistas in Nicaragua, and of pressuring the rebels in El Salvador, could be effective in the long run only if it included an escape clause. There had to be a time and a way, when the pressure got high enough, to negotiate. Any other approach would mean an open-ended and mainly military commitment. And whatever Enders may have thought about such a program, he knew enough to know Congress would never go for it. The lawmakers would not back your fight unless you made it clear you were willing, as well, to talk.

But negotiation, in the mind of the ideologues, was a synonym for weakness. Enders made the mistake of writing up his thoughts on the "two-track" approach in El Salvador—one track military and tough, the other track one of negotiation, even conciliation, if the proper conditions were met. And no sooner was it on paper than a top member of the White House staff leaked it. Enders, it was said, was going soft. Of all people. The road to his exit from Inter-American Affairs was well paved by bureaucratic rivals who resented Enders's overbearing personality and his Eastern establishment aloofness. By May, he was gone.

The tactic of the hard-liners meanwhile was to keep everything as vague as possible. Even within the Agency, where freedom of expression is a cherished tradition, the possibility of negotiating seriously with the Sandinistas was circumvented and circumscribed. Discussions were focused on matters of detail. Attempts, even at the highest levels, to broach the question of an escape from the spiral toward greater paramilitary commitments and wider wars simply were not made. Dewey had no interest in weakening his momentum. Constantine Menges, the national intelligence officer for Latin America, would spend hours with Casey in his office hashing out various aspects and details of the war. But no one talked about peace. The Sandinistas would have to give way first, and that was all there was to it.

As the House committee reviewed the testimony of Casey and Secretary of State Shultz, and conversations with the president, those who had been critical of the thinking behind the Secret War since the beginning found their fears confirmed. The Democrats on the committee were conspicuously out of patience. To try to get the purpose of the paramilitary program against the Sandinistas clearly defined, Chairman Boland had written a letter in 1981, had passed secret legislation in August 1982, and had finally sponsored the open amendment that took his name in December 1982. Funding for the paramilitary program was limited specifically to "interdiction" of arms to El Salvador's guerrillas. There was to be no money for anything that might incite border clashes between Honduras and Nicaragua, not a penny for the overthrow of the Nicaraguan government.

So the problem for the Agency and the administration was to obscure the obvious. Of course the people fighting in Nicaragua were doing so with the aim of ridding their country of the Sandinistas. "Nobody wanted to say they were going to overthrow them," recalled one CIA briefer. "But obviously that was the idea. You wouldn't get people to participate if it were just a shabby little political scheme." And from this perspective, the congressional review was a minuet of hypocrisy. The congressmen did not want Communists in Central America, but they did not want to sign on to the tactics needed to get rid of them. The Agency people, and others in the administration, began using ever more abstract terms to describe the general goals of their program.

There were too many metaphors floating around. There was a

simile about boxers in a ring: you make them look in one direction, then you hit them from another. There was the idea of symmetry: trading one little war for another little war. And there was the notion that the paramilitary program would make Nicaragua "turn inward," and concentrate on its own problems rather than create them for its neighbors. You could write a whole essay about "looking inward," a sort of omphalocentric option. "They built this whole elaborate house of cards on the idea of making a country look inward," recalled one of the skeptics present. "Maybe like a porcupine. You punch it with a pole and it rolls up."

And the original purpose for which the paramilitary program had been funded in the first place—the "interdiction" of arms shipments from Nicaragua to El Salvador's rebels—got buried by all the imagery, which was, of course, the point.

While all the metaphors had been multiplying, the contra forces seemed to be growing at a fantastic rate, their numbers doubling from about four thousand in December to more than eight thousand in the early summer of 1983. Even if some members of the committee were doubtful about the accuracy of those figures, the operation was clearly moving forward on a scale the United States could not control. It was a war that Congress had helped to start but that it could not stop. And that the administration, on its own, probably would not stop in any case. Now the question had to be asked again, Was the covert action an instrument of policy, or was it the other way around? Wasn't the whole program "inconsistent" with the law (if indeed it didn't break it), wasn't it unwise, and perhaps worst of all, wasn't it a failure?

The CIA investigation by the Church committee in 1976 had concluded that the very minimum requirement for a paramilitary operation was that it achieve its policy goal, and that it remain deniable. Otherwise, why not make the action overt? Well, this program was not stopping arms shipments and it was not likely to overthrow the Sandinistas. Meanwhile it was utterly undeniable. Reports from both sides of the front made it clear what was happening. In fact there were some suspicions that the CIA was encouraging all the publicity. So questions of U.S. prestige and U.S. interventionism were raised. And whatever the composition of the contras' rank and file, their leaders were all members of the much-detested old Guardia Nacional. Pastora's operation was slow getting off the ground. The Salvadoran rebels looked stronger than ever. If ever there was a formula for failure, the Democrats on the committee warned, this covert action was it.

Then, without warning, the Salvadoran Left did to itself what Washington had proved unable to do.

MANAGUA, NICARAGUA

On a cul-de-sac off the South Highway about seven miles outside Managua was a collection of pleasant, upper-class houses rented out to foreigners. One was occupied by the young woman who served as the political officer at the U.S. Embassy. Another was home to a frail Salvadoran lady. Hers appeared to be a closed group of friends. She did not often associate with the neighbors. When she did receive people she was usually sitting in a hand-carved rocking chair dressed in a simple cotton dress, a large black-and-white cowhide purse within easy reach. Intelligent and quick, her voice nevertheless quavered slightly in conversation. She was in her late forties, but she looked much older. Her real name was Mélida Anaya Montes and she had once been a schoolteacher and then the leader of the Salvadoran teachers' union. Now, as "Ana María," she was second-in-command of the largest single faction of the Salvadoran guerrilla front, the Popular Liberation Forces.

In the long, impassioned meetings of her organization's Central Command she was a skilled and successful politician. She knew how to manipulate the dogmas and the symbols of the revolution to reach practical ends, and when dealing with the fractious five armies of the rebel front she pushed repeatedly and successfully for greater unity. That she met with ever greater success in the early months of 1983 was also due to the increasing support she got from the Sandinistas and from Fidel. The Nicaraguan and Cuban revolutions had been through their own struggles for unity. They backed the play of any-one who could bring it successfully to the Salvadorans. Unity was the key.

Only the leader of her own organization, Salvador Cayetano Carpio, the aging "Marcial," objected strongly to her increasing influence. As number one and number two they vied for control throughout 1982 and early 1983. The war seemed to be moving strongly their way, and before they took over or entered the government, their positions had to be clear. The debates between them were intense and ideological. Marcial advocated rigid adherence to the doctrines of prolonged war and the purity of the proletariat. He was the grand old man of the revolution. These had been his grandest principles. Ana María pushed for broader alliances, more flexible political positions. Finally at a January meeting of the Central Command, by careful maneuvering, and with the support of commanders in the field, she succeeded in circumscribing Marcial's power.

On April 6, Ana María was murdered in her pleasant Managua bungalow. Despite her security people, the attackers were able to enter easily. They stabbed her more than eighty times with an awl as she struggled and screamed. Finally they slit her throat.

When word of the killing got out, Tomás Borge and Lenin Cerna, the head of State Security, held a press conference. Cerna himself was named to head up the investigation. And Borge quickly deduced what its results would be. The murder, he said, put Nicaragua in the difficult position of admitting that a member of the Salvadoran guerrilla directorate was resident in Managua. It seemed to confirm the charges constantly made by the Reagan administration that the Sandinistas were supplying command and control facilities to the Salvadorans. So, who else could have killed Ana María but the CIA? Who else would be so brutal?

"I do not need to present specific proof," said Borge. "I do not need to say: 'Here is the murderer,' because everyone knows who the murderer is."

But Ana María's followers among the Salvadoran guerrillas were not so sure. They knew the bitterness of Marcial. They urged Borge to press harder on the investigation. After two days a servant in Ana María's house confessed her complicity to the Sandinista police. The sound of the screams haunted her and would not let her sleep, she told them. She implicated other conspirators and the path quickly led to the closest friend and confidant of Marcial himself. And the implication, even indirect, of Marcial as the author of the murder was more humiliating for the Sandinistas—and for Borge especially—than anything the CIA could have devised.

Borge and Marcial were close. They were old men of the revolution who subscribed to the same dogmas, and when Marcial flew to Managua from Libya to attend Ana María's funeral the two of them sat together. When the sickly Marcial, dressed in a sweater despite Managua's heat, vowed that day that the region's revolutionaries would walk together toward victory throughout Central America, one had the sense it would be Borge walking with him.

But as the evidence came out, and Marcial's lieutenant confessed unrepentantly to doing what was necessary to save Marcial's ideals, Marcial not only refused to acknowledge any role in the crime, he accused the Sandinistas—even Tomás Borge—of plotting against him. Old and sick, he was still defiant.

On April 12, Marcial died at his own house in Managua. The Sandinistas announced that he committed suicide. The new leaders of his guerrilla faction confirmed that he killed himself when his role in Ana María's murder was discovered. But Marcial was a man with mystical charisma for young revolutionaries. He had built passionate loyalties and kept them alive with countless personal touches. He remembered birthdays and other anniversaries, was forever sending notes of encouragement and attention. His supporters certainly saw around him a revolutionary aura as magnificent as Ho Chi Minh's. However it was that he died on the night of April 12, a bullet through his heart, he did so defiantly. And before he died, he wrote to his closest friends and followers that he had been framed.

Within a month of his death his old organization was divided. Some commanders in the field, and especially those clandestine units that had survived in the cities where Marcial built his strongest loyalties, began operating on their own. Rules painstakingly established during the previous two years of fighting were suddenly broken and there were new levels—new kinds—of bloodshed. Whatever the order and rhythm of the offensive before, now it was lost as the rebel units and factions began flexing for each other and for the world, pushing for spectacle and for ever greater recognition. There was a massacre of prisoners. There was, on the same evening, the assassination of Navy Lieutenant Commander Albert Schaufelberger III in San Salvador. He was, as the press uniformly reported, "the first American advisor killed in Central America."

IX.

JALAPA, NICARAGUA

The second siege of Jalapa, Nicaragua, began on May 22. As it happened, a group of American journalists, including senior editors from *Time* magazine and *The Washington Post,* had gone there to report on a visit by the junta and suddenly were pinned by a surprise attack along the road. It was a long night and morning before they were evacuated by air. Only on the third day after that was a new collection of reporters able to get in, and the caravan of rent-a-cars under white flags made of hotel towels arrived like a liberation force. Doors opened and people peered curiously to see who had made it down the road. Then a surge of traffic began at high speed through the dusty valley as if a bridge had been lowered.

When the journalists found Lisa, she was tending her vegetable garden behind the parish house. She was good-humored but nervous. She was determined, she said, to get in this little crop before the contras could take the town.

In the living area of the little stucco house she had pinned up a hand-drawn map of the parish served by her church. Each deserted village was marked off. Together they made a hollow perimeter all along the border. The only villages marked as accessible and populated were those along the main road down toward Ocotal. When that was cut—and it was cut now every few days for a few days at a time— Jalapa was isolated, tortured, not really vulnerable behind its defenses, but not really safe.

Lisa had lived here now for more than a year and had become a kind of fixture for the Americans who visited: reporters and, increasingly, political activists from the United States who wanted to bear witness to the depredations of Central America's war as many of them had once done to Southeast Asia's. In their reports and their letters home, Lisa was always cited as an example of bravery and determination. But by May 1983 Lisa Fitzgerald's time in Jalapa was ending.

She had witnessed enough. She seemed shaken that week. By bearing witness she had become, increasingly, a target. And everyone in Jalapa had seen, at one time or another, what the contras could do to their targets.

In June, Lisa returned to the United States to talk to the press. She took with her a list of the killings and maimings committed by the commandos of the Nicaraguan Democratic Force. She presented it to congressmen. She told of the delegates of the word whose throats were slashed and of the farm workers terrorized; the busses blown and the villagers walked away at gunpoint into the night. She became, in effect, a lobbyist against the Secret War. Subsequently she served in Managua on the Sandinistas' human rights commission, calm and reasoned and sincere and disarmingly little-girlish. She confirmed, for those who were already convinced, everything they had believed all along about the Secret War and the men who waged it. The administration paid no attention to her at all.

But that afternoon in May she mentioned something slightly different from what she would recount in Washington, and in a tone she rarely used. With what seemed the slightest thrill in her voice, Lisa said that she had heard an important contra commander was killed. She was not sure, she said, because the information had come to her second or third hand. But there had been an ambush that caught one of Suicida's top people. She said she thought the name was "El Negro."

LAS TROJES, HONDURAS

About a dozen women and girls at Pino Uno wore uniforms and carried AK-47s; Aurora and Jamilet, Jacqueline and Irma among them. They were mostly in their teens and they marched alongside Suicida's commanders and slept with them in their makeshift beds. As one commander or another tired of them, the girls were passed around, but there was not much about them that was passive. In their teenage games of coyness and seduction they raised passions among men whose lives were made of killing. They shared in the danger and the thrill of the fighting and they taunted men they thought were lesser than they or their lovers. Jamilet, who had four brothers and a sister in the fight, and who was a few years older than the rest, found in the gunfire and the risk the excitement she had always looked for as the child of a landowner in the Segovias. "I can't tell you," she told me one night with a grin of dreamy satisfaction, "it just makes me happy to be in combat." Jacqueline looked like a plump, spoiled little girl of the middle class, but she bounded up and down the hillsides of the Segovias like a rabbit, the men would say, full of energy when other troops were worn to exhaustion. On her back were long scars from Caramalo's fingers. Irma was first Krill's woman, then Cancer's, and she carried a .38 revolver in her right pocket, she told a friend, to use against Krill if he ever tried to beat her again.

All this had been mostly a matter of amusement for La Negra and Suicida until early in 1983. By then, Suicida was spending more and more time inside Nicaragua and left La Negra to handle all his logistics. In a Toyota Land Cruiser pickup truck La Negra shuttled back and forth to the capital to pick up supplies with an old man called Machete and her usual driver, El Campesino. The roads were dangerous and they drove them as fast as they could even in the loneliest hours of the night. One track they took passed over a high ridge where parts of the road had washed down the mountainside and they would have to stop, get out, fill in the crevasse with wood or rocks, then drive on with one side of the truck scraping the vertical face of the cliff and the wheels on the other trembling along the edge of the precipice. When the road dipped into a valley the truck mired in pools of mud and had to be pushed out. Another part of the route near Cifuentes passed directly through the shadow of Nicaraguan mountains full of Sandinista guns. But managing the logistics was work that La Negra enjoyed. She wanted to be indispensable to Suicida in every way. She prided herself on that.

"La Negra worked like a man. She was very impressive," said a Nicaraguan woman who knew her in those days. "But, see, what happened, like it does, is that Suicida was in Nicaragua and she got news that he was going out with this girl who was much younger than her. And she started to wonder why sometimes when he was in one part of the mountains and she was in another, and she would call him to come see her, he wouldn't come," said the woman.

"That's how it all started," said the woman.

Women in Central America are sometimes referred to as *abnegadas*. Their lives are wholly given over to their men. They withstand any abuse and their husbands' adultery, even their husbands' second families, but they appear content to live as faithful mothers and keepers of the hearth. There was nothing of the *abnegada* about La Negra. For all her devotion to Suicida, as he was finding respite from combat in the arms of Jamilet or another adolescent combatant, her own relations with several members of the staff were rumored to grow very close.

When she went to Tegucigalpa she began to take Krill with her instead of old Machete, and it was with Krill she had her good times in the city. Ortiz, taking his *parientito*'s part, warned her that it looked bad. People would talk. And they did. By early 1983 there were plenty looking for something to use against El Suicida.

With Villegas continuing to back him, this mere sergeant fielded more troops than any other man in the FDN. His fame and his personal mystique were growing as well. And in the eyes of several ex-Guardia officers this sergeant did not have the background or the administrative skills needed to run an operation as large as he commanded. Suicida did nothing by the book.

In January, El Muerto left Pino Uno for the capital, reporting the worst of Suicida and particularly his faithless woman.

El Suicida was a quiet type, El Muerto said. He kept to himself and didn't mix with the troops. He sat up in the command post listening to music on his tape recorder and playing checkers with his buddies and La Negra. Ah, La Negra. There really were a lot of problems with her. She wanted to be everything there. She was commander, execu-

tive, S-2, S-4, S-3, and she didn't know anything, said El Muerto, the
veteran of Argentina. There were always problems with the personnel
of the base. She took responsibilities that she didn't have the abilities
to undertake and she interfered in your work.

She interfered in El Muerto's own work, he said. He would want
to send a commando to get some information along the border and she
wouldn't give the man enough supplies to carry out the mission. Sometimes she wouldn't let El Muerto himself leave the base. And then,
while he was in charge of base security, well, the whole world was in
and out of there. There were all these little problems about taking
decisions, said El Muerto. She was always the one who took them.
And she created—she created a kind of ménage, as you might say. She
monopolized these people, and she made them loyal to her, said El
Muerto.

Suicida's enemies, knowing how partial Villegas was to him, began
to focus their attacks on La Negra instead. And while nobody bothered
about Suicida's romances in the field, La Negra's affairs with Krill and
also with Caramalo suddenly became the focus of universal concern,
even anger. She was said to be demoralizing the troops. Suicida might
be a problem, but La Negra was *the* problem.

THE HONDURAN-NICARAGUAN BORDER

La Negra's driver, El Campesino, probably pulled to a stop in the
pine forest a few hundred yards before the stretch of road that cut along
the line of the border near Cifuentes. It was usual procedure on the trip
back from the capital. The men could jump out of the back and take a
piss, stretch out a bit, then load a round into the chamber and be ready
for action if there were an attack.

On La Negra's last trip to Tegucigalpa she had been looking for
General Gustavo Alvarez, the Honduran strongman. Suicida wanted to
talk to him and had sent him a letter through a local coffee grower
whose brother was an officer in the Honduran army. Suicida wanted a
member of the general staff to come to the combat zone to see what
was happening there, but no one would come. El Suicida and his people
had an international reputation now and were pushing to build on whatever fame they had—expand their forces, take more territory, launch
new offensives. He and his people were the new heroes of the new
revolution. But he needed more guns. He needed more money. And
Echaverry and Bermúdez in Tegucigalpa would not oblige.

Echaverry, the chief of staff, didn't know—nobody in Tegucigalpa knew—what to do with Suicida. You couldn't use force. His forces were stronger and more loyal to him than anything you could muster against him. And you couldn't use suasion. "Suicida, after the publicity, became more crazy, like a little kid in his playpen," said one of his comrades. He was his own commander. And you couldn't really cut him off at this point because he accounted for as much as half of the FDN's strength.

Some people in the FDN thought Echaverry was actually frightened of Suicida. The Sergeant-Comandante seemed perfectly capable of killing a member of the general staff, or taking him hostage if he got the chance.

Sandinista intelligence would hear him talking over his radio about "those bastards who send me here, and who order me around here." He was the single most important figure in the fight against the Sandinistas, he thought, and yet he was not even made a member of the general staff himself. "It's me who's burning his balls down here fighting the Communists," he complained.

Suicida went only rarely to the capital, now. He was not going to deliver himself into the hands of his enemies.

So La Negra was trying to talk to Alvarez for him. But it seems she failed and by the time she drove up to the operation at Radio 15 she was angry and frustrated. She and El Campesino and the others loaded the truck with guns and ammunition and money and hundreds of thousands of Nicaraguan *córdobas* and headed back to Las Trojes.

In La Negra's dirt-brown Toyota she and her men would have been exhausted by the time they reached the pine forest and stretched in anticipation of the fast run down the road near Cifuentes, where there was always the chance the Sandinistas would open up on them. Maybe they were not paying attention as they started the race along the exposed straightaway, and maybe it wouldn't have mattered if they were.

A .30-caliber machine-gun round took off a large part of La Negra's head when the ambush hit.

X.

ARENALES, NICARAGUA

"La Negra," said one of Suicida's friends, "was his eternal companion. La Negra was his secretary, his friend, his sister, his wife. This was a woman with a strong constitution, a tough temperament, who was Suicida's support. He cried a lot on the death of La Negra. After that Suicida confused everything. I mean, he had no one to help him, no one to advise him.''

Suicida's grief was indistinguishable from anger, and it quickly engulfed his forces. He was like a boxer wild with frustration, slamming his fists into a wall until his fists began to break. His men died now in numbers they had never suffered before. And still he kept pounding. The villagers in Trojes talked later about the madness that descended on them. ''It was chaos,'' said one young peasant. ''It was anarchy here,'' said an old woman. ''They thought they ran the town.'' The Honduran army had to come in to make a show of restoring order as the men grew wilder and more reckless. And then Suicida used the Honduran troops as well to push for his revenge.

Just across the border from Trojes is the settlement of El Porvenir, a collection of tobacco fields and drying sheds. For two days at the beginning of June, Honduran troops from the Sixth and the Sixteenth battalions provided mortar fire to cover the advance of Suicida's main force into the plantations of El Porvenir. And then he sat his men there with nowhere to go, no plan, it seems, to advance. The Sandinistas counterattacked with artillery, their big mortars set up in batteries, dropping one shell after another onto Suicida's people, igniting the barns and the few houses of the settlement, driving the commandos into holes, blowing them to bits before finally, after a week, Suicida pulled them back toward Trojes and the camp at Pino Uno.

It had been carnage for its own sake. It was a revenge, it seemed, as much on his own men as on the Sandinistas. Yet Suicida seemed to have found in the fighting an odd peace. He regained something of his cruel humor. Even in the first flush of his fury he found time to toy with a recruit, torment and test him.

A day or so after La Negra was killed, Suicida was waiting for supplies at Arenales when the sound of skirmishing reached him. A new man had gotten the assignment and was trying to make his way through a Sandinista ambush. The poor bastard was in the same dirt-brown Toyota in which La Negra had died. The Sandinistas knew the car well. It was a rolling target. But Suicida sent no reenforcements. He sat and waited and watched with evident amusement as the men with the supplies straggled into his camp.

His new civilian volunteer was Salvador Icaza, a former judge in Estelí who had resigned in protest against Somoza in 1977. Icaza had been something of a friend to the Sandinistas in those days. But he had fallen out with the Sandinistas during the fighting and he blamed them for torching his home and threatening his family. He had fled the country before the end of the war. He lived uneasily after that in a modest suburban house in Memphis, Tennessee, with all the members of his family working to support themselves, until, finally, he decided to come to Nicaragua to fight. In Danlí, friends put him in touch with Suicida and Suicida put him to work.

But Icaza was flabby and not up to marching in the mountains, much less fighting his way out of an ambush. By the time he arrived at Arenales one of his men was wounded in the arm. His own face was scarlet and his chest was heaving, partly from fatigue, partly from anger.

"Mr. Icaza," said Suicida, "what happened to your backpack? It looks like it has, oh, about five holes in it."

"You are a son of a bitch is what you are," said Icaza.

"Mmmm. Mr. Icaza," said El Suicida, "have you been fighting with mice? Because you've got these holes in your pack here."

It was, Icaza realized, Suicida's idea of a joke.

It was the judge's first taste of combat and it was not the war he had expected when he told his wife in Tennessee he was going back to Nicaragua to fight. "I had never been in the jungle. I had never fought with a gun, even hunting. I never fought against anybody—well, maybe against my wife. I'm not very bright, but I can see what's going on. I've got a little common sense." This fight seemed to have very little common sense to it. The borderline between bravery and madness was as vague as the frontier between Honduras and Nicaragua.

Suicida declared on the spur of the moment, "Mr. Icaza, we are going to see Caramalo, get ready." Icaza knew that Suicida and his men were talking about their every movement over the radio, and the Sandinistas must know both where they were and where they were headed. There would be an ambush. Everyone knew it. But Suicida and his men were picking up their packs and rifles and setting off "so happy to start pulling a trigger. They were so happy that they didn't want to stay in the camp. They know they are going to be in an ambush. 'We are going to have a party today.' They talked like this. It was crazy. And I am thinking to myself, 'poor Mr. Icaza.' "

"Who else knew what time La Negra was going to be passing that point in the road?" Ortiz asked Suicida soon after La Negra's death.

Ortiz was suspicious because one of La Negra's frequent traveling companions, a Dr. José, had been given an unexpected trip to Guatemala by Bermúdez. Ortiz had a theory. Bermúdez had wanted to get him out of the way.

"Parientito," said Ortiz, "it's not the Sandinistas who killed La Negra, it's the general staff."

Maybe this would have seemed incredible in another environment. But in the pervasive atmosphere of distrust and conspiracy that had settled over the Secret War in the preceding months, there was nothing implausible about the high command's plotting to murder subordinates who challenged its authority. There was El Muerto's report against her. Who could tell what was happening now? The Argentines were supposed to be out of the operations, but they were still running them. Lau was supposed to be removed as G-2, but he was still there. The Americans did not seem to have a handle on things. With no one in charge, everybody looked out for himself. You eliminated trouble as you saw fit. Maybe you punished a man through his woman.

Suicida was not convinced by Ortiz at first. But then, a few days later he came back to him. *"Parientito,"* said Suicida, "you're right. The Sandinistas are not going to kill La Negra in Honduras." And then a few days after that Suicida came back to Ortiz again. "Our people killed her," he said. Farmers who lived near the site of the ambush told Suicida they had seen two officials from Pino Uno hanging around a hut in the area of the killing on the afternoon that it happened. But while the farmers recognized them, Suicida knew these men were not supposed to have been in the area for months, ever since he drove them away as the spies of Echaverry, Bermúdez and Lau. They were the ones called B-1 and El Muerto.

"I know who did it," said El Suicida, "and I'm going to kill them."

But by then it was too late for Suicida to get his hands on either one. El Muerto and B-1 had disappeared. Among some officers of the FDN word was out that the Argentine Ribeiro had hidden them in a Tegucigalpa safe house near the soccer field not far from the U.S. ambassador's residence. Then they were infiltrated into Nicaragua to begin trying to build an urban front for the organization. They were arrested in Managua after one day.

In fact, much later, Sandinista State Security did claim credit for killing La Negra. "We prepared the ambush," said security chief Lenin Cerna.

What Suicida believed is more important, however, and he appears to have believed that Echaverry and Lau's boys were responsible for La Negra's death. And that he would be next.

XI.

DANLÍ, HONDURAS

At Xally's Hotel in Danlí the women were accustomed to the use of FDN commanders; accustomed to their drinking and rages and violence. Like the whores of any village in Central America, they were used up. They were fat from childbirth and a life as sedentary as poverty allows, except for the youngest of them, the girl of fourteen or fifteen who might be fresh enough from the countryside to have a figure. Some made the effort to show a man something sexy as they opened the beat-up refrigerator for another Nacional or poured him a shot of Ron Plata. Some few might have seemed to go crazy under a man. But in the sweat of the bare-bulb rooms, on wooden cots, they were mostly the same. They were not much to fight over, certainly, but the men always did.

On the night of May 30 the fight was worse.

Krill loved to have a good time at Xally's. Some nights he'd get some pills to keep him going with two or three of the girls—at least, that's what he told people. But when Krill drank too much the torpor in his eyes edged toward total detachment; then, as if touched by a malevolent spirit, a fury would erupt that nobody could control. Even among country people without guns a drunken rage is a bloody one. Machetes are an extension of the peasant's hand and they swing them like fighting cocks cutting each other to bits in a flurry of flashing blades. For the American-supplied commanders of the FDN, however, the Browning 9mm pistol had replaced the machete.

The incident at Xally's Hotel came only a couple of weeks after La Negra's death, and what Krill was thinking about the way she died, how he felt the loss, is nothing he ever told anyone I talked to. But an image returns of the two of them sitting in my room in the Hotel Maya the evening after they had brought James and me back up from the border. We ordered up hors d'oeuvres and snacks that stretched the limited creativity of the Maya kitchen. But they seemed pleased. And they had a couple of Flor de Cañas and Cokes. And we laughed and talked about our adventures with the easy camaraderie of recent survival. And La Negra and Krill had seemed completely comfortable in each other's presence—indeed, when, taking us into Nicaragua, they had ridden together on the same horse, and when they sat up all night laughing under the stars at the first campsite inside the border, they had seemed, at the least, like siblings. He had been at ease with her, comfortable and confident.

There are also those in the FDN who say that Krill, as much as Suicida, was affected by the fame he suddenly found in the pages of *The Washington Post* and *Newsweek*.

It was something to tell women about; something to make other soldiers envious.

On the night of May 30 there was another FDN commander at Xally's Hotel. Called Jaguar, he had come up from the schooling base where the officers in Tegucigalpa thought they had their best men and where they had wanted to send some of Suicida's people. There was a lot of tension between the commandos of the two task forces.

The fight began because of a girl, or a remark, or maybe a look in the eye. Whatever. And before anyone could stop it the men were in a bloody embrace on the floor and Jaguar got his gun out of the holster first, perforating the refrigerator (the girls would always lament that), the wall, the ceiling.

"Okay, you son of a bitch," Krill is supposed to have said, falling back and dragging his own Browning out of his belt. Taking aim. "That's the way they shoot at the schooling base? Now I'm going to show you how we shoot at Pino Uno." And he blew Jaguar away.

The shootout at Xally's Hotel was a good story that made the rounds quickly in the ranks. "It's the Wild West with submachine guns and AK-47s is what it is," said one of the officers who heard about it. And word that Krill had killed a fellow commander must have reached Tegucigalpa quickly. But there is no indication it received much attention.

Pino Uno, Honduras

Salvador Icaza kept his diary hidden and worried constantly that Krill or Cancer would come across the notes he had taken since his arrival at Pino Uno.

Suicida had made the erstwhile judge from Estelí his S-5, in charge of communications and psychological operations and morale. Icaza took his assignment seriously. He liked to talk about morality, religion, common sense. He felt those elements were important to winning the war. Icaza used to arrange for sympathetic priests to come to the camp and give communion to the soldiers "and they would feel human again." And Icaza saw the side of Suicida that made many of his men love him.

"How would you say?" Icaza wondered. "If you take the bad things, they had some good things too. They were concerned about their friendship with the people. He was concerned with sharing food with his people. He had some kind of leadership."

The commandos used to run out of cigarettes all the time. "They never smoked one cigarette; people used to smoke three packages a day." Suicida would line up the troops: "One carton for you, one packet for you"—knowing how much each man smoked—"and the people were happy, talking about how good was their commander.

"Or like soft drinks. 'Mr. Icaza is going and we need to rent a little truck and get as many soft drinks and Coca-Colas as we can.' And, yep, I went there and got it.

"Food. Bread. You know you cannot find bread, that which we call *pan dulce*. One time he almost bought the whole bakery in Danlí and sent it back to his men. Crazy things that people like, that people love.

"There was a man sick. He asked him what was wrong. And he said, Well, I'm sick. And he gave him fifty dollars. Or 'What happened to your boot?' 'I've got my toes sticking out.' So he just pulls off his boots and gives them to him. He knows he's got some others, but the gesture of doing it—you know that you are with him."

But Icaza did not know what to make of Suicida's macho games in the field, or the way that Krill and Cancer and Caramalo acted in the camp.

They drank a lot. They were "universal carburetors," said Icaza. They drank "anything from unleaded to Flor de Caña." They emptied their guns in the air, raising hell all over the place. There were fights over women, and over who was the braver and the better soldier and there were fights, as well, over power. "You see," said Icaza, "power made the people drunk." Any little argument with them when they were crazy would get you a gun shoved in your chest. And in the two months after La Negra died the tensions got steadily worse. Krill and Caramalo and Cancer talked to each other with their pistols in their hands. Every moment was unpredictable.

In retrospect some of Pino Uno's persistent problems would seem minor. There was, for instance, Suicida's padding of his troop strength.

"That is part of the business. Get more logistic money," Icaza said. "One time he told me to make a report to the staff and ask for more stuff. And he said, 'Well, we've got seventeen hundred or two thousand men.' And I said, 'I am going to make a report in fifteen days.' And he said, 'Make a report right now.' And I said, 'I am going into the field to count the troops.' He knew what I meant and he just laughed. And he made another guy make a report."

There were the punishments for the slightest infractions: two and three hours of pushups for a failure to salute.

It was what Icaza called "rumors," however, that most disturbed him. "People there are very discreet. They are not going to disclose," said Icaza. "They were so afraid even to talk to me." But as Icaza became more of a fixture in the camp—went out on more missions, proved himself—the stories began to multiply. "They started telling me stories about"—Icaza stopped himself—"rumors that Krill did such and such a thing, that La Negra did such and such a thing. But not the specifics." Then Icaza got to know Cancer, the short, wiry little Indian who vied with Krill for the laurels of killing. "Cancer was one of those men who knew all that shit," said Icaza. "And I was real close with him, so he told me all that shit."

And when Icaza was alone he wrote it down in his little book.

Icaza was told about Suicida and Krill and the Barreda couple, whom he had known in Estelí.

Icaza was told a story that Krill was interested in a woman from a family that had come to the camp as refugees, and that he had sent the husband into combat to be killed like a latter-day Uriah. But Krill did not trust the Sandinistas to do the job for him.

"That son of a bitch Krill ambushed his own troops, just to get rid of them," said Icaza, recalling the story in a burst of passion. "And Suicida knew that fucking shit."

One night during the assaults against El Porvenir, Icaza heard that new prisoners had been brought in and that Krill was going to interrogate them.

"I had been hearing rumors," as Icaza put it in his usual understatement, "that Krill was not a good guy."

The prisoners were taken to the stand of trees outside the camp where interrogations were conducted, probably the same area where the Barredas were held and tortured. The captives were boys, seventeen, eighteen years old, "young kids like my son," thought Icaza. They were barefoot and bound and had been thrown down on the dirt. Krill was half drunk, asking questions. He got an answer he didn't like.

His black-cleated jungle boot caught one of the kids under the chin and the head bobbed back on the dirt. And Icaza, who would claim later that he witnessed no murders firsthand at Pino Uno, did not want to see what would happen next. He grabbed Krill. The muscles of the commander's arm were as taut as an animal's. He looked at Icaza with sullen surprise in the forest night.

"Krill, please, quit fucking with this guy."

"Mr. Icaza, it is not your business."

"It is my business," said Icaza. He had been made S-5, and prisoners were part of his responsibility and they had to be treated like prisoners of war. The idea was to try to win these people over, he told Krill as he pulled him aside. Krill stared at him drunkenly, partly curious, partly malevolent.

"Krill, are you crazy, man? There is no way you are going to get away with that stuff. Even if we are not in the main camp there are a bunch of people looking at you."

Krill said nothing, then, suddenly, arrived at a decision, said, "Hey, go ahead. You can do what you want with him." Krill didn't give a damn if Icaza wanted to try to convert these guys.

By late June, Icaza said he had compiled a report of twenty-six handwritten pages about "what I had heard and noticed in Pino Uno. Rumors. And I investigated more than that." By his count, Krill alone was said to have murdered more than thirty commandos, prisoners and civilians.

Finally Icaza took his report to Echaverry, the chief of staff in Tegucigalpa. "And they said, you know, 'Forget it. You know what happens in this revolution. Everybody gets wild. We'll take care of it,' " Icaza recalled. What they did, he said, was "not a fucking thing."

DYING—SUMMER
AND FALL, 1983

I.

TEGUCIGALPA, HONDURAS

William Casey, along with his deputy, his national intelligence officer, the head of his international affairs division and, of course, Dewey, dropped in on Central America for a couple of days in late June 1983: one day for El Salvador, where Casey wanted to talk to the locals about toning down their death squads, and one day in Honduras to check up on the war. He held court, as it were, in Negroponte's home and his embassy, and there was a friendly dinner with General Alvarez. Central Americans who met with Casey's crew remember a flying circus of aging men in tropical shirts, looking like insurance executives at a convention in Hawaii. Confident, energetic and abrupt as ever, Casey gave the strong impression that he, at least, thought everything was under control.

"Good trip," one of the people at the embassy said to him ironically, meaning a short one.

"What else was there to do?" Casey is supposed to have answered crisply.

The problem of Suicida apparently did not come up.

Maybe there was too much information to sort through, one agent suggested, too many other details to attend to. The reports on what was happening at Pino Uno were "very fuzzy," he recalled. It seemed Suicida "had been totally enraged by something that had happened to some of his people and he went in and massacred a whole bunch of people. As I remember it it was pretty cold-blooded. Not something he did just in a rage, but he stood them up and killed them."

Another CIA man remembered "there was a little ripple of shock in the Agency when it turned up he was shooting prisoners."

At least one member of the congressional committees, a supporter of the paramilitary program, heard stories of atrocities from friends in the Agency. There was an account that said Suicida had taken several captives, as many as thirty, and killed them all. There were rumors, as well, circulating among the civilians in Tegucigalpa; rumors they did not want to believe about men buried alive, about mutilations. Nor were they limited to Pino Uno. Accounts began circulating of similar actions by the men of the FDN commando called Mack in Madriz, and Tigrillo's men in Jinotega. Rapes and murders and tortures. In Washington, Lisa Fitzgerald tried to make her point with Congress and the public about the terror that had ravaged the countryside around Jalapa. And yet none of it seemed to take hold.

One Agency veteran explained the low level of attention given Suicida's actions by the authors of the Secret War as a matter mainly of bureaucratic discretion: "I think that when Dewey and company became aware that he was being naughty, I think they kept it as quiet as they could as long as they could within the Agency."

The president, one noted, had begun to call the contras "freedom fighters" in public.

So the problem, to the extent it was noticed, was treated as a matter of technique; the kind of thing that good instruction, better discipline and training could take care of. It was suggested that the Argentines, who were still handling most of the instruction at Lepaterique and at the Quinta Escuela outside Tegucigalpa, might try their hand at straightening things out.

"They asked Osvaldo to prepare a little manual on psychological warfare," remembered one of the American agents. "It was the wildest thing you ever saw. It was about seven or eight pages and all but about half of it had to be cut. It was full of attacks with no objectives; things like calling airlines and telling them there's a bomb. That kind of thing." Later there would be other manuals. The problem as they saw it was not in the nature of the war and the men who led it but in their unfortunate inefficiency.

Meanwhile, the killing in and around Pino Uno went on.

MEXICO CITY, MEXICO

Dial Torgerson of the *Los Angeles Times* was one of the few correspondents in the Central American press corps who could be called a veteran. In his early fifties, he had spent most of his life covering the Third World's wars, and he was relaxed and good-humored as he went about his job. He seemed to have a favorite story for every unpleasant situation. For driving down deserted roads that might lead straight to combat, for instance, he told the tale of a reporter in Rhodesia who pulled into a little village on a dusty highway and waited for a local bus or truck, known to correspondents as "native mine-sweepers," to precede him on his way. None came. But there were a number of children standing around and he asked them repeatedly if there were any mines or booby traps ahead. "No sir," they assured him, one and all. He drove slowly out of town and, glancing back in his mirror, saw them all cringing and laughing with their hands clamped tight over their ears.

Laugh at a story like that and it puts you oddly at ease when you find yourself in a similar situation.

Dial was a good friend, always easy to talk to, rigorously courteous. Edgar Chamorro, the public relations executive of the Nicaraguan Democratic Force, summed him up when he said, simply, he was "a gentleman, *ese señor*." One day in late June 1983, I found myself waiting for hours for my son, flying down from the States, to emerge at immigration in the Mexico City airport. In the course of this anxious vigil Dial came through on his way back from Los Angeles. His ex-wife, the mother of his children, had died only a few months before and he was trying to spend more time with them, and succeeding. He had just been to his daughter's high school graduation and he was in a bright mood.

In his typically well-mannered style he called me a couple of days later to make sure that my son had indeed arrived all right, and to suggest that we get together at some point in the month, perhaps when he got back from his latest swing through the isthmus. He did not mention that he would be writing about the contras. Maybe at that point Dial did not know he would go looking for Suicida.

* * *

TEGUCIGALPA, HONDURAS

It was about 6 P.M. on June 20 when Edgar Chamorro went to room 406 at the Maya Hotel to talk to Dial. Marcie Johnson was there with him. The daughter of a prominent Honduran politician of the 1940s who spent much of his life in exile, she had good connections, was perfectly bilingual, and worked as a fixer, translator and stringer for ABC. When Dial was in town she worked for him as well. She was a close friend of his, and of his second wife, Lynda Shuster, who was the *Wall Street Journal* correspondent. Marcie was one of the witnesses at their little wedding in Tegucigalpa the year before.

In Dial's room that evening, as often happened when you interviewed Edgar, the conversation soon waxed theoretical and philosophical. Edgar played a game of remarkable frankness as he flacked for the Secret War. He always seemed vaguely bemused by the project, and vaguely disillusioned. But before he talked too much he would retreat into dissertations on Nicaraguan history, American invasions. That night, Edgar talked about why he thought Somoza had lost.

It was a simple analysis. He said Somoza had lost the war because of the *guardias* who killed ABC correspondent Bill Stewart. "It doesn't matter how many of *us* die," Marcie remembered his saying. "What it will take for the Sandinistas to lose will be the first American journalist that dies—that gets killed by them."

The interview began to drag out, and it must have been about a quarter to seven and no one had yet made arrangements to travel the next day, so Marcie went downstairs to the Molinari Rent-a-Car desk in the lobby.

"We were leaving at five-thirty in the morning the next day to go out there. I had been with ABC ten days before. The main highway, the Pan-American road, had been blocked off because they were doing some construction, so it took you a long time to get out there and of course Dial always got lost when he got out in the country and I was going to drive. So I went downstairs and I remember as I was walking out of the room I said, do you have any special indications about the car you want? And he said, 'No, just get a white one for peace.' " Probably it was a little joke.

Dial's newspaper was planning some sort of series. There would be one reporter down on the border with the contras, and another inside Nicaragua with the Sandinistas. It was what I had done, with Ed Cody reporting for *The Washington Post* on the opposite side, three months before. But now the action was concentrated around El Porvenir. The area had been the center of skirmishing and combats for more than a week. To get to Trojes in a regular car one had to take the road that ran right along the border, the same stretch where La Negra had been killed.

Edgar warned Torgerson that Susie Morgan had been shot at on that stretch with a mortar a few days before. "I told him to put up a flag or something—a white flag—and make it clear that you are from the press," Chamorro recalled.

"Dial wanted to do a contra story," Marcie said. "He was interested in what the situation really was. He had heard that La Negra had been killed. The FDN was saying that the Sandinistas had killed her. In Nicaragua they were saying that the FDN had killed her because Suicida was questioning how the leadership was running things and some corruption and other things—and he wanted to see what was happening.

"People were going out there," said Marcie. "It was where the story was, and he wanted to go.

"Dial had decided he wasn't going to take a whole bunch of people," Marcie recalled. "Dial was not one to get into this groupy press deal. He just wanted to get out there, do his thing and come back. He didn't have a whole bunch of time here. He had picked this to do a story and he wanted to go out and come back." He decided he would take just Richard Cross, a free-lance photographer with three years in the region, and Marcie.

Chamorro left at about 7:30 and Marcie and Dial went over mundane, vital details. Should they take a gas can with them? Where could you get black market gas if you had to? Marcie knew the place. And then there was the question of arrangements for the trip to the new U.S. training facility for Hondurans and Salvadorans at the north coast town of Trujillo. This was Monday. The flight to Trujillo would be Wednesday. The embassy was putting on one of its shows.

"Marcie, do you think that you ought to stay and arrange the trip to Trujillo?"

"Dial, I don't think there's that much to arrange. They're the ones that are going to be giving us transportation. I've given them our names, you know." Marcie figured she would be needed more for her Spanish with Dial. He had never really mastered the language, especially the peasant's language. And she knew the road and she knew the people they would be running into.

Dial "got real quiet and he started going through his papers,"

Marcie remembered. "And it was getting late and I was married at the time and lived far away from Teguc and I had the kids and I had to get home. And I remember I said to him, 'Well, if you don't need anything else I think I'm gonna go.'

"And he said to me, 'I don't want you to go on this trip.'

"I said, well, why? There was something there that I didn't understand. He didn't really have a logical explanation for me not going. And I felt I could be good use to him, and he said no, no. And he said to me, you're going to have to get up too early in the morning to come into town and it's a long trip and I think you can do better for me staying here in town. And I looked at him and I said, well, okay, if that's what you want.

"And he says, 'Aren't you afraid?'

"I said, 'Hell no, I'm not afraid. I'm telling you I'll go and I'll drive you there.'

"And he looked at me—and he always treated me like, not a daughter, but more like 'I'm the older man and I'm wise,' you know—and he said, 'No, kid, you stay. Set up the trip for Wednesday.'

"And I remember going out the door and telling him, 'You're not going to change your mind?'

"And he said, 'No.' "

II.

The Honduran-Nicaraguan Border

Icaza went out on patrol at dawn on June 21 with about twenty-five men. Among them was Coyote, the wild-eyed machine-gunner from Krill's squad who carried his M-60 like a toy and wore bandoliers of NATO rounds across his chest. They were waiting near the end of a rugged back road to Trojes for an ammunition shipment to carry in on their backs, and some new battery packs for the radios. This was now the main supply route for the FDN. The contras no longer used the border road at all, even in disguised vehicles. As Suicida had trucked all the supplies he could get into his forward camps for his attacks on Teotecacinte and El Porvenir, he had employed every kind of car and truck he could get his hands on to do the job. The Sandinistas positioned in the hills only 150 or 200 yards away had turned the dirt highway that ran past the burned-out customs house into a firing range where nothing was safe.

"What they had been doing," Icaza recalled, "is shooting every-body else because they believed that we were using those kinds of transportation."

Icaza's position among a stand of pines on the back road was about five hundred yards deeper into Honduras, with a low hill protecting it from the Sandinista guns.

"We heard the explosion at about two or two-thirty in the afternoon," said Icaza. It seemed too loud to be a rocket-propelled grenade. Icaza thought it might be a mortar round and sent one of his men up the hill.

"There is a little white car that's blown up," the commando reported.

Icaza crept to within about a hundred yards of the Toyota to take a look, but he made no effort to reach it because he didn't want to risk the Sandinista guns. "The road is an open field, man. We could get in at nighttime, but not in the day." But Icaza remembers no shooting from the Sandinista side. "They didn't need to fire any more, man. You know, twenty-five pounds of C-4 in that kind of mine blows up a tank. It was powerful enough to tear in pieces that little car.

"It was a shame to see those two Americans die," he said.

Icaza's ammunition and the battery to make his radio work did not arrive until about eight, well after nightfall, and finally he got in touch with Suicida, who knew something of what was happening.

"Hey, two Americans died on the road," Suicida told Icaza.

"Yeah," said Icaza, "I can see the car right here."

"Well, what happened?"

Icaza thought maybe it was an RPG, maybe a mine. He wasn't sure since he was not going to risk a sniper hitting anyone he sent to investigate.

"Don't move," Suicida said over the radio. "There are some soldiers around"—Honduran soldiers—"and they are going to rescue the bodies."

Icaza remembered about five minutes of heavy covering fire. The Honduran helicopter landed and picked up the corpses and left.

When I interviewed Icaza I asked him what Suicida said when it was all over.

"He said, 'Hey, man, this son-of-a-bitch war is starting to get hot. Now the Americans are involved in this shit,' is what he said. He was kind of a little glad that that happened," Icaza recalled.

"Now they are going to feel in their own flesh what we are suffering" were the words Icaza remembered from Suicida. "Now they might open their eyes."

MEXICO CITY, MEXICO

With the randomness of pure chronology, a reporter's notebooks pick up any little fact or impression that needs writing down. The one that sits in front of me at the moment is the battered spiral-bound pad in which I took notes about Dial's death the night it happened and the day afterward. On the first page, by coincidence, was Richard Cross's new address written in his own hand. I had bumped into him at a restaurant in one of Mexico City's wealthy suburbs a couple of days before he went down to Honduras. And I was still in Mexico, still trying to steal time with my wife and son, when a friend called from UPI and, in the course of asking me what I knew about Dial, told me Dial and Richard Cross were dead.

Interviews with some Guatemalan guerrillas living in Mexico City give way in the notebook to an idea for a board game called "Quagmire: The Unconventional War Game." Here is a long scrawl of phone numbers where I was trying to reach Lynda Shuster, who was out reporting a color story on mariachis in Plaza Garibaldi when the story broke about Dial's death. And then the shreds of phone conversation and misinformation and communiqués read by an embassy spokesman apparently as befuddled as anyone by what was going on. Supposedly there were three foreign journalists killed. One of them was said to be a *Time* correspondent, who was in fact in Miami and had to tell all his friends very quickly, after the first news flash, that he was still alive. A supposed witness said there were four dead, three of them "light-complexioned."

The killing was ascribed to "antitank grenades fired by the Sandinista army from the La Tabacalera hacienda in El Porvenir.

"The journalists were traveling in a tourist car on highway from Trojes to Cifuentes and in mentioned place attacked by grenades from Nica territory.

"Car was totally destroyed and its occupants killed immediately."

Then there are notes of a phone conversation with Edgar, saying he warned Dial about the danger, mentioning that it was the same place La Negra was killed.

Edgar was sorry, he said, especially about Dial. *"Es un gentleman, ese señor,"* said Edgar.

More embassy notes. Another spokesman. "Recovered about 10:30 by Honduran military."

Then some prices and phone numbers for a private jet and then this rather long entry dated June 22:

"The cabin of the Saber 60 smells of rose scent and the rubber of the body bag.

"Somehow I wound up becoming Lynda Shuster's escort in the recovery of Dial's body today.

"Carol [my wife] and I drove over to check on her in Mexico this morning a little after eight. There being no other way to get to Tegucigalpa we exercised the license that tragedy gives, or that we figure it ought to give, and we chartered a jet to go get Dial, or what's left of him.

"It seems the White House got interested in the case somewhere along the way—in a big way. And the bureaucratic obstacles that kept us awake most of the night suddenly disappeared in Tegucigalpa in the early afternoon.

"The rule that we had to have the body in a sealed coffin had seemed to stymie everything because you can't fit a coffin in a jet this size. Can't get it through the door.

"Phone calls to L.A., to Sacramento, to Washington by a suddenly hot-to-trot embassy. Turns out you can bring the body in in a body bag if it's a noncommercial flight.

"So Dial lies behind our seats now, blocking the way to the lavatory, in a green rubberized bag that might hold a set of golf clubs or a surfboard, but holds him. The people who put him on board threw the little designer pillows from the seats and my blazer and Lynda's jacket over the bag. But Lynda couldn't help but notice, she said, having already been told by a friend in Teguc, that the body inside the bag was smaller than the man she loved.

"The body, it seems, has no legs."

III.

PINO UNO, HONDURAS

Suicida poured himself another canteen cup of Veuve Clicquot champagne, mixing in some ice and Coca-Cola and rum. He had four or five cases of the stuff brought down from Danlí, but it tasted to him like *chicha*, the drink of corn and water that children drink. It didn't have much of a kick. The caviar was no better. He ate it on a tortilla. It was a bad idea, this champagne and caviar to celebrate his name day, the day of Saints Peter and Paul. It was the kind of idea La Negra would have liked, and it only made a lonely celebration more sour still in this dark cantina in Matazanos. He opened a beer. Where was Krill? He had sent Krill out to blow up one of the bridges between Ocotal and Jalapa. Now he wanted Krill there. He even wanted Icaza, who had gone out partway with Krill for some reason. Send somebody to get Icaza. This party for Pedro Pablo Ortiz Centeno, El Suicida, was going to go on and on.

It was about three in the morning when Icaza got back to Pino Uno. Some of the boys were waiting with a jeep. "Suicida wants to talk to you; he's raising hell in Matazanos."

No, Icaza said, he was tired and he was sick.

"Mr. Icaza, he wants to talk to you. Please, it's his birthday, he wants to have a talk—a drink with you."

Suicida wanted to present Sara. She was his little lady.

Icaza looked at her—a common Nicaraguan peasant girl Suicida had appropriated as he would a heifer. He looked around at the drunken commandos. There was Habakuk, one of his favorites, the recuperating El Campesino and the rest. And Icaza, the judge from Estelí, thought to himself, "This poor soldier. He doesn't have anything in his head. He is low, low class. A poor man. That is the kind of man he is."

Icaza asked if he could have a couple of bottles of the champagne to take with him.

Sure, said Suicida, as much as you want.

Icaza took the bottles down to a little stream and strung a hammock between a couple of trees. He fell asleep in the cool to the sound of the water.

Krill woke him, drunk but smiling. He'd blown the bridge and he'd stolen a couple of cows on the way back to camp. Come on, old man, drink with us. Have a piece of meat. And for the second day in a row the officers of Pino Uno got blitzed to honor El Suicida, and shot their guns in the air, shot Coca-Cola cans and raised hell, as if they celebrated the end of a season.

IV.

WASHINGTON, D.C.

The decision to send ships to the coasts of Central America and mount the biggest joint military maneuvers Honduras ever saw was taken as early as May in Washington, although President Reagan did not sign off on it until July, and Secretary of State Shultz did not know about the naval aspects until he read about them in the papers.

No one was quite certain, it seems, just who was running the policy. Since Enders had been pushed out, the Core Group had lost its core. All voices were more or less equal, and all were competing, in ways they had not been able to before, to dominate the policy. At the same time, Congress was threatening with a vengeance to shut the whole thing off.

Washington had built its policy toward Central America on the compromise idea that a little aid here, a little covert action there, would have to do the job of intimidating enemies and rescuing friends. The crux of the opposition to the policy in the United States was the fear that the region would turn into a quagmire like Southeast Asia, dragging in American troops and making them die for nothing. And the crux of the administration's policy was the insistence that this was not so. The whole idea, as explained by Ambassador Negroponte, among others, was to have the local forces do the work. This was the pitch the president made in repeated speeches, including an appeal to a joint session of Congress in April 1983.

But the problem, perfectly evident by June, was that the local forces were not, in fact, doing what they were supposed to do.

The hope had been Pastora, and Pastora was, to say the least, a disappointment.

The idea of Commander Zero still charmed some of the Agency's men and they were still pushing hard for unity. The magic chemistry of the FDN's army and Pastora's name were still seen as a formula for congressional approval and, perhaps, the kind of presence in Nicaragua that could give this faltering effort of the last two years some claim to permanence. Meetings went on throughout June, with Carlos Coronel shuttling back and forth as Pastora's emissary to the Agency and the FDN leadership.

Meanwhile Tomás Castillo, the new task force director, continued working with the FDN civilians to try to encourage them to think and talk like Edén, to pave the way for a unified effort. There was even a meeting with a Mr. Baker, an expert on the Socialist International, to get them up to speed on the thinking of the moderate left. But Pastora forged ahead on his own program. In early July, Commander Zero mounted an all-out attack to take the little garrison of San Juan del Norte. And he failed.

The military and political leaders of the fight against the Sandinistas seemed, to some of the paramilitary experts who worked with them, terribly naive and willfully inattentive to solid advice. Even Pastora, the veteran guerrilla fighter, seemed plagued by a conspicuous lack of realism. The FDN types were worse still. Shaw and Dewey had to come down on them again and again, demanding that they restructure and rethink their strategies with the emphasis on guerrilla operations. This idea of *guerrilla convencional* was going nowhere fast.

"I think these people had not yet adapted their mind to the fact that they could go in and exist inside Nicaragua without sanctuary," said one advisor from the Agency. "The FDN accepted in theory the idea of unconventional war. But many of these *comandantes* were prima donnas and while they would pay lip service to this sort of thing, what they wanted was to go in and take towns.

"As we learned from the Tet offensive in Vietnam you can't expect a civilian population to rise up and fight a conventional army. They're not going to do it. But these guys were in a sort of dream world." By some accounts, Dewey also harbored that not-so-secret dream.

But the Sandinistas were learning more quickly. And in June, Cuban General Arnaldo Ochoa, the genius of the Angolan wars, arrived to shore up whatever holes they had in their strategy. Their basic arsenal, meanwhile, was fleshed out with truck-mounted rocket launchers, the "Stalin organs" that rained explosives on insurgent forces.

Ways had to be found to rescue the contras from their own incompetence, and Washington's own brilliant General Paul F. Gorman, the newly named commander in chief of the U.S. southern command in Panama, came on the scene to fill the bill. Having served as a national intelligence officer himself during the mid-1970s, Gorman was comfortable, it seems, both with the Agency and with Casey. Gorman had guns and men for maneuvers to intimidate the Sandinistas and back them off if they had any ideas about attacking the contra camps. The ships were an extra flourish at the end. Meanwhile, United Nations Ambassador Jeane Kirkpatrick, whose voice was also heard more often on the project since the demise of Enders, advocated a special presidential commission to study options and make the tougher aspects of the program more palatable for Congress and the public. Henry Kissinger was persuaded to lend his name to that effort.

At the Pentagon there was more and more talk about concepts like "perception management" and "the mantle of inevitable victory."

A pattern was being established; means developed to salvage the contras' war even if they failed to fight it. They were means that had to be employed with increasing force in the months to come.

V.

Pino Uno, Honduras

Suicida wanted to launch one more strike against Jalapa. It did not matter what Bermúdez or Echaverry wanted anymore. July 19 was coming and he was going to mark the anniversary his own way. It would be four years, now, since the retreat to San Juan del Sur and the escape of the barges. There were four days left before the action would begin, and he and his main men went drinking in Matazanos. The old *Cascabeles*, the Rattlesnakes, together.

But something set Krill and Cancer on each other. The hate had been building for a long time. The girl, Irma, was part of it. She loathed Krill and she fed Cancer's resentments. But there had also been the retreat from Jalapa in the December offensive. There had been Cancer's call for help in March, that Krill, busy becoming a celebrity, had left unanswered. And it seems that something Cancer said that afternoon made Krill and Suicida suspicious of him. Something made them think he was a spy for Echaverry, or, at least, that is what they said later.

Why did they fight? "Because of women, because of command, who was the best shot," said one of the soldiers from Pino Uno. "They were drunk. They had some differences. Old-time differences."

And as they got very, very drunk, the differences got very violent, more quickly than any of them could imagine.

They were back at Pino Uno just before nightfall, stumbling and shouting. Cancer had left his gun somewhere. He didn't even have his Browning. Suicida had wandered off to the little barn used as his headquarters, but a crowd of commandos was gathering around to see the fight that was coming. Suddenly Krill ordered some of his men to grab Cancer and tie him up. The wiry young commander struggled in the hands of Krill's men, screaming with fury as they put the cuffs on him. "If you tie me up you're going to shoot me, you motherfucker," Cancer shouted so all the troops could hear. He knew as well as anyone what Krill did with people who were tied up: the boot and the knife or the bullet in the nape of the neck.

Country people who had joined the ranks for ideals or adventure or fear had seen these fights before, but this looked different. Krill was pushing Cancer and Cancer was still screaming at him, stumbling, now falling on himself in his semi-stupor. It could have been almost funny. He was down on the ground as Suicida came walking back from the headquarters to see what was happening.

Krill looked at the men around him and at Suicida coming to pull him back from his goal, and suddenly he dropped onto Cancer, pinning him with his knees. He put the Browning to Cancer's chest, firing again and again before anyone moved, his eyes still on the men around him ready to fend off anyone who tried to stop him.

"You son of a bitch!" shouted Suicida. "You've screwed everything."

But nobody was making any moves in those first seconds after the shots. Cancer lay dead under Krill's knee, little bubbles of blood welling up from the powder-burned holes in his chest. Nobody wanted to get in trouble with Krill. The son of a bitch was crazy. And he was quick. He grabbed an M-60 held by one of the commandos who had come to watch. "All right, sons of bitches," he shouted like the cornered killer of a B-movie, "anybody tries to fuck me, I'm going to ventilate him with this machine gun."

The commandos edged back, many of them ran, clearing the area around Krill and the corpse.

Suicida looked at Krill. He seems to have known at this moment that he was on his own again. *They* were on their own. Every man in the camp had seen this scandal. Tegucigalpa would find out and use it against him. And Cancer's own men, two or three hundred of them, were going to be a problem. There was going to be war in Suicida's own ranks because of this if he did not do something. But Krill was his own man. Krill had been with him so long.

He could come up with a story: Cancer had been paid by Echaverry—maybe $100,000—to kill him. Krill had saved him just in time. And there might have been some people who would believe that. But not those who were there in the camp.

"We're packing," he said. "We're moving Pino Uno to Arenales."

Suicida took the big tent that had been the hospital. He took radios and ammunition and guns. He had hidden more than a hundred captured rifles and other supplies against the possibility that he might ever have to set off again on his own, and in the no-man's land of Nicaragua he thought he could find safety. He could still fight the Communists better than anyone. He could trade on that with Villegas if no one else. But even before he crossed into the Segovias his men were leaving him. What had been a force of more than two thousand at that point, a third or more of the total force of the FDN, splintered into collections of a hundred men here, fifty there. Everybody kept his mouth shut. Still they were reluctant to blame Suicida himself. The problem, they told each other, was that his officers used him. Krill used him. La Negra had used him. But one could not endure this any longer. They still hated the staff in Tegucigalpa. They still loved Suicida, many of them. But they disappeared. And Suicida and Krill and the old group from the Rattlesnakes, each with a few men of his own, went back to the mountains where they had started in the days of the .22s.

TEGUCIGALPA, HONDURAS

There is a story told, but not solidly confirmed, of an incident a few weeks later:

Suicida still called on his radio demanding supplies, but he was cut off, perhaps in the hope that his command would wither and die completely. Nobody wanted to try, yet, to capture him. And nobody was going to take the responsibility of going to Arenales to talk to him.

So nobody expected him and Krill to appear in Tegucigalpa in full combat gear. They burst into the safe house of the general staff, bullets in their chambers. They weren't going to leave until their demands were met.

None of the staff appears to have been there at that moment. But any shoot-out would be disastrous. Support for the effort was already low in the United States, funds could dry up and the supplies for the coming offensive were short in any case. If this mutiny among the contras in the middle of Tegucigalpa got out—if it led to bloodshed when the town was full of reporters from the States—there could be a disaster. But Suicida and Krill were hell-bent on being a disaster.

No one could talk to Suicida but Villegas. As the story was told later the smooth, white-haired veteran of dirty wars spoke quietly to the mad commanders of the Segovias. "Calm down," he told them. "Calm down."

"No," said Suicida. "No, man. I ask for help and no one comes. I'm fighting and the other units won't give me help. Echaverry won't even answer the radio. Why won't a single member of the general staff come to the combat zone?" It was the old problem, only now it was much worse. These people were sleeping in their nice houses, going to bars and casinos here in the capital. He was fighting the war.

"No," said Villegas. Suicida knew he had always been the Argentine's favorite. They had been in this war together for so long. Villegas had taken care of him before, had gotten him what he needed to fight. And Villegas would do it again. But he couldn't if Suicida continued with this craziness. "Calm yourself," he said.

The commander of the Segovias was wary and at first refused to submit. When finally he agreed to leave he seems to have known he had put a price on his head. He went to see Ortiz at Radio 15, and Ortiz didn't know what to say when he heard what Suicida had done. "Go back to the mountains" was the only advice he could give. "Don't come back to the capital."

Word spread instantly in Tegucigalpa of Suicida's action, and the rot that had been eating away at the command for months began dissolving into chaos. Suicida was a renegade that no one could handle, and no one would take responsibility.

"He's mutinied," members of the FDN told each other.

"Against whom?" someone would ask.

"Against the general staff."

"But there is no general staff."

Shaw and Dewey were still big on the idea of command and control as the solution to their worst problems with the FDN. They had worked out a system to sidestep Echaverry and Bermúdez. Bermúdez had proved, as a young woman said years before, "mainly an office officer." He had a large collection of pictures taken in the base camps, but most of the time he was ensconced in the base at Lepaterique, a short drive from the capital, or, indeed, in the capital itself. Echaverry was worse still, and bore the added stigma of his Argentine connections. The Argentines, more than ever, were seen as a dead and possibly larcenous weight in the operation.

Now a new offensive was in the making and Dewey himself had come down, along with Monica, to help Shaw make it work. It was going to be a major push around Ocotal. It was going to put the FDN back on the map. But, most importantly, it was going to establish the new system of command and control.

The idea was to have a single officer running operations from a camp either on the frontier or, preferably, inside Nicaragua itself. He would be called a "tactical commander" or a "theater commander" and he would see to the needs and the strategies of the various task forces. He would clear up any confusion about objectives, disbursements, discipline. The theater commander would take away the motives for insubordination. He would clean up.

Bermúdez and his staff were wary. It was obvious enough that the tactical commander could be used to cut them out altogether. They rejected the first name suggested by the Americans and countered with one of their own; the bright young ex-Guardia captain Hugo Villagra, who went by the code name Visage.

Visage had led the attack on Radio Noticias for the Argentines in 1980, then spent a year in Costa Rica's jails. He won his freedom when he planned, and his buddies executed, the hijacking of a local Costa Rican airliner. But plagued by disaster, he was arrested again in El Salvador when his pilot made the mistake of setting down there rather than in a secure strip arranged for him across the border in Guatemala. Another year in prison, but this time defended and protected by the ultra-rightists of Roberto d'Aubuisson's political network. The U.S. embassy officially fought to have him extradited to Costa Rica. D'Aubuisson's people fought to have him freed. D'Aubuisson's people won. A protégé of Somoza's son. A terrorist in Costa Rica. An airplane hijacker. A close friend of the men who sponsored El Salvador's death squads. This was the man who was supposed to clean up the operations of the FDN.

The Agency accepted him.

One of his first assignments was to get Krill.

VI.

THE NICARAGUAN-HONDURAN BORDER

The jackhammer percussion of the helicopter rotors was audible several seconds before the machine itself appeared coming in low and fast across the Poteca River into Nicaragua. It landed at the edge of the ramshackle camp that Krill and his patrol had made. On the Honduran Air Force "Huey" helicopter were one of Alvarez's liaison officers and Visage, now theater commander for the FDN. The new offensive was going to begin soon and Visage was scrambling to put his forces into some kind of order. Krill was not there, the people said, but he was on his way back. He had attacked El Jícaro and it had been bad. There were a lot of dead.

Visage waited on the green hillside.

For almost two months Suicida and his men had been "in rebellion." Troops under one of his group commanders or another—
hundreds of troops, some of them the best fighters in the contra army
—were wandering all over the place. And nothing had been done.

But the time for the big new offensive, Operation Marathon, was
getting near and Suicida's troops were needed. A base was going to be
set up to try to recuperate them. And something—nobody was saying
and maybe nobody knew what it was—something was going to be done
with Suicida and Krill, Caramalo and Habakuk.

Visage could say he had seen this coming. Suicida's loss of control
had been gradual and Visage had tried to warn the general staff months
before. But then Suicida's men were fighting a lot. All the patrols were
operating fairly well; they were ambushing all over the place. They
inflicted a lot of casualties on the Sandinistas. Everyone was involved.
Pino Uno was the force that gave the greatest results.

There were reports even then, Visage recalled, about the cattle
rustling, and padding troop strengths, and failing to pay the local peasants for supplies. There were some rapes. And all that had provoked a
certain concern. You said something to Suicida and he said he was
going to correct it. But he hadn't, of course. He'd already lost control.

Krill and Caramalo were the worst of the worst. Visage considered
them complete thugs. And with Krill there was this thing of killing his
own commandos for the least cause. There were a great quantity of
them, not just two or three. It could be for any reason at all, whatever
little thing: say, for example, that one was very late bringing some
information. Visage knew that kind of thing had been common on the
Southern Front during the war of '78 and '79. But here in the FDN they
had said they weren't going to do that. You can punish a person by
demanding his attention, putting him on watch or sending him on a
hike, because you have to take disciplinary measures for certain kinds
of failings. But you don't kill the man.

Ten, twenty, thirty—there may have been as many as forty commandos killed by Krill. No one knew for certain. Their stories were
lost to confused rumor and unmarked graves. And then there had been
Jaguar. And then Cancer. And the camp had broken to bits. And now
it was weeks, months later, and Visage had to try to put it all back
together again.

The Americans were saying they didn't want to get involved, although of course they knew about these "anomalies." Shaw, the sta-

tion chief, maintained that all this was an internal affair for the FDN to resolve. The main thing the Americans seemed concerned about with Suicida, and others, was the padding of the payrolls.

The men started coming in now from the disaster at Jícaro, their ragged green shirts dark with sweat, limping from the march and staggering from wounds. Visage had been informed that this attack was going to be mounted, and Krill was ordered not to make it. Like all the other orders it was ignored. Krill had gone after the town where the American Capuchins lived. There should have been diversions and feints to throw the defenders off guard. It could have been done. But Krill had gone after it like a madman. They had lost a lot of people. Some of the dead were being carried in now. And La Niña among them, one of the commanders Visage had hoped to salvage from the Pino Uno fiasco.

Krill always moved more easily than the rest. Visage waited for him. Visage had brought with him four of the boys he had trained as his special corps to go with him to set up the new command post inside Nicaragua. They spread out slightly to cover lines of fire.

Visage ordered Krill into the copter. And Krill told him to go to hell. He was staying here in the mountains with his men. No, said Visage, these boys of his were here to establish a base where they could begin to recuperate all those from Pino Uno who were wandering the mountains without rest these last months. Krill was no longer needed here.

Krill looked around for backing from among the commandos. But Visage had chosen his moment well. There were no eyes to look into that signaled support. The hundred or so men in Krill's patrol were exhausted and beaten. They were not going to fight with the new tactical commander and these men from his staff and the Honduran liaison as well.

Krill was angry, but he swung himself into the Huey.

Caramalo was picked up the same day. Visage saw him as a bum now, not even trying to carry on the war with his little group of men. Both the prisoners were taken to the abandoned chicken farm—La Quinta Escuela—now run by the Argentines as their school just outside the capital.

El Suicida was not arrested when Captain Luque, the Honduran liaison, found him near Arenales. By some accounts he was with his woman Sara. He was invited back to the capital to talk. Suicida trusted Luque. He had heard there were changes and he went.

*   *   *

TEGUCIGALPA, HONDURAS

Ortiz did not know what had happened to Suicida until a note was smuggled to him at Radio 15. "*Parientito,* they've captured me," Ortiz remembered it saying. "My life's in danger. They want to kill me."

It had been only a few nights since they had talked, when Suicida had come up to the capital with Luque. And even then Suicida had worried. "*Parientito,* they want to kill us," he had told Ortiz. "A few days ago they asked me if I was related to you. They're going to kill us. First me and then you," he said, "because we're always criticizing the shameless bastards."

Ortiz called Villegas at La Quinta to try to get an idea of what was happening.

"Suicida has got problems," said Villegas. "Don't get into it."

Ortiz said that if there was going to be some kind of proceeding he wanted to defend Suicida.

"Don't get involved," said Villegas. "I love him, too, but don't get involved."

The manager of Radio 15, Suicida's oldest friend in Tegucigalpa, drove to La Quinta to see what he could do, and once again he confronted Villegas. Even as they talked he could hear from one of the rooms—or thought he could—the voice of a man shouting. "*Parientito! Parientito!*" But Villegas would not let him in.

Ortiz and his woman, Laura, felt helpless. They rationalized their impotence with the belief that, whatever happened, Suicida would not be harmed. They thought that Suicida might be forced out of the service, as so many of the old officers had been, or might even be jailed somewhere for a time.

VII.

TEGUCIGALPA, HONDURAS

"They were people who never accepted any of their mistakes," said one of the FDN officers who judged Suicida and Krill, Caramalo and Habakuk. "Not one. They said it was all envy, that it was a confabulation; they had done everything 'for the fatherland.' But 'for the fatherland' is not going around killing people who are fighting for you; your own comrades. 'For the fatherland' is not raping women."

Krill, especially, "never accepted his error, even though he was confronted with all the facts and the investigation: that they inter-viewed many people; that, well, it was an exhaustive investigation because we wanted to prove that the acts really had occurred. We did not want to make any mistake ourselves. Statements were taken from many people: group commanders, detachment commanders, combat-ants, women, men. All the anomalies came out, all the disasters, all the evil. It was plainly confirmed. All the charges that there were against him confirmed that he was a man who was noxious to the struggle.''

Suicida and the rest were confronted with the charges at La Quinta in a makeshift court-martial before the general staff. Some former Guardia officers, majors and lieutenant colonels, had been brought down from Miami to conduct the investigation and the proceedings. But there was about the affair an atmosphere of nervous self-righteous-ness.

"What are you going to do with them?" asked Salvador Icaza, the former judge from Estelí, when he was called to testify to the general staff. "Are you going to kill them? Are you going to execute them? What are you going to do with Krill and these other guys?"

He had tried to bring attention to the problems months before, when a lot of people who were dead now, were still alive. "You're not going to use my testimony against anybody else, because you're re-sponsible for this shit," he said.

Icaza blamed the old Guardia officers and the general staff. He remembered only one time that any one of them had visited Pino Uno while he was there, and then it was Diablo Morales, who had known Icaza as a civilian in Nicaragua and had insulted him, asking Suicida what "all these civilians were doing here," as if he believed that only the old Guardia were any good. And Icaza blamed the Argentines, the way they trained people and sent them back full of their Argentine arrogance.

Echaverry had been holding Icaza's passport for weeks to get the visa "fixed." Icaza thought of it as he stood in front of the general staff and he demanded it back. Echaverry said he would send it when the Americans returned it. "I sent it to them and it never came back," he said.

"You are a damned liar," said the sad-eyed judge. "You never sent it." He opened the drawer of the desk and took it out himself.

It was a trivial protest, perhaps, in the middle of the proceeding, but Icaza wanted to show just how little he trusted Echaverry.

And by then Icaza's was only one angry voice among many. Several of the field commanders were fed up with the high command. When they saw the new officers arriving for the trial some suspected that yet another bunch of old losers was going to be imposed on them. They wanted to run their own war their own way, and a much broader mutiny than anything Suicida alone could have led was beginning to develop. The ploy of the tactical commander was not working after all.

The long-planned Operation Marathon had been nothing but a feeble sprint. The Sandinistas had cut them to bits. And dissension was much worse as a result. Everything about it had been screwed up. El Negro Chamorro's little band had gotten into trouble quickly, called for more guns and been turned down by the CIA station. They were nearly cut to pieces and blamed the Agency for it. They were supposed to have stayed away from the border posts, to keep from embarrassing the Hondurans. Instead they attacked them. There were diversions all around as Visage had planned, but Mack's main body, the Nicarao Task Force, was hours late getting to Ocotal, so instead of taking it, all they did was shoot up the slums on its edges. Even one of their propaganda film makers got there ahead of them. The logistics problems that were predicted months before now came true. Marathon was routed after four days.

There were more questions all the time about the money. The commanders were sure that Echaverry and Bermúdez and the rest were pocketing funds meant for the war. The Agency grew so suspicious it brought in lie detectors.

And still there was Suicida.

The majors and lieutenant colonels from Miami "brought out the facts encountered and the realities and made their recommendation," said one of his captors. Death.

"We held a consultation with the three officers who made the investigation and with the general staff and arrived at the conclusion that this was the only thing you could do. We couldn't keep being mild; we had to set a good example and a good precedent—above all in the case of Krill, who had killed so many, well, commandos."

The tone of the officer suggested that the commandos alone would not have been sufficient cause for the death penalty.

"Above everything he had killed a good group commander," said Krill's captor. "Right there in the camp. For pleasure. For pleasure! That was our complaint against him. It was too much. We arrived at the conclusion that this was the only measure that you could take."

But you could not kill just one of these men. They were born to vengeance. They all had to be eliminated. Suicida, Krill, Caramalo, Habakuk.

"In accordance with the recommendations of the junta, our being in agreement on this, it was the only thing we could do. There was nothing else."

Just where the execution took place, and exactly when, is one of those elements of the story that people call a rumor even when they know the fact.

The rumor was that they were taken to El Aguacate, the big airstrip built and run by the Americans near the Nicaraguan border and from which most of the airborne supplies were flown to FDN units inside Nicaragua. Hugo Villagra—Visage—was supposed to be the executioner, with a squad of riflemen brought in from among Mack's troops at La Lodosa.

But Krill and Caramalo and Habakuk were "taken to the border" and executed a few days before Suicida, according to one of his captors. Probably they were taken inside the Nicaraguan border to die. The Americans who had tried so hard to keep their hands clean of this affair would not have wanted the executions taking place at one of their facilities.

And one member of the FDN told me that Suicida himself died at La Quinta and was buried there, then that his body was moved.

I found in my interviews one other reference to what happened to Suicida.

Early in October 1983, a member of the general staff is supposed to have taken a newly arrived American called John Kirkpatrick on a tour of the Tegucigalpa installations. Perhaps without thinking, he made a stop at La Quinta Escuela.

As other members of the FDN later heard the story, screaming could be heard as the two of them walked into the school. Villegas came out in a hurry and pulled the staff member aside. "What the hell are you doing with the American here?" La Quinta was an Argentine operation. The Americans were not supposed to show their faces there.

Suicida was being interrogated, according to the story that circulated in the FDN. For several days he had been held naked with no food, and he was tortured. Maybe it had something to do with the money.

The American, it was said, had no idea what was happening.

Epilogues

Suicida was a secret the men who fought the Sandinistas tried to keep from themselves. In August 1983, Bermúdez would threaten Edgar Chamorro for talking to reporters about Suicida's June rampage. A year after the executions Aristides Sanchez would still say in Tegucigalpa, "I don't know anything about Suicida." Even as details of what had happened did begin to leak out, and one by one men like Chamorro and Salvador Icaza, appalled by what they knew, began to talk about Suicida, they would always do so as if he were an aberration. Icaza would call the history of Suicida "something like My Lai," the infamous massacre by American troops in Vietnam. "What happened with Suicida and with Krill," he said, "whatever they did, that does not reflect the FDN. They were particular people who did crazy things." Yet, just as the special case of My Lai grew from the common horror of Vietnam—symbolized it, epitomized it—as the history of covert action against Nicaragua emerged in the months after Suicida's execution, it was clear that he represented much of what was wrong with the Secret War, and much that could never be set right with it.

Suicida's case was special, but it was not unique, and it was precisely to compensate for the failings it represented in the covert action that the CIA had to make its role ever more direct, ever more public. Covers were blown. Pretenses were dropped. As the Agency scrambled to keep the project going, it took measures that ultimately undermined the project, leading finally to the long-anticipated cutoffs of American money in late 1984 and early 1985. But by then the administration had shown itself—even if it did not declare itself—at war with Nicaragua. It would not back away, and perhaps by then with so much prestige on the line it could not. Soon enough, one by one, and often little heralded, Americans began to die in a fight that, without men like Suicida, would never have existed. Slowly the door for direct intervention widened.

THE MANUAL

Terror was always a tool the FDN commanders considered at their disposal. In earlier years they had set off bombs in airports, hijacked planes, murdered officials. "We're not using terrorism," Echaverry said in July 1983. But that "doesn't mean we don't have the capacity," he added.

The problem was to keep "implicit and explicit terror" under control, and to that end, in the wake of Suicida's rebellion, the Agency commissioned a manual on "Psychological Operations in Guerrilla Warfare."

The idea of such a book had been around for some time. It had come up at least as early as June 1983 when Casey and Dewey and their colleagues dropped in on Honduras and El Salvador. The Argentines had tried their hands at one. But after Suicida's rampages, the need was more urgent. Echaverry, probably fresh from meetings with Dewey, would say that Suicida's problem was his failure to grasp the basic principles of insurgency. Suicida himself and other commanders were attending seminars, Echaverry claimed in July 1983: "a system of immersion, a bath in the thinking of guerrillas."

The man who finally got the job of producing the manual was the CIA contract agent known as John Kirkpatrick. The Nicaraguans he worked with the most were Edgar Chamorro, Noel Ortiz, Laura Ortiz and Salvador Icaza.

Kirkpatrick was affable, if a little strange. An older man, he dressed entirely in black. He told some of the Nicaraguan exiles he worked with that it was to inspire a cult of death among the fighting men, but Laura used to tease him and call him "the umpire" and ask him if he wore black underwear, too. Shaw, the station chief, would just shake his head and smile at Kirkpatrick's eccentricity. But Kirk-patrick, like a mourner, had a right to wear black. He was a veteran of ugly, unheard-of battles where a lot of people died and few cared. His business was to convince the fighters that what they did was noble, and their causes were worthwhile.

"He was not a big deal, a big wheel," one of the Nicaraguans remembered. "He would drink a little bit. But his intentions were great. He was a good man and he did a lot of things for us. Sometimes we'd sit up long, long nights at Radio 15 de Septiembre. Sometimes he'd visit us at the camps."

In late November and early December 1983, Kirkpatrick and his Nicaraguan friends visited several of the FDN bases. Icaza told him about Suicida and what he had seen and heard. In one camp after another, as they looked into questions of morale and the conduct of the troops, new stories of brutality emerged. "There's a bunch of shit they're doing to us here," men would say, and then they would begin to tell their stories. Rape. The execution of prisoners. Mistreatment of the men. Kirkpatrick heard it all.

Other men in the Agency bureaucracy might have tried not to know. But John Kirkpatrick, this odd, aging man in black, was not really of the bureaucracy. He was part of that group of contract people working for IAD (International Activities Division) whom regular Agency personnel would sometimes describe with open contempt, and sometimes dismay.

A station chief is likely to be a generalist. He is going to know about the politics, economics and society of the country to which he is assigned, and he is supposed to know it well. He may have some background in covert action and paramilitary operations, but he also has to hold up the intelligence side of his job. The people who work for IAD, on the other hand, are support staff and specialists. They know demolition or they know psychological operations, they know air op-erations or ground or marine operations, but they may know nothing at all about the countries where they work.

"When you're not running a war, you don't know what to do with these people," the Agency's old-timers would sometimes say. "And when you are running a war they don't know how to do it."

But John Kirkpatrick thought he knew quite a bit about his end of a paramilitary operation: the psychology of it. He knew what gained you the kind of popular response the Agency was looking for from the rebels, and what kinds of things could lose it for you very quickly. He

knew about those special circumstances when an assassination might
be unavoidable, even appropriate. He knew from studying the methods
of the Communists everywhere, and from his own experience in Vietnam and from what he learned from the Phoenix program there, how
you could make even an accidental killing work in your favor. But he
also knew what a My Lai could do, and the way one massacre could
destroy your credibility. So he examined the bits and pieces of the story
no one had wanted to know, apparently hoping the damage could be
repaired.

Living at the house with Laura and Noel Ortiz, working long hours
day after day, Kirkpatrick put together a manual much like the old
course outlines used for the Green Berets at Fort Bragg back in the
1960s. The final product was a little book with a cover in the blue and
white of the Nicaraguan flag. The graphic motif was rows of heads with
large holes through them. Targets. It looked as if they were targets for
snipers. But the idea was that the targets were their minds.

Chamorro objected to some parts of the manual, where it was
suggested criminals be hired to carry out some of the FDN's dirty
work, and a few pages were ripped out of some copies. But Icaza used
the manual happily in the new classes he was teaching. Icaza was now
training psychological warfare teams to travel with the combat units. If
they did not win the hearts of the peasants, they were at least supposed
to think twice before they murdered them.

What the Agency higher-ups thought of the manual nobody knew,
and nobody seems to have asked. The administration at Langley never
bothered to read it. And Dewey, for one, could not. He didn't know
Spanish. When the storm over "Psychological Operations in Guerrilla
Warfare" broke in October 1984, almost a year after it was distributed,
it seems the Agency was utterly flabbergasted.

It was a week before Reagan and Mondale were to debate foreign
policy, and the storm was quintessentially a matter of Washington perceptions and politics. What was important to the legalistic minds of the
capital was that the manual seemed a direct contravention of a presidential directive explicitly barring the CIA from getting involved with
assassinations: "No person employed by or acting on behalf of the
U.S. government shall engage in or conspire to engage in assassinations." The manual talked about "neutralizing" Sandinista officials,
and in context that sounded like murdering them. Washington is much
more oriented toward paper than people, and the juxtaposition of two
pieces of paper—the directive and the manual—made the story.

Congress acted appalled. But Dewey had pointedly told the congressional committees months before that there were assassinations of Sandinista officials—and so what? Dewey said at a secret briefing in late 1983 that "civilians and Sandinista officials in the provinces, as well as heads of cooperatives, nurses, doctors and judges" had been killed by his rebels. But that didn't contradict the presidential directive, Dewey said. "These events don't constitute assassinations because as far as we are concerned assassinations are only those of heads of state," Dewey reportedly told the committees. "I leave definitions to the politicians," he said. "After all, this is a war—a paramilitary operation," he said.

His words reflected perfectly the attitudes of many agents. Even after the manual controversy broke, one of the CIA men who worked in Honduras said flatly, "Let's face it, our people are teaching people how to kill people, how to set up ambushes, how to set up a claymore so it can kill the most people." As another CIA veteran suggested, it wasn't a *manual* that made killers of the FDN's commanders. "Maybe if your friend Suicida hadn't had any *guns* he would have been a nice person. . . ." Shaw told people at the time of the controversy that he figured it was a "fifteen-day flap." But as often happened with Shaw in 1984, he was wrong. The manual epitomized in the eyes of Congress the crazy clumsiness and dubious morality of the covert program. It led directly to a freeze of funding in the fall of 1984.

THE MINING

The virtual disintegration of Suicida's unit, the largest in the contra army, brought an already faltering effort to a virtual standstill. No one was there to take up the slack. And some commanders were making utter fools of themselves.

In early August 1983 Comandante "Mack" was surprised by a Sandinista attack on his camp and took off running, leaving behind in a hammock his briefcase full of documents, expense receipts and photographs. On August 6 the Managua newspapers ran pictures of Mack and Bermúdez and Echaverry, Noel Ortiz and Suicida, the Argentine Villegas and other advisors. One was a group shot in front of a U.S.-supplied Honduran Air Force helicopter. Mack's telephone book had been in the briefcase, along with the numbers of General Alvarez's aide, Alexander Hernandez. There were receipts for gas and for the

C-4 explosive used to blow bridges and electrical towers. There was Mack's false Argentine passport with a multiple-entry U.S. visa, his Miami Creditbank card and his American Social Security card (No. 264-91-8946) in his real name, José B. Bravo.

In October the failure of Operation Marathon underlined both the contras' incompetence and the Agency's misguided expectations. When Dewey visited Tegucigalpa in the late summer along with Monica he had been warned by U.S. military officials connected with the program that the kind of logistical support he was planning to give for Operation Marathon—at most a pair of World War II vintage C-47 transports—was simply not sufficient to keep the troops going. But the Agency had gone ahead with the offensive, and the deficient logistics, anyway. And the offensive had, as predicted, proved disastrous.

Since the contras seemed to be doing such a poor job, the Agency decided to take more direct action.

In August and September a new "finding" was put together. On September 20, 1983, it was presented to the congressional committees by Secretary of State George Shultz, who had replaced Haig the year before, and by Casey. In a move meant to appease the legalistic minds of Washington, the new finding dropped the tired argument about interdicting arms. Now the quid pro quo about supporting Nicaragua's rebels until the Sandinistas stopped supporting subversion in other countries was made explicit. There was, an administration official said carefully, "no thought of the administration backing the insurgents in trying to overthrow the Sandinista government."

The Senate committee took the bait and voted the money the administration wanted. The House went along, too.

But what neither side of Congress knew, or was told, was that major changes were taking place in the program. The Agency was falling into an old, familiar pattern—and failing—of the American military. When the troops couldn't do the job, technology was supposed to fill the gap.

"If the FDN and Pastora's people can't really do things that hurt, it's got to be worked out another way" is the way one senior intelligence official recalls the attitude during that period. "There was constant pressure for that. Casey was pressing the IAD and Dewey Clarridge to come up with things."

"There was a push to have some kind of success in Nicaragua, something that would quell congressional criticism. To show that we were doing things.

"I supposed some of Casey's impatience was that neither the FDN nor Pastora were having any political effect. Dewey was hoping for defections of [whole] Nicaraguan units, but as far as I know that never happened."

In August and September 1983, after their futile efforts to take isolated little San Juan del Norte (Graytown), Edén Pastora's forces operating out of Costa Rica began using CIA–supplied airplanes for attacks as well as resupply missions. When one of them, a Cessna, crashed at Managua airport after dropping two 150-pound bombs, it was quickly traced back to mysterious Agency-linked companies that supplied it. The bombs were traced to El Salvador.

In high-tech operations, for obvious reasons of discipline and skill, the Agency preferred to use its own people. "Unilaterally controlled Latino assets" it called the men it contracted from Ecuador and various other South American countries. In September and October 1983 a series of attacks on Nicaragua's port facilities were begun. Before dawn on October 10, millions of gallons of fuel erupted into flames on the Corinto waterfront. Tens of thousands of residents in the flimsy wooden shacks that surrounded the area were forced to flee the city, and for hours as firefighters struggled against the flames it appeared that everything would be lost. The FDN claimed responsibility, but no Nicaraguan had anything to do with the attack. It was carried out by the "Latino assets" using speedboats to work from a CIA mother ship anchored several miles out to sea.

"There were some operations that we didn't even know about until afterwards," Edgar Chamorro later told the *Los Angeles Times*. "Calero [an FDN director and nominal commander in chief] didn't have any part in it at all. Bermúdez went once to blow up a bridge, but he wasn't taking an active part; he was just a guest on a boat. He told me that the man doing the job was an Ecuadoran who almost drowned and never found the target. The sun was coming up, the frogman wasn't back yet and everyone in the boat was very nervous. The man finally showed up at the last minute and they grabbed him and ran north. Bermúdez was very critical; he said, 'Why don't the North Americans just give us the money and let us do it?' "

Bermúdez confirmed the account to the *Times:* "That was at Paso Caballo. It didn't succeed."

But the CIA and the administration generally were feeling a new potency in the fall of 1983. They had, at relatively little cost and with amazing popular support, knocked over the chaotic, Communist re-

gime on the tiny Caribbean island of Grenada. Dewey reportedly took
to driving around with a bumper sticker that said "Nicaragua Next."
Old acquaintances of his, bumping into him at an airport, remember
him gushing about what was going on with "my war."

"Dewey would run to Casey with a report that showed something
good was happening," recalled one CIA official. "And it might not be
true. But Casey would say, 'Why isn't it?' He wanted to hear that good
things were happening down there."

On January 2, 1984, one of Shaw's assistants woke Edgar early in
the morning and gave him a press statement. The FDN had mined
Nicaragua's harbors, it said. Telegrams were to be sent to Lloyd's of
London, so insurance rates would rise. The FDN dutifully claimed
credit. But the FDN had not done any part of that job either, or other
mining operations that followed. The CIA's men working off a "mother
ship" again had planted the small explosive devices in the harbors. The
idea was to squeeze the Sandinistas' economy as the contra forces
themselves were never able to do. The effort failed. Most ships continued to come in, despite some damage from the "firecracker" mines.
Exxon had announced earlier that it would no longer send its tankers
into Nicaraguan ports but—in a now familiar pattern—the Soviet
Union soon moved to fill the gaps with its own ships. Far from pressuring the Sandinistas to pull away from Moscow, the action pushed them
closer still.

The first reports of all this went largely unremarked in Washington.
But when the French offered to clear the ports and other American
allies began to protest about the operation, Congress started to take
note. The Senate intelligence committee especially, perhaps because it
normally was more supportive of the program than the House, felt it
had been deceived. Goldwater wrote a furious letter to Casey. "This is
no way to run a railroad," he said. "I am pissed off!"

Nicaragua took the matter of the mining and the entire secret war
to the World Court and the Reagan administration had to disavow the
court's jurisdiction. The pretense of legality for the operation against
Nicaragua was being stripped away along with its secrecy.

THE DIRTY WARRIORS

After the near rebellion of the field commanders in December 1983,
partly spurred by concerns they had shared with Suicida and conster-

nation about what happened to him, the entire high command of the FDN was once again reorganized. Bermúdez managed to stay, after making a power play and threatening to take most of the civilian front men on the Directorate with him. As Shaw told one member of the Directorate, Bermúdez had been with the effort too long to let go. But Echaverry returned to Argentina.

By then a new civilian president had been elected in Buenos Aires and the last of the men who had organized the Secret War and run it for Washington went home. Names of key figures at the top of the operation surfaced in the trials of senior officers begun in the spring of 1985. Villegas's whereabouts and true identity are unknown. But Colonel Osvaldo Ribeiro served until early 1985 as second-in-command of Argentine army intelligence in Buenos Aires. Passed over for promotion, he quietly retired.

Ricardo Lau did not leave so easily. He remained a part-time resident of Tegucigalpa, working closely with Bermúdez in one shady capacity or another, at least until late 1984. "He's a man who takes care of himself," said one of his acquaintances in the FDN. "His house is in Colonia, Los Angeles, in front of the Tomy Supermarket. He has his wife in Guatemala, but another woman in Tegucigalpa. He goes around in a mustard-colored Toyota pickup with smoked windows." Finally, in January 1985 the Hondurans reportedly threw El Chino out.

On December 31, 1984, the Honduran armed forces issued a communiqué on the results of an investigation into political disappearances. In oblique language it said it "suspected that some of the persons reported missing could have been the victims of a vendetta carried out by non-Honduran irregular armed leftist and rightist groups." But in private, army officers made it clear that they were talking about some of the contras, and particularly about Lau. The Hondurans most involved with the disappearances were the ones, like Alexander Hernandez, who were most involved with the contras, and with Gustavo Alvarez.

But General Alvarez himself was no longer there. On March 31, 1984—to his enormous surprise, and the Agency's—General Gustavo Alvarez was arrested and thrown out of the country by his subordinates. Alvarez's ambitions had become ever more transparent. He was actively maneuvering to make himself president at the expense of the elected civilian Roberto Suazo Cordova. He looked as though he could do it, too, until he made the mistake of insulting several of his officers and telling them he would remove them from their commands. Their response was to remove him first. Alvarez subsequently went to live in Miami, where, in the fall of 1984, several of his closest associates—a Palestinian building contractor, an international arms dealer, and his former second-in-command of the Honduran army—were indicted for plotting to kill Suazo Cordova. Alvarez himself was not directly implicated.

THE AMERICANS

Shaw, the station chief in Tegucigalpa, was very close to Gustavo Alvarez. Everybody knew that, especially the officers who plotted the general's overthrow. At the official, public level, the U.S. commitment to Alvarez had been enormous. Military assistance to the armed forces he commanded had risen from $4 million in loans in 1980 to $77.5 million in grants in 1984. In that same period, combined U.S.–Honduran military maneuvers on an unprecedented scale were a major overt tool used to pressure the Sandinistas and protect, as a deterrent, the contra base camps. But it was at the covert and even the personal level that Shaw was closest to Alvarez. An estimated $80 million had been spent on the Secret War by 1984. And the general had been the key to the key Argentine connection that had made it all possible. On a personal level, the station chief and his wife adopted a little Honduran girl and made Alvarez the godfather.

Shaw was so plugged in to Alvarez that nobody told Shaw—or anyone else at the embassy—that Alvarez was going to be thrown out. The station chief was as completely, humiliatingly blind-sided as the general himself. Ambassador Negroponte was equally embarrassed. And by June Shaw was gone.

In October and November 1984, as the controversy raged over the CIA training manual, Shaw was one of those agents reprimanded for his part in its production. So, of course, was Kirkpatrick. At least four other agents also were chastised.

But Dewey continued to prosper. He stayed on as Latin America division chief at the Directorate for Operations to patch over differences with the new Honduran commanders, then Casey transferred him to the prestigious post of European division chief. He was given an award for his work and given, it was said, the highest bonus of the year.

Dewey, his defenders claimed, had done a great deal without a great many resources. And once he was gone, even some of his critics would find a good word for him.

"You can't criticize Dewey too much. I think if he hadn't done what Casey wanted, Casey would have had him out of there," said one CIA man.

But by 1984, Casey's war was leaving deep scars on the Agency. Such trust as had built between the CIA and Congress was all but destroyed. The disillusionment with the Secret War and its long public history was manifest among intelligence veterans.

As one said, "The sad thing is that a lot of people are going to end up feeling they were used and abused, between Congress and the Agency."

Secret wars always unravel, and this one was no exception. Veteran agents had seen it happen with the Montagnards and the Hmong and the Kurds, and now, it was probably going to happen again.

"I think," said one CIA man, "the ethical rule in warfare is that you obtain your objective with the least loss of life to your own side or the enemy. And I think that ought to apply to these sorts of operations, too. It's not some congressman's morality about overthrowing a government. I'm not sure whether it's morality or pragmatism—or if there's much of a difference. This operation has killed a lot of people without really doing anything."

Meanwhile, Americans were beginning to die.

On December 16, 1984. the *Detroit Free Press* reported that "members of a secret U.S. Army helicopter unit, wearing civilian clothes and flying at night, have ventured into hostile territory in Central America to aid pro-American forces, according to relatives of unit members." It was the relatives of the dead ones who told the stories. Sixteen members of the "Night Stalkers" 160th Task Force of the 101st Airborne Division supposedly had been killed in accidents, but many, it seems, were flying combat missions in Central America. Efforts by other journalists to follow up on this report were stifled as the sources named refused to talk, and the veil of secrecy around the already carefully sheltered unit became virtually hermetic. But even without the *Free Press* story, there are public records of at least seven American agents and soldiers killed in mysterious circumstances possibly connected with the Secret War in 1983 and 1984.

There was Navy Lieutenant Commander Al Schaufelberger III, the number two man at the U.S. Military Group in San Salvador. Trained as a SEAL (sea-air-land) commando, Schaufelberger put together Salvadoran units to operate in the Gulf of Fonseca between Nicaragua, Honduras and El Salvador. They worked out of the same kind of CIA–supplied "Piranha" speedboats used by the contras and it is conceivable, though unproved, that they were among the "unilaterally controlled Latino assets" that carried out some of the operations against Nicaragua. Their nominal mission was to interdict arms.

Many of the U.S. advisors in El Salvador were vulnerable. A grenade at the swimming pool bar of the Sheraton Hotel any Sunday would have taken out half a dozen. The machine-gunning of four Marines in a San Salvador café in June 1985 proved the point. But Schaufelberger, as it happened, was the only one targeted and killed by the Salvadoran guerrillas before 1985, and by that time the character of the war there was greatly changed.

On January 11, 1984, a U.S. Army helicopter was forced down by Sandinista ground fire after flying over Nicaraguan airspace. Official reports suggest it had strayed, but it may have been mistaken for one of several CIA flights and misguided by U.S. military air controllers at a base in Honduras called Carrot Top. It landed on the road along the border near Cifuentes, near where La Negra and Torgerson and Cross had died. Under heavy fire, the pilot, Warrant Officer Jeffrey Schwab, was killed.

On September 1, 1984, Dana Parker and James Powell died in a helicopter crash in Nicaragua while accompanying a group of contras on a mission there. One description of the mission said they were unarmed and meant to resupply FDN troops. Another version had them on a combat mission against a Cuban-run military training facility, possibly for Salvadoran rebels. The CIA told Congress it "had no advance knowledge of the specific mission" by these anti-Communist soldiers of fortune in a private group called Civilian Military Assistance and that "no CIA officers were in contact with any member" of the group prior to "the ill-fated event." But it was noted in the press at the time that Powell was a former helicopter pilot in Vietnam. And Parker was a veteran of the Huntsville police department who served in the Alabama National Guard's elite Special Forces unit. Their profiles are similar to those of many contract men.

On October 19, 1984, two CIA officers and two contract employees, all Americans, were killed when their surveillance plane crashed over El Salvador. The Agency said they were monitoring arms shipments to the Salvadoran rebels from Nicaragua at night when they flew into a volcano. U.S. reconnaissance flights also helped deploy Salvadoran troops against the rebels there. But the contras used the same Salvadoran air base for supply and attack missions both before and after the CIA crew was killed. The actual flight plan of the plane is unknown. The Agency would release none of the names of the dead.

COMMANDER ZERO

By the end of May 1984 every group Edén Pastora had ever worked with had a reason to kill him, and many had tried. They stalked him by day and by night, most often with bombs. But Pastora's luck held. In June 1983 a pair of assassins from Nicaragua made the mistake of parking their car across from the Costa Rican security ministry in San José. When they returned with a bomb prepared to drive to a visit with top members of Pastora's organization it appears that they had already armed the device and set its radio control. It also appears that the powerful police transmitters across the street set it off. They were blown all over the lot. One died.

A few months later an agent alleged to have been working for the Basque ETA was captured as he was casing Pastora's house in the San José suburbs.

The dirty warriors of the FDN, meanwhile, had long wanted to make Pastora a martyr for their cause. They suspected he represented a fifth column, a Sandinista plot to keep the insurgency divided. If so, he was a lot more valuable dead than alive. At the same time, Alfonso Robelo and the men who had joined with Pastora in ARDE (Alianza Revolucionaria Democratica) were furious about his repeated refusals to compromise with the FDN and to mollify the CIA.

On May 30, 1984, Pastora called a press conference at one of the dilapidated shacks on stilts in the jungle along the Rio San Juan, just inside Nicaraguan territory. Pastora was going to announce that he not only refused to unify with the FDN but that he was splitting with the members of ARDE who wanted to.

As ever with Edén, the conference was called on short notice and badly organized. His nephew Orion rang up a handful of reporters late at night on the twenty-ninth and few members of the international press corps heard about the conference in time to show up at the Irazú Hotel the next morning for the bus and boat trip that was supposed to take them north.

One who did show up was Susan Morgan, who was stringing for

Newsweek. She came along with ABC stringer Tony Avirgan. Susan looked a little like the British actress Sarah Miles. Weary. Worldly. She had covered El Salvador and Lebanon. She was a friend of Dial's and had been down the road where he was killed just a few days before him.

Linda Frazier was invited to the press conference. She was the wife of the Associated Press correspondent, who was out of town. When she and Joe Frazier had lived in Mexico she had been one of the hostesses who kept the wives of other correspondents sane with shopping trips and parties. Now in San José she worked as a part-time reporter for the little *Tico Times* newspaper.

Waiting to roll out of the Irazú Hotel along with them was the Swedish television reporter Peter Torbionsson, who was well known to the rest of the press corps. He had been covering the area for years. And he brought with him a Danish photographer named Hansen he had met from a free-lance outfit called Europa 7.

In all, there were twenty-four journalists, most of them local, on the little expedition north to hear Commander Zero declare, once again, his independent war against the National Directorate, and his contempt for the ex-Guardias of the FDN.

Of course the promised bus never showed up. Everyone piled into such cars as were available, cramming equipment here and there, cameras, recorders, Hansen struggling along with his metal case. Linda rode with him and Torbionsson. She was excited and expectant about the story. Having spent most of the last several years at home raising her son, now that he was settled into school she was enjoying the chance to get a little adventure, to rebuild a career.

The drive took most of the day. It was late afternoon by the time everyone started piling into dugout canoes for the hour-long trip to the little house at a place called La Penca. It was nightfall as they climbed up the stairs and crowded around Commander Zero, the television crews jockeying for position, Hansen and other photographers looking around for angles; everyone, it seemed, tripping over equipment boxes.

Rosita, one of Pastora's prettier young recruits, showed up with some coffee for him, and she was just leaning over to pour at 7:20 P.M. when the bomb went off. Pastora's luck held. The girl shielded him from the blast and only his legs were hurt seriously by burns and bits and pieces of the electronic gear that suddenly became shrapnel. He and his aide, Tito Chamorro, who was more gravely hurt, and two other wounded ARDE members, were rushed from the scene in a speedboat.

They left behind the reporters, screaming for help, for medicine, for doctors, for the love of God, and getting no answers. No one seemed to know what to do. Those farthest from the blast, like Hansen, sat stunned on the ground, or wandered aimlessly around the scene. There was only one young girl from ARDE trying to minister to the victims.

Susan Morgan was desperately hurt: burned, her hands and legs broken, her elbow shattered.

José Quiros, a local television cameraman, was dead. So was Rosita.

Linda Frazier was dying, but it was slow. Both her legs had been blown off at the thigh. It was hours before all the wounded were dragged, finally, into the boats and across the river to Ciudad Quesada, where they received some minimal attention. By then, Linda was dead.

Hansen checked out of the hospital early the next morning, took a cab down to San José, checked out of his hotel and vanished. Who he was and who he was working for have never been conclusively determined.

Five weeks later, after Pastora had been treated at a hospital in Caracas, Venezuela, he showed up in Washington once again looking to win support and, perhaps, to straighten out his relations with the Agency. I spent a long couple of days with him there in a room at the Embassy Row Hotel. Outside the door and down the hall, State Department security officers carried satchels that showed the outlines of their shotguns and Uzi machine pistols. They gossiped nervously about schedules and chase cars. But Pastora sat relaxed and easy in his bed as his wife, Yolanda, quietly worked on her nails beside him, listening to his conversation and filling in the occasional detail.

Pastora wore short pajamas that left his legs exposed and he regularly rubbed salve into the enormous, month-old burns and raspberry-colored skin grafts that covered his shins and thighs. He tweezed out bits of the bomb's wiring and slivers of aluminum that had surfaced on his skin and teased his woman when she warned him about infection.

"I'm the bionic man," he said. "I don't get infections." He extracted another piece of wire. "See, they've repaired these short circuits."

But if Pastora's luck had stayed with him, his magic had not. He had been too much trouble to too many people for too long. The members of the National Directorate now talked of him with contempt, and none of the regret that was heard when he first took up arms against them. The CIA at last had cut him adrift as well. There were no more monies to be had, and all those sources Pastora seemed to have thought, or at least had often claimed, were independent Latin American businessmen, suddenly dried up as well. The press that had helped him nurture his image for so long did not soon forgive what had happened to the reporters in the house on stilts at La Penca. Reporters would not remember Pastora for his bravery there.

Commander Zero was no longer the star of the revolution, no longer the hope of the counterrevolution.

THE SANDINISTAS

With the war against the contras as a reason and as a pretext, the Sandinistas moved steadily into the Soviet orbit with only the occasional pause along the way to test the possibilities of conciliation with Washington and find them, always, wanting. They accepted peace accords tendered by the four Latin American nations of the "Contadora Group." The United States rejected them. They held elections; Washington declared them invalid. Probably the Sandinistas were not surprised. Some may have been pleased. Often, on their own account, they seemed to act with pathological self-destructiveness.

They alienated some of the best minds in the revolution—men like Arturo Cruz, who had been part of Los Doce in 1978 and Robelo's replacement on the junta in 1980; or Alfredo César, whose renegotiation of Nicaragua's debts after the war helped save it from bankruptcy. By 1982 such men had left the country, as sad as they were bitter. Cruz almost ran for president in 1984 when the Sandinistas almost gave him a chance. But it didn't happen. The Sandinistas alienated large segments of the Catholic Church by pursuing a running battle of words and prerogatives with the Archbishop of Managua, then publicly insulting the Pope when he visited Managua and demanded that his priests, many of them revolutionaries, show more allegiance to his conservative bureaucracy than to the Sandinistas. Their excuse for having their police and their organized crowds shout down the Pope was that he refused to condemn the atrocities being committed by the contras.

The Sandinistas meanwhile continued to defend their own revolution by trying to help others. But most of their efforts were failures. In 1983 there was an attempt to get a guerrilla operation going in Honduras, the sanctuary of the contras. It would have been a little war traded for the little war that had been traded for El Salvador. It took years to plan and stage. It took only a few weeks to destroy. A special U.S.-trained counterinsurgency squad, helped out by some contra units, eliminated the Honduran insurrection. In Costa Rica a few tiny groups sprouted up sympathetic to the idea of violent revolution. They went nowhere. Costa Rican democracy was as effective against insurgents as Honduran troops.

In El Salvador, meanwhile, a heavy dose of repression—tens of thousands of people slaughtered in the name of anticommunism—combined with the leadership of Christian Democrat José Napoleon Duarte and the self-destructive propensities of the Salvadoran left to end any imminent threat from the insurgency the Secret War had been designed to stop. President Duarte, even as he called Nicaragua the cancer of Central America, had helped remove the original reason for Washington's attacks on it.

But, of course, by 1985, the rules had changed.

The problem with Managua now was said to be its conventional military buildup, and its ever more conspicuous links to Moscow.

The Sandinistas put an increasingly sophisticated and well-armed force in the field. They had Soviet rifles, Soviet antiaircraft batteries and Soviet attack helicopters. They built a major new military airbase. They were a power the likes of which Central America had never seen. They were a match for any of Washington's allies in the area, and potentially for all of them combined. And by their lights they had to be.

The determinists among them had won out, had been proved right at every turn in the road. The United States was out to destroy them, and their only routes to survival lay either in a kind of capitulation that men educated in hiding and in jail could never face, or in strength.

It might be said that a poor nation pitted against a superpower can look in only one direction for help, and that is toward the other superpower. Certainly that fit the thinking of the Sandinistas. When Congress in May 1985 flatly refused, after a furious debate, to give the contras any more money, Reagan declared an economic embargo against Managua. Daniel Ortega, now Nicaragua's president, was flying even then to Moscow for assurances the Soviets would begin, once again, making up the difference as they did when Reagan cut off the wheat in 1981, and the mines cut off the oil tankers in 1984. Congress, however, felt it had done the Sandinistas a favor with its vote. Now, embarrassed and insulted, it reversed itself again and renewed aid to the contras for "humanitarian purposes."

SUICIDA

Just as some of the best Sandinistas had left the revolution in 1982, fed up with its arrogance and its totalitarian tendencies, in 1984 the ranks of the counterrevolution's leadership were thinned by disillusionment with its crimes, its corruption, the dictates of the Agency, the inconstancy of Congress, the seeming futility of the cause. Salvador Icaza went home to Memphis. Ortiz left Radio 15 to return to flying.

It was just about Christmas time in Miami in 1983 when Tomás Castillo, the CIA liaison with the FDN directorate, dropped by Edgar Chamorro's place to pick up Chamorro's old travel documents and give him some new ones. They went to the Rusty Pelican for a drink, looking out on the speedboats in Biscayne Bay as waiters in Hawaiian shirts brought their orders. That was when Chamorro had asked about what had happened to Suicida.

"At least they court-martialed him," said Tomás. They executed him, he said.

Chamorro felt sick. It seemed that so much had gone wrong. So much had been wasted. Thousands of peasants were dead, tens of thousands homeless. In the FDN hospitals they lay without the land they worked, and without the arm or the leg they used to use to work it. No one was any closer than before to overthrowing the Sandinista Front. No one was going to get the land back for them. Edgar had found himself called a leader, but he knew he was just a tool. He was part of a package. "We were being used, like nice guys, to convince Congress." Now he found, in this comfortable bar among the Hawaiian shirts, that "we have killed people—not only that, we have sent people to kill our own people."

"This is like a Kafka world," he thought later. "You can manipulate people to the extreme, but there is no truth or reality around you. Or reality is irrelevant. Someone to whom you have no access makes the decisions, unseen."

It was getting hard to see the difference between the Sandinistas' values and those of the people who fought them. Maybe it would be better, Chamorro suggested to Tomás, just to find a way to come to terms with them—really to come to terms with them.

Tomás looked at Chamorro as if he were mad. "No," he said, "don't you see? There's no way to do that. Those people are evil."

It was a month later that Chamorro began to talk to me about the men who loved to kill.

By 1985 the contra forces, even taking into account the Agency's and their own exaggeration, certainly exceeded ten thousand combatants. The Sandinistas, in order to fight them, had imposed a draft in 1983. And many young men, when faced with the inevitability of joining one army or another, opted for the contras. The Sandinista strategies that had alienated so many of the mountain people since the 1982 state of emergency had grown more severe and ever more onerous. By the spring of 1985 they included planned relocations of tens of thousands of the independent farmers in the Segovias, and again the contra ranks were swelled. Though their leaders were still the *guardias,* the killers and the chosen front-men of the CIA, there was no place else to turn. The fight continued, now, with no end in sight and the constant threat that the Reagan administration, having committed itself to the Sandinistas' overthrow, would finally decide it had no option but open, direct U.S. military action if the contras faltered once too often or too badly.

The army was still in the field. The war was not over.

Notes

Notes on Sources:

(p. 13)

First epigraph is from Reagan's speech to the twelfth annual Conservative Political Action Conference in Washington, D.C., as quoted in *The Washington Post,* p. 1, March 2, 1985.

Second epigraph is from page 27 of an original copy of "Operaciones Sicologicas en Guerra de Guerrillas," produced by a contract agent of the Central Intelligence Agency as an instruction manual for anti-Sandinista guerrillas in the fall of 1983. The quote in Spanish reads: *"Una fuerza armada guerrillera siempre conlleva un terror implícito, porque la población, sin decirlo en voz alta, siente temor de que las armas puedan ser usadas en su contra."*

Prologue:

(pp. 15–16)

The O. Henry Bar is in the Tegucigalpa Holiday Inn. On January 28, 1984, I had a drink there with Edgar Chamorro after we had visited a Nicaraguan Democratic Force field hospital. His remarks are from my notes taken during our conversation and from my January 29, 1984, journal entry about the encounter.

(p. 16)

The description of how Sandinista prisoners are treated comes from a man who was held by them in 1981 and subsequently released. He talked about his experience in a June 1984 interview but asked not to be cited by name. His account confirmed other interviews with former prisoners and the families of prisoners in

August 1981 and May 1982 in Managua. The young man referred to in the text did not give any details of his treatment, but he stutters, and when asked about interrogations he found himself unable to get any words out of his throat for most of a minute.
(p. 17)

Both State Department and Central Intelligence Agency sources have told me on several occasions that the station in El Salvador was shut down during the 1970s. David Atlee Phillips, who was CIA Latin America Division chief in the early 1970s, confirmed this in a telephone interview in December 1984.

Endings—1979:

(pp. 19–20)

The images of San Juan del Sur at the end of the 1979 war come from interviews conducted with residents of the town in May ·1984, although several were reluctant to have me report their names. The family that lived within the old school in 1979 was still living there in 1984 and the account of their actions is the one they gave me. The woman who owns the Hotel La Estrella complained about the economic problems of 1984 as much as the fears of 1979.
(pp. 21–23)

I first met Edén Pastora in 1980 in Granada, Nicaragua. I interviewed him at length in April and December 1982 in San José, Costa Rica. But the running account of his experiences comes from two days of exhaustive tape-recorded interviews in his room at the Embassy Row Hotel in Washington, D.C., July 6 and 7, 1984. The description of Pichardo comes from meetings with him in Corinto, Nicaragua, on a July 1982 tour of the sites of various anti-Sandinista attacks. By then he was commander of the northern sector involved in most of the fighting against the contras. The description of the area between Lake Nicaragua and Rivas is from several trips through the region by car.
(pp. 23–26)

The account of the escape from San Juan del Sur was first told to me by Julio César Herrera, Pedro Pablo Ortiz Centeno and Sonia Zapata Reyes in a week spent traveling with them in March 1983. I was able to watch Herrera's behavior at close hand for several days and my description of it reflects what I saw as well as what I was told.

The townspeople of San Juan del Sur remember this period well, of course, providing several descriptive details. Other former members of the National Guard who asked not to be cited by name also provided insights into the thinking of the men at that time, and a few publications by groups sympathetic to the anti-Sandinista cause provided other details. These include *Nica Libre Centroamericana,* a magazine published by the Union de Periodistas y Escritores de Nicaragua en Exilio under Carlos A. Flores-Cuadra, Miami, July 1984. This magazine reports that Col. Montenegro, known as Sagitario, was captured and died in a Sandinista prison in October 1979.
(p. 24)

The incentives for enlisted men to join the National Guard were well known,

but they are also enumerated in Richard Millet's excellent history of that institution, *Guardians of the Dynasty,* Orbis Books, Maryknoll, N.Y., 1977. The attitude expressed toward senior officers is from interviews with Julio César Herrera, in Nueva Segovia Nicaragua, March 24, 1983.
(p. 26)

Pastora talked about his decision to go to Managua in July 1984 interviews. Also see the San José, Costa Rica, newspaper *La Nación,* July 20, 1979, "Tropas de Edén Pastora avanzan sobre Managua," by Edgar G. Fonseca and Levi Vega.
(pp. 26–28)

Antonio Calderón, the tugboat pilot, told me his story on May 26, 1984, at his house in San Juan del Sur. The account is from my notes of our conversation, observations of the house itself, and interviews with other residents of the neighborhood. The date he, other townspeople and Julio César Herrera gave for the departure is July 20, but press accounts of the time suggest it was July 19. See *El Mundo,* "Llegan Huyendo 500 Guardias de Somoza," p. 1, San Salvador, July 21, 1979.
(pp. 28–30)

The excitement of July 1979 in Managua has been recorded and retold in countless publications. The depiction of it here comes especially from interviews in Managua, March 13–19, 1980, and July 15–25, 1980, during the first anniversary celebrations.
(p. 30)

Dr. Hugo Spadáfora had resigned as Panama's deputy health minister to lead a much publicized "brigade" of 80 Panamanian volunteers. The presence of three *montonero* guerrilla columns and the role of the Argentine ERP with Sandinista intelligence were reported by *Washington Post* special correspondent Martin Andersen in interviews with former members of the Argentine guerrilla groups in Buenos Aires in December 1984. The role of the Salvadorans was reconfirmed by senior members of the Salvadoran Farabundo Marti National Liberation Front in Managua in June 1984.
(pp. 30–31)

The members of the original junta were: Daniel Ortega, a member of the Sandinista National Directorate; Sergio Ramírez, author, intellectual and longtime Sandinista associate who had been one of the group of "Los Doce"; Moisés Hassan, an urban organizer for the Prolonged Popular War faction of the Sandinistas and a U.S.–educated physics professor; Violetta Chamorro, the widow of Pedro Joaquin Chamorro and a member of the board of directors of the newspaper *La Prensa;* and Alfonso Robelo, the owner of the GRACSA vegetable oil firm, a prominent leader of the Frente Amplio Opositor and of businessmen who were pushing for Somoza's overthrow from 1977 to 1979.

The membership of the Sandinista National Directorate was apportioned three per "tendency." For the "Terceristas": Daniel Ortega, his brother Humberto Ortega and the Mexican–Nicaraguan Victor Tirado. For Prolonged Popular War: Tomás Borge, Henry Ruiz (the Soviet-schooled and Palestinian-trained guerrilla commander known as Modesto) and Bayardo Arce, a former journalist. For the Proletarians: Jaime Wheelock, Luis Carrion Cruz and Carlos Núñez.

(p. 31)

The quotation from the television reporter in the crowd is drawn from transcripts of film collected for the production of the WGBH Television-Frontline series *Crisis in Central America*.

(p. 31)

Bravo's phone number on the map in the bunker was copied down during an interview with Humberto Ortega there in July 1982.

(pp. 32–35)

The account of Pastora's revolutionary development is based on the July 1984 interviews. There is also material drawn from conversations with faculty at the Colegio Centroamerica, now in Managua, in October 1983, and from its yearbook for the class of 1956–57. Other supplementary material is from tape-recorded interviews with José Francisco Cardenal in August 1984 and Leopoldo Salazar in San José, Costa Rica, in June 1984, and notes on a conversation with Alfonso Robelo in San José in April 1982. Borge's and Daniel Ortega's prison experiences were recounted by them in videotaped WGBH interviews that I conducted in May and June 1984.

(pp. 35–37)

For a specialized but brief and readable discussion of the development of the Sandinistas' factions see *FSLN: The Ideology of the Sandinistas and the Nicaraguan Revolution*, by David Nolan, published by the Institute of Interamerican Studies, University of Miami, Coral Gables, Florida, 1984. This subject was discussed at length by Borge in the June 1984 WGBH interview and by former Nicaraguan junta member and now deputy interior minister Moisés Hassan in a February 1984 interview. The quotation and dialogue are as recounted by Pastora, July 1984.

(p. 36)

Ramírez lived in exile in Costa Rica and briefly in West Berlin, building his reputation as an academic and author. His best-known collection of short stories is *Charles Atlas Muere Tambien (Charles Atlas Also Dies)*. He served on the revolutionary junta continuously from 1979 until the 1984 elections, when he became vice-president. I interviewed him on several occasions for *The Washington Post* between 1981 and 1983 and for WGBH in May 1984.

Carlos Coronel, the son of poet José Coronel Urtecho and the brother of two prominent Sandinistas, is one of the most enigmatic characters in the annals of the revolution. In later years both Nicaraguan sides of the Pastora operation in the Secret War would suspect him of spying for the other, and both would continue talking to him. I interviewed him in June 1984, in San José, Costa Rica, when he was with the exiled Pastora.

(pp. 37–38)

The inventory of arms from José "Pepe" Figueres was recited by Pastora in the July interviews. That Figueres helped the Sandinistas with arms has often been reported. He confirmed this in a conversation at his house outside San José, Costa Rica, in June 1984.

(pp. 38–40)

The account of the taking of the National Palace is centered on Pastora's own vision of it as recorded in interviews he gave to WGBH producer Martin

Smith and to me in July 1984. A thorough account of the event from all sides can be found in Bernard Diederich's richly detailed *Somoza: American Made Dictator,* Dutton, New York, 1981, pp. 176–188.
(p. 40)

Julio César Herrera told the story of eating toothpaste to try to kill the thirst during the voyage from San Juan del Sur, and Pedro Pablo Ortiz Centeno confirmed it, in the March 1983 interviews.
(p. 41)

The Israeli ship incident is discussed in Diederich, p. 216, and in Somoza's own version of his fall, *Nicaragua Betrayed,* as told to Jack Cox, Western Islands, Belmont, Massachusetts, 1980, pp. 239–40.
(pp. 41–42)

The bazooka incident is told as recounted by Herrera and Ortiz Centeno in March 1983. But other *guardias,* including officers, have also taken credit for driving off the Sandinista boat, according to confidential interviews with former members of the Guardia in Miami, November 1984.
(pp. 42–43)

Antonio Calderón told the story of drinking his own urine in the May 26, 1984, interview.
(p. 43)

I interviewed Pezzullo regularly during his term as ambassador to Nicaragua, and specifically for this book in March and again in May 1984.
(p. 44)

Vaky was interviewed by a WGBH crew in April 1984. The quotation is from that transcript. I talked to Vaky on several occasions in 1983 and 1984 and checked specific points with him over the telephone on December 14, 1984.
(p. 45)

Murphy, who was jailed for his role in the ABSCAM scandal, was interviewed in prison by WGBH producer Martin Smith in May 1984. His remarks are taken from the transcript of that videotape.
(pp. 46–48)

In *Nicaragua Betrayed* Somoza includes transcripts of his conversations with Pezzullo and other U.S. officials as they were tape-recorded secretly in his offices. The Pezzullo conversations run from p. 333 to p. 380. Pezzullo talked about how Somoza looked and acted in the May 1984 interview.
(p. 49)

Mejia's name was picked from a list of six officers proposed by the American embassy. Another name on the list was Col. Enrique Bermúdez. See Somoza-Cox, p. 383.
(pp. 49–50)

The account of Somoza's departure comes from WGBH interviews with Pezzullo and Urcuyo in May 1984; from Somoza-Cox, pp. 388–390; Diederich, pp. 311–328; interview with Pezzullo, May 1984.
(p. 51)

The story of Bill the American was told to me by two confidential anti-Sandinista Nicaraguan sources in interviews in Miami in November and December 1984. I have his full name and contacted him by telephone on three occasions in De-

cember 1984 and January 1985. He acknowledged his broad participation in the events, said he did not want to be identified by name and declined to talk about specifics.
(pp. 52–53)

Descriptions of León cited in quotation marks are from *La Nación,* July 1979, "Implacable caceria humana en el norte de Nicaragua," by Guillermo Fernandez.
(p. 52)

The account of making bombs comes from a confidential interview in Miami, in November 1984. It was confirmed in its outlines by other confidential interviews in Miami the same month and by the reported effects of the bombs.
(p. 53)

Interview with Pedro Núñez Cabezas, Managua, June 5, 1984.
(pp. 54–55)

Durich was identified in a confidential interview in Miami in November 1984. *Washington Post* special correspondent Martin Andersen found extensive information on him in December 1984 in the files of Argentina's Center for Legal and Social Studies in Buenos Aires.

According to these files, Carlos Alberto Durich worked for the Escuela de Mecanica de la Armada Argentina (ESMA), one of the two largest concentration camps run by the Argentine government, where an estimated 4,000 "disappeared people" are believed to have been detained before they were killed. He was described as a close assistant of Benazzi Berisso, one of the more infamous torturers at the ESMA. In a bizarre career typical of the twists and turns taken in the Argentine underground he was linked both to the Libyan embassy and to the Peronist party as well as the right-wing military. He is also reported to have traveled to the Malvinas during the war against Britain, using a war correspondent's credential issued by a Navy death squad working out of the ESMA.

The photograph of Durich in the legal center files shows a man about 30–35 years old, with dark hair, neatly cut and parted on the right, a strong chin, bushy eyebrows and a prominent nose.

A former member of the AAA death squad operation in Argentina who knew Durich told Andersen that he was a navy informant and of dubious probity but that he had indeed been in Central America.
(p. 55)

Interview with Emilio Echaverry, Tegucigalpa, July 29, 1983.
(p. 55)

Interviews with confidential sources in Miami, November–December 1984.
(pp. 55–57)

This, again, is Antonio Calderón's account as told May 26, 1984. The date he gave was July 24 and this corresponds with the recollections of Ortiz Centeno and Herrera. But it appears more likely that the boats made landfall on Sunday, July 22. See *El Diario de Hoy,* "Guardias Nicaraguenses Relatan Odisea al Escapar," p. 2, San Salvador, July 25, 1979. Also see *El Diario de Hoy,* "283 Guardias Nicaraguenses Llegan al Puerto de La Unión," p. 3, San Salvador, July 24, 1979; and *El Mundo,* "Sandinistas remolcan hasta La Union 283 guardias nicas," p. 11, July 23, 1979. In these last two accounts five Sandinistas reportedly volunteered to tow the *guardias* to El Salvador. But the same Sandinistas were detained by the

Salvadorans, and this official version disseminated at the time does not correspond to the recollection of any of the participants interviewed.
(p. 57)

Confidential interview with former Guardia officer, Miami, August 1985.
(p. 57)

More than 600 guardias were reported to be arriving daily in El Salvador in the week after July 19, 1979. See *El Diario de Hoy,* "600 Nicaraguenses por Dia Llegan a El Salvador," p. 3, and "Guardias Nicaraguenses Relatan Odisea al Escapar," p. 2, San Salvador, July 25, 1979.
(p. 58)

The officer who ran the kidnapping operation, according to Salvadoran court records, was retired Major Guillermo Antonio Roeder. He was arrested in 1982 and imprisoned for more than two years before finally being released in 1984. The account of the secret cells appeared in an unpublished annex to the OAS human rights report on El Salvador issued in 1979.
(p. 59)

Gutiérrez quotation is from transcript of June 1984, San Salvador, videotaped interview I conducted for WGBH.
(p. 59)

The May 1979 slaughter on the steps of the San Salvador Cathedral was recorded by CBS contract cameraman Domingo Rex.
(pp. 59–60)

Telephone interview with Robert Pastor, December 17, 1984.
(p. 60)

Telephone interview with Viron Vaky, December 12, 1984.
(p. 61)

There are several excellent accounts of the 1979 coup. One of the best is in Ray Bonner's *Weakness and Deceit,* Times Books, New York, 1984.
(p. 61)

The scene at Danker's is from interviews with confidential Nicaraguan anti-Sandinista sources in Miami, December 1984, and telephone interviews with Betty Castillo and with Fred Danker, December 1984.
(p. 62)

El Diario de Hoy, "Desertores Llegan a El Salvador," July 19, 1979, p. 65.
(p. 62)

Although she is known as Laura, that is not her real name. I interviewed her briefly on November 24, 1984. She asked that her real name not be published.
(pp. 62–63)

For biographical note on Enrique Bermúdez see the pamphlet "FDN: Que? Quienes? Cuando? Donde? Como? Por que?" published by the Nicaraguan Democratic Force, February 1983.

The story of the press conference is taken from 1984 interviews with participants who asked not to be cited by name; from Somoza-Cox, pp. 199-200; and from an interview with Laura Ortiz, November 24, 1982.
(pp. 64–67)

The basic account of Barbara's persuasion and its result is drawn from the July 1984 interviews with Pastora, who had been seconded to Borge's interior ministry at the time and was in a position to have known. The description of Borge's office is from a visit there for an interview in November 1981. The role of Barbara in Bravo's death was confirmed by confidential sources interviewed in Miami in August 1984 and again in November 1984. The description of Bravo's actions in the hotel the day of his disappearance is from a January 1984 interview with the then-manager, who asked not to be cited by name. The clinical aspects are from the *Miami Herald*, "Bravo Believed Tortured, Slain," by Ileana Oroza and Guillermo Martinez, October 17, 1979, and from Somoza-Cox, pp. 385–86, and autopsy photos, p. 284. Also see claim by Argentine Gorriaran Merlo that his group killed Bravo, note for p. 89 below.

The Sandinistas officially deny complicity in killing Bravo.
(p. 65)

Pastora referred to the Cuban intelligence officer as "Moleón." Miguel Bo-laños Hunter, a twenty-year-old Nicaraguan defector who formerly served in State Security's counterintelligence division, told the conservative Heritage Foundation in June and July 1983 that a "Renan Montero (nom de guerre) is a commander in the Nicaraguan intelligence service who worked with the Sandinistas for fifteen years and became a naturalized Nicaraguan citizen." He is described as a former colonel in Cuba's intelligence service. See *The Heritage Foundation Back-grounder*, No. 294, September 30, 1983, p. 8.
(p. 66)

"The Hondurans have always attributed that to me," Cerna said with a smile when asked about this one afternoon five years later. It was just coincidence, he suggested, that he was in Tegucigalpa at the time Bravo was killed and that right afterward he was named publicly as head of State Security. Cerna was interviewed in Managua, May 29, 1984.
(pp. 66–67)

Borge's October 17, 1979, remarks to a youth rally were monitored on Radio Sandino by the CIA's publicly disseminated Foreign Broadcast Information Service and reprinted in Somoza-Cox, p. 386.
(pp. 67–68)

The taunts of the children and conditions of the ex-*guardias* in La Union are as reported in *El Diario de Hoy*, "Guardias Nicaraguenses Relatan Odisea al Es-capar," pp. 2, 68.

The described reaction of Suicida and his men to their situation is from inter-views with them in March 1983. His account of persuading the Honduran border guards to help him is from an interview on the evening of March 26, 1983. The generic description of the Honduran border posts is based on visits to several of them over the course of five years in the region.

Beginnings—1980

(pp. 69–70)

All quotations are drawn directly from the text of the 1980 Republican plat-form, which speaks to the Reagan administration's enduring perceptions of the subject better than any of the essays written by some of his more ideological supporters at the time.

(pp. 70–72)

I was in Managua from July 14 to 25, 1980. Observations about Fidel Castro and the Nicaraguan commandants were made firsthand and are taken from my notebooks. He commented on the Republican platform in his July 19 speech and also privately according to one confidential Sandinista source interviewed in July 1980.

(p. 72)

The *Santa Fe Document,* by Roger Fontaine, Gen. Gordon Sumner, Francis Borchey, David Jordan and Louis Tames, first published in 1980 by Council for Inter-American Security, has been distributed more widely by the left than by the right. For a typical left-wing analysis of it see *La Ultima Batalla de la Tercera Guerra Mundial,* by Horacio Verbitsky, pp. 87–91, Editorial Legasa, Buenos Aires, 1984.

(p. 72)

The description of the Salvadorans' treatment in Managua in July 1980, including the conversation, is drawn from Document G in "Communist Interference in El Salvador: Documents Demonstrating Communist Support of the Salvadoran Insurgency," United States Department of State, February 23, 1981.

These are the foundation documents for one of the most controversial of the Reagan administration's propaganda efforts, the so-called "White Paper" of the same date. They have been attacked as fabrications by such apostate former CIA men as Philip Agee and Ralph McGehee (see, for instance, McGehee's "The C.I.A. and The White Paper on El Salvador," an article with deletions by the CIA, pp. 423–25, in *The Nation,* April 11, 1981). The attacks are based on educated but highly biased guesswork. Both *The Wall Street Journal* and *The Washington Post* ran lengthy analyses of the documents in 1981 showing the way their contents were overstated, exaggerated and twisted to fit President Reagan's perceptions. There are also some egregious errors of identification apparent to students of the region. In Document F, for instance, "Ana María" is identified as Ana Guadalupe Martinez of the Salvadoran ERP. In fact "Ana María" was Mélida Anaya Montes, the second-in-command of the Popular Liberation Forces, an organization bitterly at odds with the ERP for much of its recent history. The result is very misleading about who was supposed to get what arms, and where they stood on the political spectrum.

Yet the source documents themselves appear very much in line with what Salvadoran insurgent leaders and representatives as well as Sandinistas told me privately in Managua in October 1983 and May 1984, especially insofar as the frictions between the Salvadorans and the Nicaraguans were concerned. Cuban officials acknowledged their role in supplying the Salvadoran rebels in interviews in Havana, September 1981. Fidel Castro said publicly at that time that he thought it was Cuba's moral duty to support them, but it no longer did in material terms. Sandinista National Directorate member Bayardo Arce said in a March 1982 interview that the Sandinistas had introduced the Salvadorans to their own sources of supply.

What Document G suggests, particularly, is that the Sandinistas, far from taking precipitous action to incite subversion in El Salvador, were reluctant even to help their revolutionary comrades there defend themselves at a moment when their potential for a rapid, popular uprising was being crushed by army-supported death squad operations costing hundreds of lives a month.

Also see the House Intelligence Committee statement of March 4, 1982, which calls intelligence on Nicaraguan support for the Salvadoran insurgents "convincing;" the September 22, 1982, staff report of the House Intelligence Subcommittee on Oversight and Evaluation, "U.S. Intelligence Performance on Central America: Achievements and Selected Instances of Concern," which questions degrees and amounts but concluded that "beyond doubt" Communist countries were involved in the Salvadoran insurgency; and the May 13, 1983, House Intelligence Committee report to accompany bill H.R. 2760, the dissenting view by Rep. C.W. "Bill" Young, which contains a detailed discussion of the White Paper documents that is more closely and carefully reasoned than the White Paper. Young notes, p. 38, that the Sandinista role "in the early part of 1980, according to documents, was largely facilitative." A figure tentatively identified as Comandante Bayardo Arce "arranged contact for insurgents with Panamanian arms traffickers in March." In fact, Arce admitted later in a March 1982 interview with me and *Washington Post* Assistant Managing Editor Jim Hoagland that the FSLN had introduced the Salvadoran rebels to the people who had supplied the FSLN with arms during the 1979 war. In addition, a top Cuban official interviewed in Havana in September 1981 admitted that Cuba had supplied the rebels with arms in 1980 but had since stopped the flow. The question of whether the Salvadoran insurgency stood or fell on Cuban and Nicaraguan help is, however, another matter. U.S. military advisors in Honduras and El Salvador in 1982 came to believe that the incompetence of the Salvadoran army rather than the armaments of the rebels was the main military problem they faced in shoring up the government.
(p. 74)

The description of the plot to bomb the July 19 celebration is from a confidential source who directly participated in it. He was interviewed in Miami, August 1984. Other, American sources speaking from secondhand information also talk of a failed attempt by a former Guardia pilot to bomb Fidel Castro when he visited Estelí the same week.
(p. 75)

Pezzullo interview, May 1980.
(p. 75)

See documents I, J, and K of "Communist Interference in El Salvador: Documents Demonstrating Communist Support of the Salvadoran Insurgency."
(p. 76)

Conversation with Jorge Salazar and thoughts as recounted by Pastora, July 1984.
(p. 76)

Salazar's charm and charisma were observed firsthand at press conferences and informal interviews in April 1980 and July 1980. The affectionate description of him is from an interview with his wife, Lucia Cardenal viuda de Salazar, a director of the Nicaraguan Democratic Force, in New Orleans, April 1984.
(p. 77)

The outline of Robelo's position is from interviews in Managua in April and May 1980.

(p. 77)

José Francisco Cardenal as observed in April and May 1980. His view of the Cuban revolution is from interviews in Miami, August 1984.

(p. 78)

Pastora's thoughts are from July 1984 interviews.

(p. 78)

The exact date of the Carter administration's "finding" for covert action in Central America is a matter of contradictory statements. One congressional source suggested it came as early as 1978, as things were heating up in Nicaragua. But most sources put it in 1980. CIA officials sympathetic to Reagan's Director of Central Intelligence William Casey frequently cite it as the precedent for the "secret war." But a CIA source who volunteered this bit of information in a December 1984 interview also confirmed that there was no paramilitary aspect to the Carter finding. Also see Joseph Lelyveld, "The Director: Running the C.I.A.," *The New York Times Magazine,* January 20, 1985, p. 25.

(p. 78)

Salazar's plotting and interest in a clandestine radio station was noted in interviews with a source close to José Francisco Cardenal in Miami, August 1984.

(p. 79)

The thoughts of José Francisco Cardenal at the time, and Ramírez's remark to him, are as recounted to me in an interview with him in Miami, August 11, 1984.

(pp. 78–80)

I covered the council of state affair in Managua from April 24 to May 8, 1980. The observations of events there are from my notes.

(p. 80)

Cardenal's wanderings building his conspiracy are as recounted in tape-recorded interviews in Miami, August 10 and 11, 1984. Salazar's role in the plot, detailed by the Sandinistas at a November 1980 press conference, subsequently was confirmed to me privately by a member of his family in San José, Costa Rica, in June 1984, and by U.S. diplomatic sources in interviews in May 1984. One said he advised Salazar against getting involved and warned him the whole thing might be a trap.

(p. 81)

Pastora's thoughts and remarks are as recounted in July 1984 interviews.

(pp. 81–82)

Tomás Borge's remarks are from a tape-recorded interview, November 1980.

(p. 82)

Descriptions of the early Guatemalan operations are from interviews with three confidential sources, veterans of that period, in June, August and December 1984. The quoted description of Lau is from a Nicaraguan civilian who knew him, interviewed in August 1984.

(p. 83)

The description of the OSN's files is from an interview with a confidential Latin exile source who had access to them in 1978 and 1979, interviewed in Miami, November 1984.

(p. 83)

The characterizations of Lau are from an interview with CIA source, February

22, 1985, and an interview with a former Nicaraguan National Guard officer in Miami, December 1984.

One Nicaraguan, Pedro Diaz, went to the trouble to swear out an affidavit, No. 3061696, denouncing Lau to the Honduran Army, August 20, 1982. Noting that the majority of Nicaraguans feel "revulsion and mistrust for gentlemen such as the aforementioned Ricardo Lau Castillo (a.k.a 'Chino')," Diaz charges that when Lau resided in Guatemala he sent men out to commit robberies and assaults, then denounced some of them to the Policia Judicial and ordered others killed so that he could keep the money himself.

Lau's defenders among the Nicaraguan Democratic Force hierarchy interviewed in Tegucigalpa in November 1984 said that he was maligned by people who either were paranoid or who wanted to harm the FDN. They did not deny that he was involved in such activities. Instead they said nothing was proven against him or that they did not know about them.
(p. 83)

The attitude of younger officers toward Bermúdez was described in confidential interviews with ex-*guardias* in Miami in August 1984 and November 1984.
(p. 84)

Hugo Villagra was interviewed about his escape briefly on August 12, 1984.
(p. 84)

Pedro Núñez Cabezas was interviewed in Managua on June 5, 1984.
(pp. 84–85)

The description of the Legion's arrival in Guatemala City is from interviews with confidential Nicaraguan anti-Sandinista sources in Miami in November and December 1984.
(pp. 85–86)

The CIA source cited was interviewed in September 1984.

There have been many books published on the abuses of the CIA and its major covert operations from the 1950s until the mid-1970s. Some of the best and most relevant for understanding recent events in Central America are, for an overview, Thomas Powers, *The Man Who Kept the Secrets: Richard Helms and the CIA,* Alfred A. Knopf, 1979; Stephen Kinzer and Stephen Schlesinger, *Bitter Fruit,* (Anchor-Doubleday, 1983), a detailed account of the 1954 Guatemala coup; and Peter Wyden, *Bay of Pigs,* Simon & Schuster, 1979.

But the key source material for understanding the CIA's abuses and the public's revulsion in the mid-1970s comes from fifteen months of investigations into "Foreign and Military Intelligence" in 1975 and 1976 by the Senate's Select Committee to Study Governmental Operations with Respect to Intelligence Activities, chaired by Senator Frank Church. Regarding "continuity" see especially Book I of the *Final Report,* published by the U.S. Government Printing Office, April 26, 1976, p. 158:

"The Committee found that one of the most troublesome and controversial issues it confronted was the question of the utility and propriety of the CIA's maintaining a worldwide 'infrastructure' (e.g., agents of influence, assets, and media contacts). Are these 'assets' essential to the success of a major covert action program? Or does this standby capability generate a temptation to intervene covertly as an alternative to diplomacy?'' The report goes on to say that while the CIA attaches "great importance to the maintenance of a worldwide clandestine infrastructure—the so-called 'plumbing,' '' that network had been substantially reduced since it reached a peak in the 1960s. The report noted, however, that "although the United States has no substantial covert action program in the Western Hemisphere today, the CIA does continue to maintain a modest covert action infrastructure consisting of agents of influence and media contacts.'' In a footnote, the term "agents of influence" appears to include at least three CIA assets in various parts of the world who were "involved, or contemplated for use in, plots to assassinate foreign leaders.''

The hunt for Ché Guevara, as it happened, was a story often told in 1982 and 1983 in San Salvador by the head of the U.S. Military Group there, Colonel John Waghelstein, who participated in the mop-up operations in Bolivia.
(p. 85)

The meeting of Central American interior ministers was recounted to me in interviews with former Salvadoran security chief Colonel Roberto Santivañez in Washington, D.C., March 22, 1985, and with Salvadoran General José Alberto "Chele" Medrano, in San Salvador, June 1984. Also see the exhaustive reporting on the residual networks by Allan Nairn, "Behind the Death Squads," *The Progressive,* May 1984, pp. 20–29.
(p. 86)

There are several good accounts of the Chilean secret service's assassination of Orlando Letelier and his American assistant. See especially Eugene M. Propper and Taylor Branch, *Labyrinth,* Viking, 1982, and Sol Landau and John Dinges, *Assassination on Embassy Row,* Pantheon, 1980. For a neat little summation of the Argentine role in Bolivia see the report on "Oversight on Illegal Drug Trafficking from Bolivia and U.S. Application of the Rangel Amendment,'' by the House Subcommittee on International Development Institutions and Finance of the Committee on Banking, Finance and Urban Affairs, July 1981.
(p. 86)

The role of Brigade 2506 was cited by confidential sources in Miami interviews, August and November 1984.
(pp. 86–87)

I interviewed Sandoval Alarcón and Sisniega Otero in their Movimiento de Liberacion Nacional headquarters in Guatemala City, May 1981. It was an altogether disturbing place, with its unsmiling guards everywhere, some of them carrying submachine guns that looked as if they had been around since 1954. The one bit of relief was a poster of Ronald Reagan affectionately embracing a chimpanzee from the film *Bedtime for Bonzo.* Sandoval's nickname is "Miko,'' or "Little Monkey.'' His role as godfather to the Salvadoran and Nicaraguan exiles was described in interviews with confidential Nicaraguan sources in November 1984 and with a confidential Salvadoran source in March 1985. The direct quotes from Sandoval are from WGBH film archives.
(pp. 87–88)

Exhaustive reporting on the Salvadoran death squads, with particular emphasis on the Guatemalan and Argentine connections, was done jointly by Laurie Becklund of the *Los Angeles Times* and Craig Pyes of the *Albuquerque Journal* in

stories that ran in their respective newspapers in December 1983. Becklund's were "Death Squads: Deadly 'Other War,' " December 18, and "Death Squad Members Tell Their Stories," December 19. Pyes published nine separate stories between December 18 and 22 under the series title "Salvadoran Rightists: The Deadly Patriots."
(pp. 87–88)

For further elaboration on the whys and wherefores of the slaughter in El Salvador, see my article "The Truth Behind the Death Squads," *The New Republic,* December 13, 1983.
(pp. 87–88)

The d'Aubuisson documents I worked from are photocopies of the original agenda kept by Captain Alvaro Rafael Saravia. The entry for Thursday, March 27, reads line by line as follows: "Contactar Orlando de Sola 305-El Dorado Ameri/Juan Wright/Aporte a Nicaraguenses $40,000.00/Colonel Ricardo Lao—tel—67-475/Carlos Llort 63315/Ricardo Llort 69-1846/Aporte Nica—$80,000.00." The content of the papers was also published in "The Situation in El Salvador," hearings before the Committee on Foreign Relations, United States Senate, March 18 and April 9, 1981. For some reason Lau's name is misprinted as "Ricardo La. o."

For further discussion of the papers see Craig Pyes, "Who Killed Archbishop Romero?," *The Nation,* October 13, 1984. Also see the House Intelligence Committee Staff Report, "U.S. Intelligence Performance on Central America: Achievements and Selected Instances of Concern," September 27, 1982, which talks about the Agency's failure to analyze the documents.

The specific allegations against Lau were made by Salvadoran Colonel Roberto Santivañez in an interview and at a press conference in Washington, D.C., March 22, 1985. It should be noted Santivañez received several thousand dollars in support funds from liberal American activists after he began speaking out in 1984 about the abuses of the army and intelligence organizations he had served, and also received money for a film produced about him and broadcast on Washington's public television station in March 1985.
(p. 89)

A lengthy interview with Enrique Haroldo Gorriaran Merlo, the leader of the team that murdered Somoza, appeared in several Spanish and Latin American publications in August 1983, including the Mexican newspaper *El Día,* August 21 and 22, and the Spanish magazine *Siete Días.* Gorriaran Merlo, Argentine, forty-one years old in 1983, was a leading member of the Argentine ERP before he was forced into exile in 1977 by the "Dirty War" and joined up with Nicaragua's Sandinistas, according to the interview. He claimed that his decision to kill Somoza with a team of four Argentines was not ordered by the Sandinistas. He said he saw in Nicaragua that "the people wanted him to pay for his crimes but that Somoza had escaped from their hands." Gorriaran Merlo's intention in granting the interview appears to have been to exculpate his Sandinista comrades for the murders of their enemies. He was speaking out in 1983 "because at this moment aggressions against Nicaragua are intensifying," he said. "Those of us involved have some experience in our country, in the various kinds of tasks that are implied in an operation of this kind: from the search for information to the execution of the plan." (Q. Your experience was only in Argentina?) "No. Some of us had carried

out successfully other operations in Tegucigalpa, such as the bringing to justice of Comandante Bravo, one of the heads of the Guardia Nacional, responsible for innumerable crimes." (See notes above for pp. 64–67.) In Managua in July 1983, I was offered an opportunity to interview Gorriaran Merlo by another journalist acting as an intermediary, but the offer was withdrawn without explanation.
(p. 89)

Revelations of the atrocities committed by Argentina's military continued throughout 1985. The most comprehensive indictment of the generals' regime, however, was contained in the 350-page summary of 50,000 pages of testimony collected by the twelve-member National Commission on the Disappearance of Persons (CONADEP) under the chairmanship of Ernesto Sábato and delivered to Argentine President Raul Alfonsín on September 20, 1984. Much of the contents of the report remained secret. But a digest released to the press is quoted here as it appeared in the *Buenos Aires Herald,* September 21, 1984, p. 13.
(p. 89)

Although written from a decidedly leftist perspective, a well-argued and well-documented discussion of the Argentine generals' views is Horacio Verbitsky's *La Ultima Batalla de la Tercera Guerra Mundial,* Editorial Legasa, Buenos Aires, 1984.
(pp. 90–92)

The account of the attack on Radio Noticias is drawn from an extended interview with one of the participants on August 10, 1984. Hugo Villagra, interviewed in Miami, August 12, 1984, confirmed parts of the story relating to his perceptions. Further details were found in the newspaper clippings at the morgue of *La Nación* in San José, Costa Rica, under file reference number 557.68. Not all of these bore dates, unfortunately. The quotes from Viola are as reported in an Associated Press dispatch in *La Nación* under the headline "Emisora costarricense usada para atacar a la Argentina." The radio was allegedly used to send coded messages to the *montoneros:* see "Argentina acusa a Radio Noticias del Continente," August 6, 1980. The attack and its aftermath are covered in "Asaltaron a tiros la emisora Radionoticias del Continente," December 15, 1980, p. 13A; "Identifican al jefe del comando que asalto radio," December 16, 1980; "Versiones contradictorias sobre atentado contra radioemisora;" "Capturan a presuntos miembros de comando que ataco emisora," December 19, 1980; "Procuraduria elabora denuncia contra presuntos terroristas." The participants in the attack, according to *La Nación,* were ex-Guardia Captain Hugo José Villagra Gutiérrez, Roger Benavides Castillo, who survived his wounds, Orlando Murillo Gonzáles, José E. Gutiérrez Ampié, José Luis López Gutiérrez, Luis Humberto Solórzano Gonzalez, wounded in the leg, and Roberto Núñez Martínez.

Radio Noticias was shut down finally by the Costa Rican government in March 1981 after automatic rifles and other weapons reportedly were discovered by Costa Rican authorities in a house nearby. See "Descubren armamento en cercanias de Radio Noticias del Continente," February 9, 1981, p. 16A, and "Firmado acuerdo que suspende frecuencia de Radio Noticias," March 5, 1981, p. 6A.
(pp. 92–94)

The 1979 ordeal of La Negra, Sonia Zapata Reyes, is as she recounted it in interviews and conversations March 22, 23, 24 and 29, 1983. The generic descrip-

tion of the Managua barrios is from firsthand observations. The woman friend of
La Negra was interviewed in November 1984.
(p. 94)

The recollections of the days with .22s are from interviews with Sonia Zapata
Reyes, Pedro Pablo Ortiz Centeno and Julio César Herrera in March 1983.
(pp. 94–95)

The description of the Segovias comes from visits in March 1983, May 1983,
October 1983 and June 1984.
(p. 95)

The April 1980 arrests are dealt with in statements by Tomás Borge monitored
by the Foreign Broadcast Information Service (FBIS), "Daily Report—Latin
America," May 14, 1980. p. P-11.
(p. 95)

The May 1980 shutdown of the San Pedro Sula radio is as monitored in FBIS,
May 18, 1980, p. P-16.
(p. 96)

Quotations are from "Josué," a member of Suicida's band interviewed March
23, 1983, in Nueva Segovia, Nicaragua.
(p. 96)

The killing of the Cuban teacher is as recounted in an interview with Julio
César Herrera, March 24, 1984. The account of the other two Cuban teachers is
from Radio Sandino, monitored by FBIS, October 23, 1981, p. P-7.
(p. 97)

Herrera's account of his name changes is from an interview on March 23,
1983.
(p. 97)

Herrera told his story of killing the militia commander March 26, 1983, as we
were marching in Nueva Segovia. Immediately after telling it, he stopped the
march for a moment to point out a dove sitting on a stump in the forest.

Lenin Cerna, head of the Sandinista State Security, in an interview May 30,
1984, denied that any Cuban teacher had been killed in San Francisco del Norte in
1980 or 1981, or that any militia commander had been murdered at Guasaule.

Findings—1981

(p. 99)

House Intelligence Committee hearing room is described from visit there in
October 1982.
(pp. 99–100)

The overall perception of a consensus sought, constructed, and thwarted between Congress and the administration on intelligence questions comes from interviews with CIA and congressional sources in August, September, November and
December 1984 and January and February 1985. Also see the Church Committee's
"Foreign and Military Intelligence," Final Report, Book I, pp. 13, 430–31.
(p. 100)

Casey was born March 13, 1913, according to a CIA spokesman. Several
requests for a formal interview with Casey were denied in December 1984. I talked

to several of his employees and associates, however, between August and December 1984. For obvious reasons they all asked to remain anonymous.

The characterization of Casey's oratory is well known and was invariably mentioned by congressional sources in interviews in 1982 and in the summer and fall of 1984. Some referred to him as "Mumble Joe."

There are several good profiles of Casey extant, the most thorough and accessible probably being Lelyveld's *New York Times Magazine* piece, January 20, 1985.
(p. 101)

The Hugel story was by Patrick Tyler in *The Washington Post,* May 16, 1981. Casey's reaction to Goldwater was recounted by a senior CIA official, December 1984.
(p. 102)

Before any hard and fast decisions on the Secret War were taken, several CIA "old-timers," released from service during the cutbacks of the 1970s, were in contact with anti-Sandinista forces, acting as private citizens to reassure them that once Reagan was elected, their lot would improve. See Alfonso Chardy and Juan O. Tamayo, " 'New' CIA U.S. Involvement," *Miami Herald,* June 5, 1983, p. 1C. But while some of these men eventually served as contract agents in the Secret War, their self-importance in creating it is, I believe, overstated. The paramilitary operation against Nicaragua ultimately was not just an out-of-control creation of conspiratorial ex-spies and right-wing ideologues but a conscious decision by senior administration officials who consider themselves pragmatic policymakers.
(p. 102)

The membership of the Core Group as well as its name was a matter of constant variations. But it was basically the functional, regionalized offspring of the National Security Committee subcommittee, referred to as the Group in the Church Committee's recommendations of 1976. The Group approved and reviewed all types of sensitive intelligence activities. Represented are the Secretary of State, the Secretary of Defense, the Assistant to the President for National Security Affairs, the Director of Central Intelligence, the Attorney General, and the Chairman of the Joint Chiefs of Staff. (See Church Committee final report, p. 430.) Also see Robert C. Toth and Doyle McManus, "CIA 'Cowboy' Led Covert Activity in Nicaragua," *Los Angeles Times,* March 3, 1985. McManus and Toth refer to the National Security Council's Senior Interagency Group on Central America and name "four officials who oversaw the contra operation": Enders, National Security Council staffer Colonel Oliver North; the CIA Latin American division chief whom they refer to as "Dewey Maroni" and the Defense Department's Nestor Sanchez. There were, however, other officials who sat in.
(p. 102)

For a consideration of the Vietnam mentality in Central American policy, see Dickey, "The Gang That Blew Vietnam Goes Latin," *The Washington Post,* November 28, 1982, pp. C1–C2.

Also see, in the context of Kissinger protégés and the Secret War, Kissinger's remarks to the Church Committee, November 21, 1975, p. 38, cited in the Final Report, p. 159:

"If the diplomatic track cannot succeed without the covert track, then the

covert track was unnecessary and should not have been engaged in. So hopefully, if one wants to draw a general conclusion, one would have to say that only those covert actions can be justified that support a diplomatic track."
(p. 103)

The quotations about the Core Group are from interviews with participants and sources knowledgeable about its deliberations in the Washington, D.C., area, November and December 1984 and February 1985.
(pp. 103–4)

Quotations about Haig's obsession with Cuba and Castro are from a confidential interview in the Washington, D.C., area, February 1985. But Haig's views on the subject are laid out straightforwardly enough in *Caveat: Realism, Reagan, and Foreign Policy,* Macmillan, New York, 1984. See especially pp. 96–100, 117–40. The anguishing series of meetings is referred to on p. 127. For Haig vs. Helms, see pp. 67–68, 94.
(p. 103)

Quote on ideologues is from confidential interview, Washington, D.C., area, December 1984. Quote on manhood is from a confidential interview, Washington, D.C., area, February 1984.
(pp. 103–4)

I covered the final offensive in El Salvador from January 10 to 22, 1981.
(p. 104)

Enders's decision-making process was characterized by a colleague in a confidential interview in the Washington, D.C., area, December 1984.
(p. 104)

The March 9, 1981, finding was reported by Don Oberdorfer and Patrick E. Tyler, "U.S.–Backed Nicaraguan Rebel Army Swells to 7,000 Men," May 8, 1983, and by Chardy and Tamayo in the *Miami Herald,* June 5, 1983.
(pp. 105–6)

The discussion of the aid cut-off to Nicaragua comes from an interview with Pezzullo in May 1984, and with senior State Department officials and a former member of the Core Group in December 1984. The closing of Pamplona was recounted in a confidential interview with a U.S. diplomatic source in May 1984.
(p. 105)

Haig's remarks to Ambassador Rita Delia Casco are from *Caveat,* p. 100.
(p. 106)

The full text of the April 1 statement on the cut-off of economic aid to Nicaragua appears in "Department of State Bulletin," Volume 81, Number 2050, May 1981, p. 71.
(p. 106)

The little green book and the Bulgarian celebrations were observed firsthand. The assertion of renewed aid to the Salvadorans is from U.S. diplomatic sources interviewed at the time and a confidential Sandinista source interviewed in July 1981. I also interviewed Salvadoran guerrilla and opposition leaders obviously resident in Managua in November 1981.
(p. 107)

MacFarlane's report was noted by Toth and McManus, *Los Angeles Times,* March 3, 1985.

(p. 107)

On Casey's reluctance to get the Agency involved initially in an open-ended paramilitary program, a supporter at Langley said in December 1984. "He was aware that this was going to be a problem, but it was decided there was no other way to do it. . . . But he really is deeply concerned about the Agency, deeply concerned that he not get it in trouble."

Haig also notes in passing in *Caveat,* p. 129, that Casey initially had reservations about the covert program.

(p. 107)

The quotation about the mess made by paramilitary operations is from a confidential interview in the Washington, D.C., area, November 1984.

(pp. 107–8)

Casey's discovery of Clarridge in Rome and Clarridge's educational background were reported by Toth and McManus, *Los Angeles Times,* March 3, 1985, although they only used his pseudonym. The other personal details are from interviews with Clarridge's acquaintances in the fall of 1984 and the spring of 1985. His service record is taken from copies of the Foreign Service list published by the U.S. State Department through 1973.

(pp. 108–9)

Sanchez's background is also taken from Foreign Service lists and from interviews in Washington with a source close to him in May 1983 and in February 1985. Casey's views toward him, and Clarridge's remarks about him, were recounted by senior intelligence sources in interviews in August, September and November 1984. Toth and McManus also deal with the subject.

(pp. 109–11)

Observations of the scene during Enders's August 1981 visit to Managua were made firsthand. The characterization of his remarks to the Sandinistas is from an interview with Nicaraguan Foreign Minister Miguel D'Escoto, August 12, 1981, and with confidential sources in the Washington, D.C., area in December 1984 and February 1985.

(p. 110)

The characterization of the "nun-killing" Salvadoran regime is from a conversation with a senior diplomat at the U.S. embassy, San Salvador, January 1981.

(p. 110)

A senior U.S. military advisor in El Salvador was interviewed at length in May 1981.

(p. 110)

The pilot training and the East German and Soviet involvement with State Security were confirmed to me by a confidential Sandinista source in November 1981. The Cubans also were involved and a well-informed U.S. source interviewed in May 1984 said that by 1981 "the Cubans had set up a three-tier intelligence system: one for the government, one for Tomás Borge, and one for themselves." Also see note for p. 65.

(pp. 110–11)

The specific points at issue in Enders's August visit were also addressed in the letters and "draft proposals" of possible agreements that Enders sent Daniel Ortega on September 8, September 16 and September 28 ("Let me assure you that

our actions and words have been carefully restrained to facilitate dialogue with Nicaragua. To maintain this course, however, similar restraint must be shown by Nicaragua," Enders said in a not very veiled threat signed "Tom"). D'Escoto replied in letters to Haig on September 19 and October 31 saying that his government was analyzing the proposals but that the United States had to take some concrete measures, such as ending military exercises near Nicaragua, to facilitate the normalization of bilateral relations. In both Nicaraguan letters, D'Escoto blames Washington for aggravating the situation in El Salvador with "tragic effects" and praises the Salvadoran rebels for embracing peace proposals.
(p. 111)

In New York on October 7, 1981, Ortega listed 36 "aggressions" against Central America, beginning in 1855 when "the William Walker filibusters [sic] landed in Nicaragua with the purpose of annexing the whole of Central America to the southern states of the United States" and ending with the "Falcon View" military exercises of October 1981. See "Discursos Pronunciados por el Comandante Daniel Ortega en las Naciones Unidas," Ministerio del Exterior, Managua, 1983, pp. 74–78.
(p. 111)

Interview with Core Group veteran was in Washington, D.C., area, November 1984.
(p. 111)

Clarridge's desire for a cause was noted in an interview with a confidential intelligence source in the Washington, D.C., area, August 1984.
(pp. 111–12)

The presentation of the November 1981 finding was described by congressional sources in May 1983, April 1984 and August 1984; in Oberdorfer and Tyler, *The Washington Post,* May 8, 1983; and in Chardy and Tamayo, *Miami Herald,* June 5, 1983, which adds: "Casey himself told the committees of the CIA's 'minimal' and 'optimal' plan. The minimal plan would only interdict the Cuban-Nicaraguan arms pipeline to El Salvador; the optimal plan would amount to an attempt to overthrow the Sandinistas."
(p. 113)

The account of the meeting between Suicida and Noel Ortiz is told as recounted to me in an interview with an eyewitness and another source close to Ortiz in Miami in November 1984. I tracked Ortiz down in Tegucigalpa on November 28, 1984. He confirmed the details and the dialogue.
(pp. 114–15)

The account of training in Argentina is from Nicaraguan anti-Sandinista sources interviewed in Miami in August and December 1984 and Pedro Núñez Cabezas, interviewed in Managua, June 5, 1984. The Sandinistas first reported on the Argentine training in January 1982 (FBIS, January 15, 1982) after capturing William Baltodano, a veteran of Buenos Aires, when he attempted to mount a sabotage campaign in Managua.
(p. 115)

NBC producer Maurie Moore and I interviewed General Gustavo Alvarez in his office in Tegucigalpa July 26, 1983, at which time he showed us his memorabilia from the Argentine military academy. That was also the occasion of his remark on the morality of destroying Marxist regimes.

(pp. 115–16)

Ribeiro's role was confirmed in interviews with: Edgar Chamorro on August 9, 1984; José Francisco Cardenal, August 11, 1984; confidential interviews with two U.S. right-wing contacts of Ribeiro's in August 1984; CIA sources in October and November 1984; Nicaraguan anti-Sandinista sources in Tegucigalpa, November 1984; and Argentine military sources interviewed by Martin Andersen in Buenos Aires, December 1984. Andersen attempted to interview Ribeiro himself, but Ribeiro declined.

(p. 116)

I interviewed Echaverry (who gave me this unusual spelling of his name) on March 29, 1983, and on July 29, 1983.

(p. 116)

For an account of the arrests in January 1981 and the rise of the "Argentine method" see Leticia Salomon, "La Doctrina de la Seguridad Nacional en Honduras: Analisis de la caida del General Gustavo Alvarez Martinez," *Boletin Informativo Honduras,* Especial 11, May 1984, p.6.

I reported personally on the disappearances in Tegucigalpa, November 1981, and the role of Alexander Hernandez, denounced by Alvarez's rival Colonel Leonidas Torres Arias, in October 1982.

(p. 117)

I reported on the Honduran shift in view from El Salvador as the enemy to Nicaragua as the main threat in Tegucigalpa in April 1981.

(p. 117)

The story of $50,000 going to Negro Chamorro's group was mentioned by several Nicaraguan anti-Sandinista sources. The Sandinistas reported it after the capture of William Baltodano (FBIS, January 15, 1982), p. P-6.

(p. 118)

The lack of interest in fighting by the Argentine trainees and the statistics of their dropout rate were cited in confidential interviews with Nicaraguan anti-Sandinista sources in November and December 1984.

(p. 118)

Ortiz told the story of his first camp in an interview in November 1984.

(pp. 118–19)

Suicida's problems with weapons were recounted by him and members of his group in March 1983.

(pp. 119–20)

The meeting between Cardenal and Villegas (undoubtedly a pseudonym) was recounted by Cardenal in an interview August 11, 1984. The dialogue is as he recalled it.

(p. 121)

Pastora's doubts and disillusionment as a revolutionary bureaucrat were characterized by Moisés Hassan, interviewed in July 1981. Pastora's reservations about the revolution are from interviews in April 1982 and July 1984.

(p. 121)

Descriptions of U.S.–Torrijos relations are from interviews with U.S. diplomats in Panama in November 1984 and in the Washington, D.C., area in February 1985. Pastora talked about his relationship with Torrijos in April 1982 and July 1984 interviews.

(pp. 121–23)

The account of Pastora's flight to Panama and the death of Torrijos is from July 1984 interviews. Poveda did not leave Nicaragua until several months later, according to an April 1982 interview with him.

(pp. 123–24)

Material on the Galtieri visit to Washington was reported by Martin Andersen in interviews with senior Argentine military officials in December 1984. Also see *Malvinas: Trama Secreta,* by *Clarin* reporters Oscar Raul Cardoso, Ricardo Kirshbaum, and Eduardo van der Kooy, Sudamerica-Planeta, Buenos Aires, 1984, pp. 27–31; and Verbitsky, pp. 80–107.

(pp. 124–25)

I attended the embassy party in Tegucigalpa in November 1981. The quotation is from the Exeter alumni bulletin, spring 1982. Negroponte was class of '56.

(pp. 125–26)

Negroponte's functions with regard to the Secret War often were overstated in the press in 1982 and 1983. The description of his role here is from interviews with U.S. intelligence and diplomatic sources in Tegucigalpa, Miami and Washington, January, November and December 1984.

(p. 126)

Mike served until September 1982, according to CIA sources. There are federal legal restrictions on the revelation of the names of U.S. intelligence agents. Where I believe the agents still to be in the field and hence potentially vulnerable to possible attack or retaliation I have refrained from printing their full names.

(p. 126)

The visit by Casey and Clarridge's remarks were noted in interviews with diplomatic sources in December 1984.

(p. 126)

Ribeiro's accommodations and tastes were mentioned in several interviews. (See note for pp. 115–16.)

(p. 126)

Bermúdez is quoted in McManus and Toth, "CIA Sent Contra Force—And Americans—Into Thick of War," *Los Angeles Times,* March 3, 1985.

(pp. 126–27)

The situation in the camps in late 1981 was described in interviews with Ortiz Centeno, Herrera and Sonia Zapata Reyes, "La Negra," in March 1983; with veterans of Pino Uno, Suicida's camp, Tegucigalpa, January 28, 1984; and in interviews with Nicaraguan anti-Sandinista sources in Miami, December 1984.

(pp. 127–29)

The scenes at Sagitario camp and with Villegas and the anecdote about the watch are as Ortiz recounted them, November 1984.

(p. 129)

The reorganization of the FDN high command was described in interviews with senior FDN officials in Tegucigalpa in November 1984.

The Nicaraguan Democratic Force was formed in August 1981 from a union of the September 15 Legion under Bermúdez and Lau and the Nicaraguan Democratic Union (UDN) under Cardenal. The first military general staff of the new organization consisted of Orlando Bolaños, Enrique Bermúdez, Raul Arana, Ricardo Lau, Justiniano Pérez and Carlos Rodriguez.

After the December 1981 housecleaning the new military general staff consisted of Bermúdez, chief of staff; Edgar Hernandez, personnel; Lau, intelligence; Echaverry, operations; Francisco "El Gato" Rivera, logistics; Manuel Antonio Cáceres, psychological operations. These positions were maintained until December 1982.

The Secret War—1982

(p. 131)

The brief account of the blowing of the two bridges, including the use of night-vision goggles, is from interviews with anti-Sandinista Nicaraguan sources familiar with the operation in November and December 1984. The use of claymore mines to set up a perimeter is referred to in the account of a captured guide from the Rio Negro team, presented at a press conference in Managua, April 6, 1982 (FBIS, April 9, 1982, "Security Director Lenin Cerna Press Conference," pp. P4–P11). He does not mention night-vision goggles, but he was not present at the time of the explosion itself.

(pp. 131–32)

The Miskito training was partly undertaken by Justiniano Pérez, according to FDN sources interviewed in Tegucigalpa, November 1984.

(p. 132)

The bridge-blowing as the point of no return was discussed by a source in the Washington, D.C., area, November 1984.

(p. 132)

The National Security Council document, "U.S. Policy in Central America and Cuba Through F.Y. '84, Summary Paper," on a meeting of the National Security Planning Group in April 1982, was published in its entirety in *The New York Times*, April 7, 1983.

(p. 132)

The parenthetical anecdote about the squad leader with a stomachache comes from an interview with an informed Nicaraguan source in Miami, December 1984.

(p. 132)

The notion of "symmetry" was discussed with me in detail by senior U.S. diplomatic sources in Central America in June 1983.

(p. 133)

"U.S. Approves Covert Plan in Nicaragua," by Patrick E. Tyler and Bob Woodward, appeared in *The Washington Post* on March 10, 1982, on a front page entirely dominated by Nicaraguan news. The lead story of the paper was "U.S. Shows Photos to Back Charge of Nicaragua Buildup," by John Goshko. The third story was "Nicaragua Sees Regional Revolt If Invaded," by Christopher Dickey.

(p. 133)

CIA spokesman George Lauder said in a telephone interview in December 1984 that "the Director does not leak. Period."

(p. 133)

The military official cited was interviewed in Tegucigalpa in February 1983.

(p. 133)

Summary paper in *The New York Times,* April 7, 1983.

(pp. 133–34)

Alfredo César, a member of the Sandinista party and head of the Nicaraguan Central Bank in March 1982, said in an interview in Washington, March 1985, that the Sandinista Directorate had been looking at least since late 1981 for a pretext to impose a state of emergency.

I reported on the Miskito camps in May 1982 in Nicaragua and in October 1982 in Honduras.

I attended the rally in Managua, May 1, 1982. At the time it appeared that Borge was angling to declare openly that Nicaragua was a Socialist state. However, Ortega returned from Moscow with considerably less aid than some Sandinista officials said he had expected. Nicaragua refrained from a formal declaration of a Socialist government.

(pp. 134–35)

Lisa Fitzgerald's impressions, background and attitudes are as recounted in a lengthy tape-recorded interview in Managua, Nicaragua, June 4, 1984, except for the recollections of the Philippines and the impact of that experience on her, which is from an interview *Washington Post* reporter Carla Hall had with her in June 1983.

(pp. 135–36)

Cardenal's experience and feelings upon arrival in Tegucigalpa are as recorded in an interview on August 11, 1984.

(p. 136)

Description of operation at Radio 15 is from interviews with sources who worked there in early 1982, interviewed in November 1984.

(p. 137)

Herrera and Ortiz Centeno talked frequently in their March 1983 interviews about the excitement of receiving the first FALs. The shouts they used and their exchanges with the Sandinista militias when they first got the FALs, however, were recounted by a Nicaraguan who fought alongside them, interviewed in Miami in December 1984.

(pp. 138–39)

The account of Easter Week events at Tererios and San Pablo is from Lisa Fitzgerald interview, June 4, 1984.

(p. 139)

The level of Sandinista penetration of the anti-Sandinista movement was discussed by Lenin Cerna in the May 29, 1984, interview.

(p. 139)

The captured saboteur referred to is William Baltodano. See FBIS, January 15, 1982, p. P4.

(pp. 139–40)

The depiction of Humberto Ortega is from my notes and a tape of the interview in the bunker, July 1982.

(p. 141)

The description of Pino Uno is from interviews in January 1984 with Nicaraguans who had served there.

(pp. 141–43)

The specific recruits of the FDN described and quoted here were interviewed on March 23, 24 and 27, 1983, in Nueva Segovia. Their views coincide with Nicaraguan refugees in Danlí, Honduras, interviewed in October 1982.

(p. 143)

The haircutting scene is as recounted by Laura Ortiz, November 24, 1982.

(p. 143)

The mutual enjoyment of La Negra and Suicida was evident in conversations with them both, but particularly La Negra. Their radio conversations about dentists were described by a Sandinista captain in Ocotal, Nicaragua, May 21, 1983. La Negra talked about the dinners at Pepy-Lou's and the shopping trips as we shopped in a Tegucigalpa supermarket and dined at Pepy-Lou's, March 22, 1983.

(p. 144)

The relationship between Suicida and Villegas was noted in an interview with a Nicaraguan source, November 1984.

(p. 144)

Suicida's problems with the general staff were noted in an interview with Echaverry, July 29, 1983; interviews with veterans of Pino Uno in January 1984; with Pedro Núñez Cabezas, June 5, 1984; with Nicaraguan anti-Sandinista sources who asked not to be named, in Tegucigalpa in November 1984.

(p. 144)

For brief biographies of Ramírez Zelaya and Núñez Cabezas see the Sandinista party newspaper *Barricada,* "DGSE desarticula plan terrorista de la CIA," August 19, 1983, p. 10.

(pp. 144–45)

The relationship between Clarridge and Casey was described in interviews with several CIA and diplomatic sources between August and December 1984. The main man in the middle cut out of much of the discussion was John H. Stein, the deputy director of operations, who was nominally Clarridge's boss. Part of his problem appears to have been that he had no interagency panels to sit on that were involved with running the war. "The National Security Policy Planning Group is the one Casey attends. Dewey went to the working group. Stein didn't go to either one," said a senior intelligence official in December 1984. "When Casey comes back from an NSPG meeting, sure he's going to talk to Dewey."

(pp. 145–47)

The perceptions and blind spots of the members of the congressional intelligence committees and Clarridge's reactions to them are as described by congressional sources in December 1984 and January and February 1985. The reaction to the misunderstanding by a member of the Core Group comes from an interview in December 1984.

(pp. 147–48)

I attended the Pastora press conference in the Escazú suburb of San José. The account is from my notes. The quotation in Spanish is *"les voy a sacar a balazos de sus mansiones y sus* Mercedes-Benz."

(p. 148)

The unflattering characterizations of Pastora's motives and reactions were

made by a senior Sandinista official attached to the staff of the National Directorate interviewed in May 1982. Also see "FSLN Issues Communiqué on Edén Pastora Charges," April 17, 1982, FBIS, April 19, 1982, pp. P10–P13.
(pp. 148–49)

Clarridge's predilection for Pastora was noted in interviews with U.S. intelligence officials in August and November 1984 and by congressional sources in December 1984 and January 1985.
(p. 149)

The account of Pastora's peregrinations is from the July 1984 interviews.
(pp. 149–50)

The account of Pastora's showdown in Tegucigalpa is from the July 1984 interviews with him. A CIA source interviewed in the Washington, D.C., area in October 1984 confirmed that there were serious frictions with Pastora but did not confirm or deny this specific incident.
(p. 152)

"Shaw's" physical appearance was recorded on videotape in October 1983 by an ABC camera crew in Tegucigalpa when he was set up by a group of angry, dissident anti-Sandinista rebels for a meeting in a hotel parking lot. He was also described to me by acquaintances in interviews in Miami and Tegucigalpa in August and November 1984. Shaw, under his real name, is well known to anti-CIA groups that print lists of CIA agents and their backgrounds in such publications as the *Covert Action Information Bulletin.* I reached Shaw by telephone at his new assignment in November 1984, but he declined to comment or to meet with me there. I have not named him for reasons cited in the note on p. 294.
(pp. 151–52)

The description quoted of Feldman/Mason is from an interview in Miami, August 1984. The characterization of Monica is by a U.S. intelligence source as well as by Nicaraguans. Cardenal's experience is as recounted in an interview in Miami, August 11, 1984.
(p. 153)

The quote about Lau as a bone of contention is from an interview with a CIA source in the Washington, D.C., area, November 1984. That Shaw demanded his removal was confirmed in interviews with U.S. intelligence sources in October and November 1984.

The official new FDN military general staff formed in the fall of 1982, according to senior FDN officials interviewed in Tegucigalpa in November 1984, was made up of Bermúdez, who became a member of the new FDN directorate; Echaverry, "Fiero," chief of staff; Tomás "Tito" Martinez, personnel; Edgar Hernández, intelligence; Hugo Villagra, "Visage," operations; Mario "El Diablo" Morales, logistics; Cáceres, psychological operations. See note for p. 129.

The explanation given by Aristides Sanchez, a senior FDN leader interviewed in Tegucigalpa in November 1984, was that "Lau is independent. . . . He was not retired from the movement. He left of his own free will in December [1982] because he didn't accept the restructuring."

That he did not, in fact, leave was confirmed to me in interviews with three present and former FDN officials in August, November and December 1984.

(pp. 153–56)

The narrative, dialogue and thoughts during Cardenal's ordeal in Tegucigalpa are from an interview August 11, 1984. The scene at the safe house was confirmed by another eyewitness in a later interview. FDN leaders and a spokesman questioned about this in Tegucigalpa in November 1984 said that Cardenal had been under a lot of strain and was imagining things.

(p. 154)

One copy of the Francés videotape was sent to *The Washington Post* from a fictitious address in suburban Washington about a month after Francés disappeared. I viewed another copy of the tape in Mexico City, shown December 1, 1984, in the offices of the Latin American Journalists' Federation headed by Sandinista journalist Danilo Aguirre. I have a transcript as well.

Francés also talked about Americans, especially a good ol' boy from Rutherfordton, North Carolina, named Nat Hamrick, an importer of lumber from Latin America and broom-handle machine-pistols from the People's Republic of China, a political contact and supporter of right-wing Senator Jesse Helms, who "opened doors" for the exiles in Washington. Hamrick, reached at his home, denied any political involvement with the Nicaraguan rebels but added, "I sympathize with them and empathize with them and I hope they overthrow the bastards." See "Argentine Defector Tells of Multinational Plots for Sandinistas' Ouster," reported by Christopher Dickey, Patrick Tyler and John Dinges, *The Washington Post,* December 2, 1982, p. A22.

The thinning out of Sandinista intelligence on the FDN before the Francés revelations was discussed by Lenin Cerna in his May 29, 1984, interview. Cerna did not say where Francés could now be found.

Nicaraguan defector Miguel Bolaños Hunter reported that Francés (identified as "Victor Francés") was "psychologically tortured" by Cuban-trained interrogators and forced to make his statements after being kidnapped in Costa Rica and taken to Managua. *Heritage Foundation Backgrounder,* September 30, 1983, p. 8.

(p. 154)

The exchange with Bermúdez is from an interview with an FDN military official in November 1984.

(pp. 156–57)

For "official" biographies of the all new directorate members see "FDN: Que? Quienes? Cuando? Donde? Como? Por que?," February 1983. The members were ex-Col. Enrique Bermúdez; Adolfo Calero; former Somoza vice president Alfonso Callejas; Edgar Chamorro; veterinarian Indalecio Rodríguez; Lucia Cardenal de Salazar; and businessman Marco A. Zeledón.

(p. 157)

The Ron Plata slogan was recalled by two Nicaraguans in Miami in December 1984.

(pp. 157–158)

Edgar Chamorro talked straightforwardly about the promises made to him by the CIA in tape-recorded interviews beginning August 9, 1984, with follow-ups in October and November 1984 and March 1985. But as early as March 1983, when I first met him in Guatemala City, he said he found it difficult to believe that un-

named men were saying that the FDN could triumph by July 1983. Suicida himself, in late March, clearly expected victory to come quickly. On July 29, 1983, Echaverry said in an interview, "In our mind there never has existed the idea of a prolonged war." But FDN president Adolfo Calero in Washington, D.C., and Aristides Sánchez in Tegucigalpa said in November 1984 interviews that they had understood all along that the United States did not expect them to win quickly. "One thing I can tell you about the Americans," said Sánchez. "The people who have worked with us closely have always had the intention of making a movement that was small and incapable of overthrowing the Sandinistas by force of arms." Also see Edward Cody and Christopher Dickey, "Ex-Rebel Leader Alleges CIA Vow to Aid Overthrow in Managua," *The Washington Post,* November 27, 1984.
(p. 158)

For a rundown on the legislative history of the House Intelligence Committee's concerns about the Nicaraguan operations and the legislative restraints on them leading up to and including the Boland Amendment see "Amendment to the Intelligence Authorization Act for Fiscal Year 1983: Report Together with Additional, Minority, and Additional Dissenting Views," House of Representatives, Rept. 98-122, Part 1, May 13, 1983, especially pp. 7–9.

The *Newsweek* cover story on "The Secret War" appeared November 8, 1982, pp. 42–55.
(p. 159)

The description of Suicida's grand strategy is as told by La Negra in an interview March 23, 1983.
(p. 159)

The suspicion of the general staff on the part of Suicida and his men was noted in interviews with veterans of Suicida's operation in January, October and December 1984. The account of Krill's travels is from an interview with Núñez Cabezas, June 5, 1984, as is the description of relations between Suicida and the men assigned to him from Tegucigalpa.

Also see the Sandinista party organ *Barricada,* "DGSE desarticula plan terrorista de la CIA," August 19, 1983, p. 10, reporting on statements by Sandinista prisoner Ramírez Zelaya, "B-1": "The disagreements over command and tactics, the ignorance of the chief of the task force [Suicida] and his criminal instincts, are as if 'he were making a personal war.' " By this account, Suicida also had serious differences with José Benito Bravo, "Mack," a task force commander who worked out of a camp called Nicarao near Ocotal. Suicida, angry with Mack for failing to hold up Sandinista supply lines, is said to have called him a coward.
(pp. 159–60)

Suicida and Krill talked about their thirty-three-day December offensive in general terms in March 1983. The specifics noted here, however, are from an interview with Núñez Cabezas in Managua, June 5, 1984.

The interview was conducted in Spanish in the offices of Nicaraguan State Security with one member of that organization present. These were the only circumstances in which the interview was permitted. Núñez Cabezas had, by then, spent almost ten months as a Sandinista prisoner. He was pale, nervous and stut-

tered. He asked at least twice to go to the bathroom. I tape-recorded the interview and there were no restraints on the questions, but because of the circumstances one obviously has to sift the answers carefully. I have limited my use of the material to those elements that could be independently corroborated, matters of minor detail, and Núñez Cabezas's accounts of his own personal acts and thoughts.
(p. 160)

The CIA's motives in organizing a new Directorate were discussed in interviews with U.S. intelligence sources in the fall of 1984 and by a senior administration official in November 1984.
(pp. 160–63)

The account of Lisa Fitzgerald's hearing the mortars from the shower and the rest of her perceptions as Suicida's men attacked Jalapa are taken from the June 4, 1984, interview with her in Managua except for the mention of the radio reports, which she cited in an interview in Jalapa, May 25, 1983.
(pp. 163–64)

On January 28, 1984, at an FDN field hospital off the road from Tegucigalpa to Comayagua, Honduras, I interviewed veterans of Suicida's operation. I interviewed other veterans of Pino Uno in October and December 1984. This account is taken from their recollections of the relationships in the camp. The imagery of the attack is taken from firsthand experiences with the same troops under mortar fire, although not at the location cited, and from accounts of the attack by residents of Jalapa interviewed May 25, 1983. The problem of having run out of ammunition was cited by Núñez Cabezas, June 5, 1984. In the March 1983 interviews Krill talked about problems with ambushes and briefly, at a crucial moment, about his desire to be able to help Cancer in a combat situation.
(pp. 164–65)

I covered Reagan's visit to San José on December 3, 1982. The account is from my notebooks.
(pp. 165–66)

Krill and his men talked with the mixture recorded here of sympathy and contempt about the *milicianos* and other Sandinista partisans they attacked in interviews March 23 and March 24, 1983. They did not mention the Wuambuco incident specifically, however. The description of the coffee farm at Wuambuco is drawn from experience moving through similar terrain with Krill and from the depiction in "Dieron la Vida por su Pueblo: Felipe y Mary Barreda," a special issue of the Nicaraguan magazine *El Tayacan,* by Teofilo Cabestrero, Managua, September 1984, p. 92.

Also see documentation on this incident in: "Attacks by the Nicaraguan 'Contras' on the Civilian Population of Nicaragua: Report of a Fact-Finding Mission September 1984–January 1985," reported by Reed Brody, a former assistant New York State attorney general, distributed by the Washington Office on Latin America in Washington, D.C., March 1985, pp. 8–16; and "Violations of the Laws of War by Both Sides in Nicaragua: 1981–1985," by Robert K. Goldman et al., issued by The Americas Watch Committee, Washington, D.C., March 1985.

Two Nicaraguan anti-Sandinista sources confirmed the principal events described in this section in interviews in October, November and December 1984.

(p. 166)

Initial reaction to the attack is taken from testimony of Alicia Huete Diaz in "Dieron La Vida," p. 13, as is the account of the man Felipe Barreda trying to talk on the jeep's radio. The story that Mary Barreda had a gun in her hand is from a Nicaraguan anti-Sandinista source familiar with the incident who asked not to be cited by name.

(p. 167)

For detailed descriptions of the march from pro-Sandinista sources who subsequently escaped see testimony in the Brody report, pp. 11–13, and "Dieron la Vida," p. 18.

(pp. 167–68)

The biographical material on the Barredas is from "Dieron la Vida." The quotations are on p. 91. The letter to the tobacco workers is on pp. 36–37.

(p. 168)

The bound edition of *Dieron la Vida* is called *No los Separó la Muerte*. For the quotation about saints, see "Dieron la Vida," p. 39.

(p. 168)

Suicida's description of the Barredas and his attitude are as recalled by Ortiz, interviewed November 1984.

(p. 168)

The visit of Ortiz was noted by Núñez Cabezas in the June 5, 1984, interview, and the report of Radio 15 on the Barredas is reported in "Dieron la Vida," p. 93. Ortiz confirmed in an interview that he visited the camp at that time and talked with the Barredas.

(p. 168)

The ill treatment of the prisoners cited is reported in Brody and in "Dieron la Vida." It was confirmed by Salvador Icaza, a staff member of Suicida's, with some of the qualifications cited, in interviews in Memphis, Tennessee, on October 27 and 28, 1984.

(pp. 169–70)

For the account of the escaped prisoners and treatment of deserters, see Brody, pp. 13–14, and "Dieron la Vida," p. 22.

(pp. 170–71)

Ortiz was interviewed in November 1984.

(p. 171)

The description of Suicida's attitude is from Icaza, October 28, 1984.

(p. 171)

Quotation is from Núñez Cabezas interview, June 5, 1984.

(pp. 171–72)

The get-together at Shaw's house and Shaw's marching orders are as recalled by Chamorro in August and December 1984 interviews, and by a CIA source interviewed in the fall of 1984.

Fighting—Spring 1983

(pp. 173–75)

The first-person account of travels with La Negra, Krill and Suicida is taken entirely from my notebooks, March 22 to 29, 1983.

(pp. 175–76)

The submission of the list of reporters' names to "the Phantom" was recounted by a confidential source in the United States in November 1984, as was the Phantom's remark. I am not publishing the Phantom's name for reasons cited above. That the CIA was aware James LeMoyne and I were going into Nicaragua with Suicida also was confirmed by a CIA source in an interview in October 1984.

(p. 176)

The reasoning of Edgar Chamorro and Frank Arana in giving me the opportunity to be the first reporter for a major American newspaper to go into combat with the FDN was an object of much interest to me and many questions. The reasoning recorded here is from their responses March 21 and 22, 1983, and Edgar's initial interview with me at the beginning of the same month in Guatemala.

(pp. 177–80)

Dickey notebooks, March 23, 1983.

(pp. 180–82)

Lisa Fitzgerald's experiences on and concerns about the road from Ocotal to Jalapa are as recounted in the June 4, 1984, interview, backed up by her diary of events around Jalapa. Portions of the diary, including the entry about the veterinarian and accountant, September 22, 1982, are published in Brody's report, p. 38.

(pp. 182–87)

Dickey notebooks, March 24, 1983.

(pp. 188–89)

The account of what Lisa Fitzgerald saw, heard and felt in Jalapa on March 23, 1983, is from June 4, 1984, interview with her and her diary.

(p. 189)

Dickey notebooks, March 25, 1983. The radio contact was almost two days after the March 23 engagement on the Ocotal–Jalapa road. Apparently Cancer had some trouble getting his surviving men out to Honduras.

(pp. 189–96)

Dickey notebooks, March 25 and 26, 1983.

(pp. 196–204)

Dickey notebooks, March 26, 1983.

(p. 204)

Lisa Fitzgerald interview, June 4, 1984.

(pp. 204–8)

Dickey notebooks March 26–29, 1983, and journal entry April 13, 1983.

(p. 209)

Enders's position on negotiations in the "working paper yet to be formally submitted to the NSC" that was leaked to *The Washington Post* was formulated in terms of El Salvador, where he recommended continued military aid at the same time he proposed negotiations through a third country. But the basic principle was the same that he advocated for Nicaragua, according to sources close to him interviewed in New York in the fall of 1983. (See Lou Cannon and John M. Goshko, "U.S. Weighs Plan for 'Two-Track' Policy on Salvador," *The Washington Post,* February 10, 1983, p. A1.) His abiding concept appears to have been the same as that stated by Kissinger to the Church committee in 1975: "only those covert actions can be justified that support a diplomatic track." (See third note for p. 102.)

(p. 210)

The tactics of the administration hard-liners, cited by intelligence and diplomatic sources interviewed in September and November 1984, included avoiding discussions of war—that is, an outright invasion—as much as they did avoiding talk of peace: "Negotiations were never discussed in any meetings I was in," said one member of the Core Group in a September 1984 interview. "But invasion was not discussed either. What is conventional wisdom? That we would take the towns and then there would be a protracted war, right? But what if I were to tell you that they would lay down their arms and jump for joy? And there were those who said they would. In government we normally game these things out. But [the ideologues] kept this from even being discussed."

(p. 210)

For background on the Boland Amendment, see the May 13, 1983, House Intelligence Committee report, pp. 8–9.

(p. 210)

The CIA briefer was interviewed in the fall of 1984.

(pp. 210–11)

The Agency critic who attended the briefings was a congressional source interviewed in March 1984.

(pp. 212–14)

The physical description of "Ana María" is from an interview with her in November 1981 and impressions shared with other journalists who talked to her. The political description and the account of her death are from interviews with senior officials of the Salvadoran FMLN-FDR in May 1983 and June 1984.

(p. 214)

Marcial's letter to his followers was discussed with FMLN officials in Managua in June 1984, and is referred to in the Salvadoran rebel newspaper *Venceremos,* January 1984.

(p. 214)

For a compelling account of the attack on the American journalists, see Karen DeYoung, "Rebel Ambush on a Nicaraguan Road: A Fiery Rain of Death," *The Washington Post,* May 24, 1983, p. A1.

(p. 216)

The general description of the girls at Pino Uno is from interviews with Aurora, Jamilet and Jacqueline in my March 1983 notebooks, and with Irma and Auxiliadora at the FDN field hospital in Honduras in January 1984. The detail of the .38 revolver Irma carried is from Icaza, October 27, 1984.

(p. 217)

The description of La Negra's labors and of the beginning of her jealousy is from an interview in November 1984 with a member of the FDN who knew her well, and from firsthand observations in 1983.

(p. 217)

La Negra's switch from Machete to Krill was noted in December 1984 interviews. I talked to Ortiz in Tegucigalpa in November 1984; he also mentioned it.

(p. 217)

The view of Suicida as a sergeant incapable of taking on an officer-size com-

mand was a common one, expressed in interviews with ex-*guardias* in August, November and December 1984.
(pp. 217–18)

El Muerto's evaluation of Suicida and La Negra is as he recounted it in Managua, June 5, 1984.
(pp. 218–19)

The characterization of Suicida as publicity crazy is from a senior FDN official in Tegucigalpa, November 1984.
(pp. 218–19)

The account of La Negra's death is from Icaza, October 1984. The story of her last trip to Tegucigalpa is from December 1984 interviews with FDN sources.
(p. 219)

The description of Suicida's radio conversations monitored by the Sandinistas is from an interview with state security chief Lenin Cerna, May 29, 1984.
(p. 219)

Icaza said it was a .30-caliber round. Other people, including an American military source, who saw the Toyota immediately afterward, said they thought it may have been a larger round or even a rocket.
(pp. 219–20)

Characterization of La Negra is from a December 1984 interview in Miami.
(p. 220)

Descriptions of the scene in Las Trojes and El Porvenir and the quotations from residents there are from Brian Barger, "Honduras-Based Unit Holds Town," *The Washington Post,* June 15, 1983, p. A1.
(pp. 220–21)

The account of Icaza's arrival at Arenales and his conversation with Suicida after the ambush is from Icaza interviews October 27–28, 1984. Icaza's background was confirmed by other FDN sources in November and December 1984.
(pp. 221–22)

The conversations between Ortiz and Suicida are as Ortiz related them to two close acquaintances interviewed in Miami in December 1984. Suicida's hatred and suspicion of Echaverry were also noted by Icaza, October 27–28, 1984.
(p. 222)

Cerna claimed the ambush of La Negra in May 29, 1984, interview. He said, however, that she was in Nicaraguan territory at the time.
(pp. 223–24)

The description of Xally's is based on a visit to it or a similar hotel-restaurant in Danlí with Krill and La Negra at about 1 A.M. on March 29, 1983. The description of the way Central American whores are treated is from informal conversations with them and their clients over the course of almost five years in the region. The fighting over the women at Xally's was noted in interviews with veterans of Pino Uno on January 28, 1984, who first told me about Krill's killing of Jaguar. The description of Krill taking pills to keep himself going with the girls, of his wild firing and of Krill's remarks to Jaguar before he blew him away are from Icaza, October 27–28, 1984.
(p. 224)

FDN officials interviewed in Tegucigalpa, November 1984, said that Krill and

Suicida were affected by their notoriety in the articles James and I wrote and liked
to brag about them.
(pp. 224–27)

Icaza's role at Pino Uno was confirmed independently by two Nicaraguan
FDN sources and one American intelligence source. The quotations in this section
are all taken from the October 27–28, 1984, interviews, which were tape-recorded,
except for the figure of thirty commandos, prisoners and civilians killed, which he
mentioned as we were driving to a restaurant on October 28, and which I recorded
in my notebook. It is the same approximate figure used by other FDN officials
subsequently involved with the investigation into Suicida. In October, I repeatedly
asked Icaza to see and copy his notebook. He said it was still in Honduras, hidden
near Danlí. In November when I was in Honduras I called him and asked him for
the location. He said he could not give it to me. I telephoned him again from
Washington in March 1985, at which point he said he still had not been back to
Honduras and so could not show it to me.

Dying—Summer and Fall, 1983

(p. 229)

The depiction of Casey and the rest as men in tropical shirts is from a senior
Salvadoran official who met with them, interviewed in June 1984.
(pp. 229–31)

The account of Casey's visit to Tegucigalpa and San Salvador and the quoted
conversations are from interviews with a senior U.S. intelligence official in November 1984, and with U.S. diplomatic sources in November and December
1984.
(p. 230)

To get an idea of the kinds of atrocity stories that had begun to emerge from
other areas, see the Brody report and the Americas Watch report issued in March
1985.
(p. 230)

Osvaldo's attempt to write a psychological warfare manual was talked about
by a field agent in the fall of 1984.
(p. 231)

Dial Torgerson told me the story about Rhodesian minesweepers in El Salvador, August 1981.
(pp. 232–34)

The events of June 20 and 21 recorded here are as reported in my notebook
on June 21 and 22 and as recalled by Marcie Johnson in a lengthy tape-recorded
interview in Tegucigalpa, November 1984. Marcie, since 1984, has gone by her
maiden name, Izaguirrè.
(pp. 234–36)

Icaza's account of June 21 is from the October 27–28 interviews. In the January 28, 1984, interview with veterans of Pino Uno, I encountered another witness
to the blast who told a similar, though less detailed, story.
(pp. 236–37)

As mentioned, all this material is taken directly from my notebooks.

(pp. 237–38)

The account of Suicida eating caviar and drinking champagne and his conversations that evening are from Icaza, October 27–28, 1984. The initial scene is as Icaza recalls finding him.

(pp. 238–39)

The characterization of disarray in the Central America policy is drawn from interviews with three different members of the Core Group in the fall of 1984. Negroponte's idea of the local forces doing the work is from an interview in October 1982.

(p. 239)

"Now, before I go any further," Reagan said to the joint session on April 27, 1983, "let me say to those who invoke the memory of Vietnam: There is no thought of sending American combat troops to Central America; they are not needed—indeed, they have not been requested there. All our neighbors ask of us is assistance in training and arms to protect themselves while they build a better, freer life."

(p. 239)

Carlos Coronel's role and Tomás Castillo's were discussed by Edgar Chamorro in interviews in August and October 1984. Castillo is the pseudonym of Feldman/Mason's replacement.

(p. 240)

The emphasis by Shaw and Clarridge on restructuring the war effort and reemphasizing guerrilla tactics was noted by Edgar Chamorro in August 1984; by FDN military personnel in interviews in August and November 1984; and by U.S. intelligence sources. It was the major thrust of interviews with Adolfo Calero, Emilio Echaverry and Edgar Chamorro in July and August 1983.

(p. 240)

The arrival of Gen. Ochoa Sanchez was reported in *The New York Times,* June 19, 1983, and in "Background Paper: Nicaragua's Military Build-up and Support for Central American Subversion," Department of State and Department of Defense, July 18, 1984, p. 11. I was there in July 1983 when the Stalin organs were being demonstrated in the middle of Managua leading up to the celebration of the revolution's fourth anniversary.

(p. 240)

Gorman's role was increasingly prominent in 1984, and there was talk among intelligence sources I interviewed, who told me about his intelligence background, that he might be in line for the position of deputy CIA director. But nothing came of this.

(p. 240)

"Perception management," according to intelligence sources, is related to the idea that if you look like a winner you are more likely to be one. This related closely to the idea, articulated by one officer from the U.S. Southern Command, that the contras' image profited mightily from the public side of the "secret" support given them by the administration.

(pp. 241–43)

The basic account of Krill's murder of Cancer and the date for it given here are from interviews with Irma and other survivors of Pino Uno on January 28,

1984, who witnessed it. But several details were filled in by Salvador Icaza in the October 27–28, 1984, interviews including the dialogue among Suicida, Krill and Cancer. Icaza said he was not an eyewitness but that he made extensive inquiries about what happened. Icaza was unclear, however, about the exact date.
(pp. 243–44)

The story of Suicida's trip to the capital comes from two Nicaraguan sources interviewed in November 1984. Ortiz, interviewed the same month, confirmed Suicida's contact with him. But I was unable to get any independent confirmation of this scene from Argentine or American sources. Suicida's general attitude during this period was described by Icaza, among others. The exchange about the general staff, repeated by a Nicaraguan anti-Sandinista source interviewed in Tegucigalpa in November 1984, was in reference to Suicida's general series of actions. It is not clear that it was in reference to the raid on Tegucigalpa.
(p. 245)

The appointment of "Visage" and the discussion of reasons for it is taken from interviews with Edgar Chamorro in August and October 1984. Villagra's background is documented in the Costa Rican press and other reports. For the attack on Radio Noticias, note references for pp. 90–92. For the October 29, 1981, airline hijacking see FBIS, 30 October 1981, pp. P1–P2; FBIS, 2 November 1982, pp. P2–P5; and a list prepared by the U.S. Embassy in San José of "Principal Terrorist Acts" there. Villagra described his own relationship with d'Aubuisson and his release from jail in El Salvador when questioned about it in an August 1984 interview. The position of the U.S. embassy in this regard was given by a State Department official who served there at the time who was queried on this point in March 1985.
(pp. 245–47)

The arrests of Krill and Caramalo and Villagra's thoughts are taken from a tape-recorded interview with Villagra, August 12, 1984. For a report of the August 24, 1983, attack on Jícaro observed from the other side, see Brody, p. 58.
(p. 248)

The last contact between Ortiz and Suicida, the exchange with Villegas, and the Ortizes' emotions were described by Ortiz in an interview. He did not produce a copy of the smuggled note, however.
(pp. 248–49)

The unrepentance of Suicida, Krill, Caramalo and Habakuk were described by one of the officials at the trial interviewed in the summer of 1984.
(p. 249)

Icaza's exchange with Echaverry is as he recalled it in the October 1984 interviews.
(p. 250)

Chamorro noted the problem of the lie detectors in a March 1985 interview.
(p. 250)

The failure of Operation Marathon and the near-mutiny of several field commanders in the fall of 1984 were well reported in the American press, particularly by ABC correspondent Peter Collins. El Negro's men were so angry about their treatment at Shaw's hands that they arranged to meet him in a hotel parking lot and informed Collins so Collins could film the encounter.

On January 10, 1984, forty-two FDN commanders and field officers, including Visage's replacement "Toño" and "Mack," signed an angry letter to Adolfo Calero, head of the FDN Directorate. They demanded the resignation of Bermúdez, Echaverry and Lau, among others, complaining that funds were being badly managed and that after two years no effective strategy had been designed by a general staff that spent most of its time almost 250 miles from the main theater of operations. The letter, which I had authenticated by one of the signatories, appeared in a publication circulated in Miami called *Aca Centro America,* published by Boris Leets.
(pp. 250–51)

The interview with Suicida's captor was tape-recorded in the summer of 1984.
(p. 251)

Despite the confusion about exactly where and when Suicida and his men were executed there is no question that they were killed in late 1984 by their former comrades. This was confirmed by U.S. intelligence sources as well as the anti-Sandinista Nicaraguans. High FDN officials such as Calero and Sanchez, however, continued late into 1984 to claim ignorance or to refuse to comment about the fate of Suicida.
(p. 251)

The story of the near-encounter with a tortured Suicida was told by two Nicaraguan sources in Miami in December 1984.

Epilogues

(p. 253)
The specific incident with Bermúdez was August 8, 1983, according to interviews with Chamorro in August 1984 and February 1985.
(p. 253)
Interview with Aristides Sanchez, November 30, 1984.
(p. 253)
Telephone interview with Salvador Icaza, February 1984.

The Manual
(p. 254)
Interview with Echaverry in Tegucigalpa, July 29, 1983.
(p. 254)
Implicit and explicit terror are terms from the manual.
(p. 254)
See Associated Press, "Rebel Training Book Linked to Casey Visit to Honduras," *The New York Times,* December 3, 1984.
(pp. 254–55)
Descriptions of Kirkpatrick and others' reactions to him are from interviews with Chamorro in August and October 1984; an American CIA source in October 1984; and with Icaza in October 1984.
(p. 255)
The account of visiting the camps is from Icaza, interviewed by telephone in February 1985.

(p. 255)

IAD, the International Activities Division, which combined the old paramilitary and covert actions staffs.

(p. 255)

Quote from Agency veteran is from interview in November 1984.

(pp. 255–56)

Kirkpatrick's perceptions are as noted by his Nicaraguan acquaintances and as seen in the manual itself.

(p. 256)

See Philip Taubman, "C.I.A. Manual Is Linked to Vietnam War Guide," *The New York Times,* October 29, 1984.

(p. 256)

Edgar Chamorro talked about the pages being ripped out in August 1983, which is when I first got a copy of the manual.

(p. 256)

Icaza described his use of the manual in October 1984 interviews. He has a photograph of himself with one of the classes. Most of its members are proudly holding up copies of the book.

(p. 256)

The Agency's perceptions, or lack of them, were the subject of many news articles from October to December 1984. Among others, see Bob Woodward, "Middle-Level CIA Officials Cleared Manual," *The Washington Post,* October 24, which tends to exculpate the upper reaches of the agency bureaucracy. Dewey's inability to read Spanish was noted by a senior CIA official interviewed in December 1984.

(p. 256)

The story of the manual was initially broken by the Associated Press. But *The New York Times,* particularly Joel Brinkley, ran with it. Some of that newspaper's headlines in late 1984 may suggest the furor that it provoked: "CIA Primer Tells Nicaraguan Rebels How to Kill," October 17; "President Orders 2 Investigations on C.I.A. Manual," October 19; "Nicaraguan Rebel Disputes U.S. Aide," October 20; "Legislators Ask if Reagan Knew of C.I.A.'s Role," October 21 (this was the day of the presidential debate in Kansas City); "Adviser Says Reagan Will Dismiss Officials Linked to Rebel Primer," October 22; "C.I.A. Aides Dispute Reagan on Primer," October 23; "C.I.A. Manual: A Policy Is Undermined," by Hedrick Smith, October 30; "C.I.A. Chief Defends Manual for Nicaraguan Rebels," November 2; "U.S. Says Study Found Manual Broke No Law," by Francis X. Clines; "C.I.A. Aide Is Said to Urge Punishing Manual's Authors," November 10; "House Panel Calls C.I.A. Manual Illegal," December 6.

(p. 256)

Executive Order 12333 barring U.S. personnel from involvement with assassinations was issued in December 1981, just as the United States bought in to the Secret War.

(p. 257)

Clarridge's remarks on assassination, which were independently confirmed to me by congressional sources, were first reported by Alfonso Chardy and James

McCartney, Knight-Ridder Newspapers (as published in the *Providence Journal-Bulletin*), October 20, 1984. The Defense Intelligence Agency's classified "Weekly Intelligence Summary (U)," July 16, 1982, notes the "assassination of minor government officials and a Cuban adviser" by the Nicaraguan insurgents.
(p. 257)

    Quotations from intelligence sources and indirect quotation from Shaw are from interviews in October and November 1984.
(p. 257)

    The report on Mack's briefcase is from *El Nuevo Diario,* "Abrumadoras Evidencias!!!," August 6, 1983, a report on the press conference by Comandante de Brigada Julio Ramos. The authenticity of the documents was confirmed to me by FDN sources in Miami in December 1984.
(p. 258)

    The discussion of logistics for Operation Marathon is from interviews in March and September 1984 with an American intelligence source present at the meetings.
(p. 258)

    For a discussion of the September 1983 finding, see "Report of the Select Committee on Intelligence, United States Senate, January 1, 1983, to December 31, 1984," p. 12.
(p. 259)

    Some of the best reporting on the high-tech aspects of the Secret War is by Juan O. Tamayo in the *Miami Herald:* "CIA Fights with New Technology, Old Techniques," June 5, 1983; "Hondurans Hunt Arms in Boats Bought by CIA," June 5, 1983; "Sandinistas Foes Reported Getting Salvadoran Help," October 2, 1983; "The Contra Air Force: Clues Point to CIA," October 7, 1983.
(p. 259)

    See Associated Press, "October 10 Assault on Nicaraguans is Laid to C.I.A.," *The New York Times,* April 18, 1984. The Sandinistas said from the day after the attack six months earlier that it was a direct CIA operation.
(p. 259)

    Edgar Chamorro and Bermúdez were quoted in Robert C. Toth and Doyle McManus, the *Los Angeles Times,* "CIA Sent Contra Force—And Americans—Into Thick of War."
(p. 260)

    The account of Clarridge's hubris and his actions is from acquaintances in the CIA who were interviewed in November 1984 and the spring of 1985.
(p. 260)

    The mining was announced on January 2; the controversy did not erupt until April. For a detailed chronology, see Philip Taubman, "How Congress Was Informed of Mining of Nicaragua Ports," *The New York Times,* April 16, 1984. Also see the Senate Intelligence Committee report for January 1, 1983, to December 31, 1984, pp. 7–9.

    The heat from Congress grew so intense that administration officials leaked a CIA report on a buildup for a major Salvadoran offensive in the fall, claiming that the mining was somehow aimed at thwarting this. ("CIA Views Minelaying Part of Covert 'Holding Action,' " *The Washington Post,* April 10, 1984.) The leak jeopardized sensitive intelligence sources, according to one senior intelligence official.

(p. 260)

For the Goldwater quote, see the Senate report and Toth and McManus.

The Dirty Warriors

(p. 261)

The account of Bermúdez making a power play is from interviews in Miami in December 1984.

(p. 261)

Washington Post special correspondent Martin Andersen reported on Ribeiro's whereabouts in December 1984 and January 1985.

(p. 261)

The description of Lau's address and his truck was given to me by an FDN official in Miami at the end of 1984.

(p. 000)

The text of the Honduran Armed Forces communiqué on the missing, along with a critique of it from the San Pedro Sula paper *El Tiempo,* was published in FBIS, January 2, 1985, pp. P3–P5. Aso see James LeMoyne, "Nicaragua Rebels Linked to Deaths," *The New York Times,* January 20, 1983, and "Unmasking the Death Squads," *Newsweek* (International), January 28, 1985, p. 25: "The contras operating out of Honduras knew him as 'El Chino,' the Chinese, a menacing, Asian-looking man in a Honduran Army uniform who patrolled the streets of Tegucigalpa on a motorcycle. As a top operative for the Nicaraguan Democratic Force (FDN), the largest contra group fighting to topple the Sandinista government, El Chino was theoretically responsible for the organization's counterintelligence. But apparently he was up to a lot more than spying. Officials in Honduras now suspect that El Chino, who has been asked to leave the country, used his Tegucigalpa base to mastermind the murders of the contras' enemies."

(pp. 261–62)

Good analyses of Alvarez's fall are Leticia Salomon's in "Boletin Informativo Honduras" No. 11, and Jesús Ceberio, "El general Alvarez, un paladin de la 'guerra sucia,' " *El País,* Madrid, April 8, 1984. For Alvarez's own version, see " 'Me Entregué Totalmente a Defender y Fortalecer el Gobierno,' " and "Centroamerica: Una Situación para Decisiones Inmediatas," interviews with Mirta T. Mejía in the San Pedro Sula paper *La Prensa,* May 18 and 19, 1984.

The Americans

(p. 262)

The embassy's ignorance about the impending overthrow was confirmed by Negroponte in an interview in June 1984, by a CIA source in October, and by U.S. diplomatic and military sources in November and December 1984.

(p. 262)

Statistics on U.S. military aid to Honduras were supplied by the U.S. Southern Command in Panama. The figure for aid in the covert war is from congressional sources.

(p. 262)

Several intelligence sources interviewed in October and November 1984 talked about their irritation with the way reprimands were distributed in the manual

controversy. These same sources talked about Clarridge's seeming immunity. Another source spoke about the inherent moral dangers of such operations.
(p. 263)

The *Detroit Free Press* article was by Frank Greve and Ellen Warren of the *Free Press* Washington staff.
(pp. 263–64)

Schaufelberger's background and his general activities with the Salvadorans were mentioned to me by him and by his colleagues in the "mil group" several times in early 1983. We used to play softball and go drinking together.
(p. 264)

The Schwab case was thoroughly reported by Robert J. McCartney, "CIA Is Said to Use Bases in Honduras," *The Washington Post,* January 29, 1984, and Brian Barger, "Military Sources Blame 'Carrot Top,' Not Pilot Error," Pacific News Service, January 30, 1984.
(p. 264)

The CIA's explanation to Congress about Civilian Military Assistance is in the 1983–84 Senate Intelligence Committee Report, p.12; also see "A Mystery Involving 'Mercs,' " *Time* magazine, September 17, 1984, p. 33; and John Dillon and Jon Lee Anderson, "Who's Behind the Aid to the Contras," *The Nation,* October 6, 1984. For more on civilian military assistance, see Ron Martz and Scott Thurston, " 'Just call us freedom fighters . . .' ", *Atlanta Journal–Constitution.* September 8, 1984.
(pp. 264–65)

See "4 Americans from C.I.A. Killed as Plane Crashes in El Salvador," *The Washington Post,* October 24, 1984.

From relatives, one of the dead was identified as Richard C. Spicer, a pilot from Warren, Pa. See Philip Taubman, "Pilot's Death Leads to Report of a Secret Life in the C.I.A.," *The New York Times,* October 24, 1984.

Commander Zero
(p. 265)

I was in San José when Rodrigo Cuadra Clachar and Mario Gutiérrez Serrano blew themselves up on July 3, 1983. See "Sandinistas Accused of Plot to Kill Exiles," *The Washington Post,* July 4, 1983. Gutiérrez Serrano lived.
(p. 265)

The ETA–Sandinista connections get extraordinarily complicated. According to one senior U.S. intelligence source, some administration officials hoped to exploit intelligence on them to help drive a wedge between Managua and the Socialist government of Felipe Gonzales in Spain. To do this there were two principal sources cited. One was testimony by a Salvadoran rebel leader, Arquimedes Antonio Cañada, a.k.a. Alejandro Montenegro, captured in Honduras in August 1982 and persuaded after several days to defect. The other was Gregorio Jimenez Morales, a.k.a. "Pistolas," a.k.a. Lorenzo Avila Teijón, the ETA agent arrested in Costa Rica loitering around Pastora's neighborhood.

Just as the Sandinistas may use captives like "El Muerto" for misinformation, the CIA could use Cañada and Jimenez Morales. It should also be noted that news magazines are particularly vulnerable to this approach because of their noteless style and thin attribution.

But all that said, the cover story "100 Etarras en Nicaragua," in the Spanish news weekly *Cambio 16,* No. 618, October 3–10, 1983, makes fascinating reading. The lead sentences give the flavor: "Since the fall of the dictator Anastasio Somoza, in 1979, more than a hundred terrorists of the armed Basque military organization ETA have received instruction in Sandinista Front training camps and have participated in guerrilla actions of the International Brigades that support the Popular Sandinista Army. The majority of this contingent of 'volunteer' combatants come from Mexico, Venezuela and France, the three most important sanctuaries of the ETA overseas, and were closely watched by the intelligence services of Spain, the United States and Israel. The main recruiting base, Team International, established in Mexico City, is directed by Sumi Albana, the right hand of Abu Nidal, head of the Popular Front for the Liberation of Palestine . . . ," and so on.

This article, which cited no sources for its revelations, subsequently was used extensively as the attributed source for the section "The International Connection" in July 1984 State/Defense "Background Paper: Nicaragua's Military Build-Up and Support for Central American Subversion." (See below.)
(pp. 265–67)

The running account of the press conference and its immediate aftermath is from my notes taken in Costa Rica the week afterward and from the excellent coverage by Richard Dyer and others in Linda Frazier's paper, the weekly *Tico Times,* especially the June 8, 1983, edition.
(pp. 266–67)

The name Peer Anker Hansen comes from a stolen passport. The true identity of the killer is confused by extensive misinformation in the wake of the bombing.

The Costa Rican intelligence and investigations service, the Organizacion de Investigacion Judicial (OIJ), told the press in the week after the bombing that Hansen appeared in fact to be a Basque ETA terrorist, José Miguel Lujua Gorostiola. They identified him, they said, by comparing pictures of "Hansen" with those of ETA members published in, of all magazines, *Cambio 16,* on May 28, 1984 (pictures, as it happens, taken from the files of police death squads trying to eliminate the ETA).

A month later, however, Pastora himself put no credence in this version. Among other things, it appears French intelligence said it knew perfectly well where Gorostiola was, and he was not in San José. Pastora instead said his own sources led him to believe Hansen was Rafael Samudio Pérez, "a Uruguayan who had been a Tupamaro guerrilla, was turned, and went to work for the Uruguayan police and intelligence service. He's a criminal of the right."

The search goes on, though not very actively.
(p. 267)

The interviews with Pastora were July 7–8, 1984.

The Sandinistas
(p. 268)

No Sandinista official ever told me flatly he was pleased with Washington's rejectionist position toward the elections or the Contadora draft treaties, but one senior advisor to the National Directorate did give me that impression very strongly when I met with him in New York in the fall of 1984.

The ugly affair with the Pope, I witnessed firsthand in March 1983. My impression was that he was looking for trouble—for confrontation. The Sandinistas were both foolish enough to give it to him, and to boast about it afterward—even in interviews in January 1984.
(pp. 268–69)

Hondurans in Managua talked to me about their efforts to build a guerrilla front in May 1984.
(p. 269)

One must acknowledge the role Napoleon Duarte has played trying to build a middle ground in his brutally divided country, reportedly with substantial CIA funding assuring his election in March 1984. But one should also remember all those who died in 1980 and 1981 when Duarte lent his name to the regime that killed them, claiming he could not control it, but refusing to leave it.
(p. 269)

The Soviet armaments I have seen firsthand. The Sandinistas make no extraordinary efforts to hide them. A Sandinista official told me of the airbase at Punta Huete in June 1984, remembering that such an airstrip was used as part of the reason for invading Grenada, and wondering why nobody in the United States was complaining about this one in Nicaragua. He did not have long to wait. The analysis of Sandinista thinking comes from interviews with Borge, Daniel Ortega, Sergio Ramírez and Lenin Cerna in May and June 1984.
(p. 270)

The exchange between Chamorro and "Tomás" is as Chamorro recalled it in interviews in August 1984. The description of the Rusty Pelican is from firsthand examination.

Index

About the Author

Christopher Dickey was the first American newspaper reporter to travel with Nicaragua's counterrevolutionaries in combat. As *Washington Post* bureau chief for Mexico, Central America and the Caribbean from January 1980 until September 1983, he traveled with El Salvador's guerrilla and government troops, flew into combat with Guatemala's military chief of staff, and came to know personally the region's diplomats, its presidents, its madmen and martyrs. Dickey covered the funeral of El Salvador's archbishop in 1980 and the bloody December of the same year when the American nuns were murdered. Dickey was one of the first American reporters to interview the fledgling anti-Sandinista rebels in May 1981. His sources inside the Nicaraguan government enabled him to detail the Cuban and Soviet bloc influence on the increasingly totalitarian structures and traditions of Central America's armies, uncovering the complex relations between ex-Major Roberto d'Aubuisson and his supporters, between Honduran strongman Colonel Gustavo Alvarez and his Argentine connections.

Following a nine-month leave as the Edward R. Murrow Press Fellow at the Council on Foreign Relations, Dickey is currently the Middle East correspondent for *The Washington Post*.